Filled With the Spirit

A Verse-by-Verse Commentary on
Acts of the Apostles

by
John R. Rice
Founder, THE SWORD OF THE LORD

SWORD of the LORD
PUBLISHERS
P.O. BOX 1099, MURFREESBORO, TN 37133

Printed in U.S.A.

PREFACE

Of nearly five hundred feet of shelves in my library, about sixty feet are filled with commentaries on the Bible. But those commentaries are rarely quoted here. We have felt that there was need for very careful, simple, literal Bible teaching calling attention to what the Scriptures expressly say, explaining Scriptures with other Scriptures, that the Word of God itself may have the mighty and miraculous impact God intended.

We have received great help from the books by Sir William Ramsay, from International Standard Bible Encyclopedia, Davis Bible Dictionary, and from the commentaries. The author believes the Bible, loves it, is a literalist. We have spent more study on the book of Acts than on any other in the Bible. We trust that the concern of an evangelist, our more than forty years' experience in building and in helping New Testament, soul-winning churches, and having some part in winning thousands of souls, has somewhat prepared our heart for teaching in the book of Acts about New Testament churches, soul winning, the fullness of the Spirit, and the evangelistic ministry of Peter, Paul, Barnabas and Silas.

After enormous labor and great blessing we commend this commentary on the book of Acts to the charitable interest of God's people and to the merciful blessing of God. May the Holy Spirit guide each seeking, believing, loving heart as God's people use this book.

November, 1963   John R. Rice

Table of Contents

ACTS, CHAPTER 3

TABLE OF CONTENTS 7

ACTS, CHAPTER 19

ACTS, CHAPTER 20

ACTS, CHAPTER 21

ACTS, CHAPTER 22

ACTS, CHAPTER 23

Introduction to the
Acts of the Apostles

The author of the book of Acts is "Luke, the beloved physician" (Col. 4:14). He is named also as Paul's companion in journey (Acts 16:12 and Acts 20:5). Second Timothy 4:11 tells us he was with Paul in Rome. In Philemon 24 he is called <u>Lucas</u>, who sent greetings in Paul's letter to Philemon.

There is no important controversy against Luke's writing the book of Acts. The second century Muratorian canon ascribes Acts to Luke as well as Irenaeus, Jerome, Tertullian and Clement of Alexandria.

The book of Acts is generally divided into two distinct general parts. In chapters 1 to 12 Peter is the chief character, Jerusalem is the center, the Gospel is taken principally to Jews. In chapters 13 to 28 Paul is the principal character, Antioch is the center of missionary work, the Gospel is preached to Gentiles more than to Jews. Of course in the first section, chapters 6 and 7 are about Stephen's brief but wonderful ministry. Chapter 8 is about Philip's ministry, and chapter 9 is about Paul's conversion. Also, Cornelius the Gentile at Caesarea and Ananias at Damascus enter into the narrative. But principally, the first twelve chapters center on Peter, and Jerusalem and Jews. And in chapter 13 to 28 Antioch is only a starting place, and the story follows Paul and Barnabas, then Paul and Silas, to Crete, to Galatia and Cilicia, into Macedonia, to Jerusalem, to Caesarea, and finally by shipwreck and voyage to Rome. But the central character is Paul. Always he goes first to the Jews, when he can, but the ministry is chiefly to Gentiles.

It is interesting to trace the following of the Great Com-

mission of Acts 1:8, in the book. Chapters 1 to 7 at Jerusalem; chapters 8 to 12 to Samaria; chapters 13 to 28 to the
uttermost parts of the world. But again, this is only a
rough, incomplete, suggestive outline of the book. We know
that others, not recorded in Acts, carried the Gospel far
away: Peter to Babylon, Thomas to India, and "they that
were scattered abroad went every where preaching the
word" (Acts 8:4).

Luke Wrote by Direct Inspiration From God, Not as Paul's Spokesman, Not From His Memory of Events

In the book of Acts we find that in Acts 16:10 the writer
suddenly turns from the third person to the first person.
And in that chapter the terms "we" and "us" are used ten
times (nine times in the Greek) showing that Luke was with
Paul's party in Philippi, then in Acts 20 the writer of the
book of Acts is again present with Paul, and again he re-
peatedly uses the terms "us" and "we" from verses 5 to 16.
Then in Acts 21 the writer says "we" and "us" again about
Paul, indicating that he was with Paul from Miletus on to
Jerusalem.

Some way, Luke was with Paul again two years later still,
when he went to Rome. So in chapters 21 and 27 the writer
uses the personal pronouns "we" and "us" again, showing
that Luke was with Paul on that journey, in the shipwreck,
his stay on the island of Melita and his trip to Rome.

Did Luke write his Gospel and the book of Acts as
spokesman for the Apostle Paul? We think certainly not.
The Bible gives no indication that he did, and so any tradition handed on from Papias or Eusebius has no more authority than if some present-day man should have an opinion
about it. Scholars naturally tend to seek a natural, human
source for the Scripture, aside from a plenary, wholly ade-
quate inspiration from God. It is not justified.

Jeremiah the prophet had a secretary or amanuensis who

wrote down from the mouth of Jeremiah the very words given him by the Holy Spirit (Jer. 36:4). The inspired words were given Jeremiah, and Baruch wrote them down. But nothing like that is hinted in the relation between Luke and Paul, and we have no right to give any credence to such a man-made tradition unsupported by Scripture or by any known fact.

In fact, Luke tells us how he wrote the Gospel, saying, "It seemed good to me also, having had perfect understanding of all things from above, to write unto thee in order, most excellent Theophilus" (Luke 1:3--not "from the very first," as in the King James Version).

The Greek word so translated means "from above." It was so translated in John 3:31, John 19:11, James 1:17, James 3:15-17. Luke had had perfect understanding of what he wrote, and he could only have that absolute finality and perfection of Scripture by divine revelation, written by verbal inspiration, and thus he could write Theophilus, "That thou mightest know the certainty of those things, wherein thou hast been instructed" (Luke 1:4). So what Luke wrote he got directly from God, not from Paul and not from his own memory of the events, nor not by the testimony of eyewitnesses. It is, we think, a foolish and bad interpretation of the introduction to Luke's Gospel (Luke 1:1-4) to indicate that Luke traced out by study, by interviewing witnesses, the matter he wrote. No, Luke got these matters perfectly "from above."

When Luke was present with Paul, in four chapters of the book of Acts, the matter is no more detailed, no more accurate than the matters reported when Paul could not have been present. Luke wrote by divine inspiration and not from memory of what he personally experienced.

And that fits with the clear teaching of the inspiration of Scriptures, that "Eye hath not seen, nor ear heard, neither have entered into the heart of man, the things which God hath prepared for them that love him. But God hath revealed them unto us by his Spirit..." (I Cor. 2:9, 10). So an inspired writer wrote, not what his eye had seen, not what his ear had heard, not what he has logically figured out in his heart, but what God revealed by His Spirit and "not in the words which man's wisdom teacheth, but which the Holy Ghost teacheth; comparing spiritual things with spiritual" (I Cor. 2:13).

We must remember from II Peter 1:20, 21 "that no prophecy of the scripture is of any private interpretation. For the prophecy came not in old time by the will of man: but holy men of God spake as they were moved by the Holy Ghost."

Luke's Literary Style Partly His Own, Wholly God's

The language and literary style of the Gospel according to Luke and of the book of Acts are said by some authorities to be in the finest Greek of any New Testament writings. Was Luke then a man of more culture and more natural gifts than other inspired writers? Probably so, but not necessarily so. On the one hand, it is probable that Luke's vocabulary and literary instinct were just what God wanted to use, in the main. So if we had other writings by Luke, not inspired, it might follow much the same literary style of his inspired writings; we do not know. In as far as the inspired penman understood what God had him write, and in as far as he entered into the thought and message which God's Spirit had him write down, then that far, perhaps, but only that far, the style of the penman would coincide with the style the Holy Spirit chose.

It would be a great mistake to think of Luke's style in writing the book of Acts as principally a distinctive personal style he had developed apart from inspiration, and to think that God simply supervised in some general way, and let Luke select his own forms of speech and vocabulary in writing the Scripture.

In the first place, we can be sure that God Himself

formed Luke's thinking and style and vocabulary and manner of expression long before he was used of God to write God's inspired words in the book of Acts (as in the Gospel of Luke). The Scripture plainly says, "Known unto God are all his works from the beginning of the world" (Acts 15:18). So before Luke was born, God had in mind that he would be used to write this part of Scripture. We are told that "... the children being not yet born...," God chose the elder, Esau to serve the younger, Jacob (Rom. 9:11-13). Do you think that God would be less thoughtful about those who were to write the precious, eternal Word of God in human speech? God's Holy Spirit filled John the Baptist "even from his mother's womb" (Luke 1:15). His career was all planned out ahead of time. Does God do less for others, particularly those He would use to write down the eternal words of God? Paul was inspired to write, "But when it pleased God, who separated me from my mother's womb, and called me by his grace, To reveal his Son in me..." (Gal. 1:15, 16). Oh, then the mighty hand of God prepared Luke's character and vocabulary and thinking.

And in so far that the style of the book of Acts and the Gospel according to Luke is Luke's style, it was still a style that God Himself had formed. So the style was probably largely Luke's style which God had prepared in him. But it was altogether God's style, for whether or not Luke perfectly understood what he wrote, he wrote the very words of God. Sometimes they were exactly what Luke would have written perhaps and sometimes not.

But we are clearly taught that inspired writers of the Old Testament after they had prophesied or written the Scriptures "inquired and searched diligently..., Searching what, or what manner of time the Spirit of Christ which was in them did signify, when it testified beforehand the sufferings of Christ, and the glory that should follow. Unto whom it was revealed, that not unto themselves, but unto us they did minister the things, which are now reported unto you..."

(I Pet. 1:10-12). So inspired writers never completely understood all of God's meaning in what they wrote. The Scriptures are perfect; no man's understanding is perfect. Sometimes, no doubt, they understood very little of it, or none of it, as when the high priest, Caiaphas, unwittingly prophesied that in the death of Christ one man should die for all (John 11:49-52), or as when Balaam's donkey was inspired to speak. So if the writer never completely understood the message he wrote, it is not fair to give the writer entire credit for the vocabulary or style. Was the style of the donkey his own or was his style of speech wholly God's?

In fact, in the case of the Apostle Paul it was said that "his letters...are weighty and powerful; but his bodily presence is weak, and his speech contemptible" (II Cor. 10:10). Strange! Paul's letters which were divinely inspired Scripture were "weighty and powerful" but in contrast he did not naturally have a good gift of speech; the power and weight of the inspired letters did not represent Paul's natural gifts or literary style!

So if the Greek language and style in the Gospel of Luke and Acts of the Apostles is beautiful, it is primarily simply part of God's chosen style.

If Shakespeare could form one style of language as from the blustering, ribald Falstaff and another style from the mouth of Portia, and still another from the half-demented and tragic King Lear, why should God not be able to use as great a variety of styles as He might choose? Are not lilting sonnets by Shakespeare and Hamlet's tragic soliloquy from the same pen?

In the Scriptures, as in the Son of God, the Human Is Present but Subordinated and Made Perfect by the Divine

The Lord Jesus was a man. He was born of a human mother. He ate, He drank, He worked, He slept. Sometimes He was tired, sometimes hungry. He was tempted in all points as we are, yet without sin. Jesus was a man, the Son of Adam, Son of Abraham, Son of David and Son of Mary. But Jesus was the incarnate Christ, the Christ of God, the Creator, who was pre-existent with the Father before the world began. He became flesh. He took on Himself the form of human flesh. He became obedient to death. So Jesus Christ is the God-man. He is wholly God and wholly man. As a man He is perfect, sinless and blameless. But the human was made perfect by the divine element and the human element was always subordinate to the divine element.

When Jesus was conceived in the womb of the virgin and carried for nine months and delivered as other babies are through a mother's pain, it was the God-man who was conceived and born. But we must remember that Mary was the passive, but willing and believing subject of the divine will in this matter. She did not initiate the matter of the birth of Jesus, did not condition the matter nor control it. So, since Jesus had such a human mother, He is human as well as divine. He is man as well as God. But God made the decisions in the matter and did the works, and not Mary.

So it is with the formation of Scriptures. Men willingly wrote down what God told them to write. But in the matter of inspiration, God wholly mastered the men and controlled them. Every word was the very word of God. In the Bible, even as on Mount Sinai, "God spake all these words" (Exod. 20:1). And so of the Scripture we are told, "...Every word that proceedeth out of the mouth of God" (Matt. 4:4; Deut. 8:3). In the writing of Scripture, the human scribe is not the dominant one anymore than Mary was the dominant one in making the baby Jesus. The incarnation of Jesus Christ is God's plan and God's work, not Mary's. So the inspiration and writing down of the words of Scripture is God's work and not man's, except as men are the incidental and willing tools and agents of God. The thoughts are God's thoughts and the words are God's words. He may have provided the vocabulary before, but all the way He perfectly controls it in every word written down.

In the Bible those who wrote sometimes expressed their own will and the will of God, so the brethren after council at Jerusalem could write to the Gentile converts, "For it seemed good to the Holy Ghost, and to us..." (Acts 15:28). But we must remember that the Holy Spirit made the decision first and then led them, after discussion and prayer, to the same decision. When Luke wrote his Gospel, he could say, "It seemed good to me also, having had perfect understanding of all things from above..." (not "from the very first" as in K.J.V.). Yes, it seemed good to Luke to write the Gospel, but only after he had had perfect understanding of the matter from above (anothen). God initiated and dominated the matter and Luke concurred in as far as he understood the mind of God.

Bible writers often wrote expressing their own heart throbs, desires, fears. One can see Paul's great concern over false doctrine in his letter to the Galatians or Paul's personal request to Timothy to bring the cloak and books (II Tim. 4:13). But we must remember that in every such case, the idea was first God's and then He led the emotions of the writers and used their emotions to express His own will in the matter.

So we might properly say that in every case the language, style and wording of Scripture is partly man's, but always wholly God's. That is, God dominated every word and selected it. In some cases the writer's mind coincided with God's mind and the words and God's thought would fit it also into the writer's heart and God's words were expressed in the writer's words.

So the book of Acts is altogether from God; and only partly, as God Himself provided and directed, does the writing represent Luke personally.

We will be wise in dealing with Scripture to remind ourselves that the supernatural element is dominant, the human element passive or gladly subject to the Holy Spirit. The style of each different Bible writer represents the style of the writer himself only as God chose it to do so. The Bible never discusses nor gives any weight to human sources for the Scriptures. Men may speak of prophets copying genealogies or of Mark writing from Peter's viewpoint, or of Luke's writing from Paul's; but the Bible never does.

Peter did indicate that he had actually seen and touched the risen Saviour and heard the voice of God commend Jesus on the Mount of Transfiguration (I Pet. 1:16-18), and John the apostle could say, "And the Word was made flesh, and dwelt among us, (and we beheld his glory, the glory as of the. only begotten of the Father,) full of grace and truth" (John 1:14) and again John could say, "That which was from the beginning which we have heard, which we have seen with our eyes, which we have looked upon, and our hands have handled, of the Word of life" (I John 1:1), but when it came to writing the Scripture, no Bible writer claims to be writing things which were based upon his experience or the testimony of witnesses he has heard, or things he has reasoned out from the facts known. No, the matter of Scripture is divinely revealed, "Which things also we speak, not in the words which man's wisdom teacheth, but which the Holy Ghost teacheth..." (I Cor. 2:13). On the contrary, in Luke's Gospel he tells of other gospel stories "even as they delivered them unto us, which from the beginning were eyewitnesses, and ministers of the word." But by these stories men do not "know the certainty of those things, wherein" they had been instructed; so Luke wrote, "Having had perfect understanding of all things from above ⌈the Greek word anothen ⌋, to write unto thee in order, most excellent Theophilus, That thou mightest know the certainty of those things, wherein thou hast been instructed." Here divine inspiration through Luke is correcting and making certain the hearsay gospel stories and reports of eyewitnesses given by others with only human wisdom, without divine inspiration. There were many such gospel stories written but only those we now have in the New Testament were inspired of God and certain.

Many authorities would make much of a few "medical terms" which they allege are used in the book of Acts. For example, Acts 28:3, 6, 8 are mentioned as using "medical terms." I do not think when the viper bit Paul, or when the people expected that Paul "should have swollen, or fallen down dead suddenly," or the "bloody flux" of Publius' father show any specialized medical training or vocabulary. That seems to be straining to find a human reason and explanation for language that is clearly given verbally by the Holy Spirit.

When was the book of Acts written? It closes with the first two years of Paul's imprisonment at Rome, about 63 or 65 A. D., and was probably written then. The book covers the time from the resurrection of Christ to the first two years of Paul's first imprisonment at Rome, and so covers probably thirty-three to thirty-five years' time.

"Filled With the Spirit"

The Book of Acts

A Verse-By-Verse Commentary

ACTS 1

VERSES 1, 2:

THE former treatise have I made, O Theophilus, of all that Jesus began both to do and teach,

2 Until the day in which he was taken up, after that he through the Holy Ghost had given commandments unto the apostles whom he had chosen:

The Book of Acts a Sequel to the Gospel of Luke

If it were not thoroughly established that Luke wrote the book of Acts, it could easily be discovered. "The former treatise" which the same writer prepared is the Gospel of Luke. Notice the evidence.

1. Both Luke's Gospel and Acts of the Apostles are addressed to "Theophilus." The name means "lover of God," probably a real person, some influential Christian. Some have thought the books were thus addressed to all "lovers of God."

2. Here is repeated the promise of Luke 24:49, "And, behold, I send the promise of my Father upon you: but tarry ye in the city of Jerusalem, until ye be endued with power from on high." And in Acts 1:4 and 5 we are told, "And, being assembled together with them, commanded

them that they should not depart from Jerusalem, but wait for the promise of the Father, which, saith he, ye have heard of me. For John truly baptized with water; but ye shall be baptized with the Holy Ghost not many days hence." And when we add verse 8 to it, we see that it is the same promise: "But ye shall receive power, after that the Holy Ghost is come upon you: and ye shall be witnesses unto me both in Jerusalem, and in all Judaea, and in Samaria, and unto the uttermost part of the earth."

Luke only, of the four Gospels, gives this promise of Jesus that they should be endued with power from on high for preaching and witnessing. So the first few verses of Acts 1 are a resume, a synopsis of the closing verses of Luke's Gospel.

3. This promise of the power of the Holy Spirit is given in connection with the Great Commission. But the Great Commission as given in the other Gospels does not fit with this account in Acts. In Matthew 28:16-20 the Great Commission is given, but we are specifically told that it was in Galilee some days before the ascension, and the ascension is not mentioned there. It is not the same occasion as this in Acts 1.

In Mark 16:15, 16 the Great Commission is given. But it is given when Jesus appeared in the upper room to the eleven the day of the resurrection, it seems. The ascension is mentioned in verse 19, but I believe that "after the Lord had spoken unto them" is a general term meaning the teaching of the forty days after His resurrection, and not that the ascension immediately followed the language in verses 14 to 18. So the first verses in Acts are not a synopsis of the closing part of Mark.

The Great Commission is given in John 20:21 when Jesus said to the disciples, "As my Father hath sent me, even so send I you." But that was "the same day at evening," the day of the resurrection (John 20:19). And that is not the same occasion as described in the first few verses of the Acts. So Acts 1:4-8 is a resume of the same account in the Gospel of Luke. Luke, then, wrote Acts also.

Thus, "the former treatise" had to be the Gospel of Luke.

The Inherent Kinship of the Gospel of Luke and the Book of Acts

The Gospel of Luke and the book of Acts are alike and they are that way obviously by the divine purpose. They are not alike simply because they were written by the same man, though God chose to use the same man and perhaps some incidentals of vocabulary and style. No, God intended that here we would have a continued story.

The Gospel according to Matthew was written particularly for Israel. It emphasizes that Jesus is the Son of Abraham, the Son of David, and the King of the Jews.

The Gospel of Mark pictures Jesus as the servant, the miracle-worker, but it does not set the stage for the fullness of the Spirit, the witnessing, the revivals, the world evangelism of the book of Acts.

The Gospel according to John was written later, inspired to meet some of the heresies that had arisen during the time of the book of Acts. The emphasis is on Jesus as Son of God more than as Son of man.

But the Gospel of Luke pictures Jesus as the Son of Adam, the "Son of man" as He loved to be called, and His genealogy is reckoned back, we believe, through Mary, the daughter of Heli, and on through Nathan, the son of David (not Solomon)--Luke 3:23 ff; while in Matthew 1:1-16 Jesus as King of the Jews is officially traced back through the line of kings, through His foster father Joseph, to David and Abraham.

In the Gospel according to Luke, Jesus is the Spirit-filled Son of man, who emptied Himself of the outward manifestation of His glory and did all His work in the mighty power of

the Holy Spirit after He was baptized of John in Jordan and
the Holy Spirit came upon Him in power (Luke 3:21, 22).

In the Gospel of John there is a great deal of blessed
teaching about the Holy Spirit, but it is generally about the
Holy Spirit as replacing the Lord Jesus, indwelling, comforting, guiding, teaching, helping the Christian to pray,
reminding him of the words of the Lord Jesus. In John
7:37-39 we are reminded that the Holy Spirit, in this sense
of dwelling in the Christian's body, could not come until
Christ was glorified--risen from the dead. In John 14:16,
17 Jesus promised the Comforter. That night before the
crucifixion Jesus said, "He dwelleth with you." But after
Jesus was risen from the dead it was promised that He
"shall be in you." And Christ would manifest Himself to
Christians through the Holy Spirit. John 14:26 promises
that the Comforter, the Holy Spirit, would teach Christians
all things and bring to their remembrance whatever Jesus
had said. In John 15:26 we are told that the Comforter
would testify of Jesus. In John 16:7 the disciples were told
that they ought to rejoice that Jesus was going away because
otherwise the Comforter could not come. In John 16:13 they
were told that the Holy Spirit would guide the disciples into
all truth. Then when Jesus had risen from the dead in John
20:22, "He breathed on them, and saith unto them, Receive
ye the Holy Ghost," and the Holy Spirit came into the bodies
of Christians that day of the resurrection.

And so the promise of the Comforter who would dwell in
their bodies and be in them a well of water springing up
into everlasting life, after Christ was glorified, was fulfilled.

But that is not the emphasis in the book of Acts and is not
the emphasis in the book of Luke.

In the book of Luke the emphasis is on the fullness of the
Spirit and enduement of power for soul winning. In Luke
1:15-17 it is John the Baptist who was to be "filled with the
Holy Ghost, even from his mother's womb"--and winning

souls, of course: "And many of the children of Israel shall he turn to the Lord their God. And he shall go before him in the Spirit and power of Elias...."

In Luke 1:41, 42 it is Elizabeth who "was filled with the Holy Ghost: And she spake out with a loud voice..." and witnessed. In Luke 1:67 it is Zacharias, the father of John the Baptist, who "was filled with the Holy Ghost, and prophesied...." In Luke 2:25, 26 it is Simeon--"and the Holy Ghost was upon him. And it was revealed unto him by the Holy Ghost...."

Matthew, Mark and John tell of the coming of the Holy Spirit upon Jesus when He was baptized, as does Luke 3:22. But Luke 4:1 continues, "And Jesus being full of the Holy Ghost returned from Jordan, and was led by the Spirit into the wilderness." And Luke 4:14 says, "And Jesus returned in the power of the Spirit into Galilee." And only Luke tells that Jesus in the synagogue at Nazareth quoted Isaiah 61:1. "The Spirit of the Lord is upon me, because he hath anointed me to preach the gospel to the poor; he hath sent me to heal the brokenhearted, to preach deliverance to the captives, and recovering of sight to the blind, to set at liberty them that are bruised" (vs. 18). And then Luke tells us He said unto them, "This day is this scripture fulfilled in your ears" (vs. 21).

Only Luke gives the parable of the importunate friend in Luke 11:5-8, where a man is begging for the bread of life for a sinner friend, and Jesus explains in verse 13 that He refers to the power of the Holy Spirit and said, "If ye then, being evil, know how to give good gifts unto your children: how much more shall your heavenly Father give the Holy Spirit to them that ask him?" The book of Luke talks like the book of Acts. The theme throughout the book of Luke is the Son of man filled with the Holy Spirit. In the book of Acts it is the story of the apostles and New Testament Christians filled with the Holy Spirit.

So very properly in Acts 1:1 we are told, "The former

treatise have I made, O Theophilus, of all that Jesus began both to do and teach."

Here in Acts 1:1 is an important, inspired definition of the relation of the book of Luke and the book of Acts. Dr. A. T. Pierson interpreted this verse to mean that Jesus "began to do and to teach" in the Gospels and that the Holy Spirit then continued to do and to teach in the book of Acts. I think he was mistaken. Matthew Henry thought that Jesus began to do and to teach in the Gospels and that Jesus Himself then through the apostles and others continued to do and to teach through the book of Acts. But that is not the inspired emphasis, as I understand the Scripture.

Rather it is this: Jesus, filled with the Holy Ghost, did His ministry as the perfect man, the second Adam, our pattern in the mighty power of the Holy Spirit. Then He breathed on the disciples and said, "As my Father hath sent me, even so send I you" (John 20:21). And Jesus had already told the grieving disciples in John 14:12, "Verily, verily, I say unto you, He that believeth on me, the works that I do shall he do also; and greater works than these shall he do; because I go unto my Father." So when Luke was inspired to write down, "The former treatise have I made, O Theophilus, of all that Jesus began both to do and teach," God meant that in the Gospels we have principally the story of the ministry of the Spirit-filled Son of man, the model man, the second Adam filled with the Spirit. In the book of Acts we have the continuing story about how others, with the same power of the Holy Spirit, worked the same kind of miracles, preached the same Gospel, had the same supernatural results. Jesus began in the power of the Spirit; Christians continued in the same power of the same Spirit.

Certainly only Jesus could atone for man's sins on the cross. But what men filled with the Spirit were enabled to do in the book of Acts is as truly supernatural as what happened in the personal ministry of Jesus in the Gospels. And so God connected the Gospel of Luke and the book of Acts because there is a deep and planned kinship in the theme and method of these two inspired books.

"After That He Through the Holy Ghost Had Given Commandments Unto the Apostles . . ."

It is a remarkable statement hard for our minds to understand and accept that all Jesus did in His ministry, He did through the Holy Spirit. Jesus who "thought it not robbery to be equal with God" (Phil. 2:6) and laid aside the manifestations and outward garments of deity and had taken on Himself the form of a servant. So Jesus came to be born as a man, to live as a man, perfect and sinless, but He was still tempted in all points like as we are. So Jesus preached and did His ministry as a man. But it was the God-Man, the perfect man, the model man, the second Adam, our pattern. So Jesus was filled with the Holy Spirit and all His works were done, not in the power of His own deity as the second person of the Trinity, the power with which He created the world, but in the power of the third person, the Holy Spirit.

Not until Jesus was filled with the Holy Spirit in the baptismal waters had He ever preached a sermon or worked a miracle or won souls. The beginning of miracles, the turning of water into wine in John 2:11 at Cana of Galilee, was after that.

Hebrews 9:14 tells us that Christ "...through the eternal Spirit offered himself without spot to God...." Now after Jesus is risen from the dead and in a glorified body it is still "through the Holy Ghost" that He had given commandment unto the apostles whom He had chosen.

And when Jesus comes back to reign on the earth it is prophesied, "And the spirit of the Lord shall rest upon him, the spirit of wisdom and understanding, the spirit of counsel and might, the spirit of knowledge and of the fear of the Lord; And shall make him of quick understanding in the fear of the Lord: and he shall not judge after the sight of his eyes, neither reprove after the hearing of his ears: But with righteousness shall he judge the poor, and reprove with equity for the meek of the earth: and he shall smite the earth with the rod of his mouth, and with the breath of his lips shall he slay the wicked" (Isa. 11:2-4). Jesus was a Spirit-filled man during His ministry. He, after His resurrection, gave commandments "through the Spirit." On earth again He will reign as a Spirit-filled King.

VERSE 3:

3 To whom also he shewed himself alive after his passion by many infallible proofs, being seen of them forty days, and speaking of the things pertaining to the kingdom of God:

Importance of Christ's Resurrection

Here, in the first sentence in the book of Acts and in the third verse, is stated a fundamental issue of Christianity. Jesus Christ is risen from the dead. Historic Christianity must stand or fall on that basis. The emphasis which is introduced so early is continued throughout the book of Acts and, in fact, throughout the New Testament. Note how vital to Christianity is the resurrection of Christ.

1. He Himself gave that as the only sign and miraculous proof of His deity. "But he answered and said unto them, An evil and adulterous generation seeketh after a sign; and there shall no sign be given to it, but the sign of the prophet Jonas: For as Jonas was three days and three nights in the whale's belly; so shall the Son of man be three days and three nights in the heart of the earth" (Matt. 12:39, 40).

Again Romans 1:4 gives the same evidence. "And declared to be the Son of God with power, according to the Spirit of holiness, by the resurrection from the dead." The deity of Jesus Christ is proven by His resurrection from the dead.

Many writers think that all the miracles of Jesus were to prove His deity, but they are mistaken. Miracles prove that God was with Him just as the miracles of Moses, Joshua, Gideon, Elijah, Elisha, and the miracles attending Peter and Paul prove God was with them, but it did not prove their deity. The deity of Christ is proven by His bodily resurrection from the dead.

2. Christ must have risen from the dead for the Scriptures to be fulfilled. The Gospel, as Paul was inspired to define it, is "...how that Christ died for our sins according to the scriptures; And that he was buried, and that he rose again the third day ACCORDING TO THE SCRIPTURES" (I Cor. 15:3, 4). The apostles understood that the Old Testament clearly prophesied the resurrection of Jesus Christ. Jesus had said that the emergence of Jonah from the belly of the whale was, in type, a prophecy of His resurrection. Peter in Acts 2:25-32 quotes Psalm 16:8-11 as prophesying the resurrection of Jesus Christ. Abraham in a figure received his son Isaac from the dead (Heb. 11:17-19) and that surely pointed toward the resurrection of Christ, since Isaac is a type of Christ. Besides, the whole trend of Scriptures with the triple line of prophecies--one, that Christ must suffer and die for the sins of the world; two, that He must have a priesthood forever after the order of Melchisedec (Heb. 5:6); three, that He must reign forever on the throne of David (Isa. 9:6 and 7, II Sam. 7:16, Jer. 23:5, Ezek. 37:25)--meant that Jesus must rise again.

And let us remember that the only resurrection discussed in the Bible is the literal, bodily resurrection. It was the body of Jesus which was buried in Joseph's tomb, and at the resurrection Joseph's tomb was emptied. One who says he believes in a "spiritual resurrection" but not a bodily resurrection is an unbeliever and a spiritual charlatan. The Bible knows nothing about a resurrection except a literal, bodily resurrection. Spurgeon had a sermon on "The Spir-

itual Resurrection," but he did not mean a spiritual resurrection instead of a bodily resurrection.

3. The resurrection of Christ was as prominent in the
preaching of the apostles as the death of Christ! They are
parts of the same Gospel according to I Corinthians 15:3
and 4. It would have been useless for the apostles to
preach the death of Christ unless they knew He was risen
from the dead.

Note how often the resurrection was mentioned in the
preaching in the book of Acts. Matthias was elected "to be
a witness with us of his resurrection" (Acts 1:22). Peter's
sermon at Pentecost centered on the resurrection of Christ
(Acts 2:24-32). In his second sermon Peter preached that
God "...hath glorified his Son Jesus" (Acts 3:13) "Whom
God hath raised from the dead; whereof we are witnesses"
(vs. 15) "Unto you first God, having raised up his Son Jesus,
sent him to bless you..." (vs. 26).

Note the references to the resurrection in Acts 4:10;
Acts 4:33; Acts 5:30, 31; Acts 7:56; Acts 10:40, 41; Acts
13:29-37; Acts 17:31, 32, and many more. On trial before
the Sanhedrin Paul said, "Of the hope and resurrection of
the dead I am called in question" (Acts 23:6). Before Felix
he preached that he had "hope toward God, which they
themselves also allow, that there shall be a resurrection of
the dead" (Acts 24:15). Festus told King Agrippa that
Paul's arrest hinged on Paul's teaching "of one Jesus, which
was dead, whom Paul affirmed to be alive" (Acts 25:19).
And before Agrippa Paul insisted, "Why should it be thought
a thing incredible with you, that God should raise the
dead?" (Acts 26:8). Again, he preached the resurrection to
King Agrippa in verses 22 and 23.

In Acts we find that Peter, Paul, and Stephen stressed always the resurrection of the crucified Saviour. In the only
two epistles of Paul written to congregations where he had
not yet ministered personally, Paul gave the strongest pos-

sible emphasis to the resurrection (Rom. 1:4; Col. 1:18; Col. 2:12). The resurrection, as we have said, was part of the saving Gospel which Paul preached and defined (1 Cor. 15:3 and 4). And he reminded Timothy of that (II Tim. 2:8).

4. Baptism, commanded for every disciple, every convert, pictures and declares the burial and resurrection of Jesus Christ (Rom. 6:3-5; Col. 2:12).

Note that Acts 1:3 claims "many infallible proofs" for the resurrection.

"Many Infallible Proofs" of Christ's Resurrection

In the Greek text the one strong Greek word tekmerion is translated here "infallible proofs." Berkley's Translation says "many convincing proofs." Young's Literal Translation has it "in many certain proofs." The Twentieth Century New Testament says "with abundant proofs," and William's Translation says "by many convincing proofs."

Consider the infallible proofs of Christ's resurrection.

1. Joseph's tomb was empty. His worst enemies could not find a dead body anywhere.

2. There were many eyewitnesses as given by Paul the apostle in I Corinthians 15:5, 6. He was seen first of Peter, then of all the twelve, and then of above five hundred disciples at one time, and most of these were living many years later.

3. He was seen of them daily for forty days in the most intimate contact. He taught them, ate with them.

4. They felt His body, flesh and bones. So John could speak of Him as that "which we have looked upon, and our hands have handled, of the Word of life" (I John 1:1). They saw Him eat broiled fish and honeycomb (Luke 24:42). Doubting Thomas put his hands in the nailprints and in the wound in His side and was convinced (John 20:27, 28).

5. They saw His miracles. He filled the empty net with fish in John 21. He came through closed doors. He van-

ished out of their sight. Then they all saw Him ascend bodily to Heaven.

6. One of the most profound proofs of Christ's resurrection is that He convinced every single gainsayer among the disciples. Every doubt disappeared. They had not believed, but now they were convinced.

7. The marvels that followed in the church at Jerusalem, in the lives of the apostles and New Testament Christians showed the power of the resurrected Christ. And every person who has trusted that Saviour for salvation knows a certain proof that Christ is risen from the dead, as the Bible says.

A man could be stoned in the Old Testament under the testimony of two or three witnesses (Deut. 17:6; Num. 35:30). A jury of twelve men can now condemn a man to the electric chair. Practically every action of the Supreme Court of the United States, every decision, is based on lesser evidence than the resurrection of which literally hundreds of people were eyewitnesses. No wonder Jesus said that those who did not believe in His resurrection according to the Scriptures were "fools, and slow of heart to believe all that the prophets have spoken" (Luke 24:25).

"Speaking of the things pertaining to the kingdom of God" (vs. 3) a more detailed discussion is given in John 21:15-25--Jesus' discussion with Peter. Luke 24:44, 45 indicates that Jesus, after His resurrection, talked about all the Old Testament Scriptures which prophesied His crucifixion and His resurrection, the things "which were written in the law of Moses, and in the prophets, and in the Psalms, concerning me." So He would spend many hours in the forty days explaining Old Testament Scriptures.

To the two on the road to Emmaus He talked, "And beginning at Moses and all the prophets, he expounded unto them in all the scriptures the things concerning himself" (Luke 24:27). Included in His discussion were clear instructions to wait in Jerusalem for the power of the Holy Spirit and then the all-important Great Commission which He stressed again and again.

VERSES 4, 5:

4 And, being assembled together with *them*, commanded them that they should not depart from Jerusalem, but wait for the promise of the Father, which, *saith he*, ye have heard of me.

5 For John truly baptized with water; but ye shall be baptized with the Holy Ghost not many days hence.

This was "the promise of the Father" which they had already heard. In Matthew 3:11 John the Baptist had said,"I indeed baptize you with water unto repentance: but he that cometh after me is mightier than I, whose shoes I am not worthy to bear: he shall baptize you with the Holy Ghost." John 3:16 tells us, "For God so loved the world, that he gave his only begotten Son, that whosoever believeth in him should not perish, but have everlasting life." In John, chapter 1, John the Baptist gives much discussion of the coming Saviour and verse 33 says, "And I knew him not: but he that sent me to baptize with water, the same said unto me, Upon whom thou shalt see the Spirit descending, and remaining on him, the same is he which baptizeth with the Holy Ghost." So we see that John the Baptist had been inspired to give great emphasis to the fact that Jesus Himself would pour out the Holy Spirit upon His people, a baptism, an overwhelming, a burial in the Spirit.

But the term "the promise of the Father" about the Holy Spirit must indicate that there were Old Testament prophecies also about the pouring out of the Holy Spirit. Isaiah 44:3 and Joel 2:28 certainly speak of what would happen later at Pentecost. Isaiah 61:1, Isaiah 11:1-4 and other Scriptures speak of the fullness of the Spirit upon Jesus. And other Scriptures indicate the great pouring out of the Holy Spirit upon Israel when the remnant shall be saved at the close of the tribulation time.

In the ministry of Jesus, too, there had been clear teaching of this fullness of the Spirit that He would give (Luke 11:5-13). This outpouring of the Holy Spirit in power is mentioned as "the promise of the Father" in Luke 24:49; Acts 1:4; Acts 2:33; Acts 2:39; Ephesians 1:13 and Ephesians 3:6.

They should "wait for the promise" of the Holy Spirit. In Luke 24:49 He had commanded them, "...but tarry ye in the city of Jerusalem, until ye be endued with power from on high." They waited, they tarried. Meantime, they "continued with one accord in prayer and supplication" (Acts 1:14). They waited and prayed in that upper room until the day of Pentecost came ten days later (Acts 2:1).

"Baptized With the Holy Ghost"

A great confusion has been caused by false interpretation here. To understand this Scripture we should remember that the Bible uses the term "baptism" in a literal, physical sense to refer to the immersion of the believer in water, and then uses the term in four different ways as a figure of speech. So the Bible never speaks of "water baptism." Physical baptism is baptism in water and the term is always so to be understood, unless the context clearly indicates otherwise. Now at the close of the ministry of Christ the term "baptism" had been widely used throughout Israel. John the Baptist had baptized many thousands. So that Matthew 3:5 and 6 says, "Then went out to him Jerusalem, and all Judaea, and all the region round about Jordan, And were baptized of him in Jordan, confessing their sins." Not, we suppose, literally every person, but some of all Israel, some from every community and area. But Jesus, through His disciples "made and baptized more disciples than John" (John 4:1). So literal, physical baptism in water was a household word.

Literal baptism is the immersion of a believer in water in New Testament language.

But the word "baptism" is used in a figurative sense four ways.

1. Baptized in, or overwhelmed, in suffering. Jesus said, "I have a baptism to be baptized with; and how am I straitened till it be accomplished!" (Luke 12:50).

2. Baptized into, or immersed in, or buried into, the body of Christ. "For by one Spirit are we [saved people] all baptized into one body" (I Cor. 12:13). That is, at regeneration the Holy Spirit fills us as living stones into the body of Christ, that temple and habitation of God through the Spirit which He is building. We are incorporated, buried in, covered, made a part of that body and so immersed or baptized into it in a figurative sense. Notice the Holy Spirit here is the agent who baptizes, and the element in which we are immersed is that body of Christ, into which we are put or placed, becoming a part of it.

3. The children of Israel are said to have been "baptized unto Moses in the cloud and in the sea" (I Cor. 10:2). The Red Sea stood up in walls on either side, we suppose, and the cloud covered them above, protected them from the pursuing Egyptians, with black darkness behind, and led them as a light before them. So physically, indeed, but more clearly figuratively they were "baptized" or covered or buried "in the cloud and in the sea."

4. Another figurative use of the term "baptism" is "baptized with the Holy Ghost," that is, overwhelmed, covered, buried in, surrounded with the Holy Spirit in power. Notice here that it is Christ who pours out the Holy Ghost upon us (Acts 2:33, Matt. 3:11, etc.). Christ is the agent. The Holy Spirit is not the agent here, but the substance in which we are surrounded and buried and covered. This is a figure indicating a great enduement of power. I think it is a mistake to confuse Acts 1:5, the promise that was fulfilled with these apostles on the day of Pentecost, with I Corinthians

12:13, which refers to the Christians at Corinth who were not even saved at Pentecost. No, baptized into the body of Christ by the agency the Holy Spirit which happens at conversion is one figure, and the floodtide or overwhelming enduement of power by the Holy Spirit for soul winning is another matter entirely. There are two different figurative uses of the term "baptism"; baptized in the body of Christ and baptized in the Holy Ghost. The teaching of Darby, Kelley, and Scofield on this matter goes against the position of Moody, Torrey, Spurgeon and other great teachers and soul winners.

No, the baptism of the Holy Spirit in Acts 1:5 means the same as "endued with power from on high" in Acts 1:8, the same as "filled with the Holy Ghost" in Acts 2:4 and the gift of the Holy Ghost in Acts 2:38, 39.

VERSES 6, 7:

6 When they therefore were come together, they asked of him, saying, Lord, wilt thou at this time restore again the kingdom to Israel?

7 And he said unto them, It is not for you to know the times or the seasons, which the Father hath put in his own power.

Christians Are Not "to Know the Times and Seasons" About the Second Coming

Just before Christ's arrest and the crucifixion, before the last supper together, the disciples had been asking Jesus about "the sign of thy coming, and of the end of the world?" (see Matthew, chapters 24 and 25, and Mark 13).

Remember these apostles were Jewish Christians, but they were Jews. They were not asking about the rapture, the time when Christ would come and call out all of the redeemed to meet Him in the air and take us away for a honeymoon in Heaven. Little had been said about that in the Scripture and in the teaching of Jesus up to this time. In

John 14:3, after the Olivet discourse, Jesus had said, "And if I go and prepare a place for you, I will come again, and receive you unto myself...." The parable of the pounds seems to picture "the return" of a nobleman who will be gone away, returning only after he will "receive for himself a kingdom, and to return" and the reward, "have thou authority over ten cities" and "Be thou also over five cities," refers to Christ's return to reign (Luke 19:11-27). And so with the parable of the talents (Matt. 25:14-30).

In the Olivet discourse the question was threefold: about the destruction of Jerusalem, about the sign and marvel or wonder of Christ's coming, and then "of the end of the world," that is, of the consummation of the age. It is the same phrase used in the Great Commission "even to the end of the world" (Matt. 28:20). But this consummation of the age is not to occur with the rapture when Christ comes to call His own out to meet Him in the air as foretold in I Thessalonians 4:13-18; I Corinthians 15:51, 52. We are now in an age or era or dispensation called in Scripture "the times of the Gentiles," when there is no Jewish king reigning at Jerusalem. The times of the Gentiles began with a Babylonian captivity. In Luke 21:20-24 Jesus foretold a future time, we think, after the rapture, when the Man of Sin and his armies will compass Jerusalem "...and Jerusalem shall be trodden down of the Gentiles, until the times of the Gentiles be fulfilled." The reign of the Antichrist, foretold in Daniel 7:25 and 26 and in Revelation 13:1-10, will still begin "the times of the Gentiles." And during that time of great tribulation even the court of the temple "is given unto the Gentiles: and the holy city shall they tread under foot forty and two months" (Rev. 11:2).

In the Olivet discourse in Matthew 24, Mark 13 and Luke 21, this second coming of Christ is principally treated as one great event, not divided into the various phases, and while the rapture is included by inference, it is not directly discussed.

The question of the apostles in Matthew 24:3 was about "the sign of thy coming, and of the end of the world," that is, the marvel of Christ's appearing when He should come back to reign at the end of the times of the Gentiles and when Christ Himself would assume the throne of David as promised (II Sam. 7:10-16; Ps. 2:6; Isa. 11:1-12; Isa. 9:6, 7; Jer. 23:3-8; Dan. 2:44; Ezek. 37:21-28). Note also the explicit promise to Mary, "...and the Lord God shall give unto nim the throne of his father David: And he shall reign over the house of Jacob for ever; and of his kingdom there shall be no end" (Luke 1:32, 33). Peter mentioned this prophecy in Acts 2:30. He says that David knew "that God had sworn with an oath to him, that of the fruit of his loins, according to the flesh, he would raise up Christ to sit on his throne." The times of the Gentiles will end when the throne of David is restored in Palestine. See the author's book, The Coming Kingdom of Christ, and the pamphlet, The Second Coming of Christ in Daniel.

The twelve apostles, then, when they asked, "Wilt thou at this time restore again the kingdom to Israel?" (Acts 1:6) did not refer to the rapture but to the final event of the series of events when Christ shall return with saints and angels to set up His kingdom and reign on the earth after the rapture of the saints, the Great Tribulation, the judgment seat of Christ, etc.

"It Is Not for You to Know" the Time for Future Events, Says Jesus

The Bible doctrine of the premillennial, personal, bodily return of Christ has been brought greatly into disfavor because of the very human but carnal tendency to try to set dates for Christ's return. Yet the one thing the Lord Jesus emphasized most clearly with reference to Second Coming matters is that the time is to be utterly unknown. Men do not know when Christ will return, not exactly nor even approximately, because it is not given us to know! The time of the Second Coming is a part of those "secret things" which "belong unto God."

How often did Jesus stress this truth that no one is to know the time of His return! Note these Scriptures.

> "But of that day and hour knoweth no man, no, not the angels of heaven, but my Father only."-- Matt. 24:36.

His coming will be as the days of Noah were:

> "For as in the days that were before the flood they were eating and drinking, marrying and giving in marriage, until the day that Noe entered into the ark, AND KNEW NOT UNTIL THE FLOOD CAME, AND TOOK THEM ALL AWAY; so shall also the coming of the Son of man be."--Matt. 24:38, 39.

> "Watch therefore: for ye know not what hour your Lord doth come."--Matt. 24:42.

> "Therefore be ye also ready: for in such an hour as ye think not the Son of man cometh."-- Matt. 24:44.

> "Watch therefore, for ye know neither the day nor the hour wherein the Son of man cometh."-- Matt. 25:13.

> "Take ye heed, watch and pray: for ye know not when the time is. For the Son of man is as a man taking a far journey, who left his house, and gave authority to his servants, and to every man his work, and commanded the porter to watch."--Mark 13:33, 34.

> "Watch ye therefore: for ye know not when the master of the house cometh, at even, or at mid-

> night, or at the cockcrowing, or in the morning:
> Lest coming suddenly he find you sleeping. And
> what I say unto you I say unto all, Watch."--
> Mark 13:35-37.

New Testament Christians were taught to watch continually for Christ's coming which might be at any unknown
time.

> "For our conservation is in heaven; from
> whence also we look for the Saviour, the Lord
> Jesus Christ."--Phil. 3:20.

The Thessalonians "turned to God from idols to serve the
living and true God; And to wait for his Son from heaven,
whom he raised from the dead, even Jesus, which delivered
us from the wrath to come" (I Thess. 1:9, 10).

This constant expectation of Christ's coming at any unknown, unannounced time was held by Paul personally who
expected Christ to come in his lifetime. First Thessalonians 4:15, "We which are alive and remain unto the coming
of the Lord..." and I Corinthians 15:52, "And the dead shall
be raised incorruptible, and we shall be changed."

In fact, the insisting on signs or wonders or evidences
and knowledge of future events is regarded in the Scriptures
as sinful. As Jesus said, "An evil and adulterous generation seeketh after a sign" (Matt. 12:39).

In I Corinthians 1:22 and 23 Paul says, "For the Jews require a sign, and the Greeks seek after wisdom: But we
preach Christ crucified, unto the Jews a stumblingblock
and unto the Greeks foolishness."

Israel was strictly warned that they were not to have diviners or observers of times or enchanters or witches or
consultors with familiar spirits, etc. who would foretell the
future, "For these nations, which thou shalt possess,
hearkened unto observers of times, and unto diviners: but

as for thee, the Lord thy God hath not suffered thee so to do" (Deut. 18:14). And it was "because of these abomina- tions the Lord thy God doth drive them out from before thee" (Deut. 18:12). King Saul lost the kingdom for himself and his dynasty "for his transgression which he committed against the Lord, even against the word of the Lord, which he kept not, AND ALSO FOR ASKING COUNSEL OF ONE THAT HAD A FAMILIAR SPIRIT, TO ENQUIRE OF IT" (I Chron. 10:13). It is sinful to try to find out what God has hidden in the future.

We Are Not to Know Even Approximately the Time of Christ's Return

"It is not for you to know the TIMES or the SEASONS, which the Father hath put in his own power." A "time" in the Bible sometimes means one year. So in Daniel 7:25 and Revelation 12:14 the three and half times is evidently the same as the forty-two months of Revelation 13:5, and the thousand two hundred and threescore days of Revelation 11:3. So no one can know what year the Lord will return.

"And seasons" evidently indicate eras or ages.

One of the arguments Jesus used showing that no one could know when He would return is, "But know this, that if the goodman of the house had known in what watch the thief would come, he would have watched, and would not have suffered his house to be broken up" (Matt. 24:43). Jesus uses a similar illustration to show the unpredictable time of His return in Mark 13:35. "Watch ye therefore: for ye know not when the master of the house cometh, at even, or at midnight, or at the cockcrowing, or in the morning." Here are named the four watches of the night as represent- ing the whole New Testament age, and if the whole New Testament or church age were divided into quarters or night watches, none of us could tell ahead of time in what period the Lord Jesus would return. For example, if the whole time, we will say, between Pentecost and the return of Christ should be two thousand years, then the matter is kept so secret that no one could know whether He would come in the first five hundred years or in the second five hundred years or in the third five hundred years or in the last five hundred years.

In other words, no one can know even approximately when Christ will return. There are no prophesied events which must occur before Jesus comes. He could have come before World War I or before World War II, before the rise of communism. New Testament Christians expected Christ's return (as they were commanded to expect it) during their lifetime.

VERSE 8:

8 But ye shall receive power, after that the Holy Ghost is come upon you: and ye shall be witnesses unto me both in Jerusalem, and in all Judea, and in Samaria, and unto the uttermost part of the earth.

The Great Commission

We would call this another statement of the Great Commission, Jesus' command that the disciples should take the Gospel to all the world. In this case the Great Commission is given on the Mount of Olives, immediately before His ascension. In Matthew 28:18-20 the Great Commission is given when "the eleven disciples went away into Galilee, into a mountain where Jesus had appointed them" (Matt. 28:16), and we suppose soon after His resurrection. It appears from the context that Jesus gave the Great Commission as expressed in Mark 16:15 when "he appeared unto the eleven as they sat at meat..." (Mark 16:14), we suppose in that upper room where they had observed the last supper with Jesus.

The Great Commission as given in Luke 24:46-49, was

spoken just before they went out to Bethany on the Mount of Olives where He ascended. So probably this Great Commission, many times repeated, was discussed before they went out to the Mount of Olives and then after they assembled there before His ascension.

The Great Commission as given in John 20:21, "As my Father hath sent me, even so send I you," etc., was on the day of the resurrection, "the same day at evening" (John 20:19). So we may be sure that in all those forty days Jesus spent with the disciples teaching them, He repeated again and again the Great Commission. His command to His disciples was to go into all the world and preach the Gospel to every creature. He did it the very day, the evening of His resurrection; He did it when He appeared again as they sat at meat. He gave the Great Commission when they assembled in Galilee. He gave them the same command before going out to Bethany on the Mount of Olives where He ascended. And then on the Mount itself, the last words He spoke to His disciples, we understand, was this same Great Commission!

Was the Great Commission Given to the Church as an Institution or to Every Individual Christian?

It is clear from three evidences that the Great Commission was given to every individual Christian and not to any organization or institution as such.

First, in Matthew 28:20, after giving the command to the apostles to make disciples and baptize them in all the world, Jesus added, "teaching them [the converts] to observe all things whatsoever I have commanded you." Every convert was to get exactly the same Great Commission given the apostles.

Second, the Great Commission as given by Jesus was recorded at least five times in the New Testament and it seems, on five different occasions. And in every case "the eleven" (Judas is dead) are mentioned as "the disciples" and never any group as a church when the Great Commission was given.

Consider these five occasions.

1. Jesus gave the Great Commission in Matthew 28:19, 20, but in verses 16 and 18 we read, "Then the eleven disciples went away into Galilee, into a mountain where Jesus had appointed them....And Jesus came and spake unto them, saying, All power is given unto me in heaven and in earth," and He gave the Great Commission. It was to the eleven disciples, and then through them, to every individual converted and baptized.

2. Again, in Mark 16:14 and 15 we find that the Great Commission commandment was given to "the eleven as they sat at meat, and upbraided them with their unbelief and hardness of heart, because they believed not them which had seen him after he was risen. And he said unto them, Go ye into all the world, and preach the gospel to every creature."

Thus the Commission was not given to any institution or organization: none was present. It was given to the eleven and through them, to every Christian.

3. In Luke 24:33-35 we read how the two who had met Jesus on the road to Emmaus "returned to Jerusalem, and found the eleven gathered together, and them that were with them." The eleven disciples were together and some others were with them, possibly the mother of Jesus and His brothers, as mentioned in Acts 1:14, and possibly Mary Magdalene. We do not know. But to this group verse 36 says, "And as they thus spake, Jesus himself stood in the midst of them." He comforted them, and then in verses 47 and 48 He gave them the Great Commission. No mention is made of a church.

4. In John 20:19 we find that when Jesus rose from the dead, "Then the same day at evening, being the first day of

the week, when the doors were shut where the disciples were assembled for fear of the Jews, came Jesus and stood in the midst, and saith unto them, Peace be unto you." Who were present? "The disciples were assembled for fear of the Jews." And to them Jesus said in verse 21, "As my Father hath sent me, even so send I you." It was not a church meeting as such. They were addressed as individuals, not as an institution.

5. In Acts 1:2 we read that Jesus "through the Holy Ghost had given commandments unto the apostles whom he had chosen." And verse 4 says, "And being assembled together with them, commanded them that they should not depart from Jerusalem, but wait for the promise of the Father, which, saith he, ye have heard of me." They were to be baptized with the Holy Ghost and then in verse 8 the promise is combined with the command of the Great Commission, "But ye shall receive power, after that the Holy Ghost is come upon you: and ye shall be witnesses unto me...." Here it is clearly stated that the Great Commission was given "unto the apostles whom he had chosen" and according to the clear statement of Matthew 28:20 every new convert was to be baptized and to have passed on to him exactly the same command as given the apostles.

Now we must make it clear: God's usual unit in every place is a local church.

1. Local congregations or churches of Christians are greatly emphasized in Acts. Certainly all Christians should associate themselves with local churches sound in faith.

2. Local churches should certainly try to carry out the Great Commission. Since every member has an obligation to win souls, certainly the group as a whole should win souls.

3. Much of soul-winning work can be done better by united effort. Jesus sent out the seventy two by two. The palsied man of Mark 2 was carried by four. A congrega-

tion can maintain a pastor or pastors, send a missionary, build a building, provide for the poor, maintain fellowship, sing or be taught the Word, in groups. Baptism, the Lord's Supper, the decision to exclude a brother in gross sin, as in I Corinthians 5, can all be done more impressively and reputably by group approval.

Local churches are important, and all Christians, in Bible times, were members of local assemblies. Often the best way to win souls is in some connection with a local church. But the Great Commission is given to every Christian in the local church, not to the local church as an official body. If the group as an organization or institution fails, that does not excuse the individual Christian. According to Jesus' words in Matthew 28:19, 20, new converts are to be baptized and then taught to carry out all the commands given the apostles.

Soul winning can only be done as people are endued with power of the Holy Spirit. "Ye shall receive power, after that the Holy Ghost is come upon you: and ye shall be witnesses unto me..." (Acts 1:8). No congregation is endued with the power of the Holy Spirit as an institution but only as individuals present are filled with the Spirit. Those who are won to Christ must come as individuals, and those who win souls to Christ must do it as individuals.

"Ye Shall Receive Power, After That the Holy Ghost Is Come Upon You"

Acts 1:8 is of tremendous importance in defining what happened at Pentecost. When the Holy Ghost came on the disciples, they simply received power to witness for Jesus. And the same thing is stated in Luke 24:49, "But tarry ye in the city of Jerusalem, until ye be endued with power from on high." And in both cases, in Luke and in Acts, this promise of soul-winning and witnessing power is given in connection with the Great Commission.

How foolish for anyone to misunderstand what God is talking about here! The disciples were not to tarry for some gift of tongues. Of course, the Gospel must be preached in some language or more than one language, but the preaching of the Gospel with power is the matter here promised. There were incidental miracles in connection with Pentecost, the sound of a rushing, mighty wind, and visible tongues of fire that sat on the people. But that is not what is promised and not that for which they waited. Those miracles were incidental, unpredicted, and unrepeated. What they were to wait for was power from on high. They were to receive power to witness for Jesus. Jesus had just, throughout the forty days, pressed upon His disciples the command to go into all the world and preach the Gospel. And the command was not only to them, but to all Christians who should follow, "even unto the end of the world," and even "to every creature." The Lord firmly joined together the duty to preach the Gospel and the command to be filled with the Holy Spirit, to be endued with power from on high. No one should separate them. The one great equipment required for witnessing is to be filled with the Holy Spirit.

There are many errors and misunderstandings of the meaning of Pentecost. But note the disciples did not wait for the origin of the church. We believe that that "general assembly and church of the first-born which are written in heaven" will be called out at the rapture and assembled in Heaven and will include all the saved of all ages. The Bible never tells us when the church began, never speaks of its "origin" or "founding." Certainly that is not what the Scriptures are speaking about at Pentecost. Rather, the disciples are commanded to wait, to be endued with power from on high when the Holy Ghost is to come upon them, and then they are to witness and win souls carrying out the Great Commission.

The disciples did not wait to speak in tongues. The talking in whatever language was simply witnessing with power as the Lord had promised and they were given power to speak in the languages of the people who were gathered so they could witness and win souls. And so they did.

The disciples were not waiting to seek "a second work of grace." At Pentecost there is no hint that the carnal nature was destroyed in these disciples or that they were "sanctified." No, they had been given a task to carry the Gospel to all the world. Now they were plainly commanded to wait upon God for enduement of power for this task. And the meaning of Pentecost is as simple as that. "Ye shall receive power, after that the Holy Ghost is come upon you: and ye shall be witnesses unto me...."

Here is the key that explains all the terms used about what happened at Pentecost. When the disciples were "baptized with the Holy Ghost" as promised in Acts 1:5, they were simply surrounded, overwhelmed, submerged in the mighty power of God to enable them to witness. This is what it means to be "filled with the Holy Ghost," the more usual term, and the more literal term used throughout the book of Acts, but referring to what happened at Pentecost in Acts 2:4. So to be filled with the Holy Spirit and to be baptized with the Spirit mean the same thing.

Pentecost was the time when God had promised to "pour out of my Spirit" (Joel 2:28; Acts 2:17, 18). This enduement of power from on high for witnessing is "the gift of the Holy Ghost" of Acts 2:38, promised to all whom "the Lord our God shall call" (Acts 2:39).

What happened at Pentecost is that the disciples were endued with power to witness for Christ and they won some three thousand souls. And that was a "specimen day" as D. L. Moody said. Just as Joel prophesied that Pentecost was included in "the last days," so the enduement of power on that day is promised throughout this age for all Christians who will meet God's requirement.

VERSES 9–11:

9 And when he had spoken these things, while they beheld, he was taken up; and a cloud received him out of their sight.

10 And while they looked steadfastly toward heaven as he went up, behold, two men stood by them in white apparel;

11 Which also said, Ye men of Galilee, why stand ye gazing up into heaven? this same Jesus, which is taken up from you into heaven, shall so come in like manner as ye have seen him go into heaven.

Christ's Coming as He Went Away

Note how literal was the ascension of Jesus. The resurrection of Jesus was a literal, physical resurrection. Joseph's new tomb was empty. Jesus ate and drank before the disciples. They touched Him, handled Him. Now Jesus with His physical body ascended literally, visibly to Heaven. Now in Heaven He has that physical body and when He returns to the earth again, He will have that same physical body, and with the visible wounds in His hands (Zech. 13:6). And then it is said of Israel, "and they shall look upon me whom they have pierced" (Zech. 12:10).

Oh, how glad Heaven must have been to receive Him! How the millions of angels delighted to see Jesus in His physical body and to see His wounds! And how glad Jesus must have been to get back home again! This is part of "the joy that was set before him" (Heb. 12:2) for which He endured the cross and despised the shame. But that joy will not be completed until all the redeemed of all ages, saved by His precious blood, will be gathered home with Jesus and when they come from the North and East and South and West to sit down with Abraham and Isaac and Jacob in the kingdom of God.

But here standing by them were two "men" in white apparel. We believe that these "men" were angels. The two angels in Genesis 19:1 and 15 are called men in verses 5, 10, 12, and 16. And the Lord and two angels who appeared to Abraham in Genesis 18 are called "three men" in verse 2. The Angel that appeared to the woman who was to become the mother of Samson in Judges 13:3 is called "a man of God" in verses 6 and 8 and "the man" in verse 10. The angel that appeared to Daniel in Daniel 10:5 is called "a certain man" and in verse 18 another angel, "one like the appearance of a man," is mentioned. Angels, then, look like men, are often called men. And we suppose that these two were heavenly angels who stood by the disciples and announced that Christ would come again as He went away.

So since Christ will return in the way He went away, He will come visibly, bodily, literally. "The Lord himself shall descend from heaven" (I Thess. 4:16). Jesus meant the same thing when He said, "And if I go and prepare a place for you, I will come again, and receive you unto myself" (John 14:3).

I take it that the similarity of Christ's second coming to His going away refers to His return to reign on the earth (not His coming into the air to call us away).

"A cloud received him out of their sight," says Acts 1:9. And Revelation 1:7 says, "Behold, he cometh with clouds; and every eye shall see him."

Jesus ascended "from the mount called Olivet" (Acts 1:12). And when He returns again we are told, "And his feet shall stand in that day upon the mount of Olives, which is before Jerusalem on the east, and the mount of Olives shall cleave in the midst thereof toward the east and toward the west..." (Zech. 14:4).

To explain away the very explicit promise that Christ will personally return again to the earth is wicked unbelief.

VERSES 12–14:

12 Then returned they unto Jerusalem from the mount called Olivet, which is from Jerusalem a sabbath day's journey. 13 And when they were come in, they went up into an upper

room, where abode both Peter, and James, and John, and Andrew, Philip, and Thomas, Bartholomew, and Matthew, James *the son* of Alpheus, and Simon Zelotes, and Judas *the brother* of James.

14 These all continued with one accord in prayer and supplication, with the women, and Mary the mother of Jesus, and with his brethren.

The Upper Room Pre-Pentecostal Prayer Meeting

The disciples returned from the Mount of Olives, less than a mile to Jerusalem. They went not to an upper room but into the upper room (the Greek article is definite), the same one where they had had the last supper and there, we suppose, they lived during the days before Pentecost.

In this prayer meeting were the eleven apostles, Mary the mother of Jesus, and the half brothers of Jesus (born of Joseph and Mary after Christ was born). We suppose they were James and Jude or Judas (who wrote the books of James and Jude in the Bible) and Joses and Simon (Matt. 13:55, Mark 6:3). These brothers of Jesus had not believed in Him and had not been converted before Christ's crucifixion (John 7:5). To them Jesus sent a special message after His resurrection that they should meet Him in Galilee (Matt. 28:10). There, we suppose, when they saw the resurrected Saviour, they trusted Him. Or possibly they had trusted Him in connection with His death and those three sad days He lay in the grave. Now they are in the prayer meeting before Pentecost.

The total number present were "about an hundred and twenty" (vs. 15).

Note these did not simply tarry or wait passively; rather they "continued with one accord in prayer and supplication."

There they prayed with "supplication" or pleading. This is the "importunity" of the man pleading for bread of life for others in Luke 11:8. We suppose this is the time when, after the bridegroom has been taken away, the children of the bridechamber fasted in Mark 2:19 and 20.

Prevailing Prayer for Holy Spirit Power

"These all continued with one accord in prayer and supplication...."--vs. 14.

We dare not dismiss these ten days of persistent prayer and supplication in the upper room as an incidental matter, or as peculiar to that time and place. No, there is a Bible principle that always those who need the fullness of the Holy Spirit, power to do God's work, need to wait on Him and plead till they be endued with power from on high.

I. GOD REQUIRES AND CHRISTIANS OFTEN NEED TO PLEAD WITH GOD FOR ANY WANT FOR SUPPLY, FOR DELIVERANCE, FOR WISDOM, FOR POWER.

1. That is the specific teaching of the parable in Luke 18:1-9. "And he spake a parable unto them to this end, that men ought always to pray, and not to faint."

2. Jacob wrestling all night with the angel, 'prevailed with God and with men' (Gen. 32:26 ff).

3. Samuel "cried unto the Lord all night" (I Sam. 15:11).

4. Queen Esther and her maidens fasted and prayed three days and nights for deliverance of the Jews from destruction (Esther 4:16).

5. The Canaanitish woman who persistently pleaded for her devil-possessed daughter (Matt. 15:21-28) shows that God is pleased at such persistent pleading.

6. Jesus Himself "went out into a mountain to pray, and continued all night in prayer to God" (Luke 6:12). If there were no specific instructions that we should wait on God and plead for Holy Spirit power, it is still clearly God's will for His people to seek His face. Again and again in the Scriptures are such terms as "wait on the Lord," "seek my face"; terms like "supplication" and "importunity."

7. In Ephesians 6:18 we are commanded, "Praying al-

ways with all prayer and supplication in the Spirit, and watching thereunto with all perseverance and supplication for all saints."

8. Elijah is a classic example of persistent prayer (James 5:17, 18; I Kings 17:19-22; I Kings 18:42-44).

II. THERE ARE SPECIFIC INSTRUCTIONS AND PROMISES ABOUT PRAYING FOR HOLY SPIRIT POWER.

1. Isaiah 40:29-31 clearly refers to the power of the Holy Spirit, given in answer to persistent prayer. "He giveth power to the faint; and to them that have no might he increaseth strength....But they that wait upon the Lord shall renew their strength...."

2. Second Chronicles 7:14 gives God's people the way to revival including if they "humble themselves, and pray, and seek my face, and turn from their wicked ways; then will I hear from heaven...."

3. In Luke 11:5-13 the Lord Jesus particularly teaches His disciples how to pray for the bread of life for sinners, that is, how to prevail for soul-winning power. Verse 8 says that the one essential of this kind of prayer is "importunity." In verses 9 and 10 the Lord urges continuing to ask and seek and knock. In verse 13 He promises, "If ye then, being evil, know how to give good gifts unto your children: how much more shall your heavenly Father give the Holy Spirit to them that ask him?" The verb for ask is present tense, indicating continued action. And the Holy Spirit ministry for which one is here taught to pray is not the indwelling of the Spirit, but the enduement of power, to carry bread for sinners.

4. In Luke 24:49, after Jesus had given the command that repentance and remission of sins should be preached in all nations and instructed these disciples that they were the witnesses to tell it, He commanded, "But tarry ye in the city of Jerusalem, until ye be endued with power from on high."

5. In Acts 1:4 Jesus commanded the disciples "that they

should not depart from Jerusalem, but wait for the promise of the Father, which, saith he, ye have heard of me." And in the light of verse 14 we know that the waiting was to include "prayer and supplication."

III. THERE ARE MANY BIBLE EXAMPLES OF PEOPLE WHO PRAYED FOR AND RECEIVED THE POWER OF THE HOLY SPIRIT TO WITNESS FOR JESUS.

1. The insistence of Elisha in following Elijah on the day he was translated, asking that "a double portion of thy spirit be upon me" must be regarded as persistent prayer for the power of the Holy Spirit (II Kings 2:1-9). And the sons of the prophets saw that "the spirit of Elijah doth rest on Elisha" (II Kings 2:15).

2. It was in answer to the prayers of his father and mother that John the Baptist was "filled with the Holy Ghost, even from his mother's womb" (Luke 1:15). But his own persistent prayer to be anointed for the prophesied ministry seems certainly implied in the statement of Luke 1:80, "And the child grew, and waxed strong in spirit, and was in the deserts till the day of his shewing unto Israel."

3. The angel appearing to Zacharias to announce the coming birth of John the Baptist said, "Thy prayer is heard" (Luke 1:13). And the indication is that he meant years of prayer on the part of Zacharias and Elisabeth for a son who would be a great prophet. So this praying woman, "Elisabeth was filled with the Holy Ghost, and prophesied..." (Luke 1:67).

4. The apostles, with a group of about 120, "continued with one accord in prayer and supplication..." for the power of God in Acts 1:14.

5. The same group later prayed and were filled with the Spirit again in Acts 4:31.

6. Paul, converted on the road to Damascus, continued three days and nights in fasting and prayer before Ananias laid his hands upon him and he was "filled with the Holy Ghost" (Acts 9:9, 11, 17).

7. Paul the apostle prayed for the converts at Ephesus to be filled with the Spirit. In Ephesians, chapter 1, he said, "Making mention of you in my prayers; That...God...may give unto you the spirit of wisdom and revelation in the knowledge of him...that ye may know...what is the exceeding greatness of his power" (vss. 16-19). In Ephesians 3 he prayed, "That ye might be filled with all the fulness of God" (vs. 19). So it is proper to pray for the fullness of the Spirit, that is, for power to witness for Christ.

VERSES 15–26:

15 ¶ And in those days Peter stood up in the midst of the disciples, and said, (the number of names together were about a hundred and twenty,)

16 Men *and* brethren, this Scripture must needs have been fulfilled, which the Holy Ghost by the mouth of David spake before concerning Judas, which was guide to them that took Jesus.

17 For he was numbered with us, and had obtained part of this ministry.

18 Now this man purchased a field with the reward of iniquity; and falling headlong, he burst asunder in the midst, and all his bowels gushed out.

19 And it was known unto all the dwellers at Jerusalem; insomuch as that field is called, in their proper tongue, Aceldama, that is to say, The field of blood.

20 For it is written in the book of Psalms, Let his habitation be desolate, and let no man dwell therein: and, His bishoprick let another take.

21 Wherefore of these men which have companied with us all the time that the Lord Jesus went in and out among us,

22 Beginning from the baptism of John, unto that same day that he was taken up from us, must one be ordained to be a witness with us of his resurrection.

23 And they appointed two, Joseph called Barsabas, who was surnamed Justus, and Matthias.

24 And they prayed, and said, Thou, Lord, which knowest the hearts of all *men*, shew whether of these two thou hast chosen,

25 That he may take part of this ministry and apostleship, from which Judas by transgression fell, that he might go to his own place.

26 And they gave forth their

lots; and the lot fell upon Mat- | with the eleven apostles.
thias; and he was numbered |

The Election of Matthias as a Witness

Judas is dead. It would seem proper, since all the apostles represented Israel and there were twelve tribes of Israel and the number twelve had a special meaning to Jews, that there ought to be twelve witnesses to the resurrection of Christ. Judas had failed, had fallen from his apostleship; now they needed another witness.

His requirement was that he must "have companied with us all the time that the Lord Jesus went in and out among us, Beginning from the baptism of John, unto that same day that he was taken up from us" (vss. 21, 22). And then he was to "be ordained to be a witness with us of his resurrection." The great theme of New Testament preachers was the resurrection of Christ which proved His deity and proved that His coming, His death, and all were "according to the scriptures." So they must have another witness. He must have been baptized by John the Baptist, must have been present in the entire earthly ministry of Christ, must have seen Christ after His resurrection and must have seen the ascension. Such a one could give solemn witness that any intelligent and open heart could believe when he told them of Christ's resurrection.

Here is a strange combination. The disciples selected two men, both suitable, both meeting the requirements. They seemed not to have clear leading as to which of the two would be the better witness. So they prayed for God to take part and show His will "by lot." Unless God Himself supervised the matter, the choice would have been left entirely to chance. This way of finding the will of God is never suggested to us in the Bible, and probably would usually be dangerous, particularly with unspiritual people.

Note that Matthias "was numbered with the eleven apostles." He is never called an apostle. He is numbered with the eleven apostles as one of the official and chosen witnesses of Christ's resurrection. We suppose the need for such a witness was in Jerusalem and in the days immediately after the resurrection. Matthias is not heard from again.

It is true in verse 25 that the apostles wanted a man "that he may take part of this ministry and apostleship, from which Judas by transgression fell." But we believe the part of the apostleship which he took was simply to witness to Christ's resurrection. He may have gone with a certain authority, as did the eleven apostles in teaching and preaching until the canon of Scripture should be fulfilled. But if so, we are not told of his ministry.

It is interesting that seventeen people are mentioned as apostles if we count Matthias. Besides the original twelve, there is Matthias, Barnabas and Paul (Acts 14:14), James the brother of Jesus (Gal. 1:19), and then Jesus who is called "the Apostle and High Priest of our profession" (Heb. 3:1). So there were more than twelve apostles, whether Matthias is called an apostle or not. But there were needed twelve to be witnesses of the resurrection of Christ. What twelve of the apostles "shall sit upon twelve thrones, judging the twelve tribes of Israel"? (Matt. 19:28). We do not know.

The Fall of Judas

Notice that it was "part of this ministry and apostleship, from which Judas by transgression fell." He fell from an official position. It is not hinted that he fell from salvation.

On the contrary, Judas was never saved. In John 6:64 Jesus said, "But there are some of you that believe not. For Jesus knew from the beginning who they were that believed not, and who should betray him." Here it is clearly inferred that Judas himself had never trusted Christ, was not saved.

Again, in the same chapter, in verses 70 and 71 we are told, "Jesus answered them, Have not I chosen you twelve, and one of you is a devil? He spake of Judas Iscariot the son of Simon: for he it was that should betray him, being one of the twelve." Judas was an unsaved professor.

Does it seem strange that an unsaved man would be allowed to go with Jesus as an apostle? Remember that the betrayal by Judas was foretold in the Old Testament and that is referred to by Peter in Acts 1:16 and 20.

Besides, Judas was typical of many, many others in all ages who have 'a form of godliness without the power thereof' (II Tim. 3:5). Jesus warned us that there would be many such. In Matthew 7:15 He warned, "Beware of false prophets, which come to you in sheep's clothing, but inwardly they are ravening wolves." In Matthew 7:21-23 He said:

> "Not every one that saith unto me, Lord, Lord, shall enter into the kingdom of heaven; but he that doeth the will of my Father which is in heaven. Many will say to me in that day, Lord, Lord, have we not prophesied in thy name? and in thy name have cast out devils? and in thy name done many wonderful works? And then will I profess unto them, I never knew you: depart from me, ye that work iniquity."

And Jude 4 warns us of "ungodly men, turning the grace of our God into lasciviousness, and denying the only Lord God, and our Lord Jesus Christ." It should not be surprising, then, that Judas is typical of thousands of others unconverted in the churches, even in places of leadership in churches who are unconverted sinners deceiving and being deceived, blind leaders of the blind.

ACTS 2

VERSE 1:

AND when the day of Pente- | were all with one accord in one
cost was fully come, they | place.

Did the Church Begin the Day
of Pentecost?

Israelites were required when they should reap their harvest that they should "bring a sheaf of the firstfruits of your
harvest unto the priest" (Lev. 23:10). Then numbering fifty
days from that offering they were to bring "a new meat offering unto the Lord" (a food offering of loaves, with seven
lambs and a kid, Lev. 23:16-19). That day of "an holy con-
vocation" (Lev. 23:21) is Pentecost. But the resurrection of
Christ is pictured by that first sheaf of the harvest. "But
now is Christ risen from the dead, and become the firstfruits of them that slept" (I Cor. 15:20). And so it is supposed that Pentecost came fifty days after the resurrection
of Christ. If that be true and since Jesus appeared to the
disciples after His resurrection for some forty days (Acts
1:3), then, the time of waiting in the upper room and of
prayer and supplication was ten days.

But neither in the Old Testament feasts, which were typical, nor in the New Testament discussion of Pentecost, is
anything said about the origin of the church at Pentecost.
We believe that the Scofield Reference Bible, that most valuable and helpful of all reference Bibles, is in this matter
mistaken in the notes about Pentecost.

On pages 156 and 157 Dr. Scofield has a note on Leviticus
23:16 saying:

> "The feast of Pentecost, vs. 15-22. The anti-
> type is the descent of the Holy Spirit to form the
> church. For this reason leaven is present, be-

> cause there is evil in the church (Mt. 13:33;
> Acts 5:1, 10; 15:3). Observe, it is now loaves;
> not a sheaf of separate growths loosely bound to-
> gether, but a real union of particles making one
> homogeneous body. The descent of the Holy
> Spirit at Pentecost united the separate disciples
> into one organism (I Cor. 10:16, 17; 12:12, 13,
> 20)." On the following verse Leviticus 23:17 the
> Scofield note says: "The wave-loaves were of-
> fered fifty days after the wave-sheaf. This is
> precisely the period between the resurrection of
> Christ and formation of the church at Pentecost
> by the baptism of the Holy Spirit (Acts 2:1-4; I
> Cor. 12:12, 13)...."

There is very widespread understanding that the church, the body of Christ, began at Pentecost. That is remarkable, particularly since the Bible never mentions anything of the kind! I think that idea, that the church was formed at Pentecost, comes perhaps from at least three errors.

1. A misunderstanding of what the church is.

2. A misunderstanding of Pentecost and what happened then.

3. A misunderstanding of some Scriptures, particularly I Corinthians 12:13, and the baptism of the Holy Spirit.

Why We Believe the Church Could Not Have Been Formed at Pentecost

Our Catholic friends have led the world wrong on the meaning of the word church. In the Encyclopedia Britannica, a Catholic scholar in the article on the Roman Catholic Church says concerning the word church, "By it we mean the visible body or organization which Christ Himself set up to perpetuate for all time the authoritative teaching of the truth which He came on earth to reveal to mankind." Then he says, "A more technical definition would be as follows: 'the church instituted by Jesus Christ is the visible society of men who, having received baptism, united in the profession of the same faith and in one communion, and are seeking the same spiritual end under the authority of the Roman pontiff, the successor of St. Peter, and of the bishops who are in union with him.' "

All of the major Protestant denominations which have a connectional system in the ministry, an episcopacy or hierarchy, are in that matter patterned after Rome. The idea of one world-wide society visible to men being called a church is utterly foreign to Bible usage. The word church in the Bible never refers to a denomination. It never refers to the sum of the denominations joined together. The church, the body of Christ, including all the saved, is another matter. To understand what the Bible teaches, we must rid ourselves of the idea of a denomination or a group of denominations in connection with the word church.

The little Greek word ekklesia, translated church in the New Testament, simply means a called-out assembly. So Israel gathered out of Egypt at Mount Sinai is called "the church in the wilderness" (Acts 7:38), and it was a church: not a Christian organization, not a local New Testament church, of course, and not particularly a church of God, but it was a called-out assembly.

In Acts 19, the word ekklesia is (the only times in the New Testament) translated "assembly" in verses 32, 39, and 41. That mob at Ephesus was a church in the simple meaning of the term. Not a Christian church, of course, but they were a called-out assembly.

So a local congregation of Christians is, in a more specialized sense, a church. The word is used referring to local congregations about ninety times in the New Testament.

But that "general assembly and church of the firstborn, which are written in heaven" (Heb. 12:23), "the body, the church" (Col. 1:18), including all the saved, will be a called-out assembly at the rapture and hence this body of all the saved of all ages is called "the church."

This church could not have been formed at Pentecost because the word church, referring to that mystical body of Christ, must include all those at the rapture. All were not present, of course, at Pentecost and Old Testament saints will be called out at the rapture also, for we are told, "The dead in Christ shall rise first: Then we which are alive and remain shall be caught up together with them in the clouds, to meet the Lord in the air..." (I Thess. 4:16, 17). Old Testament saints are among "the dead in Christ," will be in the rapture, part of the "called-out assembly" or ekklesia, the church which is Christ's body.

Then again Hebrews 12:23 says that all of us come to face that "general assembly and church of the firstborn, which are written in heaven." And Old Testament saints are written in Heaven just as much as New Testament saints. Any point of origin for the church which leaves out part of the body of the called-out assembly, which will be raptured, is inaccurate.

Again, that church is described in Ephesians 5:25-27 in words that must include all who are saved.

> "Husbands, love your wives, even as Christ also loved the church, and gave himself for it; That he might sanctify and cleanse it with the washing of water by the word, That he might present it to himself a glorious church, not having spot, or wrinkle, or any such thing; but that it should be holy and without blemish."

The Lord Jesus loved the church and gave Himself for it. Evidently the church, then, includes all for whom Christ died and who accepted Him. It includes all the Christians that He labors to cleanse with the Word of God. And according to verse 27, the Lord clearly refers here to the rapture, "That he might present it to himself a glorious church, not having spot, or wrinkle...." So, then, the church which will be presented to Christ at the rapture must include all those saved by His blood.

Someone objects that Jesus promised, "Upon this rock I will build my church" (Matt. 16:18) and, hence, they think the building of the church was then future. But note carefully that Jesus spoke not of the origin of the church, but of the long process of construction. He spoke not of a ground breaking, the origin, but of extended building and what He really said was, "On this rock I will be building my church" with continued action involved. And He is still building that body which will be called out at the rapture. First Peter 2:5 says, "Ye also, as lively stones, are built up a spiritual house, an holy priesthood...."

Again, speaking of this body which is continually building by the addition of new converts, Ephesians 2:19-22 says:

> "Now therefore ye are no more strangers and foreigners, but fellow citizens with the saints, and of the household of God; And are built upon the foundation of the apostles and prophets, Jesus Christ himself being the chief corner stone; In whom all the building fitly framed together groweth unto an holy temple in the Lord: In whom ye also are builded together for an habitation of God through the Spirit."

That building "groweth unto an holy temple." It is still being builded.

Remember that the mystical body of Christ, the church, has a right to that term only in view of the rapture. Then when Christians are called out to meet Christ in the air, they will be literally a called-out assembly, a church. They are now that in prospect. But that body must involve all the saved of all ages, not just those since Pentecost, for Abel and Abraham and Elijah and David have the same right in that body and will be as prominent in the body as those saved in New Testament times.

Dr. Scofield on this matter of the church has a note on Ephesians 3:6. He says, "That the Gentiles were to be saved was no mystery (Rom. 9:24-33; 10:19-21). The mystery 'hid in God' was the divine purpose to make of Jew and Gentile a wholly new thing--'the church, which is his [Christ's] body.' "

However, Dr. Scofield thus missed the point of Ephesians 3:6. That verse says: "That the Gentiles should be fellow-heirs, and of the same body, and partakers of his promise in Christ by the gospel." The mystery revealed here is not that there will be a new body, but that the Gentiles will be admitted along with godly Jews to the same body. And that is the sense of nearly all the second chapter preceding, that Gentiles are now brought nigh by the blood of Christ and are made partakers of the same blessings with Jews, and "now therefore ye are no more strangers and foreigners, but fellowcitizens with the saints, and of the household of God" (Eph. 2:19). The church, then, is not primarily a New Testament body. It includes all the saved of all ages. So it was not formed nor begun at Pentecost.

A Misunderstanding of Pentecost Leads to a Misconception of the Origin of the Church

Many scholars think that at Pentecost there began a new dispensation. In Old Testament times the Holy Spirit was with Christians, but did not dwell in the bodies of Christians. As Jesus said in John 14:17, "He dwelleth with you, and shall be in you." He was with Christians before; now at a future time He would be in them.

And now the Holy Spirit dwells in the body of every Christian. "What? know ye not that your body is the temple of the Holy Ghost which is in you, which ye have of God, and ye are not your own? For ye are bought with a price: therefore glorify God in your body, and in your spirit, which are God's"(I Cor. 6:19, 20). And Romans 8:9 says, "But ye are not in the flesh, but in the Spirit, if so be that the Spirit of God dwell in you. Now if any man have not the Spirit of Christ, he is none of his." So the Holy Spirit now dwells in every Christian. BUT THIS DID NOT BEGIN AT PENTECOST! NO, the indwelling of the Spirit began on the day Jesus rose from the dead.

In John 7:37-39, this was foretold:

> "In the last day, that great day of the feast, Jesus stood and cried, saying, If any man thirst, let him come unto me, and drink. He that believeth on me, as the scripture hath said, out of his belly shall flow rivers of living water. (But this spake he of the Spirit, which they that believe on him should receive: for the Holy Ghost was not yet given; because that Jesus was not yet glorified.)"

That is, the Holy Spirit could not yet be given in the sense of dwelling in the body of Christian people and flowing out from the Christian body as His headquarters on earth, until Christ should be glorified. But the day that Jesus rose from the dead in the glorified body, then "the same day at evening" Jesus came to the disciples, spoke peace to them and showed them His hands and feet. "Then said Jesus to them again, Peace be unto you: as my Father hath sent me, even so send I you. And when he had said this, he breathed on them, and saith unto them, Receive ye the Holy Ghost" (John 20:21, 22). Jesus breathed on the disciples on the day He rose from the dead. That day they received the Holy Spirit. So any change in dispensation happened at the resurrection, not at Pentecost. The Holy Spirit from that time on dwelt in the body of all Christians.

What was the meaning, then, of Pentecost? Jesus explained it very simply: "But ye shall receive power, after that the Holy Ghost is come upon you: and ye shall be witnesses unto me both in Jerusalem, and in all Judaea, and in Samaria, and unto the uttermost part of the earth" (Acts 1:8). They waited in the upper room till they were endued with power from on high. Then as the Holy Spirit came upon them in witnessing power, they spoke to many and three thousand people were saved and added to them that day.

So Pentecost was not the day of "the descent of the Holy Ghost." As far as moving his headquarters from Heaven to earth, he had done that on the day of the resurrection of Christ. And those who were filled with the Spirit in Acts 2:4 were filled again in Acts 4:31. That is, they were endued with power for witnessing. Pentecost was simply a great "specimen day" as the disciples started out filled with the Spirit to obey the Great Commission. So the church was not formed by the descent of the Holy Spirit at Pentecost, as good men have thought.

A Misunderstanding of the Baptism of the Spirit and of I Corinthians 12 and 13 Has Led Many to Believe That the Church Was Formed at Pentecost

Further in this study of the book of Acts, I think that the earnest student will find that the great enduement of power they received at Pentecost is variously called 'baptized with the Spirit,' 'filled with the Spirit,' 'the gift of the Spirit,' and 'the pouring out of the Spirit.' It is certain that Jesus told His disciples, "Ye shall be baptized with the Holy Ghost not many days hence" (Acts 1:5). People do not understand the meaning of the word baptism as used in the Bible when they think that "being baptized with the Spirit" at Pentecost meant the formation of the church.

1. There is one literal, physical baptism. It is the immersion of a believer in water. And so Ephesians 4:5 says "one baptism." But baptism is used in a figurative sense as

follows: Jesus overwhelmed in suffering said, "I have a baptism to be baptized with..." (Luke 12:50).

2. A believer overwhelmed, covered, buried in the Holy Spirit in an enduement of power for witnessing is "baptized with the Spirit" (Acts 1:5).

3. But the believer is made a part of the body of Christ, buried in it, made a part of it, by the Holy Spirit at conversion, is thus in a figurative sense "baptized into one body by one Spirit," as all of us are.

4. In I Corinthians 10:2 we are told that the Israelites "...were all baptized unto Moses in the cloud and in the sea." Again, that is a figurative use of the term. But with the sea walls high on either side, with a cloud fore and aft and above, they were "baptized in the cloud and in the sea."

Now I think one who notices carefully will see that to be baptized with the Holy Spirit for soul-winning power as at Pentecost, is an entirely different matter from being taken by the Holy Spirit and placed in the body of Christ and buried there, amalgamated there, as in I Corinthians 12:12-14.

That passage reads: "For as the body is one, and hath many members, and all the members of that one body, being many, are one body: so also is Christ. For by one Spirit are we all baptized into one body, whether we be Jews or Gentiles, whether we be bond or free; and have been all made to drink into one Spirit. For the body is not one member, but many."

I think the obvious meaning is regeneration. Everyone who is saved is made, then, a part of the body of Christ. This could not refer to Pentecost because the people at Corinth were not at Pentecost. But it was true of them as it is of all Christians in the world, that everyone of us has been made to drink in one Spirit and has been put into one body by this same Holy Spirit who regenerated us.

Now we agree that according to I Corinthians 12:13, "For by one Spirit are we all baptized into one body, whether we be Jews or Gentiles, whether we be bond or free; and have been all made to drink into one Spirit." But that matter of being buried into and becoming a part of the body of Christ, that group called prospectively the church which will be called out and assembled in Heaven at the rapture--that baptism happens to each individual when he is regenerated and made a Christian. When the Holy Spirit takes one and buries him into the body of Christ and makes him a part of that body at regeneration, it is not the same as "baptized with the Holy Ghost" promised to the disciples by the Lord Jesus in Acts 1:5 and fulfilled at Pentecost. That baptism or overwhelming with the Holy Spirit power at Pentecost happened only to those who were there, not to us, and it did not weld them into one body. Nothing like that is said in the Scriptures. No, as I Peter 2:5 tells us by expression, "Ye also, as lively stones, are built up a spiritual house, an holy priesthood, to offer up spiritual sacrifices, acceptable to God by Jesus Christ." There speaking of salvation the Apostle Peter tells us every Christian is built into that building, that spiritual house, at salvation. And Ephesians 2:19-22 tells us also that Christians, born of God and put into this body which will be called out at the rapture, "are builded together for an habitation of God through the Spirit" (Eph. 2:22). But building a building is a process and that process is still continuing, and living stones are still built into the building when people are born of God. The two wave-loaves required as an offering by Jews on the feast of Pentecost may represent God's people; I think they do. Perhaps they represent Jewish Christians and Gentile Christians who now will be combined together in one body. But it is always a mistake to form a doctrine by a type when there is no clear statement of the doctrine in the Scriptures, and there certainly is no clear statement that the church was founded at Pentecost or "formed by."

By a misunderstanding, I Corinthians 12:13, where baptism is used as a figure of what happened when the converts at Corinth had been put into the body of Christ by the Holy

Spirit at their conversion, is thought to mean the same thing as Acts 1:5, where it is said that the apostles and others were to be baptized of the Holy Ghost, flooded, immersed in, overwhelmed with the power of the Holy Spirit at Pentecost. But the two are not the same. The people at Corinth were not present at Pentecost. For a new convert to be placed into the body of Christ and made a part of that building at the time of salvation is not the same as for one already saved and a member of the body of Christ to be filled, covered, overwhelmed with the Holy Spirit.

The Christians "were all with one accord in one place." A similar language is used five times about that young church at Jerusalem in Acts 1:14, Acts 2:1, Acts 2:46, Acts 4:24, and Acts 5:12. They were so thoroughly of one mind in setting out to obey the Great Commission, in waiting for God's power upon them to witness, of one accord in happy, sacrificial Christian living, in prayer and so of one accord in public meetings.

VERSES 2–4:

2 And suddenly there came a sound from heaven as of a rushing mighty wind, and it filled all the house where they were sitting.

3 And there appeared unto them cloven tongues like as of fire, and it sat upon each of them. 4 And they were all filled with the Holy Ghost, and began to speak with other tongues, as the Spirit gave them utterance.

"Filled With the Holy Ghost"

God's time had come for the mighty enduement of power which Jesus had promised. We are not surprised, then, to find three miraculous outward manifestations.

1. The "sound from heaven as of a rushing mighty wind."
2. The "tongues like as of fire, and it sat upon each of them."

3. The miraculous power to speak in the languages of those present.

The "Sound of a Rushing Mighty Wind"

The sound as of a cyclonic wind was miraculous. It was not promised before, was not repeated again. In Acts 4:31 an earthquake attended the filling with the Spirit. But neither the sound of a mighty wind, nor the miraculous, visible tongues like fire, nor the miraculous gift of "ability to speak in the languages of those who heard, had any essential connection with the enduement of power from on high," the fullness of the Holy Spirit. We repeat, these miracles were all three incidental, they were not what was promised nor what the disciples waited for, and they were not repeated when others were filled with the Spirit.

A man declared to me he "received the Holy Ghost just like at Pentecost." But I found there was no "sound of a rushing mighty wind," no "cloven tongues as of fire." And the "tongues" he said he received were not those of anyone present to whom he could witness; and no sinner was converted. So I told him he had been deceived, he had only an imitation, not what the disciples received at Pentecost.

Of course, we are not to expect the same incidental miracles of the cyclonic wind, the tongues like as of fire, the supernatural gift of foreign language of someone else present, the earthquake of Acts 4:31, or the visible form of the Holy Spirit like a dove, and the audible voice of God from Heaven as when Jesus was baptized. They are not promised. We are never encouraged to ask for nor expect these incidental miracles. If God has a reason for a miracle when one is filled with the Holy Spirit, well and good. Usually, of course, as in Bible times, there will be none-- then well and good. Let us not be enamoured of some incidental, special demonstration not promised. But we are promised and should seek to be filled with the Spirit for soul-winning testimony.

There Was Also the "Cloven Tongues Like as of Fire and It Sat Upon Each of Them"

Note the terminology. Dr. Scofield, in the margin, has this reading, "Tongues, as of fire, parting and sitting upon each of them." The indications are that the Holy Spirit came not on the group as a mass, but on each individual separately. Individuals, not crowds, are filled with the Spirit. Individuals, not churches, are soul winners, and individuals, not churches as corporate bodies, must have God's power for soul winning. If there was power on a congregation, it was because some individual Christians were filled with the Spirit. Remember the temple of the Holy Spirit is not a church building, but a Christian's body. So likewise, Holy Spirit power comes upon individual Christians, not on bodies of people, except as individuals in the group are filled with the Spirit.

Pentecost Did Not Begin the Indwelling of the Holy Spirit in Christians' Bodies

"And they were all filled with the Holy Ghost."

Notice clearly what this does not mean.

Do not confuse the fullness of the Spirit with the indwelling of the Holy Spirit. No new dispensation began at Pentecost. No different way of God's dealing with men began here. The fullness of the Spirit for soul-winning power is one thing; the fact of the indwelling of the Spirit in every Christian is an entirely different matter. The following scriptural facts about the indwelling of the Holy Spirit are important.

1. The indwelling of the Holy Spirit, making His headquarters in the bodies of Christians, was foretold by Jesus in John 7:37-39:

"In the last day, that great day of the feast,

Jesus stood and cried, saying, If any man thirst, let him come unto me, and drink. He that believeth on me, as the scripture hath said, out of his belly shall flow rivers of living water. (But this spake he of the Spirit, which they that believe on him should receive: for the Holy Ghost was not yet given; because that Jesus was not yet glorified.)"

Note that "the Holy Ghost was not yet given" in the sense of dwelling in the bodies of Christians and flowing out from the Christian's body, as headquarters on earth, not yet given "because that Jesus was not yet glorified." When Christ should be raised from the dead, glorified with the resurrection body never to be again abused by men, then the Holy Spirit would be given.

2. When Christ was glorified and raised from the dead, the same day He breathed upon the disciples and said, "Receive ye the Holy Ghost" (John 20:19-22). They did, that day, 'receive the Holy Ghost.' That is, He personally came into the bodies of Christians to dwell. We believe that it occurred for every Christian living at that time.

3. Now all Christians have the Holy Spirit dwelling in the body. First Corinthians 6:19 and 20 says, "What? know ye not that your body is the temple of the Holy Ghost which is in you, which ye have of God, and ye are not your own? For ye are bought with a price: therefore glorify God in your body, and in your spirit, which are God's."

Romans 8:9, 10 says:

"But ye are not in the flesh, but in the Spirit, if so be that the Spirit of God dwell in you. Now if any man have not the Spirit of Christ, he is none of his. And if Christ be in you, the body is dead because of sin; but the Spirit is life because of righteousness."

First Corinthians 3:16 and 17 says:

> "Know ye not that ye are the temple of God,
> and that the Spirit of God dwelleth in you? If any
> man defile the temple of God, him shall God de-
> stroy; for the temple of God is holy, which tem-
> ple ye are."

The promise of John 14:17 that the Holy Spirit "dwelleth with you [before the death of Christ] , and shall be in you" (after the resurrection) was now already fulfilled before Pentecost. All these apostles and other Christians who waited at Pentecost for the enduement of power already had the Spirit of God dwelling within them. Whatever dispensational change there was in relation to the Holy Spirit occurred the day of the resurrection, not at Pentecost. The fullness of the Holy Spirit is not the same as the indwelling of the Spirit. No Christian ever needs to pray now for the Holy Spirit to come and dwell within. He does. That is a part of salvation. He is "Christ in you, the hope of glory," that is, Christ as represented by the Holy Spirit manifesting Himself within the Christian.

"Filled With the Spirit" Is Not a New Way of Working

Other people before Pentecost have had the power of the Holy Spirit come upon them. John the Baptist was "filled with the Holy Ghost, even from his mother's womb" (Luke 1:15). Elizabeth "was filled with the Holy Ghost" (Luke 1:41). Zacharias was "filled with the Holy Ghost" (Luke 1:67). And we are clearly told that when John the Baptist was filled with the Holy Spirit that he should "go before him in the spirit and power of Elias" (Luke 1:17). So Elijah was filled with the Spirit, too, in the same fashion as these New Testament Christians. And so we are told in many Old

Testament Scriptures that the Spirit of the Lord came upon various ones so they could prophesy or speak and witness for God with power. See Exodus 35:31; Numbers 11:25, 26, and 29; I Samuel 10:6 and 9; I Samuel 16:13; Judges 14:6, 19; Judges 15:14, and II Kings 2:9, 15. So the coming of the Holy Spirit upon people to fill them or anoint them or empower them was not a new thing at Pentecost.

"And They. . .Began to Speak With Other Tongues, as the Spirit Gave Them Utterance"

A great deal of confusion, misunderstanding and false doctrine have centered around the matter of "speaking in tongues." Surely at this first great occasion of the pouring out of the Holy Spirit after the giving of the Great Commission and Christ's ascension, we should find a typical and definitive case of "speaking in tongues." So we do. The word tongue here in the Greek New Testament is glossa, a simple word meaning the literal tongue and so by inference as in English and other languages meaning a language or speech.

VERSES 5–11:

5 And there were dwelling at Jerusalem Jews, devout men, out of every nation under heaven.

6 Now when this was noised abroad, the multitude came together, and were confounded, because that every man heard them speak in his own language.

7 And they were all amazed and marvelled, saying one to another, Behold, are not all these which speak Galileans?

8 And how hear we every man in our own tongue, wherein we were born?

9 Parthians, and Medes, and Elamites, and the dwellers in Mesopotamia, and in Judea, and Cappadocia, in Pontus, and Asia,

10 Phrygia, and Pamphylia, in Egypt, and in the parts of Libya about Cyrene, and strangers of Rome, Jews and proselytes,

11 Cretes and Arabians, we do hear them speak in our tongues the wonderful works of God.

The "Tongues" Were Natural Languages
for Preaching the Gospel

Notice the following facts:

1. "Every man heard them speak in his own language" (vs. 6). These are no unnatural or heavenly tongues. In verse 8 the hearers said, "And how hear we every man in our own tongue, wherein we were born?" And then follows a list of the nationalities of those present, about fifteen nationalities. In verse 11 they said, "We do hear them speak in our tongues the wonderful works of God." The languages used were languages known and understood by those present. The idea of Neander, of Dr. G. Campbell Morgan and other commentators who follow Neander, that New Testament Christians sometimes fell into an ecstasy and talked in some heavenly language unknown to men, is utterly foreign to the Scriptures. Nothing like that happened at Pentecost, nor, as far as we know, at any other Bible time. The word unknown in the discussion of "unknown tongue" in I Corinthians 14 is not in the Greek. In every case here at Pentecost the language spoken was heard and understood by someone who regularly spoke that language.

2. Note that the speaking here was for the purpose of preaching the Gospel. "We do hear them speak in our tongues the wonderful works of God." The speaking in the power of the Spirit was the important thing. People were convicted and converted through the testimony of those who spoke. The matter as to whether one preaches the Gospel in Aramaic or Latin or English or German or Spanish is incidental. It takes the same Gospel, it takes the same power of the Holy Spirit, and the language is incidental. Speaking in tongues here, not previously learned, was miraculous, but it was an incidental miracle. The object was to get the Gospel to sinners who otherwise would not understand it.

This, no doubt, is the speaking "with new tongues" foretold in Mark 16:17.

In I Corinthians 14 those at Corinth had a tongues heresy. They were using foreign languages to make a show in the services, and so Paul was inspired to instruct them that one should not testify in a language unknown to others, unless someone should interpret, and that was to be an incidental part of the service with not more than two or at the most three speaking in some foreign language unknown to the crowd and never unless someone should interpret to them. And then followed instruction that women were to be silent in such services (I Cor. 14:34). What Paul rebuked was not miraculous but natural, not spiritual but carnal, a wrong use of language as if it were spiritual to talk in some language others could not understand. That it was natural languages they used is clear from I Corinthians 14, verses 16 and 24 where are mentioned "the unlearned" who would not understand their talk in foreign languages. Paul said, "I thank my God, I speak with tongues more than ye all" (vs. 18). Or in the Greek it is singular "with a tongue," that is, Paul everywhere taught in the Koine Greek and wrote his epistles in Greek. He does not here refer to some heavenly language or even a miracle of tongues as at Pentecost. But he always spoke to be understood and said, "I had rather speak five words with my understanding, that by my voice I might teach others also, than ten thousand words in an unknown tongue," that is, in a foreign language not understood by those present. There is no teaching in the Bible of some heavenly language not regularly used by men somewhere.

Besides, the miracle of Pentecost in which people were given the power to speak in the language of other people present was not intended for everybody. "Do all speak with tongues? do all interpret?" (I Cor. 12:30). Obviously most Christians do not need the miracle languages as at Pentecost. We are not taught anywhere in the Bible to seek the gift of tongues, but rather we are to seek to prophesy, that is, to speak in the power of the Spirit in a language people can understand (I Cor. 14:1).

The important thing to remember is that at Pentecost the disciples were setting out to carry out the command of the Great Commission and preach the Gospel. In this case there were incidental miracles that helped them preach to others who did not understand the Aramaic which they regularly spoke. (On this matter see the author's book, The Power of Pentecost, or the pamphlet, Speaking in Tongues, for more detailed teaching.)

VERSES 12-21:

12 And they were all amazed, and were in doubt, saying one to another, What meaneth this?
13 Others mocking said, These men are full of new wine.
14 ¶ But Peter, standing up with the eleven, lifted up his voice, and said unto them, Ye men of Judea, and all *ye* that dwell at Jerusalem, be this known unto you, and hearken to my words:
15 For these are not drunken, as ye suppose, seeing it is *but* the third hour of the day.
16 But this is that which was spoken by the prophet Joel;
17 And it shall come to pass in the last days, saith God, I will pour out of my Spirit upon all flesh: and your sons and your daughters shall prophesy, and your young men shall see visions, and your old men shall dream dreams:
18 And on my servants and on my handmaidens I will pour out in those days of my Spirit; and they shall prophesy:
19 And I will shew wonders in heaven above, and signs in the earth beneath; blood, and fire, and vapour of smoke:
20 The sun shall be turned into darkness, and the moon into blood, before that great and notable day of the Lord come:
21 And it shall come to pass, *that* whosoever shall call on the name of the Lord shall be saved.

The Prophecy of Joel Begins to Be Fulfilled

What happened at Pentecost was foretold in Joel 2:28-32. This passage explains Pentecost and is quoted here by divine inspiration with that in mind. Note carefully the things that are taught here.

1. The New Testament age here is called "the last days." It includes Pentecost, "This is that," and goes right on through the signs and wonders of the tribulation time to "that great and notable day of the Lord" (vs. 20). The term "the last days" and "the latter times" in the New Testament never means the closing days of the age, but rather the whole New Testament age. See Hebrews 1:1, 2 where "time past" refers to the Old Testament time and "in these last days" includes the time when God has "spoken unto us by his Son." So the personal ministry of Jesus was in the period the Bible calls "the last days."

So I John 2:18 says, "Little children, it is the last time: and as ye have heard that antichrist shall come, even now are there many antichrists; whereby we know that it is the last time." That is, the term is used about the whole New Testament age. So "the latter times" in I Timothy 4:1 refers to the whole New Testament age, the rise of the Catholic church with celibate monks, priests and nuns, with Lent and forbidding to eat meat on Fridays. In II Timothy 3:1, "In the last days," the perilous times mentioned, refer to characteristics of a whole New Testament age. Notice the present tense verbs in the command to Timothy, "From such turn away," and "for of this sort are they."

"Now as Jannes and Jambres withstood Moses, so do these also resist the truth...." The commands were pertinent to Timothy, the conditions existed at that time and are characteristic of the whole New Testament age.

The scoffers that "shall come in the last days" in II Peter 3:3 again refer to the whole New Testament age and not to any particular time which is supposed to mark the closing days of this age. No, in New Testament language the term "the last days" includes all the time from the personal ministry of Christ, from Pentecost, and from the ministry of

John the beloved on down to the "Day of the Lord" when Christ will come back to reign!

2. The pouring out of the Holy Spirit "upon all flesh," that is, we believe, upon all kinds of people and not literally on every individual. The pouring out of the Holy Spirit, of course, is a blessed privilege available to every Christian. In Old Testament times the Holy Spirit came on a few prophets of God. Now the power of the Holy Spirit for witnessing and prophesying is available to sons and daughters, servants and handmaidens, young men and old men. See the promise in Acts 2:39.

3. Note the meaning of the term "prophesy." It means to speak in the power of the Holy Spirit. Sometimes it may be foretelling the future. Sometimes it may be rebuking sin or telling people how to be saved, but always it will be speaking in the supernatural power of the Holy Spirit.

Matthew 26:67 and 68 tells us that when they abused Jesus before His crucifixion, "Then did they spit in his face, and buffeted him; and others smote him with the palms of their hands, Saying, Prophesy unto us, thou Christ, Who is he that smote thee?" That is, if Jesus had the Spirit of God upon Him, He could, while blindfolded, tell who it was that smote Him. To prophesy is to speak with the power and wisdom of God when one is moved by the Holy Spirit.

It is important to notice that "prophesying" does not necessarily mean preaching to a congregation. In Acts 11:28 Agabus stood up and prophesied publicly to a crowd. In Acts 21:10 and 11 the same man prophesied personally to Paul the apostle. So the sons and daughters, servants and handmaidens, men and women alike may all be filled with the Spirit and may witness personally for Christ, although women are elsewhere forbidden to teach or usurp authority over the men, but to be in silence in mixed congregations including men (I Tim. 2:11, 12). Every Christian can witness and every Christian can be filled with the Spirit for this witnessing.

4. Note that the blessed promises about preaching the Gospel and witnessing in the power of the Holy Spirit and of people being saved, go right on through the time of the rapture, through the time of the Great Tribulation until "that great and notable day of the Lord come." "The day of the Lord" means the time when Jesus comes in judgment to reign. Just as the Great Commission given in Matthew promises, "And, lo, I am with you alway, even unto the end of the world," that is, the consummation of the age, so is the fullness of the Spirit promised for the witnessing and soul winning here commanded.

5. The purpose of the prophesying, the speaking in the Spirit to win souls, is told. Verse 21, quoting Joel's prophecy, says, "And it shall come to pass, that whosoever shall call on the name of the Lord shall be saved." As everywhere this power of the Holy Spirit is promised for witnessing (Luke 24:46-49; Acts 1:8), so here the fullness of the Spirit prophesied by Joel and which began to occur at Pentecost was to result in people being saved.

Let us note further that as in the Great Commission so here the Gospel has in mind "whosoever," Jew or Gentile, in any country, in any age.

Notes on Peter's Sermon at Pentecost

Peter's sermon began with verse 14. Notice these worthwhile points about the sermon.

1. He began with the thing before the people's minds. "These are not drunken, as ye suppose."

2. He explained the pouring out of the Holy Spirit with the supernatural manifestations of saving power, along with incidental miracles by showing from Joel 2:28-32 that this was fulfillment of prophecy. A new age had begun and this was the public inauguration of the age, the first massive public attempt to carry out the Great Commission. Now God offered the Holy Spirit power to all Christians for that purpose.

3. Notice Peter's bold facing of the sin question. In verse 23 they had taken Jesus "and by wicked hands have crucified and slain" Him. All true evangelism must deal early and definitely with sin. In verse 38 he will command them to repent, so he shows the wickedness of their hearts in hating, rejecting and crucifying Jesus.

4. It was a Bible sermon. First, he shows from Joel that the present pouring out of the Holy Spirit was prophesied and is a part of God's plan for getting out the Gospel. Then he quotes from Psalm 16 to show that David had foretold the resurrection of Christ. Then he quotes from Psalm 110 to show that the Father has Jesus at present sitting on the right hand in Heaven until the time when He will come back to reign (vss. 34, 35).

5. Peter drives straight to his main conclusion, "That God hath made that same Jesus, whom ye have crucified, both Lord and Christ." Jesus is the prophesied Christ, the Messiah of Israel. He is the only Saviour.

6. Then Peter gives the urgent conclusion that they should repent.

7. Then there was an extended period of testifying, exhorting, answering questions and applying the truth of the Scriptures he had quoted (vs. 40).

8. It is important to notice that Peter's sermon was a topical sermon. Bible preachers never simply expounded a passage of Scripture without an immediate application. They did not simply "gather around the Word." Bible preachers used the Scriptures as a means to a holy end, to instruct in righteousness, to reprove and rebuke sin, to bring people to repentance, to lead to salvation or assurance of salvation. Expository preaching is often good, but it is not usually the way Bible preachers preached nor the usual way for the best evangelists such as Moody, Finney, Torrey, Spurgeon and Billy Sunday. The Bible is not a

museum piece for examination for one's own interest without any regard for its spiritual impact. The Bible is a sword, a hammer, a fire in the hands of God's prophet. And Bible preachers so used it to bring about certain holy ends as God intended. Expository preaching is sometimes to be preferred, but often not.

VERSES 22–24:

22 Ye men of Israel, hear these words; Jesus of Nazareth, a man approved of God among you by miracles and wonders and signs, which God did by him in the midst of you, as ye yourselves also know:

23 Him, being delivered by the determinate counsel and foreknowledge of God, ye have taken, and by wicked hands have crucified and slain:

24 Whom God hath raised up, having loosed the pains of death: because it was not possible that he should be holden of it.

Peter Clearly Presents His Case

Argument will come later, but here Peter clearly states three things:

1. The marvelous ministry of Jesus "approved of God among you by miracles and wonders and signs." They knew this. God approved Jesus.

2. They had wickedly delivered Jesus to be slain. The Sanhedrin had planned it. The mob of people had gone along with them choosing Barabbas to be released and Jesus to be crucified. Then the Roman governor, Pilate, had given authority to kill Jesus. Peter was addressing a whole crowd of murderers, Christ-rejecters, lost sinners.

3. But God had raised Jesus from the dead. And that brought Peter to the main point of his sermon. Jesus Christ was raised from the dead and, therefore, proved to be the promised Christ, Messiah, of the Old Testament, the only Lord and Saviour.

"Jesus of Nazareth, a Man Approved of God Among You. . ." (Vs. 22)

Here Peter is proving that Jesus, a man, is God; that is, "both Lord and Christ" (vs. 36). It is a soul-damning heresy to hold Jesus as less than God. But the Creator now has humbled Himself and become a man. He has humbled Himself and taken on "the form of a servant, and was made in the likeness of men: And being found in fashion as a man, he humbled himself, and became obedient unto death, even the death of the cross" (Phil. 2:7, 8). Certainly Jesus is God, is Creator, but He was a real man. He is no less man because He is God. And He called Himself "the Son of man" fifty-nine times in the Gospels. He is a man born of woman, He is of the seed of David, of the tribe of Judah. He will return as man to sit on David's throne and reign on this earth. He is the model man, the second Adam. Jesus of Nazareth is the Lord of glory! So Peter preaches here.

"Ye Have Taken, and by Wicked Hands Have Crucified and Slain" (Vs. 23)

Peter and other New Testament preachers pressed hard on the wickedness of all who rejected Christ. In verse 36 he says, "That same Jesus, whom ye have crucified...." In Acts 3:13-15 Peter accused these Jewish people, "whom ye delivered up, and denied him in the presence of Pilate...But ye denied the Holy One and the Just, and desired a murderer to be granted unto you; And killed the Prince of life...."

See how Stephen addressed the people in Acts 7:51-53:

"Ye stiffnecked and uncircumcised in heart and ears, ye do always resist the Holy Ghost: as your fathers did, so do ye. Which of the prophets have not your fathers persecuted? and they have slain them which shewed before of the coming of the Just One; of whom ye have been now

the betrayers and murderers: Who have received the law by the disposition of angels, and
have not kept it."

Some would excuse the rejection of Christ by Jewish people and Jewish leaders saying that they were under a mis-
apprehension, that they expected a secular king to deliver
them from Roman rule, etc. Such teaching ignores the
universal record in the Scriptures of the wickedness of the
human heart. It is true that unconverted men such as these
Jewish leaders and other people are spiritually blind, but
there is no excuse for their sin. It was wickedness, not ignorance, that rejected the Saviour, hated Him, chose a
murderer instead of Him, crucified Him and mocked Him
while He died. The Roman scourge, the crown of thorns,
the spittle in His face, the plucking out of His beard, the
perjured witnesses, the fake trial before the Sanhedrin, the
cries of the mob, "Crucify him," manifested the attitude of
unregenerate, wicked hearts, enemies of God. Their
trouble was not ignorance, but sin--heart wickedness.

Even so now all infidelity, all unbelief in Christ and in
the Bible is from "an evil heart of unbelief" (Heb. 3:12). In
the Old Testament Scriptures fulfilled, in the miraculous
ministry of Jesus, in His teaching "as never man spake,"
Jesus left no room for honest unbelief. So it is today. No
fact of science or history or archeology, no intelligent reason and logic can justify turning away from the Bible as
God's Word or rejection of Christ Jesus as God's own Son,
our atoning Saviour. Jesus said after His resurrection, and
this applies to all unbelief, "O fools, and slow of heart to
believe all that the prophets have spoken," particularly with
reference to Himself (Luke 24:25). There is a moral wickedness to unbelief. Jesus said in John 3:19-21:

"And this is the condemnation, that light is
come into the world, and men loved darkness

rather than light, because their deeds were evil. For every one that doeth evil hateth the light, neither cometh to the light, lest his deeds should be reproved. But he that doeth truth cometh to the light, that his deeds may be made manifest, that they are wrought in God."

Jesus properly complained, "Ye <u>will not</u> come unto me...," not that they could not come, but would not. Their trouble was not with their comprehension but with their wicked wills, choosing to go away from God and reject Christ.

VERSES 25–31:

25 For David speaketh concerning him, I foresaw the Lord always before my face; for he is on my right hand, that I should not be moved:

26 Therefore did my heart rejoice, and my tongue was glad; moreover also my flesh shall rest in hope:

27 Because thou wilt not leave my soul in hell, neither wilt thou suffer thine Holy One to see corruption.

28 Thou hast made known to me the ways of life; thou shalt make me full of joy with thy countenance.

29 Men *and* brethren, let me freely speak unto you of the patriarch David, that he is both dead and buried, and his sepulchre is with us unto this day.

30 Therefore being a prophet, and knowing that God had sworn with an oath to him, that of the fruit of his loins, according to the flesh, he would raise up Christ to sit on his throne;

31 He, seeing this before, spake of the resurrection of Christ, that his soul was not left in hell, neither his flesh did see corruption.

From Psalm 16 Peter Proves That the Resurrection of Christ Was Foretold, and Christ's Lordship

Peter quotes from memory Psalm 16:8-10. It is a remarkable fact that as far as we know in every case but two in the New Testament preachers preached without a copy of Scripture before them, quoting Scriptures from memory. The two exceptions are Jesus in the synagogue at Nazareth in Luke 4:16-22, and in the case of the Ethopian eunuch who had opened before him Isaiah 53 when "Philip opened his mouth, and began at the same scripture, and preached unto him Jesus" (Acts 8:35).

Notice Peter's argument from Scripture.

1. David was still dead and his sepulchre was at Jerusalem. Therefore, David could not have been writing about himself in prophesying that God would not leave someone's soul in Hell nor suffer his holy body to see corruption in the grave.

2. But David was a prophet, and so this was a prophecy about the coming Saviour.

3. God had made an oath to David that according to the flesh, He would raise up the Messiah to sit on David's throne. This shows that Peter was familiar with God's covenant to David recorded in II Samuel 7:8-16 and I Chronicles 17:7-14, and in other Old Testament Scriptures, that David's seed should sit on his throne forever in the future.

4. So David had it revealed to him and was inspired to write down in Old Testament Scripture about the resurrection of Christ. "His soul was not left in hell [rather the realm of the dead], neither his flesh did see corruption [did not decay in Joseph's tomb]."

"Thou Wilt Not Leave My Soul in Hell" (Vs. 27)

In verse 27 Peter is quoting from Psalm 16:10. He says it applies to Christ, "that his soul was not left in hell, neither his flesh did see corruption" (vs. 31). "Hell" here is the Greek word <u>hades</u>, translating from the Psalm the Hebrew word <u>sheol</u>. It literally means the place of the dead. <u>Sheol</u> is sometimes translated the grave, but it never means a literal grave or any particular sepulchre, but only a grave as used for a figure of death. It was simply prophesied that God would not leave Jesus in the unseen world, among those of the other world and would not leave His body to decay. There is a gradual evolution in the meaning of words. It seemed that originally the Hebrew word, sheol, here translated "Hell," referred to the realm of the dead, whether saved or lost. However, as the Scriptures advanced, the tendency was to use the term and its New Testament equivalent, hades, to refer to the realm of the damned, as "Hell" generally means in English. The meaning among Christians is largely colored by the history of the rich man in Hell in Luke 16:19-31. However, the Apostles' Creed, referring doubtless to this Scripture, says that Christ "descended into hell," by which it simply means that He descended into the realm of the dead. He died.

Jesus did not go to the place of the damned. He did not suffer after death, but went immediately to be "in paradise" (Luke 23:43). He went immediately to be with the Father, praying, "Father, into thy hands I commend my spirit" (Luke 23:46). Even before He died on the cross Jesus cried out, "It is finished" (John 19:30). In an agony of separation from God and taking the place of a doomed sinner, Jesus had prayed, "My God, my God, why hast thou forsaken me?" (Mark 15:34). But after that, atonement being made and fellowship with the Father restored, He could pray, "Father, into thy hands...." The whole matter of atonement for sin was settled on the cross. Jesus did not go into what we call Hell. He did go into death. He did not suffer after death, but went immediately to be with the Father in Paradise.

Some have interpreted I Peter 3:18 and 19 as teaching that Jesus, during His three days with His body in the grave, went to Hell and there preached to the spirits in prison. That is a misunderstanding of the Scripture. Rather, I Peter 3:18 and 19 teaches that Jesus "...by the Spirit...he went and preached...in the days of Noah" to those now in Hell. That is, the Holy Spirit in Noah and through Noah re-

presented Christ, and men then rejected Him and are now
in Hell.

"According to the Flesh, He Would Raise Up
Christ to Sit on His Throne" (Vs. 30)

The resurrection of Christ proves His deity (Rom. 1:4).
That was the "sign of the prophet Jonas" (Matt. 12:39, 40),
the one conclusive evidence of His deity. But here we learn
that Christ was raised up "according to the flesh" to sit on
David's throne. Peter says that is meant in the inspired
sixteenth Psalm, and that the resurrection according to the
flesh, a literal, bodily resurrection, proves that Christ
will reign literally, bodily on David's throne at Jerusalem.
It is foolish and wicked to speak of a so-called "spiritual
resurrection," meaning that the body did not literally,
physically come out of the grave. It is equally unbelieving
and a perversion of Scripture to teach that the reign of
Christ on David's throne as promised Mary in Luke 1:31,
32, as promised in Isaiah 9:6 and 7, and many other Scriptures, is less than a literal, physical reign on earth on the
very throne of David at Jerusalem. The physical resurrection of Christ--how Satan hates it! How the carnal, human
heart rebels against it! For if this be true, then all the
Bible says is true, Christ is God, and every sinner will be
held accountable for rejecting Him.

In the same vein, in Acts 17:31, 32 Paul, preaching at
Athens, said that the bodily resurrection of Christ proves a
coming day of judgment for unrepentant sinners.

Concerning the physical reign of Christ on David's
throne, see the author's pamphlet, Christ's Literal Reign
on Earth, or chapters in the large book, The Coming Kingdom of Christ.

VERSES 32–36:

32 This Jesus hath God raised up, whereof we all are witnesses.

33 Therefore being by the right hand of God exalted, and having received of the Father the promise of the Holy Ghost, he hath shed forth this, which ye now see and hear.

34 For David is not ascended into the heavens: but he saith himself, The LORD said unto my Lord, Sit thou on my right hand,

35 Until I make thy foes thy footstool.

36 Therefore let all the house of Israel know assuredly, that God hath made that same Jesus, whom ye have crucified, both Lord and Christ.

The Resurrected Christ Sitting at the Right Hand of the Father Has Poured Out the Holy Spirit on His Own; He Is the Only Lord and Saviour

Here is the great theme of all the Bible preachers: the resurrection of Christ. God has raised Jesus from the dead!

1. Jesus is now "by the right hand of God exalted."

2. The promise of the Holy Spirit, made often in the Old Testament, repeated by John the Baptist and repeated in the ministry of Jesus, is now fulfilled, the pouring out of the Holy Spirit in special enduement of power and now dwelling in the bodies of Christians. The pouring out of the Holy Spirit as at Pentecost is a further evidence that Christ is God raised from the dead, fulfilling Old Testament promises.

3. Peter uses Psalm 110:1 to show that this period when the resurrected Christ is seated at the right hand of the Father on high is foretold in Scripture. "The Lord said unto my Lord, Sit thou at my right hand, until I make.thine enemies thy footstool."

4. Now the inescapable conclusion. This same Jesus (the human name, the "man name" Jesus) is "both Lord and Christ." The one they have crucified is the only Saviour!

"Let All the House of Israel Know. . ." (Vs. 36)

Note how Peter's sermon is addressed in some sense to
the nation Israel. Jews were present out of all the countries
mentioned in Acts 2:9-11. The feast day Jerusalem was
filled with Jews from all over Palestine and beyond, "Out of
every nation under heaven" (Acts 2:5). So in verse 14 Peter
addressed them, "Ye men of Judaea, and all ye that dwell at
Jerusalem." In verse 22 he addresses, "Ye men of Israel."
In verse 36 he said, "Therefore let all the house of Israel
know assuredly, that God hath made that same Jesus, whom
ye have crucified, both Lord and Christ." The whole nation
Israel is held accountable for the crucifixion. So the command here is to the whole nation Israel to repent. See also
Acts 4:10 when Peter is addressing particularly the high
priest and the Sanhedrin, "Be it known unto you all, and to
all the people of Israel, that by the name of Jesus Christ of
Nazareth, whom ye crucified, whom God raised from the
dead, even by him doth this man stand here before you
whole." This addressing the whole nation gives some color
to the prophetic character of the statement in Acts 2:19-21.

VERSES 37-40:

37 ¶ Now when they heard *this*, they were pricked in their heart, and said unto Peter and to the rest of the apostles, Men *and* brethren, what shall we do?

38 Then Peter said unto them, Repent, and be baptized every one of you in the name of Jesus Christ for the remission of sins, and ye shall receive the gift of the Holy Ghost.

39 For the promise is unto you, and to your children, and to all that are afar off, *even* as many as the Lord our God shall call.

40 And with many other words did he testify and exhort, saying, Save yourselves from this unto- ward generation.

They Were to Repent for Salvation

There was a wonderful response to Peter's sermon.

"They were pricked in their heart." This is the supernatural work of the Word of God, empowered by the Spirit
of God. It does not matter much that at Pentecost the people
spoke in several languages (to people who heard the Gospel
in their own tongue). The important thing is that they spoke
with the power of the Holy Spirit. What we are to seek is
not some incidental or outward manifestation, but God's
power on His Word and on our testimony.

So these convicted people said to Peter and t1e rest of the
apostles, "Men and brethren, what shall we do?"

Notice the question carefully. They did not say, "What
must we do to be saved?" or "What shall we do to be
saved?" No, that question is asked clearly by the Philippian
jailer in Acts 16:31 and there is clearly answered. But
these people want to know what to do, not only to be saved
but to partake of this marvelous outpouring of the Holy
Spirit which has shaken the whole city and made ignorant
and unlearned fishermen and other Christians into mighty
soul winners. The question involves not only how to be
saved, but how to have the power of God. And Peter answers their need distinctly.

"Then Peter said unto them, Repent...." This is not a
different plan of salvation from the plan to "believe on the
Lord Jesus Christ" as the Philippian jailer was instructed
and as otherwise given often in the Gospels (John 1:12; John
3:14-16; John 3:18; John 3:36; John 5:24; John 6:40; John 6:47;
Acts 13:38, 39). The saving Gospel as to how men are to be
saved is once described as "repentance toward God, and
faith toward our Lord Jesus Christ" (Acts 20:21). But usually where one is mentioned as the way to salvation, the
other is implied, not mentioned. Actually saving repentance and saving faith are simply two ways of saying the
same thing. The Greek word for repentance is metanoia,
meaning literally a change of mind. That is, a change of
heart attitude. But the change is from unbelief to faith. To
repent means to turn from sin. Saving faith means to turn

to Christ, relying on Him for salvation. So one turns from sin in the heart to Christ, and the same saving faith turns from sin and turns to trust Christ. So to believe on Christ in saving faith and to honestly turn the heart from sin against God, to love and trust Him, is the same thing. Repentance and faith are different names for, or different aspects of, the same heart turning.

Sorrow is not repentance. However, "godly sorrow worketh repentance" (II Cor. 7:10). The Bible does not prescribe any period of mourning before one can trust Christ for salvation. One who hates his sin and turns from it in his heart at the same moment turns to Christ. There are not two steps nor several steps in the plan of salvation. This step, turning from a love of sin to dependence on Christ for forgiveness and cleansing of this sin, is one, simple, instantaneous step and the Bible may speak of the step as repentance, or as faith.

Compare two statements of the Lord Jesus and you will see that faith certainly includes repentance, and repentance certainly includes faith. "I tell you, Nay: but, except ye repent, ye shall all likewise perish" (Luke 13:3, 5). "He that believeth on him is not condemned: but he that believeth not is condemned already, because he hath not believed in the name of the only begotten Son of God" (John 3:18). Except you repent you shall perish. But one who has believed in Christ, depended upon Christ, has already repented and, therefore, is not condemned.

The above Scriptures, Luke 13:3, 5 and John 3:18, also show that an honest heart repentance, turning to trust in Christ, means that one is already saved. In Acts 2:38 Peter gives two different conditions for two different results. One is to repent and be saved. That is one condition for one result. The second condition and result, we are told, "and be baptized every one of you in the name of Jesus Christ for the remission of sins, and ye shall receive the gift of the Holy Ghost."

They Were to Be Baptized in Obedience to "Receive the Gift of the Holy Ghost"

The King James translation of Acts 2:38 "...be baptized every one of you in the name of Jesus Christ for the remission of sins" is unfortunate and inaccurate. The little Greek preposition eis, translated for, is an indefinite preposition of reference. It does not mean in order to. If Peter had commanded the people to be baptized in order to receive the remission of sins, he would have needed to use the Greek preposition hina, which means in order to. He did not.

This little preposition eis, used about 1,800 times in the New Testament in Greek, is variously translated, for, at, toward, unto, into, etc. so it could be translated for, as here, only in the sense of "on the basis of," or "on the ground of," so Dr. A. T. Robertson explains.

Even in English the preposition for does not necessarily mean in order to. Often for means "on the basis of," or "on the ground of." Thus one is scolded for being late, or arrested for stealing, or praised for beauty, or rewarded for bravery, or paid for work. In that sense only is one "baptized for the remission of sins," that is baptized for remission of sins already obtained when one repented.

Acts 2:38 does not give a new plan of salvation. Acts 10:43 says, "To him give all the prophets witness, that through his name whosoever believeth in him shall receive remission of sins." So John 3:36 says, "He that believeth on the Son hath everlasting life." So say many other Scriptures. One who trusts in Christ has, immediately, everlasting life.

Mark 16:16 says, "He that believeth and is baptized shall be saved." That is no different plan than that so often and so plainly stated. One who believes on Christ is saved. When he is baptized, professing that faith, as is immediately commanded and as was regularly the case with New Testament converts, he is still saved, of course.

So Acts 2:38 simply means two things the people of Jerusalem were to do, to have all that Peter and the other disciples had. First, they were to repent, and so have remission of sins. Second, they were to be baptized, so publicly confessing Christ and offering themselves as dead with Christ and raised to walk in newness of life, and so to receive the gift of the Holy Ghost.

Read Acts 2:38 again and do not stop until the period. What is the result promised? Not only that those who repent shall be saved; but those who go on to baptism, openly professing their faith and aligning themselves with these who are filled with the Holy Spirit, and giving themselves to the soul-winning activities of Peter and the other Christians --they "shall receive the gift of the Holy Ghost."

We must remember that when the hundred and twenty were filled with the Holy Spirit, it is recorded, "Now when this was noised abroad, the multitude came together, and were confounded..." (Acts 2:6). The multitude, including many thousands of people, were of some fifteen different nationalities as listed in verses 8 to 11. Verse 12 says "And they were all amazed, and were in doubt." Here in the most public way possible, in the presence of thousands, was fulfilled the promise of Joel, the great pouring out of the Holy Spirit with amazing results. Peter had in some detail explained that this was the fulfillment of Joel's prophecy and of the great significance of this day. He had showed them that the pouring out of the Holy Spirit was another attestation of the resurrection of Jesus Christ who was now at the right hand of the Father and "hath shed forth this, which ye now see and hear" (vs. 33). So when they asked, "What shall we do?" they meant, "What shall we do to be saved and to be filled with the Holy Spirit as these Christians are?"

So the conditions named in Acts 2:38 are the steps that lead to "the gift of the Holy Ghost." They should repent and then and there, they would be saved. But they ought to go on to be baptized in public profession of their faith, identifying themselves with these Christians and with Christ Himself and with His great agelong, soul-winning program, by being filled with the Holy Ghost for witness. So baptism mentioned here is not a condition of salvation. It often is connected, in the Bible, with the fullness of the Holy Spirit.

Jesus was baptized and there praying the Holy Ghost came upon Him in a form like a dove (Luke 3:22). Certainly baptism had nothing to do with salvation for Jesus Himself, who needed no saving. But it did mean His surrender to the crucifixion route of death and resurrection, for the purpose of saving sinners. And so He had the gift of the Holy Ghost, was anointed for His ministry.

In Acts 19:1-7 the Apostle Paul found some "disciples" at Ephesus. They had "believed." The Scofield Reference Bible and some others speak of these "so-called disciples." But when God says "disciples" no one else has a right to say "so-called disciples." However, Paul indicates that when they were baptized they should have been taught to expect the fullness of the Holy Spirit. He explained that to them and they were baptized again. Then Paul laid his hands upon them and "the Holy Ghost came on them."

Evidently it is not baptism which is essential to the gift of the Holy Ghost, but a certain surrender and burden for souls and willingness to count self dead and to count one's self raised up to the new life of soul winning which is a condition, along with prayer, of Holy Spirit power.

Remember that John the Baptist preached repeatedly at his baptizings that "I indeed baptize you with water unto repentance: but he that cometh after me is mightier than I, whose shoes I am not worthy to bear: he shall baptize you with the Holy Ghost, and with fire" (Matt. 3:11; see also Mark 1:8; Luke 3:16; John 1:33; and Acts 1:5). It is evident that the standard set up for New Testament Christians is that everyone, as soon as he is saved, ought to be baptized as an open profession of his faith in Christ and his surrender to the soul-winning work of Jesus Christ; and then ought to be filled with the Spirit and have power on his witnessing.

Baptism Is Not a Condition of Salvation

It is clear from the Great Commission in Matthew 28:19 and 20 and Mark 16:15 and the universal practice of New Testament Christians, that converts ought to be baptized. Baptism was not essential to salvation, but it was essential and is essential to obedience. Baptism did not procure salvation, but it declared salvation one had already received.

Since many Scriptures expressly declare that one who trusts in Christ for salvation instantly has everlasting life (John 3:15, 16, 18, 36; John 5:24; John 6:47; Acts 13:38, 39), then the one who has trusted Christ is immediately saved and the baptism which followed could only declare that which had already occurred.

Baptism is a work of righteousness (as Jesus stated in Matthew 3:15). But Titus 3:5 declares, "Not by works of righteousness which we have done, but according to his mercy he saved us, by the washing of regeneration, and renewing of the Holy Ghost." Salvation is "not of works, lest any man should boast" (Eph. 2:9). (See the author's book, Bible Baptism, same publishers.)

Jesus never needed to repent. He could not repent as our example. Jesus never was in unbelief and never needed to come trusting for forgiveness. He needed no forgiveness. If baptism were a way of securing salvation, then Jesus could not be our example in baptism. But since baptism is a token of heart surrender to the soul-saving work of the Lord and pointing toward the death, burial and resurrection of Christ, then Christ could be our example in baptism. So He was baptized and immediately the Holy Spirit came on Him in an anointing for His ministry and so we may be baptized like Christ and receive the gift of the Holy Ghost, as Acts 2:38 says.

The Offer of "the Gift of the Holy Ghost" Made to Every Christian

"...Ye shall receive the gift of the Holy Ghost. For the promise is unto you, and to your children, and to all that are afar off, even as many as the Lord our God shall call." The promise of the fullness of the Spirit here is for all the Jews who heard, if they would repent and meet God's requirements. The promise was also to their children, the next generation of Jews. And the promise then was for "all that are afar off," that is, Gentiles far off from the blessings of the Jews and from God's dealings with Israel (Eph. 2:11-13, 17). And to those also far off in time, even down through all generations--"even as many as the Lord our God shall call." Everyone who is ever called to be saved is called also to have the power of the Holy Spirit upon him for witnessing.

When the soldier pierced the side of the Saviour after His death, "forthwith came there out blood and water" (John 19:34). The blood of Jesus made the atonement for our sins and meant that all could be saved. But the water pictures something also for every one. "For I will pour water upon him that is thirsty, and floods upon the dry ground: I will pour my spirit upon thy seed, and my blessing upon thine offspring" (Isa. 44:3). Jesus had promised, "He that believeth on me, as the Scripture hath said, out of his belly shall flow rivers of living water. (But this spake he of the Spirit, which they that believe on him should receive...)" (John 7:38, 39; see also John 4:14). "But whosoever drinketh of the water that I shall give him shall never thirst; but the water that I shall give him shall be in him a well of water springing up into everlasting life."

Compare the promise of Acts 2:38 and 39 with Acts 1:8. That promise of power for witnessing was to hold good "in Jerusalem, and in all Judaea, and in Samaria, and unto the uttermost part of the earth." Oh, as I have preached the

Gospel to heathen people in Japan, in Korea, in India, I found it true, as it is true in America.

So in Ephesians 5:18, "And be not drunk with wine, wherein is excess; but be filled with the Spirit," is the command for every Christian in every generation. And Peter continued then (vs. 40) to testify and exhort, answering questions, pleading for decision.

VERSE 41:

41 ¶ Then they that gladly received his word were baptized: and the same day there were added *unto* *them* about three thousand souls.

Souls Saved the Inevitable Result of Spirit-Filled Witnessing

There is a direct connection between verse 4 and verse 41. "And they were all filled with the Holy Ghost, and began to speak...as the Spirit gave them utterance...Then they that gladly received his word were baptized: and the same day there were added unto them about three thousand souls." Remember that the fullness of the Spirit (or baptism of the Holy Ghost or the gift of the Holy Ghost) was to the purpose that "ye shall receive power...and ye shall be witnesses unto me." Soul-winning power on our witnessing and on our preaching and teaching is the blessed result God has promised when we are filled with the Spirit.

Notice how often in the Bible the connection is obvious between Spirit-filled witnessing and sinners being saved.

1. Of John the Baptist it is said that "...he shall be filled with the Holy Ghost, even from his mother's womb. And many of the children of Israel shall he turn to the Lord their God" (Luke 1:15, 16). The boldness and power is always apparent. Often the soul-winning results follow.

2. Connect Acts 4:31, "And they were all filled with the Holy Ghost, and they spake the word of God with boldness,"

with verse 33, "And with great power gave the apostles witness of the resurrection," and with Acts 5:14 following: "And believers were the more added to the Lord, multitudes both of men and women."

3. There is a connection between the Spirit-filled witness of Stephen in Acts 7:55 and following, with the conviction of the young man, Saul, who was soon saved on the road to Damascus.

4. In Acts 9:17 the young convert Saul was "filled with the Holy Ghost." In verse 20, "And straightway he preached Christ in the synagogues, that he is the Son of God." And the context shows his increasing strength and power to confound the unbelievers so that his life was threatened.

5. Barnabas: "For he was a good man, and full of the Holy Ghost and of faith: and much people was added unto the Lord" (Acts 11:24).

So at Pentecost when "they were all filled with the Holy Ghost" and spoke out for God, some three thousand people turned to God and were baptized.

VERSES 42-47:

42 And they continued steadfastly in the apostles' doctrine and fellowship, and in breaking of bread, and in prayers.

43 And fear came upon every soul: and many wonders and signs were done by the apostles.

44 And all that believed were together, and had all things common;

45 And sold their possessions and goods, and parted them to all *men,* as every man had need.

46 And they, continuing daily with one accord in the temple, and breaking bread from house to house, did eat their meat with gladness and singleness of heart.

47 Praising God, and having favour with all the people. And the Lord added to the church daily such as should be saved.

The Wonderful Life of the Young Converts

It is amazing when we consider that this young church in Jerusalem had almost none of the things we now often think to be essential in our church services. They had no church building. (Not a one is mentioned in the whole New Testament!) They met in people's homes, in porches of the temple, in a borrowed synagogue, in a vacant lot or by the seaside!

The preachers were unlearned and ignorant men, though they had been with Jesus and had mighty power and spiritual wisdom. They had no organization, no officers except the apostles. There were thousands of members before deacons were even elected. As far as we know, they had no musical instruments, no songbooks, no libraries.

In the author's pamphlet, The Seven Secrets of a Happy, Prosperous Christian Life, we have from this passage listed the following happy steps to Christian success, followed by these young converts.

1. They had assurance of salvation. "They that gladly received his word were baptized" (vs. 41). They believed that they were saved on the assurance of the Word of God.

2. They were baptized. They openly committed themselves to Christ and identified themselves with Christ and His people.

3. They joined themselves together. They had a church membership, though they may not have had a church membership roll or a filing system or a record book. However, some quorum of Christians passed on the eligibility of those who came to be baptized, if there were any question about it (Acts 10:47). Paul "assayed to join himself to the disciples" (Acts 9:26), but they put him off until others vouched for him. The brethren wrote letters to other Christians to "receive" Apollos when he came (Acts 18:27) and Phebe, a servant of the church at Cenchrea when she should come (Rom. 16:1). So "there were added unto them about three thousand souls" means that many became accepted as mem-

bers of the congregation, received as Christians. And that church membership included fellowship and breaking bread in the Lord's Supper (vs. 42).

4. "They continued stedfastly in the apostles' doctrine," that is, in the teaching which the apostles gave, which we now have in the Bible. That was equivalent to daily study of the Word of God.

5. They continued daily and regularly in earnest prayers (vs. 42).

6. They learned to give and share joyfully "and sold their possessions and goods, and parted them to all men, as every man had need," that is, when a need arose that required it.

There was no communism here among these New Testament Christians. In the first place, they only sold their property and gave the money when it was needed immediately. They did not divide up their property or have it all belong to the state. Each one shared what he had with others out of love and as the need arose.

This is different from communism in that it was voluntary, it was done only as occasion required it immediately, and when the need was passed, each went on in private enterprise and private ownership of his property. It is clear from Acts 4:34-37 that the case of Barnabas, who sold what he had and brought all the money to the apostles, was an exception. Others sold property when it was necessary to help other people but not otherwise all of it. The case of Ananias and Sapphira in Acts 5:1-11 shows that "Whiles it remained, was it not thine own? and after it was sold, was it not in thine own power?" (vs. 4). For an individual to give to the needs of others voluntarily and at great sacrifice during some temporary time of stress is not the same as the principle of atheistic communism.

Every young Christian ought to learn the joy of giving both tithes and offerings and of trusting the Lord daily about material needs.

7. We are told, "And the Lord added to the church daily such as should be saved" (vs. 47). Their testimony: "Continuing daily with one accord in the temple, and breaking bread from house to house" (vs. 46). It is not surprising, then, that souls were saved and received for membership daily.

Some churches receive members at Easter. That is not the Bible way. Some receive members when the membership committee meets once a month (if there are any to receive). Other churches which have a vigorous soul-winning program try to win souls every week and receive members every Sunday. The big Highland Park Baptist Church in Chattanooga, Dr. Lee Roberson, pastor, has an evangelistic service every Wednesday night also, and usually an invitation for people to receive Christ and claim Him openly and to receive members. But the church at Jerusalem with thousands of members saw new converts added to the church daily! Soul winning is not only important: it was almost the sole aim and end of the Jerusalem church and of New Testament Christians!

ACTS 3

VERSES 1–11:

NOW Peter and John went up together into the temple at the hour of prayer, *being* the ninth *hour*.

2 And a certain man lame from his mother's womb was carried, whom they laid daily at the gate of the temple which is called Beautiful, to ask alms of them that entered into the temple;

3 Who, seeing Peter and John about to go into the temple, asked an alms.

4 And Peter, fastening his eyes upon him with John, said, Look on us.

5 And he gave heed unto them, expecting to receive something of them.

6 Then Peter said, Silver and gold have I none; but such as I have give I thee: In the name of Jesus Christ of Nazareth rise up and walk

7 And he took him by the right hand, and lifted *him* up: and immediately his feet and ankle bones received strength.

8 And he leaping up stood, and walked, and entered with them into the temple, walking, and leaping, and praising God.

9 And all the people saw him walking and praising God:

10 And they knew that it was he which sat for alms at the Beautiful gate of the temple: and they were filled with wonder and amazement at that which had happened unto him.

11 And as the lame man which was healed held Peter and John, all the people ran together unto them in the porch that is called Solomon's, greatly wondering.

The Healing of the Lame Man

It was "at the hour of prayer, being the ninth hour." So in Jewish time it was about 3:00 p.m. There were said to be three times of prayer--at the third, sixth and ninth hours.

"Went up together in the temple." This is the temple as rebuilt by Herod. First, there had been Solomon's temple, destroyed by Babylonians at the final captivity (II Chron. 36:19). Then, the returning remnant after the captivity rebuilt the temple (Ezra 5:2; 6:15). Then Herod the Great rebuilt and restored the temple on a grand scale, beginning about 19 or 20 B.C., finished 46 years later (John 2:20).

The miracle took place "at the gate of the temple which is called Beautiful"; not the city gate now called by that name. The gate by this name is not named elsewhere in the Bible but is thought to be the gate of Nicanor looking toward the brook Kidron on the east side. Josephus said it was made of Corinthian brass, magnificent.

People came running together "in the porch that is called Solomon's" (vs. 11). Perhaps the term portico would be a better term than porch. It was a roofed colonnade along the eastern wall in the Court of the Gentiles of Herod's temple. Here Christ had taught the people at the Feast of Dedication in John 10:23. It was an open court or plaza where crowds gathered. Acts 5:12 tells us that the Christians "were all with one accord in Solomon's porch" where the apostles wrought signs and wonders.

Here is an amazing miracle of a man "lame from his mother's womb" with such lack and deformity of his bones that he could not walk. At Peter's word he was instantly healed. It is not that he felt better or that fever was reduced or that his body became adjusted, but a miraculous change took place in his tissues, a creative miracle, without the use of any natural processes. Compare this miracle with the one very much like it in Acts 14:8-10. There, too, was a man "impotent in his feet, being a cripple from his mother's womb, who never had walked." And Paul there, like Peter here, commanded the man, "Stand upright on thy feet." Paul, "perceiving that he had faith to be healed," commanded the man, just as we are sure Peter had it revealed to him by the Holy Spirit that this man would have faith to be healed. And in both cases the man would have faith to be healed. And in both cases the man "leaped and walked" and was happy. And in both cases the apostles, Peter and Paul, respectively, preached to the crowd that assembled.

Note that this is a bold and instant miracle without recourse to a season of prayer. Peter was like Joshua who suddenly commanded the sun to stand still or like Elijah who said, "If I be a man of God, then let fire come down from heaven, and consume thee and thy fifty" (II Kings 1:10). It is like Moses who commanded the earth to open and swallow Korah and his adherents (Num. 16:30-33). So did Peter here command the lame man to become whole. It is the kind of a miracle that Jesus Himself did when He cursed the fig tree. It is the kind of miracle that Jesus promised the disciples, if they should have faith, that "whosoever shall say unto this mountain, Be thou removed, and be thou cast into the sea; and shall not doubt in his heart, but shall believe that those things which he saith shall come to pass; he shall have whatsoever he saith" (Mark 11:23).

The lame man was laid daily at the Beautiful Gate of the temple to ask alms. He had been lame "from birth" and was "above forty years old" (Acts 4:22). If he had lived at Jerusalem long it is nearly certain he had seen and heard Jesus in person. Jesus healed many others--why not this man?

It seems unlikely that he would have faith to expect healing and to attempt to rise and walk as Peter commanded, had he not known ahead of time about Jesus and His power. He may have, probably did, hear the Gospel at Pentecost. Possibly then he became convicted of his sins, perhaps had been saved. Or he may have trusted Christ for salvation here and now as Peter talked to him. "Faith cometh by hearing, and hearing by the word of God" (Rom. 10:17). So we may be sure that somewhere, either from Jesus or the apostles, he had heard the Gospel before.

And a blessed truth is here: Some who were not saved when they heard Jesus, were saved when they heard the apostles. Jesus had promised them, "Verily, verily, I say unto you, He that believeth on me, the works that I do shall he do also; and greater works than these shall he do; because I go unto my Father" (John 14:12). They have the same power of the Holy Spirit that Jesus had, and each Christian can win some one others might not win.

The Miracles of Jesus in the Gospels Carried on by Christians in the Book of Acts

In the first verse in the book of Acts Peter says that in his former treatise (the Gospel according to Luke) he wrote "of all that Jesus began both to do and teach." Now the clear inference is that in the book of Acts he is going to tell of all that the apostles and other New Testament Christians continue to do and to teach, even as Jesus did, in the same power of the Holy Spirit.

Jesus, after being anointed with the Holy Ghost at His baptism (Luke 3:22), set out in the power of the Holy Spirit to teach and preach and do miracles from the first miracle, the turning of water into wine in Cana, on till the miracles after His resurrection, the miraculous gathering of fish in John 21, and His bodily ascension to Heaven. Now the New Testament Christians, filled with the Holy Ghost at Pentecost, are to expect and to have the same miraculous power as Jesus had.

That is what Jesus promised the night before He was betrayed. In the upper room He told His disciples, "Verily, verily, I say unto you, He that believeth on me, the works that I do shall he do also; and greater works than these shall he do; because I go unto my Father" (John 14:12).

The same night, in the high priestly prayer, Jesus prayed, "As thou hast sent me into the world, even so have I also sent them into the world" (John 17:18). Then when He was risen from the dead, "the same day at evening" He came to that upper room where the disciples were assembled and said to them, "Peace be unto you: as my Father hath sent me, even so send I you. And when he had said this, he breathed on them, and saith unto them, Receive ye the Holy Ghost" (John 20:21, 22). New Testament Christians are to have the same power Jesus had, do the same kind of preaching Jesus did, see the same kind of marvelous conversions that Jesus had, and work the same kind of miracles that Jesus worked! So is the plain teaching of these Scriptures as we understand them.

Thus throughout the book of Acts we find a succession of wonderful miracles in almost every chapter. In Acts 2 we have the miraculous sound of a rushing mighty wind, the visible tongues of fire, the gift of languages; in chapter 3 the marvelous healing of this lame man; in chapter 4 the earthquake in verse 31; in chapter 5 the punitive death of Ananias and Sapphira at Peter's word and the healing of multitudes in verses 15 and 16 and the release of James and John from prison by an angel (vs. 19). In Acts 6 we find that "Stephen, full of faith and power, did great wonders and miracles among the people" (vs. 8). In Acts 7:55 we have the miraculous vision of Jesus at the right hand of God seen by Stephen; in Acts 8:6, 7 miracles and healings; in Acts 9 the miraculous vision appearing to Paul at his conversion. In Acts 10 we have the miraculous vision to Peter which led him to go to Cornelius, and the angel appearing to Cornelius; in chapter 12 the miraculous release of Peter from prison and the instant death of Herod. In chapter 13:8-11 Elymas the sorcerer was struck blind. In Acts 14 we find the impotent man at Lystra healed; in Acts 16 the demon cast out and the earthquake at Philippi; in Acts 18:9 a miraculous vision to Paul at night; in Acts 19:11 and 12, "special miracles by the hands of Paul"; in Acts 21:10 and 11 the miraculous revelation to a prophet, Agabus. In Acts 27, we read of a miraculous vision to Paul and the whole company spared from shipwreck, and in Acts 28, Paul miraculously healed of a snakebite, and Publius' father healed. So the God of the Gospels is the God of the book of Acts. The power of the Holy Spirit resting on Christ is the same power of the Holy Spirit resting on New Testament Christians. The approval of God on Christ was shown by miracles and wonders. The approval of God on Christ is still shown by miracles and wonders in His name. So Peter preached in Acts 3 (vs. 16).

Are Miraculous, Physical Healings to Be Expected Throughout This Age?

Some Plymouth Brethren teachers speak of the book of Acts or of part of the period covered by the book of Acts as "a transitional period." Even Dr. Scofield says in his introduction to the book of Acts, "Chapters 11, 12, and 15 of this section are transitional, establishing finally the distinction, doctrinally, between law and grace."

Those who overemphasize dispensationalism think the ministry of John the Baptist was legal and under law and not Gospel and not grace; they think that John the Baptist had more emphasis on repentance than is proper now and that the baptism of John was not Christian baptism. In this we believe they are mistaken. Mark begins his story about John the Baptist in these words, "The beginning of the gospel of Jesus Christ, the Son of God" (Mark 1:1). The only baptism Jesus and the twelve apostles had was that administered by John. The preaching of John the Baptist on repentance (Matt. 3:2) and of Jesus (Matt. 4:17) was the same. Their preaching on salvation (Jesus in John 3:16; John in John 3:36) was the same.

Out of this overemphasis mentioned the Bullingerites and other ultradispensationalists have gone farther to say sometimes that baptism is not for this age and some even declare the Lord's Supper is not for this age, etc. Some even think that the plan of salvation was different in the Old Testament. But against that see Acts 10:43, "To him give all the prophets witness [Old Testament and New Testament prophets]; that through his name whosoever believeth in him shall receive remission of sins."

So many good men have a tendency to say that the book of Acts is not a proper picture of Christianity for today. They say that the age of miracles is past. Some, like G. Campbell Morgan, say that talking in tongues in apostolic times was some mysterious ecstasy and talk in a heavenly language having no gospel use, but now that is no more. However, speaking in tongues never was anything but simply the power to speak in the language of people present who understood and thus heard the Gospel. Some even interpret I Corinthians 13:8-13 as teaching that the miracles and gifts of the Spirit recorded in the book of Acts are done away now that the canon of Scripture is fulfilled. But, we think that is a false interpretation of that passage, and believe that "when that which is perfect is come" refers to the resurrection of the body, a perfect knowledge and perfect love.

No, we do not believe that the age of miracles has past. We believe that God often heals the sick miraculously in answer to prayer. Note first some false teachings and false emphases about miracles and healing which we do not believe.

1. The Bible does not teach that it is always God's will to heal the sick. It is often God's will for a Christian to die. Other times it is God's will for him to stay sick for some great spiritual blessing. Paul "besought the Lord thrice" for the removal of his thorn in the flesh (II Cor. 12:7-10), but this thorn in his body was not removed and he was taught to "take pleasure in infirmities." Paul instructed Timothy, "Drink no longer water [not only water], but use a little wine for thy stomach's sake and thine often infirmities" (I Tim. 5:23). Those infirmities were not healed. Paul said, "Trophimus have I left at Miletum sick" (II Tim. 4:20). All the healings in New Testament times were relative and temporary: all those healed eventually died. Those "healing evangelists" and others who say it is always God's will to heal the sick misinterpret Scripture. It is true that healing is in the atonement, as He paid for all the results of sin, but "the adoption to wit, the redemption of our body" (Rom. 8:23) waits for the resurrection time and

no man can before the resurrection possess all that is purchased by Christ's death for us.

2. Healings were relatively infrequent, even in the time of Christ and in the time of the apostles. As far as we know, Peter raised only Dorcas from the dead (Acts 9:36-42). And Paul raised only Eutychus, if he was really dead (Acts 20:9, 10). And even Jesus, as far as we know, raised only three from the dead. If only twenty or thirty miracles are recorded in the book of Acts for the church at Jerusalem and all Peter's and Paul's journeys, we may properly suppose that miracles were wonderful but infrequent. Only as miracles would honor God and further the Gospel and as God gave faith for them, did New Testament Christians have miracles.

3. It is not wrong to use medicine and doctors. No Scripture indicates that. God usually uses means, even in the saving of souls. So He uses means of doctors, medicines, treatment, diet, exercise in maintaining health or in curing disease. But God can heal without doctors and medicine and sometimes does. God can heal and usually does through normal bodily processes, but He can also heal in spite of conditions and contrary to probabilities.

Reasons Why We Think God Wants to Answer Prayer for Healing of the Sick in This Age

1. We think that the closing passage in Mark 16:9-20 is authentic. Verses 17 and 18, connected with the Great Commission, say, "And these signs shall follow them that believe; In my name shall they cast out devils; they shall speak with new tongues; They shall take up serpents; and if they drink any deadly thing, it shall not hurt them; they shall lay hands on the sick., and they shall recover." Note that these particular signs or miracles were to be given to those who believed for these particular miracles. The Scripture here does not mean that every person who trusts Christ for salvation gets these other things. If God gives the faith, He gives the wonderful answer to prayer or the

wonderful answer to faith. This Scripture simply says that where faith is given for a miracle healing of the sick, God will do the healing.

2. But other promises in the Bible indicate no restriction as to what God is able and willing to do in answer to the prayer of faith. Mark 9:23 expresses a permanent truth for all ages. "Jesus said unto him, If thou canst believe, all things are possible to him that believeth."

Mark 11:24 is not addressed only to the apostles, for the preceding verses specify the promises for "whosoever." So when Jesus said, "Therefore I say unto you, What things soever ye desire, when ye pray, believe that ye receive them, and ye shall have them," it is still the promise of God applicable today. So John 14:13, 14; John 15:7; John 16:24; so Ephesians 3:20 and many other promises are so unlimited in scope that they provide miracles wherever God gives the faith for miracles or wherever they can be asked on the authority of Jesus and in His name.

3. James 5:14 and 15 instructs one who is sick to call for the elders to pray over him and says, "And the prayer of faith shall save the sick, and the Lord shall raise him up...." So it is still proper to pray for the sick. Where God gives the faith, He will give the healing.

On this subject read the chapters on "Does God Work Miracles Today?" and "Healing in Answer to Prayer" in the author's book, Prayer--Asking and Receiving, and read The Ministry of Healing by A. J. Gordon.

And let the author here testify that he has seen healings which he regards as nothing less than miraculous: a little girl, five years old, was healed of diphtheria with a fever going in two or three hours from 105 down to normal; my father, given up by doctors to die before morning, at 7:00 a.m. awoke, put on his clothes and went about his business in normal health after some of us prayed into the night; a woman, after two years in a T. B. sanatorium, given up to die with the next hemorrhage, was healed in answer to prayer, in two weeks doing all of her own housework and thirty years later very active, with no recurrence of T. B.

All healings now are temporary and relative. Compared with the saving of a soul they are relatively unimportant. But God still has compassion on our infirmities; He invites every troubled heart to pray, and where it is for the glory of God and so He will give faith for it, then God can and often does heal the sick in answer to prayer.

VERSES 12–26:

12 ¶ And when Peter saw *it*, he answered unto the people, Ye men of Israel, why marvel ye at this? or why look ye so earnestly on us, as though by our own power or holiness we had made this man to walk?

13 The God of Abraham, and of Isaac, and of Jacob, the God of our fathers, hath glorified his Son Jesus; whom ye delivered up, and denied him in the presence of Pilate, when he was determined to let *him* go.

14 But ye denied the Holy One and the Just, and desired a murderer to be granted unto you;

15 And killed the Prince of life, whom God hath raised from the dead; whereof we are witnesses.

16 And his name, through faith in his name, hath made this man strong, whom ye see and know: yea, the faith which is by him hath given him this perfect soundness in the presence of you all.

17 And now, brethren, I wot that through ignorance ye did *it*, as *did* also your rulers.

18 But those things, which God before had shewed by the mouth of all his prophets, that Christ should suffer, he hath so fulfilled.

19 ¶ Repent ye therefore, and be converted, that your sins may be blotted out, when the times of refreshing shall come from the presence of the Lord;

20 And he shall send Jesus Christ, which before was preached unto you:

21 Whom the heaven must receive until the times of restitution of all things, which God hath spoken by the mouth of all his holy prophets since the world began.

22 For Moses truly said unto the fathers, A Prophet shall the Lord your God raise up unto you of your brethren, like unto me; him shall ye hear in all

things whatsoever he shall say unto you.

23 And it shall come to pass, *that* every soul, which will not hear that Prophet, shall be destroyed from among the people.

24 Yea, and all the prophets from Samuel and those that follow after, as many as have spoken, have likewise foretold of these days.

25 Ye are the children of the prophets, and of the covenant which God made with our fathers, saying unto Abraham, And in thy seed shall all the kindreds of the earth be blessed.

26 Unto you first God, having raised up his Son Jesus, sent him to bless you, in turning away every one of you from his iniquities.

Peter's Second Sermon

Note the features of Peter's second sermon.

1. The healing is made an occasion to get the attention of the people and bring up the subject of Christ and salvation. As the sermon at Pentecost grew out of the amazement of the people and their comments on the pouring out of the Holy Spirit, so here the healing of the lame man draws a crowd and Peter starts with that event. It is not "by our own power or holiness" that man was healed, but through the name of Christ (vss. 12, 16).

2. Again, Peter goes back to the crucifixion. He faced these men with their sin in verses 13 to 15. They delivered Jesus up, denied Him, asked for a murderer and killed the Prince of life. Every sermon to the unsaved ought to stress the wickedness of the Christ-rejecting heart and their guilt before God.

3. God "hath glorified his Son Jesus." Jesus is the Son of God, that is, the Son of the God of Abraham, Isaac, and Jacob. He has been raised from the dead, and now Peter and all these people (above five hundred brethren, I Cor. 15:6) are witnesses. Remember that the resurrection of Jesus Christ is the principal doctrine preached throughout the book of Acts.

4. It is through faith in Christ's name that this man was healed (vs. 16). I take it that it was through Peter's faith

and the faith of the lame man, just as in Mark 2: "When Jesus saw their faith," the combined faith of the four men who brought the sick man and of the sick man, He saved him and healed him (Mark 2:5). But remember, the healing was in the name of Jesus and through faith in Jesus Christ.

5. The crucifixion was only a part of the plan of God so clearly outlined in the New Testament: "those things, which God before had showed by the mouth of all his prophets, that Christ should suffer, he hath so fulfilled" (vs. 18).

6. Now comes the plan of salvation. "Repent ye therefore, and be converted, that your sins may be blotted out...." Note the progress: first, he gets their attention and interest, then this healing glorifies Jesus, then they are wicked sinners because they killed Him, but God has raised Him from the dead. And this is all prophesied in the Bible --now they should repent and be saved!

Note that to "repent" here involves faith in the Saviour, just as repentance and faith are used almost interchangeably in the plan of salvation throughout the Bible.

7. See the promise to the nation Israel of Christ's return and the restoration of David's kingdom (vss. 20, 21).

8. Note the appeal to Moses whom the Jews loved and pretended to follow. As Moses led them out of Egypt and to the land of promise, so Christ would fulfill what is yet prophesied for the nation Israel returning to reign.

9. But to reject Jesus would mean one's soul would be destroyed (vs. 23).

10. Note the tender appeal in verses 25 and 26. God promised under Abraham that in his seed all nations of the earth would be blessed. Jesus is that seed and God has sent Him to bless these Jews by turning them from their sins and saving them!

The National Appeal

Again, note that in Acts 2:14 Peter addressed, "Ye men of Judaea"; in Acts 2:22, "Ye men of Israel"; in Acts 2:36, "Therefore let all the house of Israel know assuredly...."

Even so in Acts 3:19 and following verses, the appeal is made not only to individuals to repent, but with some promise to the nation as a whole, if all of them would repent, as well as salvation to individuals.

Note some ways in which this promise is to the nation as a whole.

1. "That your sins may be blotted out, when the times of refreshing shall come from the presence of the Lord; And he shall send Jesus Christ...." An individual who repents has his sins blotted out immediately. But the national sins of Israel will be blotted out and the nation returned to favor only at the return of Christ. Then a nation will be converted in a day (Isa. 66:8). Then Israel "shall look upon me whom they have pierced" and repent nationally (Zech. 12:10). Then "there shall be a fountain opened to the house of David and to the inhabitants of Jerusalem for sin and for uncleanness" (Zech. 13:1). Then God will give them a new heart and take away the stony heart from Israel and put His Spirit within them (Ezek. 36:26, 27). Then when the nation returns to God with all their soul, Christ will return "and the Lord thy God will circumcise thine heart, and the heart of thy seed, to love the Lord thy God with all thine heart, and with all thy soul, that thou mayest live" (Deut. 30:1-6). So when Peter spoke of that time of refreshing from the Lord when God would send Jesus again, He referred to a restoration of the nation Israel and the conversion of all the Jews left alive on the earth after Christ's second coming.

2. Note the reference that the Heaven must receive Christ "until the times of restitution of all things, which God hath spoken by the mouth of all his holy prophets...." That is, the land of Palestine will be restored according to Isaiah 35, Israel will be restored to the land according to many prophecies, David's throne will be restored, the nation itself will be restored to favor with God. That time of the kingdom age, the millennium, of blessing with Christ on David's throne reigning over the whole earth, is "the times

of restitution." That is the time that Jesus spoke of "in the regeneration when the Son of man shall sit in the throne of his glory" (Matt. 19:28), when the apostles will rule with Him judging the twelve tribes of Israel.

3. Note particularly the reference to the Abrahamic covenant in verse 25. These could be the true children of Abraham only by accepting the Saviour. It is only in Jesus that all nations shall be blessed through Abraham's seed. So Jesus had taught in John 8:37-40. Those unconverted Jews were not spiritually Abraham's seed but were of their father the Devil. Only in Christ can Abraham's covenant be fulfilled.

4. It is important to see that according to this passage, the Abrahamic covenant cannot be fulfilled just by preaching the Gospel. It will take the return of Christ in person and the "restitution of all things" which were promised and that Abraham and his seed Christ shall possess the literal land of Canaan before that Abrahamic covenant is consummated. To spiritualize and thus make of no special moment those covenants with Abraham and with David and with Israel is not honest dealing with the Word of God.

5. But remember that Peter in this passage is not preaching any kingdom on earth except for born-again people who take Christ as Saviour through penitent faith.

Was the Davidic Kingdom on Earth Offered to the Jews Then in Apostolic Times?

The Scofield Reference Bible, which is the most useful and helpful reference Bible in the world, is sometimes in the notes overdispensational, we believe. However, there is some virtue to the claim of some Plymouth Brethren teachers and the Scofield Reference Bible that the kingdom was offered in the ministry of Christ, and in the early days of the apostles, and postponed. Some facts we should note clearly.

1. Certainly God had no intention to prevent and made no

promises that would prevent the arrest, trial and crucifix-ion of Christ. The whole plan of salvation and the fulfill-ment of all Old Testament Scriptures centers around the coming of Christ to die for sinners and to be raised from the dead.

2. See the insistence of John the Baptist and of Jesus in Matthew 3:2 and Matthew 4:17 that "the kingdom of heaven is at hand." That indicates that the kingdom of Christ on earth was very near (in the sense of possibility, not uncondition-ally) and that it could have begun very soon, had the Jews as a whole nation turned to Christ.

3. In that case, Judas could still have betrayed Jesus to the Roman government, and the Great Tribulation could have come with the destruction of Jerusalem, the hounding of the Jews. And then Christ would have gone to Heaven and then returned, according to the Scriptures, with saints and angels. There had to be not only the crucifixion and resur-rection, but also the Great Tribulation and the time of the Antichrist, because these are foretold in Scripture.

4. Many Bible teachers have noticed that this present church age, from Pentecost on to the second coming of Christ, is not clearly prophesied in the Old Testament. In many Scriptures the first coming of Christ and the second coming of Christ are taught in the same passage, as if they could be very near to each other.

Let us say then that it appears that God has offered the nation Israel that if the whole nation would repent and be converted now, their sins could be blotted out and the nation restored by Christ's Second Coming, and that it might have been soon after the time Peter was preaching.

At any rate, we can clearly say that the only way these present could ever have part in the blessings of Abraham, in the kingdom of David, in the national fulfillment of Israel's destiny, was by turning to Christ and being saved.

Before we close the chapter, notice that "the covenant which God made with our fathers, saying unto Abraham..."

is a covenant that Abraham and his seed shall possess the land of Canaan forever.

God's Covenant With Abraham Involves the Land of Canaan and an Earthly Possession

Remember that the covenant with Abraham mentioned in verse 25 is a covenant that involves the land of Canaan, and with Abraham and Christ, his seed, inheriting the land of Canaan.

In Genesis 13:15-17 we read:

> "For all the land which thou seest, to thee will I give it, and to thy seed for ever. And I will make thy seed as the dust of the earth: so that if a man can number the dust of the earth, then shall thy seed also be numbered. Arise, walk through the land in the length of it and in the breadth of it; for I will give it unto thee."

Again, in Genesis 17:6-8 we read:

> "And I will make thee exceeding fruitful, and I will make nations of thee, and kings shall come out of thee. And I will establish my covenant between me and thee and thy seed after thee in their generations for an everlasting covenant, to be a God unto thee, and to thy seed after thee. And I will give unto thee, and to thy seed after thee, the land wherein thou art a stranger, all the land of Canaan, for an everlasting possession; and I will be their God."

And this covenant was only incidentally and partly with nation Israel as they inherited the land under Joshua and others, for Galatians 3:16 makes clear that the seed of Abraham to whom the promise was made was Christ. "Now to Abraham and his seed were the promises made. He saith not, And to seeds, as of many; but as of one, And to thy seed, which is Christ." So the Abrahamic covenant involves the return of Christ to reign in Palestine with Abraham participating.

Abraham has not yet inherited the land of Canaan, as we learn from Hebrews, chapter 11, nor did Isaac and Jacob. "These all died in faith, not having received the promises, but having seen them afar off, and were persuaded of them, and embraced them, and confessed that they were strangers and pilgrims on the earth" (Heb. 11:13).

But then Hebrews 11 discusses many great people who lived after the nation Israel came into the land of Canaan, including Joshua, Rahab, Gideon, Barak, Jephthae, David, and Samuel. And then Hebrews 11:39 says, "And these all, having obtained a good report through faith, received not the promise."

That eleventh chapter of Hebrews also indicates that the eternal promises to the land of Canaan will involve that heavenly Jerusalem which will come down from God out of Heaven, for Abraham "looked for a city which hath foundations, whose builder and maker is God."

The Abrahamic covenant means that born-again people will come back with Christ when He comes to reign on the earth and that He will establish the Davidic kingdom again and will reign over the whole earth.

ACTS 4

VERSES 1–4:

AND as they spake unto the people, the priests, and the captain of the temple, and the Sadducees, came upon them,

2 Being grieved that they taught the people, and preached through Jesus the resurrection from the dead.

3 And they laid hands on them, and put *them* in hold unto the next day: for it was now eventide.

4 Howbeit many of them which heard the word believed; and the number of the men was about five thousand.

The First Persecution

The captain of the temple is mentioned here. We are told that twenty-four bands of Levites guarded the temple in orderly succession. The commander of each band was called a captain. Josephus says that he was next to the high priest. He was something of a captain of police keeping order about the temple during his watch. "It was now eventide" (vs. 3). The healing at the gate of the temple had taken place at "the ninth hour," that is, about 3 o'clock (Acts 3:1). Then had followed rejoicing by the man healed, a gathering crowd and Peter's sermon. We suppose that the evening sacrifices took place about three and would be finished about four, and the temple gates would be closed. Hence Peter and John were confined, imprisoned, until tomorrow.

We label this "the first persecution" because more is bound to follow. The religious leaders in Jerusalem are the same crowd that had Jesus crucified. Jesus had warned the disciples plainly in John 15:18-20:

"If the world hate you, ye know that it hated me before it hated you. If ye were of the world, the world would love his own: but because ye are not of the world, but I have chosen you out of the world, therefore the world hateth you. Remember the word that I said unto you, The servant is not greater than his lord. If they have persecuted me, they will also persecute you; if they have kept my saying, they will keep your's also."

Jesus said that the persecution came because the persecutors are lost souls who "know not him that sent me" and they will persecute Christians "for my name's sake." And because the preaching of Christ's crucifixion and the Gospel rebukes their sin, "now they have no cloke for their sin" (John 15:21-23). The preaching of Jesus Christ, His death and resurrection and ascension to the right hand of God, brings men face to face with God and with their sin, and so they hate the Spirit-filled, evangelistic preaching about Christ, the crucified and risen Saviour.

Note the basis of the persecution. It was that "the Sadducees...being grieved that they taught the people, and preached through Jesus the resurrection from the dead." This preaching of the resurrection offended the Sadducees because they had insisted there is no resurrection. It offended them more because if Christ were raised from the dead, then they were wicked to have crucified Him. Further yet, if Christ were raised from the dead, they still had to deal with Him as the living God who knew of their sins, who had preached to them and warned them and commanded them to repent!

Peter and John were not persecuted for being Christians. They were not persecuted because they believed the Old Testament, tried to live right, paid their honest debts, quit getting drunk, loved their neighbors. No, persecution does not come to people simply because they are Christians. But aggressive witnessing for Jesus in the power of the Holy Spirit, calling men to repentance, insisting that Jesus is very God proved by His resurrection, brings resentment and rebellion in the wicked heart. People are not persecuted primarily because they are Christians, but because they are fervent, Spirit-filled witnesses trying to carry out the Great Commission of Jesus.

Note the rapid increase in the number of Christians; now "the number of the men was about five thousand," probably "beside women and children," as were the five thousand fed miraculously by Jesus (Matt. 14:21).

VERSES 5–12:

5 ¶ And it came to pass on the morrow, that their rulers, and elders, and scribes,

6 And Annas the high priest, and Caiaphas, and John, and Alexander, and as many as were of the kindred of the high priest, were gathered together at Jerusalem.

7 And when they had set them in the midst, they asked, By what power, or by what name, have ye done this?

8 Then Peter, filled with the Holy Ghost, said unto them, Ye rulers of the people, and elders of Israel,

9 If we this day be examined of the good deed done to the impotent man, by what means he is made whole;

10 Be it known unto you all, and to all the people of Israel, that by the name of Jesus Christ of Nazareth, whom ye crucified, whom God raised from the dead, *even* by him doth this man stand here before you whole.

11 This is the stone which was set at nought of you builders, which is become the head of the corner.

12 Neither is there salvation in any other: for there is none other name under heaven given among men, whereby we must be saved.

Peter Preaches to the Sanhedrin

This is an unofficial meeting of the Sanhedrin, I suppose, "the rulers," and with them are elders, and scribes, and Annas the former high priest, and Caiaphas, his son-in-law, now high priest (Matt. 26:57) and the kindred of the high priest." So it is not properly an unbiased holy group of men acting officially for the nation Israel. Rather, it is a party meeting of leaders who hated Jesus and had conspired to kill Him.

The Sanhedrin was composed of seventy men, the official ruling body of Israel in religious matters. We are told that there were twenty-four rulers or chief priests who were Sadducees; twenty-two scribes, usually Pharisees; and twenty-four elders, neither Pharisees nor Sadducees.

Both Annas and Caiaphas were present.

Annas had been the high priest from A.D. 7 to 14; was the father-in-law of Caiaphas who succeeded him, appointed by the Roman government. The Jews, however, regarded Annas as still having high priestly authority. When Jesus was arrested in Gethsemane they "...bound him, And led him away to Annas first; for he was father-in-law to Caiaphas, which was the high priest that same year" (John 18:12, 13). In John 18:19 Annas is called "the high priest" as many still regarded him so. But in John 18:23 the Scripture says, "Now Annas had sent him bound unto Caiaphas the high priest."

One tremendous thing has brought these people together. The lame man instantly healed had leaped and walked and held Peter and John and no doubt had praised the Lord. A crowd had assembled. Peter had preached to them. Like wildfire it ran through the city not only that Peter was preaching, but that the lame man whom everybody had seen for many years incapable of walking was now leaping and walking and praising God with "complete soundnes;" physically. So in the midst of the circle they put Peter and John, who had spent the night in jail, and asked them, "By what power, or by what name, have ye done this?"

Peter Again Preaches the Resurrection and Salvation Through Christ

1. His sermon follows a familiar pattern and a good one. The miracle was done in the name of Jesus Christ of Naza-

reth. Peter claimed no gift, no power for himself. It was the living Christ who worked this miracle.

2. And Peter solemnly charged them again, "whom ye crucified." Don't let them forget that, Peter! And preachers everywhere should not let poor sinners forget that they have been the enemies and murderers of Christ and that God requires repentance.

3. "Whom God raised from the dead." Since the resurrection of Christ proved His deity (Rom. 1:4) and therefore proves the authenticity of the Gospel, the resurrection will be preached throughout the book of Acts in New Testament times and ought to be preached everywhere today. There is no Gospel without a literal, physical, bodily resurrection of Jesus Christ. And Christianity loses all its saving power when that essential of the faith is left out. It is then a perverted Gospel, an "other gospel," for which anyone, man or angel, who preaches it is to be accursed (Gal. 1:8, 9).

4. Again, Peter uses a Scripture. This time it is Psalm 118:22--"The stone which the builders refused is become the head stone of the corner." Jesus had quoted the same Scripture in Matthew 21:42 to these "chief priests and Pharisees." A tradition says that when the stones were prepared for Solomon's temple and brought to the site ready for laying, so that there might not be the sound of a hammer in the building, one stone was brought which could fit nowhere and the builders shoved it contemptuously aside as not cut to fit, a mistake of the stone cutters. But when they came to finish the walls, they found that the head stone of the corner was missing. It was the same despised and rejected stone. Peter applies it and says that the Psalm refers to them, Jewish leaders, who rejected Christ who is not only the foundation but the capstone of all God's plan.

Christ is often pictured in the Bible as a stone. He is that great rock which, smitten by Moses, yielded water to thirsty Israel (I Cor. 10:4). He is that smiting stone cut out of the mountains that will fall on the image representing all the world powers and governments destroyed at Christ's Second Coming (Dan. 2:34, 35, 44). He is the chief corner stone, and He is the stone of stumbling and rock of offense (I Pet. 2:6-8 quoting Isaiah 28:16). He is the rock upon which the church is builded (Matt. 16:18)--not the small stone Peter, but the bedrock Christ. "For other foundation can no man lay than that is laid, which is Jesus Christ" (I Cor. 3:11). Jesus is "the shadow of a great rock in a weary land" (Isa. 32:2). God is mentioned as a rock a number of times in Deuteronomy, in I and II Samuel, and in the Psalms.

"Neither is there salvation in any other." Here is the clear summation of the matter. Jesus is the only way of salvation. Men are lost. They need "saving." By the name of Jesus men may be saved--not through the law of Moses, not as seed of Abraham, not as Pharisees or Sadducees, but only by personally taking Christ as Saviour.

The Gospel must always deal with men as lost ones who need to be saved. And always the Gospel holds up Jesus as the only way of salvation. Church membership, confirmation, baptism, rites and ceremonies have no part in the plan of salvation except to proclaim the Gospel.

Here is stated again what Jesus said in John 14:6--"I am the way, the truth, and the life: no man cometh unto the Father, but by me." It is the same as taught in I John 5:11 and 12: "And this is the record, that God hath given to us eternal life, and this life is in his Son. He that hath the Son hath life; and he that hath not the Son of God hath not life." Not by living a life, not by accepting a creed, not by partaking of holy rites, not by deeds or merit, but simply and only by personal faith in Christ can men be saved.

VERSES 13, 14:

13 ¶ Now when they saw the boldness of Peter and John, and perceived that they were unlearned and ignorant men, they

marvelled; and they took knowledge of them, that they had been
with Jesus.

14 And beholding the man

which was healed standing with
them, they could say nothing
against it.

Powerful Preaching by "Unlearned and Ignorant Men"

These cultivated leaders were astonished "when they saw the boldness of Peter and John." The boldness of New Testament preachers, often mentioned, had a great part in their blessed success.

1. Note the boldness of Peter here as in Acts 2, boldly condemning these Jewish leaders for the murder of Christ, announcing His resurrection and deity. See also the same boldness in Acts 3. See Acts 4:19, and His boldness in announcing the death of Ananias and Sapphira in Acts 5, his defiance of the Sanhedrin in Acts 5:29, and his zeal not quenched by the beating in Acts 5:40-42. The coward has been made bold as a lion.

2. Consider the boldness of Stephen, "full of faith and power," doing "great wonders and miracles" (Acts 6:8), and the irresistible "wisdom and the spirit by which he spake" (Acts 6:10). See him facing death boldly accusing the Jews in Acts 7:51-53, and his tenderness, boldness, and faith in dying!

3. Note the boldness of Paul in Acts 9:20-22, 27, 29; his boldness in Acts 13:9-11, 41, 46; Acts 14:3; Acts 19:8; I Thessalonians 2:2. Even Paul's imprisonment made others the more bold to preach the Gospel without fear (Phil. 1:14).

This holy boldness was brought by a definite enduement of power of the Holy Spirit. This is implied in the case of John the Baptist (Luke 1:15-17). And in every case the boldness followed definite anointing of the Spirit. Acts 4:31 says, "And they were all filled with the Holy Ghost, and they spake the word of God with boldness." This was true in the cases of Peter, Stephen, Paul and others.

4. Note that they earnestly prayed for this boldness (Acts 4:29). And Paul besought prayer that he might be bold (Eph. 6:19, 20).

A Christian in the will of God, doing God's work, has much reason to be bold.

1. One reason is a good conscience, for "the righteous are bold as a lion" (Prov. 28:1).

2. The comfort of the Holy Ghost and of answered prayer gives boldness (II Cor. 7:4-7).

3. Christ our High Priest, maintaining a throne of grace and mercy, invites "let us therefore come boldly unto the throne of grace, that we may obtain mercy, and find grace to help in time of need" (Heb. 4:16).

4. A Christian should be bold in assurance of salvation, completely done by the blood of Christ alone which gives us great assurance of faith: "Having therefore, brethren, boldness to enter into the holiest by the blood of Jesus" (Heb. 10:19).

5. God's love shed abroad in our heart, making us feel our unity and identity with Christ, giving us the witness of the Spirit, means that "herein is our love made perfect, that we may have boldness in the day of judgment: because as he is, so are we in this world" (I John 4:17).

Oh, the Spirit-filled Christian, depending wholly on the blood of Christ for salvation, in touch with the living Christ, having prayers answered, filled with the Spirit and to preach God's message ought to have great boldness as New Testament Christians did.

A great part of the boldness of Peter and John is that the living Christ manifested His power, answered their prayers, and here before them was the living proof of the power of God.

The evangelist who preaches the truth without power cannot be very bold. For "the letter killeth," even the letter of the blessed Word of God, if it be not carried by the Spirit's power to the hearts of people! Orthodoxy does not give boldness. The fullness of the Spirit, the daily life of an-swered prayer and the demonstration of God's power does give boldness.

Elijah could be bold when he could pray and God would shut up Heaven for three and a half years and tell Ahab "there shall not be dew nor rain these years, but according to my word" (I Kings 17:1). Elijah could be bold when he could pray down fire from Heaven and demonstrate to the waiting multitude that he served the true God and that all these things were done at his command! He could be bold when he could pray and the parched earth after three and a half barren, desolate years should gladly receive the flood-ing rain from Heaven (I Kings 18)!

Peter and John could look at the lame beggar and say, "Silver and gold have I none," but that did not matter as long as they could say, "but such as I have give I thee: In the name of Jesus Christ of Nazareth rise up and walk" (Acts 3:6). Peter could be bold when he was so near to God that at Peter's word Ananias and Sapphira should be struck dead.

Paul could be bold when Elymas the sorcerer could at a word be struck blind (Acts 13:8-12) or when in the midst of the mighty storm at sea, the angel of God had stood by him and made a glad promise of deliverance for every person on board the ship (Acts 27:21-25)! The holy boldness of New Testament Christians was the boldness which came from being filled with the Spirit and daily manifestation of God's presence and power and of answers to prayer.

VERSES 15–22:

15 But when they had com-manded them to go aside out of the council, they conferred among themselves,
16 Saying, What shall we do to these men? for that indeed a notable miracle hath been done by them is manifest to all them that dwell in Jerusalem; and we cannot deny it.

17 But that it spread no further among the people, let us straitly threaten them, that they speak henceforth to no man in this name.

18 And they called them, and commanded them not to speak at all nor teach in the name of Jesus.

19 But Peter and John answered and said unto them, Whether it be right in the sight of God to hearken unto you more than unto God, judge ye.

20 For we cannot but speak the things which we have seen and heard.

21 So when they had further threatened them, they let them go, finding nothing how they might punish them, because of the people: for all *men* glorified God for that which was done.

22 For the man was above forty years old, on whom this miracle of healing was shewed.

God's Use of Miracles to Authenticate the Gospel

Can you see the nonplused Jewish leaders? They must have secret consultation: Peter and John were made to stand aside and they said, "What shall we do to these men? for that indeed a notable miracle hath been done by them is manifest to all them that dwell in Jerusalem; and we cannot deny it." Thus we see illustrated a principle manifested many times in the Bible.

1. Peter reminded Jewish leaders that "Jesus of Nazareth, a man approved of God among you by miracles and wonders and signs, which God did by him in the midst of you, as ye yourselves also know" (Acts 2:22). God publicly approved the ministry of Jesus by miracles and wonders and signs. The miracles did not prove Christ's deity. That was to be proven by His resurrection (Rom. 1:4), the sign of the Prophet Jonas (Matt. 12:39, 40). God approved publicly other men who were not deity by the gift of miracles but the miracles did authenticate the words of Jesus.

So with the palsied man in Mark 2:1-12, Matthew 9:1-8, Luke 5:18-26, Jesus first said to the man let down through the roof, "Son, thy sins be forgiven thee." And noting the doubting and unbelief in the hearts of the people who scornfully said, "Who can forgive sins but God only?" (Mark 2:7),

Jesus said, "But that ye may know that the Son of man hath power on earth to forgive sins, (he saith to the sick of the palsy,) I say unto thee, Arise, and take up thy bed, and go thy way into thine house." The healing was not as important as the forgiveness. Salvation is always more important than physical healing. But the healing was an open public evidence that Christ had the power and the right to forgive sins.

Jesus has used the same argument more than once. In Matthew 12:22, Jesus cast out one possessed with the devil, blind and dumb. But to the unbelieving, blaspheming Pharisees who said, "This fellow doth not cast out devils, but by Beelzebub the prince of devils," He showed that Satan could not cast out Satan and said, "But if I cast out devils by the Spirit of God, then the kingdom of God is come unto you" (Matt. 12:28).

Certainly the miracles of Jesus were intended not only as an expression of His compassion for people who are sick and troubled and devil-possessed and bereaved, but also to authenticate His ministry as one come from God. And Nicodemus knew and expressed this when he said, "Rabbi, we know that thou art a teacher come from God: for no man can do these miracles that thou doest, except God be with him" (John 3:2).

2. Miracles at the hand of Moses were clearly to prove to Pharaoh and to the children of Israel that Moses was sent and empowered of God (Exod. 3:18-20; Exod. 4:1-9).

3. The miracle of the living almond branch authenticated God's choice of Aaron to be high priest (Num. 17:8).

4. When Gideon was called to deliver Israel he said, "Oh my Lord, if the Lord be with us, why then is all this befallen us? and where be all his miracles which our fathers told us of, saying, Did not the Lord bring us up from Egypt?" (Judg. 6:13). Then in answer to Gideon's request God gave him the signs of fire out of the rock (Judg. 6:21) and the miracle of the dew on the fleece only and dry on the

earth and then the opposite with the dry fleece on wet earth (vss. 37-40).

5. Elijah prayed for the fire from Heaven to consume the sacrifice, "Let it be known this day that thou art God in Israel, and that I am thy servant, and that I have done all these things at thy word" (I Kings 18:36). The miracle authenticated the message of Elijah. It is noteworthy that when Elijah challenged the people for halting between God and Baal there was no answer, no conviction. When he offered to prove God by a miracle, they assented and later were convinced.

I believe that such miracles as listed here were the exception, not the everyday events. Yet I want to leave that door open for anybody who may need divine intervention in some miraculous and marvelous way.

Usually the ministry of a man of God is attested by the life-changing power in his messages. Drunkards are made sober, harlots made pure, infidels made into believers, lives transformed. Regeneration is a supernatural manifestation as truly as a physical miracle. Yet connected with the ministry of great soul winners down through the centuries there has been many amazing manifestations that seem to be miraculous. A. J. Gordon in Ministry of Healing lists many. And W. B. Riley in his pamphlet on Healing tells of some of which he knew. In Getting Things From God, Dr. Blanchard mentions specific instances of which he knew. R. A. Torrey knew of a good many wonderfully healed, eyesight restored, etc. Charles G. Finney tells of a woman miraculously given the power to read in answer to prayer. I have known of several cases that as far as I am able to judge were miraculous interventions of God of the New Testament fashion. The one miracle we should constantly expect is the mighty power of the Spirit of God to convict and save and change men. But on occasion God gives faith for physical miracles for those who trust Him.

The literature of the China Inland Mission tells of many

demons cast out and other amazing answers to prayer that
seem miraculous. Every Christian's testimony ought to be
authenticated by the mighty power of God on his witness and
sometimes God gives faith to expect physical miracles and
gives the needed help as He did in New Testament times.

Commanded "Not to Speak at All Nor Teach in the Name of Jesus" (Vs. 18)

What authority had these Jewish leaders? Only a nominal
religious authority. It is true they were regarded as the
appointed leaders of the nation spiritually. Paul later publicly recognized that there was some authority in the high
priest, some respect due him as "the ruler of thy people"
(Acts 23:3-5). But the Roman Empire had the secular authority. They allowed the government on ordinary matters
of morals to be carried on by the priests and the Sanhedrin,
but they reserved to the Roman governor the rights of the
death penalty (John 18:31). Later Jewish leaders angrily
took Stephen and stoned him to death, so we know that the
Jewish leaders were allowed to exercise a good deal of authority. Pilate had said about Jesus, "Take ye him, and
judge him according to your law. The Jews therefore said
unto him, It is not lawful for us to put any man to death"
(John 18:31). And only the death of Jesus would satisfy
them.

"But Peter and John answered and said unto them,
Whether it be right in the sight of God to hearken unto you
more than unto God, judge ye. For we cannot but speak the
things which we have seen and heard" (vss. 19, 20). Later
when arrested again, "Then Peter and the other apostles
answered and said, We ought to obey God rather than men"
(Acts 5:29).

"The powers that be are ordained of God" (Rom. 13:1).
The authority of rulers is from God just as is the authority
of parents over children, the authority of master over
servant, the authority of a husband over his wife. However,

it is always true that the final authority is God. Only rarely will a human authority openly command us to go against the plain command of God. In such cases, of course, the command of God has precedence. However, children are never warned to obey God rather than their parents. Wives are never warned in the Bible to obey God rather than their husbands. And only rarely does a case occur in the Bible when it was necessary to disobey secular authority to obey God. In fact, the wife is plainly commanded to obey her unbelieving husband in order to win him (I Peter 3:1, 2).

Victory for the Common People

The Sanhedrin was afraid to further punish Peter and John "because of the people" who glorified God for the miracle that was done.

So Bible preachers preaching in the power of God ought to expect to so move the hearts of multitudes of common people that everywhere good people would see the blessing of his ministry. A Christian who is true to Christ may be persecuted as were the apostles, but they do not have to fail as far as reaching people for Christ is concerned. The Gospel was successful. We must remember that "the harvest truly is plenteous, but the labourers are few" (Matt. 9:37; Luke 10:2; John 4:35, 36). Bible preachers sometimes were persecuted, but when they preached in the power of God they reached many people. We have a right to expect souls saved, lives changed wherever we go, even though some will not hear.

VERSES 23-31:

23 ¶ And being let go, they went to their own company, and reported all that the chief priests and elders had said unto them.

24 And when they heard that, they lifted up their voice to God with one accord, and said, Lord, thou *art* God, which hast made

heaven, and earth, and the sea, and all that in them is;

25 Who by the mouth of thy servant David hast said, Why did the heathen rage, and the people imagine vain things?

26 The kings of the earth stood up, and the rulers were gathered together against the Lord, and against his Christ.

27 For of a truth against thy holy child Jesus, whom thou hast anointed, both Herod, and Pontius Pilate, with the Gentiles, and the people of Israel, were gathered together,

28 For to do whatsoever thy hand and thy counsel determined before to be done.

29 And now, Lord, behold their threatenings: and grant unto thy servants, that with all boldness they may speak thy word,

30 By stretching forth thine hand to heal; and that signs and wonders may be done by the name of thy holy child Jesus.

31 ¶ And when they had prayed, the place was shaken where they were assembled together; and they were all filled with the Holy Ghost, and they spake the word of God with boldness.

Christians Again Filled With the Spirit

Here again is a prayer meeting involving many of the same people in that immortal prayer meeting of Acts 1:14 before Pentecost. There they had prayed some ten days-- the apostles, Mary, the mother of Jesus, and the brothers of Jesus, a final total of about 120 people. The power of God came mightily at Pentecost and, filled with the Spirit, they began their witness and three thousand were saved.

Now they go again to prayer.

1. There is great unity of heart. Peter and John go to their own company, report the whole matter, the threatenings of the chief priest and Sanhedrin. But they still have the same aim they had before Pentecost--to preach the Gospel to every creature. They are to tarry till they be endued with power from on high (Luke 24:49; Acts 1:4, 5). So they want to preach and witness boldly in the power of the Holy Spirit. They want God to show His power and authenticate their message so their prayer is "with one accord." Surely someone must have been inspired to pray aloud and the

hearts of the people were all united by the Holy Spirit to say Amen to the same prayer.

2. They remember the sufferings, the persecution and death of the Lord Jesus. It is prophesied in the second Psalm, "Why do the heathen rage, and the people imagine a vain thing?" That was fulfilled in the way Herod and Pontius Pilate and the soldiers and the mob came together demanding the death of Jesus! Yet they know that this was ordained and planned and they do not resent it. Jesus died and rose again. They ought to be willing to die with Him if necessary.

3. Note their request. "Lord, behold their threatenings: and grant unto thy servants, that with all boldness they may speak thy word" (vs. 29). Oh, let not our hearts be frightened! Let us not trim our message! Let us not set out to please wicked men. "The fear of man bringeth a snare" (Prov. 29:25). So they plead for boldness to keep on speaking the word though they have been forbidden to speak in Jesus' name at all.

4. And they asked that God would authenticate their message and give them reason for boldness "by stretching forth thine hand to heal; and that signs and wonders may be done by the name of thy holy child Jesus." They are a little bunch of Christians, a lonely island in the midst of a sea of a wrathful, wicked race of men. Oh, for boldness and for God's intervention to prove that Christ is the Saviour, the Lord and Christ! So they prayed. And so they were wonderfully filled with the Holy Spirit.

Filled With the Holy Spirit a Second Time Exactly as Before at Pentecost

Verse 31 here is a mountain peak of Scripture like Acts 2:4. In Acts 2:4, "And they were all filled with the Holy Ghost," and so they began their witnessing in the power of the Holy Spirit to win souls. In Acts 4:31 the same group of

Christians again prayed, "...and they were all filled with the Holy Ghost."

In the King James version the same identical nine words tell what happened at Pentecost in Acts 2:4 and what happened in Acts 4:31. Notice the similarity.

1. Before Pentecost "these all continued with one accord in prayer and supplication..." (Acts 1:14). Here "when they had prayed" they had the same anointing of the Spirit again!

2. In both cases the purpose was the same: they wanted power to witness boldly for Christ. That is another way of saying they prayed for the fullness of the Spirit and it was given them. In both cases they could have claimed and perhaps did claim the promise of Jesus in Luke 11:13, "...How much more shall your heavenly Father give the Holy Spirit to them that ask him?" In both cases they doubtless considered the plain command, "But tarry ye in the city of Jerusalem, until ye be endued with power from on high" (Luke 24:49), and "But ye shall receive power, after that the Holy Ghost is come upon you: and ye shall be witnesses unto me..." (Acts 1:8).

3. The Spirit-filled witnessing at Pentecost resulted in three thousand people saved and added to them (Acts 2:41). In this case the same train of blessing came. "They spake the word of God with boldness...And with great power gave the apostles witness of the resurrection of the Lord Jesus: and great grace was upon them all" (vss. 31, 33). And in the next chapter, "And by the hands of the apostles were many signs and wonders wrought among the people..." (Acts 5:12). "And believers were the more added to the Lord, multitudes both of men and women" (Acts 5:14).

4. There were incidental miracles in each case: a sound of a rushing, mighty wind and tongues like as of fire at Pentecost. Here "the place was shaken where they were assembled together," an earthquake. Perhaps this was given to encourage their hearts that God was with them in

power. It was not promised ahead of time. Disciples never asked for it specifically, though they did ask that "signs and wonders may be done by the name of thy holy child Jesus." We do not know that it was ever repeated, just as we do not know that the tongues like as of fire and the sound of a rushing, mighty wind and the other languages of Pentecost were ever repeated.

They prayed, the Holy Spirit came upon them in great power, "they were all filled with the Holy Ghost," there were wonderful evidences of God's power and multitudes were saved in both cases.

Here is a principle, then, clearly taught. Christians can pray and be filled with the Holy Spirit whenever they need God's power for witnessing. What happened at Pentecost was simply a sample occasion and the same people were filled in the same manner again and witnessed in the same power again. In fact, it is mentioned that Peter was also filled with the Holy Spirit in Acts 4:8. It is fair to infer that the fullness of the Spirit or the gift of the Spirit or the baptism of the Spirit (do not shrink from that term: it is in the Bible and it refers to what happened at Pentecost) is given to people who seek God's power for witnessing and soul winning.

There is a favorite saying with some, "One baptism, but many fillings." But the Bible says nothing like that. The term baptism is a figure of speech used occasionally for the enduement of power which is more often referred and regularly referred to as "filled with the Spirit." It is true that baptism is used as a figure of speech in another matter when the Holy Spirit takes a new convert and makes him a part of the body of Christ, burying him into and making him a part of that spiritual building God is preparing. But that is a figure of speech which has no reference to Pentecost, as you see from I Corinthians 12:13.

It is important to remember that what the disciples sought at Pentecost was power to witness for Christ, and

that is what they got. The great central fact of Pentecost
was that God gave power to win three thousand souls in a
day. The central fact in Acts 4:31 is that when they had
prayed and the Holy Spirit came and filled them, "they
spake the word of God with boldness" and "believers were
the more added to the Lord, multitudes both of men and
women." We are not told how the disciples felt, because
that did not matter. They did not ask for any "experience."
They wanted boldness to witness and they wanted God's
power and God's results.

VERSES 32–37:

32 And the multitude of them that believed were of one heart and of one soul: neither said any *of them* that aught of the things which he possessed was his own; but they had all things common.

33 And with great power gave the apostles witness of the resurrection of the Lord Jesus: and great grace was upon them all.

34 Neither was there any among them that lacked: for as many as were possessors of lands or houses sold them, and brought the prices of the things that were sold,

35 And laid *them* down at the apostles' feet: and distribution was made unto every man according as he had need.

36 And Joses, who by the apostles was surnamed Barnabas, (which is, being interpreted, The son of consolation,) a Levite, *and* of the country of Cyprus,

37 Having land, sold *it*, and brought the money, and laid *it* at the apostles' feet.

Unselfish Sharing of the Multitude of Christians

It is evident that there was a great economic upset among
the converts at Jerusalem.

1. Consider first that the leaders themselves were poor
fishermen from the despised province of Galilee. They
would not attract many men of great wealth. Joseph of
Arimathaea, a rich man, was a disciple (Matt. 27:57; John

19:38), but he was a timid man, not an outspoken disciple, and we do not hear of him through the entire book of Acts.

2. Then it is usual that when the Gospel first reaches an area, it is the "poor, and the maimed, and the halt, and the blind" who come willingly when the well-to-do refuse (Luke 14:21). One of the signs given John the Baptist that Jesus was the anointed one foretold in Isaiah 61:1 is that "the poor have the gospel preached to them" (Matt. 11:5; Luke 7:22). So the mass of converts at Jerusalem, especially at first, would be the poor people.

3. A little later in Acts 11:27-30 an empire-wide dearth was prophesied by Agabus. Then the disciples at Antioch "every man according to his ability, determined to send relief unto the brethren which dwelt in Judaea: Which also they did, and sent it to the elders by the hands of Barnabas and Saul." But the need among the saints at Jerusalem seems already to have been obvious. And it seems to have continued for years as it is mentioned and Paul took offerings in all the churches of Galatia and elsewhere "for the saints" in I Corinthians 16:1, in II Corinthians 8:4, 14, in II Corinthians 9:1 and following.

Doubtless the persecution that arose at Jerusalem brought severe hardship on Christians. Those who would arrest Peter and John, threaten them with death, jail them and beat them would not hesitate to have young Christians fired from their jobs, Christian renters put out of their homes. Also it may well be that many of the thousands who crowded into Jerusalem for the passover time and were saved at Pentecost and following were poor people who decided to stay in Jerusalem and added to the financial insecurity of the multitude.

However, these Christians counted what they possessed as not their own: it belonged to Christ and so they shared with all.

Note again that the sharing of their possessions was each one as he purposed in his own heart, voluntarily. There was no command of God nor of men against owning property. People only gave their property as it was needed, and some certainly did not do so. Barnabas was counted "the son of consolation" because he sold land and brought the money "laid it at the apostles' feet."

Earth-shaking events were taking place. Their own salvation and the salvation of thousands of others were matters of so great importance that they rejoiced being poor, shared what they had, and continued "of one heart and one soul" (vs. 32).

ACTS 5
VERSES 1–11:

BUT a certain man named Ananias, with Sapphira his wife, sold a possession,

2 And kept back *part* of the price, his wife also being privy *to it*, and brought a certain part, and laid *it* at the apostles' feet.

3 But Peter said, Ananias, why hath Satan filled thine heart to lie to the Holy Ghost, and to keep back *part* of the price of the land?

4 While it remained, was it not thine own? and after it was sold, was it not in thine own power? why hast thou conceived this thing in thine heart? thou hast not lied unto men, but unto God.

5 And Ananias hearing these words fell down, and gave up the ghost: and great fear came on all them that heard these things.

6 And the young men arose, wound him up, and carried *him* out, and buried *him*.

7 And it was about the space of three hours after, when his wife, not knowing what was done, came in.

8 And Peter answered unto her, Tell me whether ye sold the land for so much? And she said, Yea, for so much.

9 Then Peter said unto her, How is it that ye have agreed together to tempt the Spirit of the Lord? behold, the feet of them which have buried thy husband *are* at the door, and shall carry thee out.

10 Then fell she down straightway at his feet, and yielded up the ghost: and the young men came in, and found her dead, and, carrying *her* forth, buried *her* by her husband.

11 And great fear came upon all the church, and upon as many as heard these things.

The Sin and Death of Ananias and Sapphira: The Fake Liberality

Ananias and Sapphira sold their possession. It was their own idea, not commanded, not required. But evidently the honor that had come to Barnabas (preceding verses) and to other good men made them seek the approval of the apostles and popularity among Christians. But they agreed to give a certain part and keep part back for their own use while pretending to give it all. Their sin was not in withholding part of the money. "Whiles it remained, was it not thine own? and after it was sold, was it not in thine own power?" (vs. 4). The sin was in deception and a false claim to generosity. They lied to men, but more, they lied to God! Their sin had no special reference to the money, but to their deceit.

Let us be careful how we make claim to sacrifice. That widow who cast her two mites into the treasury, all her living, "gave more than they all" because she gave everything (Mark 12:42, 43). And many a Christian may give large gifts without ever missing a suit of clothes or a steak dinner or a new car or luxurious furnishings or a vacation. Let us not claim to give all when we hold back part of the price.

It was a conspiracy "to tempt the Spirit of the Lord," said Peter.

"A Sin Unto Death"

We suppose that Ananias and Sapphira were converted, saved people.

In I John 5:16 we are told, "If any man see his brother sin a sin which is not unto death, he shall ask, and he shall give him life for them that sin not unto death. There is a sin unto death: I do not say that he shall pray for it." Note that it is a sin of a "brother," a Christian, a sin unto death. That does not mean a spiritual death but death of the body. Sometimes Christians, because of sin, die prematurely. That was true of many at Corinth. "For this cause many are weak and sickly among you, and many sleep" (I Cor. 11:30). Divisions, strife, worldliness, approaching the Lord's Supper with sin, brought sickness to many and to many it brought "sleep." But sleep is never used as a term for the death of the unsaved, only for the saved. Christians sometimes sin and die for their sins. So, I think, did Ananias and Sapphira.

The man of God who went to warn King Jeroboam of his sin and to prophesy of King Josiah's destruction of the altar, that prophet himself was commanded to go home and not eat nor drink in that place. But a prophet of Bethel deceived him; he went home with a man and ate, and a lion killed him, as we learn in I Kings, chapter 13.

I believe that where God's prophets preach clearly against sin and the power of God is manifested, God will back up their preaching with power and bring judgment on sin, even to killing Christians and taking them home to Heaven prematurely in some cases. I have known of numerous cases of Christians who were rebellious and disobedient and who caused trouble in the churches, dying suddenly, evidently at the hand of God, dying prematurely because of sin.

Such occasions happen rarely now because seldom are there Spirit-filled preachers who set a clear standard and Spirit-filled Christians who live by these standards so that God can afford to act for His people in such immediate public judgment on sin. But, thank God, I have known and other evangelists greatly used of God have known of a number of such cases.

VERSES 12–16:

12 ¶ And by the hands of the apostles were many signs and wonders wrought among the people; (and they were all with one accord in Solomon's porch.

13 And of the rest durst no man join himself to them: but the people magnified them.

14 And believers were the more added to the Lord, multitudes both of men and women;)

15 Insomuch that they brought forth the sick into the streets, and laid *them* on beds and couches, that at the least the shadow of Peter passing by might overshadow some of them.

16 There came also a multitude *out* of the cities round about unto Jerusalem, bringing sick folks, and them which were vexed with unclean spirits: and they were healed every one.

Mighty Power Among These Spirit-Filled Christians

Note that the prayer of Acts 4:30 is being answered. God is stretching forth His hand to heal "and that signs and wonders may be done by the name of thy holy child Jesus."

Note the wonderful unity. "They were all with one accord in Solomon's porch." That is, they were in the area outside the temple proper, the colonnade called Solomon's porch. They gathered in this, something like a plaza or market place, for preaching, testimony and fellowship.

The miracles included healing of the sick (vs. 15). The people were laid in the pathway "that at least the shadow of Peter passing by might overshadow some of them." Doubtless the power was not in the shadow, but in the Holy Spirit who so surrounded and overwhelmed Peter that the power of God went with his presence everywhere. The healing of "every one" reminds us of a few occasions in the ministry of Jesus. There ought to be a few such occasions in the book of Acts, since these apostles and Spirit-filled Christians are doing the same kind of work and having the same kind of results that Jesus had, according to His promise in John 14:12 and the commission in John 17:18 and John 20:21, 22.

The multitudes of believers added to them in verse 14 is a blessed result of the fullness of the Spirit and the witness of Acts 4:31.

The great respect of the general public "and of the rest durst no man join himself to them..." was brought about partly by the report of the death of Ananias and Sapphira. The God of these people judges sin!

VERSES 17–28:

17 ¶ Then the high priest rose up, and all they that were with him, (which is the sect of the Sadducees,) and were filled with

indignation,

18 And laid their hands on the apostles, and put them in the common prison.

19 But the angel of the Lord by night opened the prison doors, and brought them forth, and said,

20 Go, stand and speak in the temple to the people all the words of this life.

21 And when they heard *that*, they entered into the temple early in the morning, and taught. But the high priest came, and they that were with him, and called the council together, and all the senate of the children of Israel, and sent to the prison to have them brought.

22 But when the officers came, and found them not in the prison, they returned, and told,

23 Saying, The prison truly found we shut with all safety, and the keepers standing without before the doors: but when we had opened, we found no man within.

24 Now when the high priest and the captain of the temple and the chief priests heard these things, they doubted of them whereunto this would grow.

25 Then came one and told them, saying, Behold, the men whom ye put in prison are standing in the temple, and teaching the people.

26 Then went the captain with the officers, and brought them without violence: for they feared the people, lest they should have been stoned.

27 And when they had brought them, they set *them* before the council: and the high priest asked them,

28 Saying, Did not we straitly command you that ye should not teach in this name? and, behold, ye have filled Jerusalem with your doctrine, and intend to bring this man's blood upon us.

Note that the high priest and those of the rulers who were Sadducees, denying the resurrection and miracles, "were filled with indignation" because multitudes were saved and increasingly miracles and wonders were done by the hands of the apostles. So violent persecution began again.

The Apostles "in the Common Prison"

Now this is beginning to look like the kind of Christianity Jesus had described to His disciples! It seems they were surprised. They should not have been because Jesus in Luke 6:21-23 said:

> "Blessed are ye that hunger now: for ye shall be filled. Blessed are ye that weep now: for ye shall laugh. Blessed are ye, when men shall hate you, and when they shall separate you from their company, and shall reproach you, and cast out your name as evil, for the Son of man's sake. Rejoice ye in that day, and leap for joy: for, behold, your reward is great in heaven: for in the like manner did their fathers unto the prophets."

According to this definition by the Lord Jesus, the Bible kind of Christians should hunger now, should weep now, should be hated and shunned now and have their name cast out as evil for Jesus' sake. That is the way godly prophets have always suffered!

Consider the beatitudes as given in Matthew 5:3-12. The first seven of the beatitudes take nine words in one, ten words in each of two, eleven words in one, thirteen words in two each, and fifteen words in one. But the final and crowning beatitude, "Blessed are they which are persecuted" takes sixty-two words! This is an emphasis by the Lord Jesus which we dare not ignore! Persecution is not only inevitable for Spirit-filled, soul-winning, bold, triumphant Christians, but it is the crowning blessing!

So now the apostles are in jail. From verse 18 we think all of them were. In verse 29 it is "Peter and the other apostles" who answered.

Well, Jesus had warned them in Matthew 10:21, 22:

> "And the brother shall deliver up the brother to death, and the father the child: and the children shall rise up against their parents, And ye shall be hated of all men for my name's sake: but he that endureth to the end shall be saved."

Again He told them in Matthew 10:23-25:

"But when they persecute you in this city, flee
ye into another: for verily I say unto you, Ye
shall not have gone over the cities of Israel, till
the Son of man be come. The disciple is not
above his master, nor the servant above his
lord. It is enough for the disciple that he be as
his master, and the servant as his lord. If they
have called the master of the house Beelzebub,
how much more shall they call them of his
household?"

They are to be faithful, they are to preach what they are
commanded to preach, "And fear not them which kill the
body, but are not able to kill the soul: but rather fear him
which is able to destroy both soul and body in hell" (Matt.
10:28).

In that passage the twelve apostles were sent forth to
cover the cities of Israel where Jesus Himself would come
(vs. 23). And to the careful student of prophecy, there
seems to be a foretaste here of the prophecy in the Olivet
discourse in Matthew 24 of the persecution during the tribulation time. But honest students must believe that it was
certainly intended for those particular disciples, and that in
some sense it is a foretaste of what New Testament Christians, filled with the Spirit, bold in their witness, pressing
at any cost for holy decisions, are to suffer during the
whole age. Paul the apostle was inspired to say:

"But we have this treasure in earthen vessels,
that the excellency of the power may be of God,
and not of us. We are troubled on every side,
yet not distressed; we are perplexed, but not in
despair; Persecuted, but not forsaken; cast
down, but not destroyed; Always bearing about in
the body the dying of the Lord Jesus, that the life
also of Jesus might be made manifest in our
body. For we which live are alway delivered

unto death for Jesus' sake, that the life also of
Jesus might be made manifest in our mortal
flesh."--II Cor. 4:7-11.

Certainly this is a clear picture of Christian life and
aggressive evangelism in a wicked world that hates Jesus
Christ.

And two chapters later in II Corinthians 6:4-6 Paul
writes:

"But in all things approving ourselves as the
ministers of God, in much patience, in afflictions, in necessities, in distresses, In stripes,
in imprisonments, in tumults, in labours, in
watchings, in fastings; By pureness, by knowledge, by longsuffering, by kindness, by the Holy
Ghost, by love unfeigned."

How are we to approve ourselves as the ministers of
God? Good ministers are to be manifested in patience, in
afflictions, in necessities (or poverty), in distresses, in
stripes, in imprisonments, in tumults (or riots), as well as
in labors, in sleepless nights, in days without food!

And in verses 8 to 10 Paul describes himself just as he
describes these apostles and Christians at Jerusalem about
whom we are now studying:

"By honour and dishonour, by evil report and
good report: as deceivers, and yet true; As unknown, and yet well known; as dying, and, behold, we live; as chastened, and not killed; As
sorrowful, yet alway rejoicing; as poor, yet
making many rich; as having nothing, and yet
possessing all things."

The apostles were wonderfully delivered by the angel of
God, and went back to preach in the courts of the temple,

but they will be cruelly beaten and this matter of imprisonment and death is to be the haunting probability for everyone of them as they go about serving God in the future. Like Paul they could say, "I die daily" (I Cor. 15:31).

Oh, it is wicked to suppose that God no more wants His people to be persecuted and suffer to His glory. Down through the ages it has been true that "all that will live godly in Christ Jesus shall suffer persecution" (II Tim. 3:12).

> Faith of our fathers! living still
> In spite of dungeon, fire, and sword:
> O how our hearts beat high with joy
> Whene'er we hear that glorious word!
>
> Our fathers, chained in prisons dark,
> Were still in heart and conscience free:
> How sweet would be their children's fate,
> If they, like them, could die for thee!

Miraculous Deliverance by an Angel

Verse 19 tells us, "But the angel of the Lord by night opened the prison doors, and brought them forth...." The apostles were commanded, "Go, stand and speak in the temple to the people all the words of this life."

It is a marvelous truth that no human government nor power can keep behind bars God's man if God wants him to be free. Only as God permits it (and He often does) can God's prophets be jailed or beaten. But the main thing with God is that sinners be reached with the Gospel. And these apostles feel the same way. So the angel brings them out of prison in a miraculous deliverance.

They are not done with persecution. These apostles will be severely beaten before the day is over (vs. 40). In chapter 8 there will be a great persecution so that all the aggressive Christians will be scattered abroad "except the apostles" (Acts 8:1). In Acts, chapter 12, the Apostle

James will be killed by Herod, and Peter will be imprisoned (Acts 12:2, 3). And again an angel would deliver Peter out of prison, but we have every reason to believe that the persecution and imprisonment followed Peter all of his life and it may well be that he died a martyr's death, although the Roman tradition about his death at Rome is certainly unreliable. There is no evidence that Peter was ever at Rome.

Peter was inspired to write:

> "Beloved, think it not strange concerning the fiery trial which is to try you, as though some strange thing happened unto you: But rejoice, inasmuch as ye are partakers of Christ's sufferings; that, when his glory shall be revealed, ye may be glad also with exceeding joy. If ye be reproached for the name of Christ, happy are ye; for the spirit of glory and of God resteth upon you: on their part he is evil spoken of, but on your part he is glorified."--I Pet. 4:12-14.

But, thank God, always there are angels about the Christian. "The angel of the Lord encampeth round about them that fear him, and delivereth them" (Ps. 34:7). God allows us to enter into the sufferings of Christ and the reproach of Christ. That is not bad but good. Fiery trials are normal for New Testament Christianity. It is only a decadent Christianity, with a lost evangelistic zeal, too much concern with the properties and pleasures and popularities of this world, which does not find the great joy of suffering for Jesus and bearing His reproach. And always there is the sweet assurance that God's angel will never let us suffer more than we ought to suffer and God's cause will never suffer for lack of God's power and God's intervention for His own.

We should remember that angelic deliverances, like the fiery persecutions, come only to Spirit-filled Christians who are willing to leave all for Jesus and enter into His crucifixion. Whenever God's people go back to this kind of witnessing with boldness and power and love and tears, day and night soul winning, boldly pressing the sin of Christ-rejection, demanding repentance and new hearts, then Satan's power will be shown and God's power will be greater than Satan's.

"Ye Have Filled Jerusalem With Your Doctrine" (Vs. 28)

That is an amazing statement. These unlearned, ignorant men have pressed the matter of salvation on everybody in Jerusalem, the center of Palestine, and that while the city has been flooded with visitors from all over the nation and beyond. Note these elements in their witnessing.

1. They had set out literally to obey the Saviour's command in the Great Commission to "preach the gospel to every creature." They did not build a nice church building and confine their religious activities to that building. As far as we can tell, they were telling literally everybody that Jesus Christ is risen from the dead, that men should repent, that there is no other name under Heaven by which people may be saved.

2. They were evidently taking every occasion. The healing of the lame man at the temple was not only the result of compassion for a poor cripple: it was that, but it was an occasion for preaching the Gospel to those who crowded around as the healed man held on to Peter and John and praised the Lord and walked and leaped in exuberant joy! I think they knocked at every door, they buttonholed every passer-by, they stopped to witness to every little group. They took seriously the command of Jesus.

3. They set out to carry out their orders without regard to the cost. They had no thought for financial security or safety from bodily harm. Slander, abuse, jail, beatings could not stop them. They were so obsessed with soul-winning witnessing that it is no wonder some people had to sell their land and property to feed them, and Paul and others

must send the offerings to the saints at Jerusalem! Oh, for a Christianity that forgets the incidentals for the main business of getting out the Gospel!

4. Note that there was a supernatural enablement that brought results. People listened because they must listen. There was divine, miraculous intervention often enough to astonish the multitudes. There was a boldness and power in the witnessing of these unlearned men, the power of the Holy Spirit. One cannot understand New Testament Christianity until he faces this fact: the preaching and witnessing was in supernatural power and the results were not human but divine. The equipment of New Testament Christians was not seminary degrees, not stately buildings and beautiful services; rather, they were "endued with power from on high" (Luke 24:49).

5. And always their pressure was upon this point: the wickedness of rejecting Christ and the awful sinfulness of the human heart which could be cleansed only by coming to Christ personally and trusting in His blood. The high priest complained that the apostles "intend to bring this man's blood upon us!" I am sure his guilty conscience, stirred by the Holy Spirit, specially resented the pressure on the wickedness of rejecting Christ. The high priest was not ready to repent, so there was a wicked rebellion in his heart against the Gospel and against these who preached it. So it ought to be today. The Gospel ought to get two results: repentance from those who will repent and violent rejection by some others who refuse to repent. It is a sin to witness so calmly or so weakly that no one is changed and no one is angered.

VERSES 29–33:

29 ¶ Then Peter and the *other* apostles answered and said, We ought to obey God rather than men.

30 The God of our fathers raised up Jesus, whom ye slew and

hanged on a tree.
31 Him hath God exalted with his right hand *to be* a Prince and a Saviour, for to give repentance to Israel, and forgiveness of sins.
32 And we are his witnesses of these things; and *so is* also the Holy Ghost, whom God hath given to them that obey him.
33 ¶ When they heard *that*, they were cut *to the heart*, and took counsel to slay them.

Another Opportunity to Witness!

As the crowd which rushed together at Pentecost, drawn by the sound of a cyclonic wind and visible tongues like as of fire and the powerful witness, was an occasion for Peter to preach, and his arrest before the Sanhedrin before had been such an occasion, now all the apostles before the Sanhedrin have a chance to witness again.

1. They plainly state, "We ought to obey God rather than men." They do not intend to quit witnessing. They make no effort to appease the anger of wicked men.

2. Jesus has been raised from the dead! He lives! These men in the council must still give account to Him, the Lord and Christ!

3. And again, "Whom ye slew and hanged on a tree." They cannot get away from these stern prophets who press upon them their guilt.

4. But God has exalted Christ Jesus "to be a Prince and a Saviour." He is to give repentance to Israel, forgiveness of sins. Salvation is offered.

5. This repentance is offered to these men not only as individuals, but as representatives of Israel. The nation ought to receive her Messiah, ought to receive her Prince who is to sit one day on David's throne. There should have been national repentance and turning to God. And the inference is that then, all the sooner the nation Israel would have been restored to Palestine, that "times of restitution of all things, which God hath spoken by the mouth of all his holy prophets..." (Acts 3:21).

6. These apostles standing up plainly say, "We are his witnesses of these things." They had been with Jesus all the

way from His baptism on to the crucifixion. They had seen
Him forty days after His resurrection, handled Him, eaten
with Him, talked with Him. They had seen Him ascend to
Heaven. The resurrection of Jesus they must face as a fact,
attested by unanswerable proof.

7. And the marvelous secret of their power was the Holy
Ghost of God "whom God hath given to them that obey him."
Oh, here is the secret! They were so obsessed with the
command of Christ to win souls, to witness for Him, that
they dare not lose the anointing, the power "whom God hath
given to them that obey him."

8. Note the result of this witnessing to these rulers:
"They were cut to the heart, and took counsel to slay
them." Preaching ought to get the salvation of hearers or
it ought to be so fervent, so earnest, that a man cannot
calmly reject it.

It is noteworthy that when Jesus went back to Nazareth
filled with the Holy Spirit and preached in the synagogue in
Luke 4 and there for the first time spoke to them filled with
the Holy Spirit in that village where He had lived so many
years as the respected and model young man, then they
soon took Him to the brow of a hill to cast Him down and
kill Him! Spirit-filled witnessing should bring either salvation or such conviction as people are cut to the heart. Now
they want to kill these apostles!

VERSES 34–39:

34 Then stood there up one in
the council, a Pharisee, named
Gamaliel, a doctor of the law,
had in reputation among all the
people, and commanded to put
the apostles forth a little space;

35 And said unto them, Ye men
of Israel, take heed to yourselves
what ye intend to do as touching
these men.

36 For before these days rose
up Theudas, boasting himself to
be somebody; to whom a number of men, about four hundred,
joined themselves: who was
slain; and all, as many as obeyed him, were scattered, and
brought to nought.

37 After this man rose up Judas of Galilee in the days of the taxing, and drew away much people after him: he also perished; and all, *even* as many as obeyed him, were dispersed.

38 And now I say unto you, Refrain from these men, and let them alone: for if this counsel or this work be of men, it will come to nought:

39 But if it be of God, ye cannot overthrow it; lest haply ye be found even to fight against God.

God Uses Gamaliel's Unwise Counsel

The plan of the high priest and his friends is to kill these apostles. But God intervenes, as He often does, even by using some unsaved man. Gamaliel was a greatly respected doctor of the law, that is, a teacher of the Pentateuch. This man was the teacher of Saul of Tarsus who became Paul the apostle, and it was a matter of prestige with Paul that Gamaliel was his teacher (Acts 22:3).

Gamaliel, doubtless was used of God to prevent the killing of the apostles. As God "makes the wrath of man to praise him" (Ps. 76:10), so He also makes the illogical arguments of men to serve Him when He wishes.

Gamaliel made the mistake of trying to deduce a principle from two illustrations. Theudas, the false prophet, raised about four hundred men, but he was slain and his workers were scattered. Then Judas of Galilee also led away many people, but he perished and his followers were dispersed. Therefore, reasons Gamaliel, if the religion of Jesus Christ is not of God, it will perish also. So they should not kill the apostles, but leave it to God. If He is no: with the apostles, He will bring the movement to nought.

I am glad that the apostles' lives were spared and God used Gamaliel's weak argument to do it. But remember it is the argument of an unsaved man, and it was not a good argument for Christians to use.

Gamaliel declared, "Refrain from these men, and let them alone: for if this counsel or this work be of men, it will come to nought."

The principle declared here is a false principle. An evil work will not always come to nought left to itself. Communism did not come to nought. Mohammedanism did not come to nought. Romanism, Jehovah's Witnesses, Christian Science and other heresies have not come to nought by being left alone. Modernism does not come to nought by being left alone. So a Christian ought not to follow the advice of Gamaliel about dealing with false cults and false doctrine and sin.

Gamaliel, an unsaved man, gave poor advice as far as these Jews were concerned, but God used it to save His apostles. However, let no one suppose that God endorses the principle stated that we should leave false doctrine and false religion alone, that we should not contend for the faith, that we should not try to put down evil. The contrary is plainly taught in the Scriptures. "Them that sin rebuke before all, that others also may fear" (I Tim. 5:20).

The command of Jude 3 and 4 is very clear:

> "Beloved, when I gave all diligence to write unto you of the common salvation, it was needful for me to write unto you, and exhort you that ye should earnestly contend for the faith which was once delivered unto the saints. For there are certain men crept in unawares, who were before of old ordained to this condemnation, ungodly men, turning the grace of our God into lasciviousness, and denying the only Lord God, and our Lord Jesus Christ."

We should "earnestly contend for the faith." We should resist the men who bring in false doctrine "denying the only Lord God, and our Lord Jesus Christ." And Paul was inspired to command Titus: "For there are many unruly and vain talkers and deceivers, specially they of the circumcision: Whose mouths must be stopped, who subvert whole houses, teaching things which they ought not, for filthy lucre's sake" (Titus 1:10, 11). And Paul commands, "Wherefore rebuke them sharply, that they may be sound in the faith" (vs. 13). God used Gamaliel's poor advice to save His apostles, but it is not good advice for us as to our method of dealing with false cults and false doctrines.

Gamaliel continued in his advice, "But if it be of God, ye cannot overthrow it...." It is true that they could not overthrow the Christian religion, but it is not true that they could not do harm to the cause. The business of getting out the Gospel to all the world is not an automatic process which God Himself runs without reference to men. God uses men to preach the Gospel. If men fail God, the Gospel fails. If men do not have a revival, do not win souls, do not build spiritual churches in any local area, the fault is not God's. It is never correct to say, "It seemed not God's will at this time to give revival." The failure is on the part of men, not on the part of God.

The principle of II Chronicles 7:14 is that "if my people, which are called by my name, shall humble themselves, and pray, and seek my face, and turn from their wicked ways; then will I hear from heaven, and will forgive their sin, and will heal their land." God depends upon His people. The success of God's Gospel depends largely on God's people. At Nazareth the unbelief of the people made it so that Jesus "could there do no mighty work, save that he laid his hands upon a few sick folk, and healed them. And he marvelled because of their unbelief..." (Mark 6:5, 6). God has power to get His work done, but in getting out the Gospel He chooses to do it through surrendered, willing, obedient vessels.

VERSES 40–42:

40 And to him they agreed and when they had called the apostles, and beaten *them*, they commanded that they should not speak in the name of Jesus, and let them go.

41 ¶ And they departed from the presence of the council, rejoicing that they were counted worthy to suffer shame for his name.

42 And daily in the temple, and in every house, they ceased not to teach and preach Jesus Christ.

The Apostles Beaten, Rejoice!

Gamaliel's counsel prevailed: they will not kill the apostles. But the rulers still hate these apostles. They are still cut to the heart with conviction, so they call the apostles forth and beat them and command "that they should not speak in the name of Jesus, and let them go."

> Must Jesus bear the cross alone,
> And all the world go free?
> No; there's a cross for every one,
> And there's a cross for me.

Jesus was manhandled, abused, scourged, crucified. Should not a Christian sometimes suffer physical pain for Him?

Paul, boasting of his faithful ministry, is inspired to write: "Are they ministers of Christ? (I speak as a fool) I am more; in labours more abundant, in stripes above measure, in prisons more frequent, in deaths oft. Of the Jews five times received I forty stripes save one. Thrice was I beaten with rods, once was I stoned, thrice I suffered shipwreck, a night and a day I have been in the deep" (II Cor. 11:23-25). In these three verses he mentions "in stripes above measure," "five times received I forty stripes save one," and "thrice was I beaten with rods." And these were all in addition to the stoning, the shipwreck, the perils, weariness, sleeplessness, hunger and thirst and nakedness. So these apostles were not depressed and were not ashamed. Rather "they departed from the presence of the council, rejoicing that they were counted worthy to suffer shame for his name." They took literally the command of Jesus to "rejoice ye in that day, and leap for joy: for, behold, your reward is great in heaven" (Luke 6:23). Ah yes, they will have great reward in Heaven, but even better than that, the cause of Christ is prospered by the testimony of good men who do not shun the beatings and disgrace and imprisonment in order to get out the Gospel! They are not ashamed of Jesus! To suffer shame for His name is joy! Oh, that we might learn it.

A Key Verse of New Testament Christianity

In Acts 5:42 we have one of the most revealing verses about New Testament Christians. "And daily in the temple, and in every house, they ceased not to teach and preach Jesus Christ."

They had almost none of the equipment, conveniences and attractions of today. They had not a single church house: not a church building is mentioned in the New Testament. They had no organs or pianos, no hymn books, not even a printed Bible. They had no auditorium for the crowds. They must meet in homes, in a borrowed synagogue for a bit until they get kicked out, or they may meet in a public plaza or porch of the temple. Or they may meet by the seaside or in a vacant loft. But meeting places are incidental. Every home in town is a church house where the Gospel is preached! Every day is the Lord's day. Every conversation is a religious conversation! Here they are taking seriously the command to get the Gospel to every creature.

So it was in Acts 2:47 when "the Lord added to the church daily such as should be saved." So it will be later when persecution scatters these Christians abroad. "Therefore they that were scattered abroad went every where preaching the word" (Acts 8:4). Here was Paul's method, the method by which he went around the Mediterranean and Asia Minor, Greece and Rome, and set the Roman Empire on fire. As he reminded the elders of Ephesus where he had preached three years, "How I kept back nothing that was profitable unto you, but have shewed you, and have taught you publickly, and from house to house" (Acts 20:20). And again, "Therefore watch, and remember, that by the space of three years I ceased not to warn every one night and day with tears" (Acts 20:31). Publicly and from house to house, night and day with tears! That is the plan for New Testament Christianity. Every Christian a preacher, every house a church, every gathering a congregation to hear the Gospel, every incident that occurs another occasion to draw men to Christ.

Many a preacher hides behind the pulpit and thinks that is his ministry. It is not the New Testament ministry and if much of the time spent in preparation of elaborate sermons and official public ministry were spent in house-to-house soul winning, nearly every preacher would be a better preacher and a better representative of Jesus Christ and the work of God would prosper more in his hands.

Every local congregation, then, should set out to visit every home in the area, seek out every lost sinner, and reach every creature by every available means!

ACTS 6

VERSES 1-7:

AND in those days, when the number of the disciples was multiplied, there arose a murmuring of the Grecians against the Hebrews, because their widows were neglected in the daily ministration.

2 Then the twelve called the multitude of the disciples *unto them*, and said, It is not reason that we should leave the word of God, and serve tables.

3 Wherefore, brethren, look ye out among you seven men of honest report, full of the Holy Ghost and wisdom, whom we may appoint over this business.

4 But we will give ourselves continually to prayer, and to the ministry of the word.

5 ¶ And the saying pleased the whole multitude: and they chose Stephen, a man full of faith and of the Holy Ghost, and Philip, and Prochorus, and Nicanor, and Timon, and Parmenas, and Nicolas a proselyte of Antioch;

6 Whom they set before the apostles: and when they had prayed, they laid *their* hands on them.

7 And the word of God increased; and the number of the disciples multiplied in Jerusalem greatly; and a great company of the priests were obedient to the faith.

The First Deacons

It is obvious that there were thousands of members in the church at Jerusalem. They had not elected deacons until deacons were needed. They were not needed to complete the organization of a church, for this church had been functioning grandly for an extended time without deacons. There were thousands of poor people in the church, and many, many widows who would now receive no help through ordinary means of charity as some had received perhaps through the synagogues. But Christians who had means were loyally taking care of their own.

However, the work was disorganized and "there arose a murmuring of the Grecians against the Hebrews, because their widows were neglected in the daily ministration." The Grecian Jews, probably not well integrated because of the language barrier, were somewhat neglected and their widows not adequately cared for in the daily giving out of food and of money as needed to widows. Someone was needed to look after the temporal wants of these poor Christian widows, greatly loved, so they elected deacons. And so we would be wise in our churches to elect deacons only as deacons are needed for specific work.

The Work of Deacons

Deacons are servants. In fact, the word <u>deacon</u> is simply an Anglicized version of the Greek word which means servant. These seven men were elected as the apostles said, "whom we may appoint over this business." They were to work under the direction of the apostles and were thus to lighten the load of these apostles who acted as elders of that great congregation. Deacons had no authority over the preacher nor over the business of the church. They were workers under the direction of the church and of the pastors caring for work that needed to be done but did not require the attention of the apostles or pastors.

Note carefully they were not an "official board." There never was an "official board" to a church in the New Testament.

Contrast the work and authority of deacons with that of the pastors, and authority of deacons with that of the pastors or bishops. The apostles were also elders or preachers, and at Jerusalem they acted officially as bishops for the time being.

While the deacon is a servant, bishops or pastors are rulers. First Timothy 3:4 and 5 says that one who desires the office of bishop must be "one that ruleth well his own house, having his children in subjection with all gravity; (For if a man know not how to rule his own house, how shall he take care of the church of God?)"

Hebrews 13:7 commands, "Remember them which have the rule over you, who have spoken unto you the word of God: whose faith follow, considering the end of their conversation."

In Hebrews 13:17 the command is to "obey them that have the rule over you, and submit yourselves: for they watch for your souls, as they that must give account...." Obviously these bishops or pastors are the rulers mentioned. In the same chapter, verse 24 commands, "Salute all them that have the rule over you, and all the saints." Bishops were the divinely appointed rulers or overseers of the local church. The term in its present usage, referring to supervision over the churches of an area or over other pastors, is utterly unknown in the Bible. The idea grew with the unscriptural Roman hierarchy. The local congregations of New Testament churches were independent, the connectional form of church government with bishops, supervisors, and popes over pastors and churches was unknown. But the local bishops ruled or supervised the congregation, even as did the apostles acting as bishops at Jerusalem.

But it is never hinted that a deacon should rule. The word simply means servant and the practice in the New Testament was that deacons were under the supervision of the bishops and were servants of the church.

There were deaconesses, too, for Phebe was a "servant of the church which is at Cenchrea" (Rom. 16:1). The word servant is the feminine form of the word translated deacon. A woman could carry bread to a poor widow or do other duties of a servant. But a woman was not allowed to have a place of rulership. "Let the woman learn in silence with all subjection. But I suffer not a woman to teach, nor to usurp authority over the man, but to be in silence" (I Tim. 2:11, 12). That itself shows that the office of deacon was not a ruling office.

A church may properly ask the deacons to serve as a committee to attend to some matter for the church, but in such case they are servants of a church, carrying out instructions of the church. So deacons could have no duty of calling or discharging a pastor, nor of handling the finances of a church, nor deciding on a church building, except as the church might ask them to make some report as a committee. So trustees of a church are simply people elected to sign papers officially under the instruction of a church and they should have no authority over church property nor church people.

The only two officers mentioned in the New Testament for a local church are the elders (preachers) who are selected as bishops or overseers, and the deacons, men who are elected as servants to carry out lesser duties under the direction of the church and the pastors.

The Qualifications of a Deacon

Note the men selected were not selected because they were prominent in the community, nor because they would bring prestige to the church, nor because they would have financial wisdom. Rather, "look ye out among you seven men of honest report, full of the Holy Ghost and wisdom, whom we may appoint over this business." So "the multitude of the disciples," the whole congregation, talked among themselves and either by tacit agreement of these Spirit-led people or by public vote they selected the men. And these men selected by "the whole multitude" were "set before the apostles." And the apostles prayed for them, "laid their hands on them" and then supervised them and appointed them in the matter at hand. These deacons were Spirit-filled men, men of practical wisdom and looking after the poor widows.

God deliver us from church officers who are selected because they have money or official position or worldly wisdom! They hinder the whole cause of Christ; they grieve the Holy Spirit, they hamstring the efforts of godly preachers. They usurp authority like "Diotrephes, who loveth to have the preeminence among them" and would not receive the Apostle John (III John 9). For one who is not filled with the Spirit, not a soul winner, to have any place of preeminence and authority in a church is a calamity. First Timothy 3:1-13 gives the qualifications of both bishops and deacons and the qualifications are very similar. After naming these requirements for a bishop the Scripture says, "Likewise must the deacons...." He is to "be grave, not double-tongued, not given to much wine, not greedy of filthy lucre; holding the mystery of the faith in a pure conscience." And the deacons' wives are to be "grave, not slanderers, sober, faithful in all things." Possibly I Timothy 3:11 refers not to the deacons' wives, but could be read, "even so women, grave...." That is, deaconesses, female servants of the church.

It is noteworthy that men ought, first, to be found blameless in Christian life and service. "Let these also first be proved; then let them use the office of a deacon, being found blameless" (I Tim. 3:10). The great requirements of a deacon, then, are that they be good men, Spirit-filled men, proven and found blameless and faithful.

The Deacons Were Soul Winners, Bold Witnesses for Christ

One of the requirements of these deacons set by the apostles was that they must be "full of the Holy Ghost." "But ye shall receive power, after that the Holy Ghost is come upon you..." (Acts 1:8). The fullness of the Spirit is given for soul-winning witness.

So seven men were elected and of the seven Stephen is mentioned first--"a man full of faith and of the Holy Ghost." And then we find in verse 8, "And Stephen, full of faith and power, did great wonders and miracles among the people." And in verse 10 we find that many disputed with Stephen but "they were not able to resist the wisdom and the spirit by which he spake." So the Spirit-filled deacon was put on trial by wicked men. He preached a sermon in the seventh chapter of Acts. God's power was on him for we are told in Acts 7:55, "But he, being full of the Holy Ghost, looked up stedfastly into heaven, and saw the glory of God, and Jesus standing on the right hand of God." And even in his death he was like the Lord Jesus praying, "Lord, lay not this sin to their charge," as they stoned him and he saw the Lord Jesus standing at the right hand of the Father to receive him. Yes, and that day God used the witness of Stephen to cut deep into the heart of a young man who stood by holding their garments, Saul of Tarsus.

The deacons were soul winners. Another of them, Philip, turned out to be a great evangelist, as we see in Acts 8. And we know that Philip was a good father for Acts 21:9 tells us he had "four daughters, virgins, which did prophesy," that is, filled with the Spirit they witnessed for Jesus (not preaching, but witnessing).

The Deaconate as a Step Toward the Ministry

Nearly always one must serve some kind of apprenticeship to prepare for the ministry. The deaconate is a step often used of God to prepare a man for preaching. A man was to "first be proved" and then to use the office of deacon (I Tim. 3:10). And then in I Timothy 3:13 we are told, "For they that have used the office of a deacon well purchase to themselves a good degree, and great boldness in the faith which is in Christ Jesus." So it turned out with two of these deacons, Stephen and Philip, that they became mighty preachers.

And we find that these Spirit-filled men helping the apostles, looking after the needs of poor widows and witnessing everywhere for Jesus, led to a great upsurge of revival, "And the word of God increased; and the number of the disciples multiplied in Jerusalem greatly; and a great company of the priests were obedient to the faith" (vs. 7).

VERSES 8-15:

8 And Stephen, full of faith and power, did great wonders and miracles among the people.

9 ¶ Then there arose certain of the synagogue, which is called *the synagogue* of the Libertines, and Cyrenians, and Alexandrians, and of them of Cilicia and of Asia, disputing with Stephen.

10 And they were not able to resist the wisdom and the spirit by which he spake.

11 Then they suborned men, which said, We have heard him speak blasphemous words against Moses, and *against* God.

12 And they stirred up the people, and the elders, and the scribes, and came upon *him*, and caught him, and brought *him* to the council,

13 And set up false witnesses, which said, This man ceaseth not to speak blasphemous words against this holy place, and the law:

14 For we have heard him say, that this Jesus of Nazareth shall destroy this place, and shall change the customs which Moses delivered us.

15 And all that sat in the council, looking steadfastly on him, saw his face as it had been the face of an angel.

The Third Persecution: Stephen on Trial

1. Note again that the persecution of Stephen came not because he was a Christian, but because he was a Spirit-filled witness. "They were not able to resist the wisdom and the spirit by which he spake." Stephen, "full of faith and power, did great wonders and miracles among the people." Satan and the carnal mind hates the witness of the Spirit, the burning in heart and conscience, the sense of guilt brought by the Holy Spirit in bold witnessing.

2. Certain Jewish leaders of importance arose "disputing with Stephen." Controversy is inescapable for good Christians who obey the Lord in witnessing. In Acts 9:29 Paul "spake boldly in the name of the Lord Jesus, and disputed against the Grecians [Greek Jews]: but they went about to slay him" as enemies here did with Stephen. With Christian men who were wrong in doctrine, "Paul and Barnabas had no small dissension and disputation with them" (Acts 15:2). At Athens Paul "disputed...in the synagogue with the

Jews, and with the devout persons, and in the market daily with them that met with him" (Acts 17:17). Then there is the plain statement of Jude 3 that "ye should earnestly contend for the faith which was once delivered unto the saints." Paul openly rebuked Peter for his compromise with the Judaizers (Gal. 2:11-14).

Many who want to avoid the reproach of Christ which comes with defense of the faith, say, "Preach the Gospel, do not defend it." But that is not the teaching of the Scriptures nor the practice of Spirit-filled, New Testament Christians. Controversy is inevitable when we face sin and sinners and when we face heresy and false teaching. And controversy goes with being filled with the Spirit and with soul-winning witness.

3. False witnesses are bribed to testify. "Then they suborned men, which said, We have heard him speak blasphemous words against Moses, and against God" (vs. 11). So it was in the trial of Jesus by these same wicked leaders and others like them. "Now the chief priests, and elders. and all the council, sought false witness against Jesus, to put him to death...At the last came two false witnesses, And said, This fellow said, I am able to destroy the temple of God, and to build it in three days" (Matt. 26:59-61). To suppose that there was any honesty in the opposition to Jesus by the chief priests is foolish. These were wicked men. They did not simply misunderstand Jesus. They hated Him, as wicked, Christ-rejecting sinners always do. There is a wicked immorality in unbelief. One who hates Jesus Christ may be expected to lie, to bribe, to slander, or to murder. To suppose that unbelief in Christ and the Bible is ever the result of an honest heart seeking the truth is nonfactual folly.

So Jesus said that false prophets would "come to you in sheep's clothing, but inwardly they are ravening wolves" (Matt. 7:15). Jesus repeatedly said to the Pharisees, "Woe unto you, scribes and Pharisees, hypocrites!" (Matt. 23).

In I Timothy 4:1 and 2 we are told that those who "depart from the faith, giving heed to seducing spirits, and doctrines of devils" will come "speaking lies in hypocrisy; having their conscience seared with a hot iron." There is a moral guilt in heresy and in unbelief. Modernists, liberals who pretend to be Christians but "denying the only Lord God, and our Lord Jesus Christ" are described as "ungodly men, turning the grace of our God into lasciviousness" (Jude 4).

And II Peter 2:1 and 3 tells us that false teachers will come "who privily shall bring in damnable heresies, even denying the Lord that bought them...And through covetousness shall they with feigned words make merchandise of you." Every modernist is an intentional rejecter of Christ. When he comes to speak on spiritual matters and deal with spiritual people, no Christ-rejecter can be relied upon to tell the truth. They use "feigned words." Liberals claim to be Christians "through covetousness" for the salaries and honors of the ministry. Their words are "feigned words," deceitful words. A man who will trample on the blood and spit on Jesus Christ cannot be trusted to tell the truth.

Also it is a sad truth that those who are against Spirit-filled witnessing, red-hot evangelism so commit themselves against God's program that they cannot be trusted. There is moral decline in anybody who opposes the Spirit-filled teaching and preaching of the Word. So these who suborn witnesses in order to kill a Spirit-filled Christian are typical of the opposition that Spirit-filled, aggressive Christians and soul winners may expect as they preach the Gospel and defend the faith.

4. Note the perversion and the appeal to prejudice in these who hate Stephen. The people set great store by Moses, so they would accuse Stephen of blaspheming Moses. It is true that Christ goes far beyond Moses, but Moses pointed to Christ. The law was never intended to save

but as a schoolmaster to bring men to Christ (Gal. 3:24). Men in an evil cause do not face the matter on its own merits but deliberately pervert the truth and appeal to prejudice and slander the witnesses. Those who oppose the doctrine of salvation by grace alone through faith and not of works accuse those who preach salvation by grace alone without works as advocating "a sinning religion," and of "encouraging sin." Modernists accuse those who are true to Christ and the Bible of being "unbrotherly, disturbers, and Pharisees."

5. In the midst of this controversy Stephen was still filled with the Spirit, conscious of God's presence, and "his face as it had been the face of an angel" (vs. 15). To be true to Christ and the Bible, to boldly preach against sin and to defend the faith does not hinder the sweetest fellowship with God, does not hinder soul-winning results.

ACTS 7

VERSES 1–53:

THEN said the high priest, Are these things so?

2 And he said, Men, brethren, and fathers, hearken; The God of glory appeared unto our father Abraham, when he was in Mesopotamia, before he dwelt in Charran,

3 And said unto him, Get thee out of thy country, and from thy kindred, and come into the land which I shall shew thee.

4 Then came he out of the land of the Chaldeans, and dwelt in Charran: and from thence, when his father was dead, he removed him into this land, wherein ye now dwell.

5 And he gave him none inheritance in it, no, not *so much as* to set his foot on: yet he promised that he would give it to him for a possession, and to his seed after him, when *as yet* he had no child.

6 And God spake on this wise, That his seed should sojourn in a strange land; and that they should bring them into bondage, and entreat *them* evil four hundred years.

7 And the nation to whom they shall be in bondage will I judge, said God: and after that shall they come forth, and serve me in this place.

8 And he gave him the covenant of circumcision: and so *Abraham* begat Isaac, and circumcised him the eighth day; and Isaac *begat* Jacob; and Jacob *begat* the twelve patriarchs.

9 And the patriarchs, moved with envy, sold Joseph into Egypt: but God was with him,

10 And delivered him out of all his afflictions, and gave him favour and wisdom in the sight of Pharaoh king of Egypt; and he made him governor over Egypt and all his house.

11 Now there came a dearth over all the land of Egypt and Chanaan, and great affliction: and our fathers found no sustenance.

12 But when Jacob heard that there was corn in Egypt, he sent out our fathers first.

13 And at the second *time* Joseph was made known to his brethren; and Joseph's kindred was made known unto Pharaoh.

14 Then sent Joseph, and called his father Jacob to *him*, and all his kindred, threescore and fifteen souls.

15 So Jacob went down into Egypt, and died, he, and our fathers,

16 And were carried over into Sychem, and laid in the sepul-

chre that Abraham bought for a sum of money of the sons of Emmor, *the father* of Sychem.

17 But when the time of the promise drew nigh, which God had sworn to Abraham, the people grew and multiplied in Egypt,

18 Till another king arose, which knew not Joseph.

19 The same dealt subtilely with our kindred, and evil entreated our fathers, so that they cast out their young children, to the end they might not live.

20 In which time Moses was born, and was exceeding fair, and nourished up in his father's house three months:

21 And when he was cast out, Pharaoh's daughter took him up, and nourished him for her own son.

22 And Moses was learned in all the wisdom of the Egyptians, and was mighty in words and in deeds.

23 And when he was full forty years old, it came into his heart to visit his brethren the children of Israel.

24 And seeing one *of them* suffer wrong, he defended *him,* and avenged him that was oppressed, and smote the Egyptian:

25 For he supposed his brethren would have understood how that God by his hand would deliver them; but they understood not.

26 And the next day he shewed himself unto them as they strove, and would have set them at one again, saying, Sirs, ye are brethren; why do ye wrong one to another?

27 But he that did his neighbour wrong thrust him away, saying, Who made thee a ruler and a judge over us?

28 Wilt thou kill me, as thou didst the Egyptian yesterday?

29 Then fled Moses at this saying, and was a stranger in the land of Madian, where he begat two sons.

30 And when forty years were expired, there appeared to him in the wilderness of mount Sina an angel of the Lord in a flame of fire in a bush.

31 When Moses saw *it,* he wondered at the sight: and as he drew near to behold *it,* the voice of the Lord came unto him,

32 *Saying,* I *am* the God of thy fathers, the God of Abraham, and the God of Isaac, and the God of Jacob. Then Moses trembled, and durst not behold.

33 Then said the Lord to him, Put off thy shoes from thy feet: for the place where thou standest is holy ground.

34 I have seen, I have seen the affliction of my people which is in Egypt, and I have heard their groaning, and am come down to deliver them. And now come, I will send thee into Egypt.

35 This Moses whom they refused, saying, Who made thee a ruler and a judge? the same did God send *to be* a ruler and a de-

liverer by the hand of the angel which appeared to him in the bush.

36 He brought them out, after that he had shewed wonders and signs in the land of Egypt, and in the Red sea, and in the wilderness forty years.

37 ¶ This is that Moses, which said unto the children of Israel, A Prophet shall the Lord your God raise up unto you of your brethren, like unto me; him shall ye hear.

38 This is he, that was in the church in the wilderness with the angel which spake to him in the mount Sina, and *with* our fathers: who received the lively oracles to give unto us:

39 To whom our fathers would not obey, but thrust *him* from them, and in their hearts turned back again into Egypt,

40 Saying unto Aaron, Make us gods to go before us: for *as for* this Moses, which brought us out of the land of Egypt, we wot not what is become of him.

41 And they made a calf in those days, and offered sacrifice unto the idol, and rejoiced in the works of their own hands.

42 Then God turned, and gave them up to worship the host of heaven; as it is written in the book of the prophets, O ye house of Israel, have ye offered to me slain beasts and sacrifices *by the space of* forty years in the wilderness?

43 Yea, ye took up the tabernacle of Moloch, and the star of your god Remphan, figures which ye made to worship them: and I will carry you away beyond Babylon.

44 Our fathers had the tabernacle of witness in the wilderness, as he had appointed, speaking unto Moses, that he should make it according to the fashion that he had seen.

45 Which also our fathers that came after brought in with Jesus into the possession of the Gentiles, whom God drave out before the face of our fathers, unto the days of David;

46 Who found favour before God, and desired to find a tabernacle for the God of Jacob.

47 But Solomon built him a house.

48 Howbeit the Most High dwelleth not in temples made with hands; as saith the prophet,

49 Heaven *is* my throne, and earth *is* my footstool: what house will ye build me? saith the Lord: or what *is* the place of my rest?

50 Hath not my hand made all these things?

51 ¶ Ye stiffnecked and uncircumcised in heart and ears, ye do always resist the Holy Ghost: as your fathers *did*, so *do* ye.

52 Which of the prophets have not your fathers persecuted? and they have slain them which

shewed before of the coming of the Just One; of whom ye have been now the betrayers and murderers:

53 Who have received the law by the disposition of angels, and have not kept *it*.

Stephen's Address Before the Council

1. This is an address recounting the dealings of God with Israel all the way from Abraham down to the present Jewish rulers. It tells of God's wonderful mercies, blessings, guidance and deliverance. It tells of the sins and failures of Israel. In this it is somewhat like the first three chapters of Deuteronomy in which Moses recounts the blessing of God on Israel, describing the forty years in the wilderness, God's blessings and provision and Israel's unbelief, rebellion and sin. It is somewhat like the seventy-eighth Psalm also which recalls God's blessings on Israel and their failures and unbelief.

2. We know that the record given here is an inspired, correct record of what Stephen said. Whether he was infallibly inspired in his message is not stated, but presumably, since God still saw fit to record the address as a whole in the Bible, the statements are generally reliable and approved of God. However, there are some problems here. The Bible does not claim infallible knowledge for Stephen, does claim perfect accuracy in the record of his speech.

3. Notice the divisions of the sermon. From verses 2 to 19 he takes them from Abraham through Jacob, down to the times of the enslavement in Egypt. This is the story of the development of the race.

From verses 20 to 41 is the story of the leadership of Moses. There is a particular reason for this. The opposition to him has been on the basis that "this man ceaseth not to speak blasphemous words against this holy place, and the law..." and "the customs which Moses delivered us" (Acts 6:13, 14). He shows them God's blessings on Moses, then how Israel had turned away from the leadership of Moses, in their own unbelief, a nation constantly backsliding and turning away from God and His leader, Moses!

These twenty-one verses are given to Moses in order to emphasize that Moses himself pointed to Jesus Christ. In verse 37, "This is that Moses, which said unto the children of Israel, A prophet shall the Lord your God raise up unto you of your brethren, like unto me; him shall ye hear." That is a quotation from Deuteronomy 18:15, 18, 19. Moses prophesied that Jesus should come. He should lead the whole nation Israel as Moses did. He is a second Moses and a greater Moses. To reject Jesus Christ was to reject the leadership and teaching of Moses.

Verses 42 and 43 tell of the constant recurring idolatry among the Israelites which led to their captivity in Babylon.

Verses 44 to 50 tell about the tabernacle and the temple of Solomon which succeeded it, and then show that actually God Himself is greater than any human building. "Heaven is my throne, and earth is my footstool," he quotes from Isaiah 66:1 and 2. Thus the worship of the true God could not be confined simply to rules and regulations of the Mosaic law. The temple at Jerusalem pictured the eternal temple of God in Heaven. All these sacrifices given by Moses pictured a greater sacrifice. Moses himself was the picture of the greater leader, Jesus, God's own Son. So is the progress of the thought expressed by Stephen here.

4. Notice the shocking boldness of verses 51 to 53. Evangelistic preaching always starts on the basis of sin and calls for repentance. Spirit-filled witnessing accuses the Christ-rejecter. This kind of preaching is expected to "cut to the heart" (Acts 5:33). And so, as the same Sanhedrin had felt about Peter and John, they "took council to slay them."

These people are called "the betrayers and murderers of the Just One." They are like their fathers who stoned the prophets. That is like the words of Jesus in Luke 11:47-51. The rejection and slaying of Jesus Christ is the natural culmination of wicked men who turned down God's prophets. And Stephen is in the holy succession of apostles and prophets who follow Jesus and are persecuted.

5. Note the "church in the wilderness" of verse 38. That simply means Israel, called out of Egypt and assembled in the wilderness, was an ekklesia. There is no connection here with the term church as used of the body of Christ which will be called out at the rapture, that "general assembly and church of the firstborn, which are written in heaven" (Heb. 12:22, 23). Some of Israel were saved, some were not. Israel is no pattern for the church. To spiritualize the term Israel as meaning the church is wholly foreign to the scriptural idea. Circumcision is not a prefigure of baptism. The Jewish Sabbath is not the same as the Lord's Day. The preacher is not a priest. The pulpit is not an altar. The church building is not a temple. The Lord's Supper is not a sacrifice like the Old Testament sacrifices, but simply an object lesson, a memorial. Note in Acts 19, verses 32, 39 and 41, the word assembly in our King James translation is the Greek word ekklesia for church. It simply means a called-out assembly and it had no necessarily Christian connotation.

Usually the word church in the New Testament refers to local congregations like "the church of God which is at Corinth" (I Cor. 1:2), or "the seven churches which are in Asia" (Rev. 1:11), or "the churches of Galatia" (Gal. 1:2). A few times it refers to that great assembly that will be called out at the rapture and assembled in Heaven, including all the saved of all ages. But remember there is no special connection between "the church in the wilderness," Israel assembled in the wilderness with the assembly of Christians who will be called out at the rapture. Both are called-out assemblages and that is all, just as the mob at Ephesus was a called-out assembly and in that sense fitted the Greek word translated church. Incidently, no other word is ever translated church in the New Testament than ekklesia except one time in Acts 19:37 where "robbers of churches" ought to be translated "robbers of temples." The word church in the New Testament never refers to a building nor to a denomination, but always to a congregation or called-out assembly of some kind.

VERSES 54–60:

54 ¶ When they heard these things, they were cut to the heart, and they gnashed on him with *their* teeth.

55 But he, being full of the Holy Ghost, looked up steadfastly into heaven, and saw the glory of God, and Jesus standing on the right hand of God,

56 And said, Behold, I see the heavens opened, and the Son of man standing on the right hand of God.

57 Then they cried out with a loud voice, and stopped their ears, and ran upon him with one accord,

58 And cast *him* out of the city, and stoned *him :* and the witnesses laid down their clothes at a young man's feet, whose name was Saul.

59 And they stoned Stephen, calling upon *God*, and saying, Lord Jesus, receive my spirit.

60 And he kneeled down, and cried with a loud voice, Lord, lay not this sin to their charge. And when he had said this, he fell asleep.

The Stoning of Stephen the Martyr

Stephen is sometimes called "the first Christian martyr." Instead we believe that Abel was the first Christian martyr (see Luke 11:50). We believe that Old Testament Christians were saved exactly as were New Testament Christians (Rom. 4:1-12; Acts 10:43). Abraham saw Christ's day and was glad (John 8:56), and Abraham trusted in Christ and was a Christian and so we believe was Abel, who was killed as a prophet by wicked Cain.

1. Note the insane rage of these. They were "cut to the heart" and "they gnashed on him with their teeth." And of the Lord Jesus it was prophesied, "They gaped upon me with their mouths, as a ravening and a roaring lion" (Ps. 22:13).

2. Stephen is again "full of the Holy Ghost" (vs. 55). We should expect, then, that his testimony would be in saving power. And it seems that the words he said burn deep into the heart of young Saul (vs. 58 and Acts 8:1). That Spirit-filled testimony bore fruit, too. The nagging conviction was like the pricks of an oxgoad which he resisted setting out to arrest Christians (Acts 9:5). "Filled with the Spirit" is not simply an expression of happiness. It is an enduement of power for witnessing, and God's power was on the witness of Stephen at his death.

3. Stephen saw Jesus, "the Son of man standing on the right hand of God." The regular position of Jesus now is seated on the right hand of the Father (Ps. 110:1; Heb. 1:13). Oh, but He who notes the fall of every sparrow and keeps a record of every hair of a saint and has His angels always around us, would not let His faithful martyr die without a glad sense of His presence! So Stephen speaks boldly to Jesus and with Jesus as One present, saying, "Lord Jesus, receive my spirit." And again, "Lord, lay not this sin to their charge." We are reminded that "if we suffer, we shall also reign with him" (II Tim. 2:12). Some heroes of the faith, we are told, "were tortured, not accepting deliverance; that they might obtain a better resurrection" (Heb. 11:35). And all of us are warned not to think it strange concerning the fiery trial that comes to such Christians. "But rejoice, inasmuch as ye are partakers of Christ's sufferings; that, when his glory shall be revealed, ye may be glad also with exceeding joy" (I Pet. 4:13).

Stephen followed in the steps of Jesus, as we are called to do. "For even hereunto were ye called: because Christ also suffered for us, leaving us an example, that ye should follow his steps" (I Pet. 2:21). So on the cross Jesus said, "Father, forgive them; for they know not what they do" (Luke 23:34), while Stephen said, "Lord, lay not this sin to their charge." On the cross Jesus prayed, "Father, into thy hands I commend my spirit," and Stephen prayed, "Lord Jesus, receive my spirit." What a wonderful disciple was Deacon Stephen, filled with the Holy Ghost, who so closely followed the pattern of His Saviour!

ACTS 8

VERSES 1–4:

AND Saul was consenting unto his death. And at that time there was a great persecution against the church which was at Jerusalem; and they were all scattered abroad throughout the regions of Judea and Samaria, except the apostles.

2 And devout men carried Stephen *to his burial*, and made great lamentation over him.

3 As for Saul, he made havoc of the church, entering into every house, and haling men and women committed *them* to prison.

4 Therefore they that were scattered abroad went every where preaching the word.

The Fourth Persecution Introducing Saul

1. Note that "Saul was consenting unto" Stephen's death. He had already some prestige in the city for those who stoned Stephen "laid down their clothes at a young man's feet, whose name was Saul." He was a Jew from Tarsus of Cilicia (Acts 21:39). He was a Roman citizen, born of a father who had obtained this great privilege and prestige (Acts 22:25-28; Acts 16:37, 38). Early he had been brought to Jerusalem and had been trained and educated under Gamaliel, their famous teacher of the law (Acts 22:3). And although a young man, already his zeal and knowledge and training had gained him great respect.

Now Saul became greatly convinced of the danger that these Christians would multiply. He thought the observance of the law as the Jewish leaders taught it would be endangered and diminished. He determined to help stamp out this movement of Christians. So Saul "made havock of the church, entering into every house, and haling men and women committed them to prison." Doubtless he was a favorite of the Sanhedrin!

2. "They were all scattered abroad" (vs. 1). All the Christians except the apostles or perhaps all the active

Christian workers besides the apostles were scattered throughout Judaea and Samaria. And verse 4 tells us that they "went every where preaching the word." No doubt Satan and the Sanhedrin meant it for evil, but God means it for good. Thus the Gospel began to be widely spread everywhere among the Jews. It was the plan of the Lord Jesus, plainly revealed, that "ye shall receive power, after that the Holy Ghost is come upon you: and ye shall be witnesses unto me both in Jerusalem, and in all Judaea, and in Samaria, and unto the uttermost part of the earth" (Acts 1:8). Well, they have all they can do just now. A little later God will make it clear to them they should go to the Gentiles (Acts 10). First, Jews everywhere must learn that their Messiah has come, that God has made Jesus both Lord and Christ and raised Him from the dead, so they should repent and trust Him. How blessed that persecution, trouble, dislocation, and poverty did not stop them, but they "went every where preaching the word."

3. "Except the apostles." The apostles stayed in Jerusalem. There was no denominational headquarters: the Lord did not establish bishops or popes over the churches. But Jesus has trained and authorized these apostles, mature, experienced, holy men of God, to supervise the work of young Christians while the canon of Scripture is being written and completed. It will be to these apostles and elders at Jerusalem that the appeal will be made as to whether it is necessary for Gentile converts to be circumcised and keep the law of Moses (Acts 15:1-29). Now such matters are forever settled for all of us by the Scriptures.

Paul had his Gospel given to him by divine revelation as the Holy Spirit had him tell us carefully (Gal. 1:11-17). However, Paul did go to Jerusalem after three years to see Peter and James, the Lord's brother (Gal. 1:18) and then after fourteen years he says, "I went up by revelation, and communicated unto them that gospel which I preach among the Gentiles, but privately to them which were of reputa-

tion, lest by any means I should run, or had run, in vain"
(Gal. 2:2). But as the body of revealed truth became clearly
defined and the canon of Scriptures completed, then the dis-
tinctiveness of the apostolic ministry declined.

They, still great preachers and soul winners, were
widely used, Thomas in India, Peter in Babylon (I Pet.
5:13). But they did not need to maintain a court of appeal to
settle problems of Christian doctrine and conduct after the
Scriptures were completed. And the apostles had no suc-
cessors. The idea of apostolic succession, of apostolic
authority passing down by the laying on of hands or by the
succession of popes and cardinals, is utterly foreign to the
idea of Scripture.

However, all were scattered abroad "except the apostles." Why did the apostles stay in Jerusalem? For several
reasons doubtless.

First, Jesus had plainly commanded them that the Gospel
"should be preached in his name among all nations, BEGIN-
NING AT JERUSALEM" (Luke 24:47).

Second, the truth must be emphasized that "salvation is
of the Jews" (John 4:22). The God of the New Testament is
the God in the Old Testament. Jesus the Saviour is Christ
the Messiah of the Jews. Those who are saved are spiritual
Jews. And "they which are of faith, the same are the children of Abraham...So then they which be of faith are
blessed with faithful Abraham" (Gal. 3:7, 9). God has not
cast away His people Israel through whom came the law and
through whom, according to the flesh, came the Saviour
(Rom. 9:4, 5; Rom. 11:1, 2). The Jewish law was "our
schoolmaster to bring us unto Christ" (Gal. 3:24). So
Christianity is not a new religion. Christ is the one
Abraham knew and trusted, the one Moses foretold, the one
preached by the prophets, the one pictured by all the sacrifices. He is the Creator, the Jehovah of the Old Testament. So the Gospel must be thoroughly preached, first at
Jerusalem and identified with the Old Testament believed by

the Jews, and the God worshipped by true Jews. So the apostles remained at Jerusalem.

Again, darkness is descending upon the Jewish mind. A veil will soon cover their understanding. The Jewish leaders have rejected and crucified the Saviour. Now they are rejecting the Gospel preached by the apostles. Everywhere Paul and others of these Christians go, they will first preach to the Jews, but then as many Jews reject it, they will turn to the Gentiles (Acts 13:46-48; Acts 17:17-31; Acts 18:6; Acts 20:21; Acts 28:28). So these apostles must continue in Jerusalem for a season. And Jerusalem must be the center from which the Gospel is spread, although persecution has driven the mass of Christian witnesses out into all Judaea and Samaria.

VERSES 5–8:

5 Then Philip went down to the city of Samaria, and preached Christ unto them.

6 And the people with one accord gave heed unto those things which Philip spake, hearing and seeing the miracles which he did.

7 For unclean spirits, crying with loud voice, came out of many that were possessed *with them:* and many taken with palsies, and that were lame, were healed.

8 And there was great joy in that city.

Deacon Philip, Evangelist

Philip the deacon has now become an evangelist. He was already filled with the Spirit, a great witness and soul winner, when elected a deacon. He is an example of the truth of I Timothy 3:13. "For they that have used the office of a deacon well purchase to themselves a good degree, and great boldness in the faith which is in Christ Jesus." He is named in Acts 21:8 as "Philip the evangelist." And the following verse mentions his four daughters, Spirit-filled Christians who witnessed for Jesus, that is, "did prophesy." Note Philip's preaching.

1. He "preached Christ unto them." No sermon is given, but we are sure he followed the New Testament pattern. He preached the wickedness of men to reject Christ. He preached that God had raised Jesus from the dead. He preached repentance, a heart turning away from sin and trusting Christ "the only name whereby men could be saved." And we are sure that he preached in the power of the Holy Spirit for he was selected as a man "full of the Holy Ghost and wisdom," and second only to Stephen among the deacons chosen in Acts 6.

2. Note the "miracles" attending Philip's ministry in verse 6, and the unclean spirits cast out and the sick healed (vs. 7). This is not surprising. Spirit-filled Stephen, too, had done "great wonders and miracles" (Acts 6:8). So had Peter and John, but miracles are not for apostles only. We had as well face it that miracles, healings, demons cast out, attended the Spirit-filled ministry of Christians throughout the book of Acts on many typical occasions. They were not often enough to become common, and certainly all did not have gifts of miracles and healings (I Cor. 12:29, 30). But equally certain God had set in the church after apostles, prophets and teachers, "miracles, then gifts of healings, helps, governments, diversities of tongues" (I Cor. 12:28). So for one reason God always has compassion on the troubled, the afflicted, the demon-possessed, the suffering. For another, New Testament Christians prayed for and expected God to approve their ministry with some special signs and wonders as He did the ministry of Jesus. (Compare Acts 2:22; Acts 3:16; Acts 4:30; Acts 5:12 with John 14:12.)

3. "And there was great joy in that city" (vs. 8). And that joy comes only in great breaking-out revival, obvious demonstration of the power of the Holy Spirit. Many people struggle so hard to find Christian joy in "the deeper life," in "the Keswick experience." They long for an ecstasy in "speaking in tongues." But the proper joy for Christians is

the joy of revival and soul winning. "They that sow in tears shall reap in joy. He that goeth forth and weepeth, bearing precious seed, shall doubtless come again with rejoicing, bringing his sheaves with him" (Ps. 126:5, 6). The proper joy for a Christian is to be expected when we carry out the Great Commission and find that, as Jesus promised, "Lo, I am with you alway, even unto the end of the world." It is true. In soul winning there is the joy of the Holy Ghost, joy of prayers answered, joy of seeing sinners saved. Such joy enters into that joy of Heaven in the presence of the angels "over one sinner that repenteth, more than over ninety and nine just persons, which need no repentance" (Luke 15:7, 10).

VERSES 9–25:

9 But there was a certain man, called Simon, which beforetime in the same city used sorcery, and bewitched the people of Samaria, giving out that himself was some great one:

10 To whom they all gave heed, from the least to the greatest, saying, This man is the great power of God.

11 And to him they had regard, because that of long time he had bewitched them with sorceries.

12 But when they believed Philip preaching the things concerning the kingdom of God, and the name of Jesus Christ, they were baptized, both men and women.

13 Then Simon himself believed also: and when he was baptized, he continued with Philip, and wondered, beholding the miracles and signs which were done.

14 Now when the apostles which were at Jerusalem heard that Samaria had received the word of God, they sent unto them Peter and John:

15 Who, when they were come down, prayed for them, that they might receive the Holy Ghost:

16 (For as yet he was fallen upon none of them: only they were baptized in the name of the Lord Jesus.)

17 Then laid they *their* hands on them, and they received the Holy Ghost.

18 And when Simon saw that through laying on of the apostles' hands the Holy Ghost was given, he offered them money,

19 Saying, Give me also this power, that on whomsoever I lay hands, he may receive the Holy Ghost.

20 But Peter said unto him, Thy money perish with thee, because thou hast thought that the gift of God may be purchased with money.

21 Thou hast neither part nor lot in this matter: for thy heart is not right in the sight of God.

22 Repent therefore of this thy wickedness, and pray God, if perhaps the thought of thine heart may be forgiven thee.

23 For I perceive that thou art in the gall of bitterness, and in the bond of iniquity.

24 Then answered Simon, and said, Pray ye to the Lord for me, that none of these things which ye have spoken come upon me.

25 And they, when they had testified and preached the word of the Lord, returned to Jerusalem, and preached the gospel in many villages of the Samaritans.

Simon the Sorcerer; Apostles and Laying on of Hands

Simon "used sorcery, and bewitched the people" (vs. 9). He convinced the people of some supernatural power saying, "This man is the great power of God." We do not think it was all fraud. Satan does sometimes give wicked men more than human power. So the sorcerers before Pharaoh in Egypt cast down their rods and they became serpents (Exod. 7:11-13). The magicians "brought up frogs upon the land of Egypt" (Exod. 8:7). These magicians tried to bring the plague of lice "but they could not" (Exod. 8:18). Bible believers cannot doubt that Jesus cast out demons miraculously as in the case of the Gadarene demoniac (Matt. 8:28-34; Mark 5:1-17; Luke 8:26-39), and in many other cases. And Christians are warned to put on the whole armor of God "that ye may be able to stand against the wiles of the devil. For we wrestle not against flesh and blood, but against principalities, against powers, against the rulers of the darkness of this world, against spiritual wickedness in high places" (Eph. 6:11, 12). Missionaries among people in darkest heathendom often find demonstrations of demoniac power and the China Inland Mission in the book, Pastor

Hsi, tells of demoniac demonstrations and demons being cast out in many, many cases. No doubt there were enough spirit manifestations, of more than human power and wisdom, to convince all the populous that "this man is the great power of God."

Simon Converted

Many of the victims of Simon's sorcery "believed Philip preaching the things concerning the kingdom of God, and the name of Jesus Christ" and they were baptized.

And then we are told, "Simon himself believed also." I believe we should take the Scriptures here at face value. As the others believed and were saved, so Simon believed and was saved also. Many have supposed that Simon was not saved simply because he wished to buy the power to lay hands on people so they would receive the Holy Spirit. But born-again Christians have done far worse than that. David's adultery and murder, Peter's denying Christ and cursing and quitting the ministry, were, I think, worse sins, going against plainer commands and greater light. And the selling out of many to denominational authority, to popularity, place and prestige are more deliberate sins than Simon's. At any rate, it is no safe nor proper attitude towards Scripture to say that those who believed in verse 12 were saved and that when "Simon himself believed also," he was not saved. One who trusts in Christ is saved. So says John 1:12; John 3:14-16; John 3:18, 36; John 5:24; John 6:40; John 6:47; Acts 13:38, 39; Acts 16:31, etc. Here we part with even the beloved Dr. R. A. Torrey, one of the most spiritual and blessed of Bible interpreters, who believed that Simon was not saved.

The Holy Spirit Given With the Laying on of Hands by the Apostles

The apostles at Jerusalem had a proper concern about the great revival at Samaria. Philip was only a deacon. How well taught was he in the Word? How wise was his direction of the great campaign? And the new converts--were they being established in the faith? So these men, properly looked up to as specially trained apostles of Christ, sent Peter and John to see the work and to publicly approve it, and add what help they could.

These apostles in seeing the multitude of new converts "prayed for them that they might receive the Holy Ghost." It is not the indwelling of the Holy Spirit mentioned here. It seems certain that ever since the day of the resurrection of Christ when Jesus breathed on the disciples and they received the Holy Ghost (John 20:21, 22), the Holy Spirit now had come into every convert's body at the time of salvation. In fact, the Holy Spirit is the one who convicts and then the one who regenerates so that one who is saved is "born of the Spirit" (John 3:6). So these converts who had believed in Christ already had the Holy Spirit dwelling within them. But in the sense of the coming of the Holy Spirit upon them in power, they had not received the Holy Ghost.

What the disciples received in John 20:21, 22, these Samaritan converts received at conversion. What the disciples received at Pentecost--the fullness of the Spirit, the pouring out of the Spirit, the Holy Spirit upon them, the gift of the Holy Spirit--they had not received. The work of the Holy Spirit in salvation, they already had. The work of the Holy Spirit as anointed witnesses, they did not have. So the disciples prayed for them "that they might receive the Holy Ghost." After they had prayed, the apostles "laid their hands on them, and they received the Holy Ghost."

We disagree with Dr. Scofield's note that "after Pentecost, so long as the Gospel was preached to Jews only, the Spirit was imparted to such as believed by the laying on of hands." That idea is nowhere stated in the Bible, and is an unwarranted conclusion. The Holy Spirit was given in power in answer to prayer, probably the prayers of the new converts, too, and certainly the prayers of Peter and John.

Dr. Scofield seems to have confused the coming in of the

Holy Spirit to dwell in the body of one who is regenerated, and enduement of power, an entirely different matter. I think it certain that according to the promises in John, chapters 14, 15 and 16 and the clear statement of I Corinthians 6:19, 20 and many other Scriptures, that the Holy Spirit, since Christ's resurrection, comes in to dwell in the body of every person who is saved, when Jesus breathed on the disciples and said to them, "Receive ye the Holy Ghost" (John 20:22).

And that God used the apostles' hands in giving the fullness of the Spirit in answer to prayer is not unusual. God uses the voices of Christians continually in getting out the Gospel and in edifying Christians. The fullness of the Spirit on a Christian often influences others near him without a word being spoken. I have walked down the aisle in a great congregation and laid my hand upon the shoulder of some man utterly unknown to me and have seen him begin to tremble and then to weep under conviction.

Charles G. Finney tells in his Memoirs how, when he went into the presence of a certain mill, the workers became agitated and some wept, powerfully moved by the Holy Spirit through his presence. Many a godly man has had the experience of a young Christian who, in fighting some battle, conquering some habit, could have great strength and help simply by being for a time in the presence of the man of God.

That is the spiritual truth back of the laying on of hands in ordination. It is certain that Timothy received certain spiritual gifts at ordination. And Paul admonished him to "stir up the gift of God, which is in thee by the putting on of my hands" (II Tim. 1:6). And again to "neglect not the gift that is in thee, which was given thee by prophecy, with the laying on of the hands of the presbytery" (I Tim. 4:14). When a council of good men, godly prophets, after proper examination, lay hands upon the head of some man called to the ministry or to other work of God, and pray for him, they only signify with their hands their approval and their prayer that God will give the needed gifts and power for the work to which He had called him.

So the deacons had hands laid upon them, though they were already men "full of the Holy Ghost" (Acts 6:5, 6). So Christians are taught to lay hands on the sick when they pray for their recovery (Mark 16:18), and the anointing with oil is simply another human symbol used to illustrate and encourage faith in the work of the Holy Spirit (James 5:14). So it is not surprising if some godly, Spirit-filled man should put his hands upon the head of a young convert and pray for him to be filled with the Holy Spirit. And just so, God has led thousands of preachers to invite a sinner who will hear and now take Christ as Saviour to grasp the preacher's hand as a token of that decision of faith. God chooses to use human voice and hands and presence, even as He used the shadow of Peter passing by to heal some (Acts 5:15). The apostles' laying hands on these new converts was not a dispensational matter.

However, we should note the anxiety of the apostles that every Christian in New Testament times have the fullness of the Spirit for witnessing and soul-winning power. So with the Apostle Paul in Acts 19:1-7.

Simon Seeks to Buy the Power to Give the Holy Spirit Through Laying on of Hands

Simon had dealt with evil powers. But he had "wondered, beholding the miracles and signs which were done" under Philip (vs. 13). Just as the sorcerers and magicians under Pharaoh saw that the power of God was far greater than that of devils and said, "This is the finger of God" (Exod. 8:16-19), so Simon saw that the wonderful power of the Holy Spirit was supernatural power beyond the power of demons, He was foolish and wrong to offer money for spiritual usefulness. But it is only fair to say that uncounted thousands have thought that because they gave liberally to the church they had certain spiritual prestige and authority.

A Roman Catholic came to me for instruction on how to be saved. He had become convinced that he needed to know Christ personally and forgiveness and salvation. Step by step I led him to see that he was a sinner, that Christ had died for him, that salvation was offered freely to all who would personally trust Jesus Christ for forgiveness. He had trusted Christ and claimed Him. Then he reached for his billfold and said to me, "How much do I owe you, Father?" I was startled and indignant and told him, "You don't owe me anything, and quit calling me Father!" But he meant no ill. He was accustomed to paying for confession and masses. So Simon, the ignorant new convert, carried over ideas from his profession in the past and offered to buy the right to give the Holy Ghost with the laying on of hands! The gift of God cannot be purchased with money. Salvation cannot be purchased by gifts of money, and no office in the church ought to be reward for liberal gifts.

Peter said, "Thy money perish with thee." Money is temporal, material, and like Simon's body, would perish. The work of the Holy Spirit is intangible, spiritual, eternal.

"Thou hast neither part nor lot in this matter: for thy heart is not right in the sight of God," Peter said. Simon had no part nor lot in the fullness of the Holy Spirit and in laying hands on others. His heart was not right in the matter. That does not prove he was unsaved, but certainly his attitude in this matter was wrong.

But was it more wrong than millions of others who never seek and never have the power of the Holy Spirit? Was it more wrong than others who think that college and seminary training or natural talent and pleasing personality are requirements for the ministry? Simon was wrong, as many others are wrong. He was still "in the gall of bitterness, and in the bond of iniquity," that is, enslaved in the old worldly, sinful habits, thoughts and principles. And we should not be too surprised for John Vassar, the blessed soul winner, friend of A. J. Gordon, was saved and active in his testimony for months while he continued working in a brewery! And Charles Spurgeon did not give up tobacco until a year or so before he died. All the denominational hierarchies are patterned after the world and human government, not after the Bible. We all have a tendency to carry over into the Christian life the concepts and ways of the natural, unconverted man and of the world about us.

"Repent therefore of this thy wickedness," he was told. He was not commanded to repent in the general sense for salvation, but to turn from this particular wickedness and pray for forgiveness, just as every Christian is taught to pray daily for forgiveness and cleansing (Luke 11:4; I John 1:9).

The humility of Simon and his obvious penitence in verse 24 indicate that the immature Christian is sorry for his sin and wants help and deliverance.

Notice that the apostles "preached the word of the Lord" here at the city of Samaria and "in many villages of the Samaritans" en route back to Jerusalem. So, although the Gospel had not yet been taken directly to the Gentiles and Peter will have to have direct teaching and a shocking experience to reconcile him to that (Acts 10), already the apostles and others are reconciled to preaching to the Samaritans, half-breed Jews, half-breed in religion, and usually despised by the Jews so that "the Jews had no dealings with the Samaritans" (John 4:9). The Samaritans did claim to worship the true God, rejoiced that they had Jacob's well at Sychar, had some Scriptures (the Pentateuch), but did not worship at Jerusalem, nor, we suppose, did they acknowledge the priesthood and Sanhedrin there. But these who are not true Jews are receiving the Gospel.

VERSES 26-35:

26 And the angel of the Lord spake unto Philip, saying, Arise, and go toward the south, unto the way that goeth down from Jerusalem unto Gaza, which is desert.

27 And he arose and went: and, behold, a man of Ethiopia, a eunuch of great authority under Candace queen of the Ethiopians, who had the charge of all her treasure, and had come to Jerusalem for to worship,

28 Was returning, and sitting in his chariot read Esaias the prophet.

29 Then the Spirit said unto Philip, Go near, and join thyself to this chariot.

30 And Philip ran thither to *him*, and heard him read the prophet Esaias, and said, Understandest thou what thou readest?

31 And he said, How can I, except some man should guide me? And he desired Philip that he would come up and sit with him.

32 The place of the Scripture which he read was this, He was led as a sheep to the slaughter; and like a lamb dumb before his shearer, so opened he not his mouth:

33 In his humiliation his judgment was taken away: and who shall declare his generation? for his life is taken from the earth.

34 And the eunuch answered Philip, and said, I pray thee, of whom speaketh the prophet this? of himself, or of some other man?

35 Then Philip opened his mouth, and began at the same Scripture, and preached unto him Jesus.

"The Angel of the Lord Spake Unto Philip"

The term angel is often indefinite in the Bible. Jacob used the word angel as if it referred to God. "The Angel which redeemed me from all evil, bless the lads" (Gen. 48:16). "The angel of the Lord" camps around Christians to protect them (Ps. 34:7). A number of times in the Old Testament "the angel of the Lord" seems to have been preincarnate appearances of Jesus Christ. In Revelation, chapters 2 and 3, the letters of the seven churches are each addressed to "the angel" of each respective church. So here "the angel of the Lord" may mean a particular heavenly being who might have appeared visibly to Philip, as angels did a good many times in the Bible. Or it may mean that the

Spirit of the Lord spoke to him, for the word angel means messenger and does not always mean the heavenly spirit beings called angels. In verse 29, "The Spirit said unto Philip." In verse 39, "The Spirit of the Lord caught away Philip."

At any rate, here came clear leading, the Word of God to Philip, telling him exactly where to go. Just as a Christian can have the power of the Holy Spirit in witnessing, he can have clear leading of the Spirit as to where he is to go and what he is to say. So Jesus "must needs go through Samaria" (John 4:4), and knew, by the Holy Spirit who filled Him, about the woman's five husbands. So Paul's company "were forbidden of the Holy Ghost to preach the word in Asia," and "They assayed to go into Bithynia: but the Spirit suffered them not," and in a vision a man called to Paul, "Come over into Macedonia, and help us" (Acts 16:6-10). So Paul and his helpers knew they were to go into Macedonia and start preaching in Europe.

Christians ought to seek and have, day by day, clear leading from God about all the Lord's work. If Philip was to go toward the South from Samaria, there would be a road leading West from Jerusalem to Gaza and on toward Egypt. He was to intercept this road and he did. And there was the eager inquirer God had prepared for him!

The Ethiopian Eunuch

Here was an unnamed man, an eunuch, high in the government of Ethiopia, treasurer under Queen Candace. He was a Jewish proselyte, that is, he had been convinced about the true God and the Old Testament Scriptures and he had gone to Jerusalem to worship. Possibly at Jerusalem he had bought this handwritten scroll of the Prophet Isaiah or possibly he had obtained it before. At any rate, now his eager heart was reading in Isaiah and he had reached the part now designated as chapter 53, foretelling the sacrifice of the Lord Jesus Christ for the sins of the world.

It seems strange that at Jerusalem, where all the apostles were, this man with a seeking heart did not find anyone to tell him about Jesus! Perhaps the apostles were so busy that they let this man slip through their fingers. They could not possibly see every person who came to Jerusalem and the man would not know to seek out the apostles. Perhaps, too, God has specially chosen the Spirit-filled Philip, so that he, eager for soul winning, should win this man.

It may seem strange that God took Philip from the great revival at Samaria on a long journey to talk to one man. But it is significant that Philip went immediately without question, that when "the Spirit said unto Philip, Go near, and join thyself to this chariot," that "Philip RAN thither to him." We are always wise to obey God without judging whether or not some other way would be best. And it may well be that this Ethiopian eunuch spread the Gospel widely in Ethiopia and other parts of Africa and that the Coptic Church in Ethiopia, degenerate now as it is, is a remaining testimony of many thousands of Christians who were brought to Christ through the salvation and ministry and influence of this Ethiopian eunuch.

It is blessed that when God leads Philip to go, He has the Ethiopian eunuch just at the right place, and reading the right Scriptures. God works at both ends of the line. One may safely go wherever God leads, knowing that He has prepared the way. And how blessed that the man already had open before him the Scriptures.

It is rather remarkable that this foreign prince, this important statesman, possibly with an armed escort, certainly with servants, would ask a stranger on the road to sit by him in the chariot and explain the Scriptures! But God led the seeking heart as well as the soul winner and so Philip was asked to come and sit by him in the chariot and to explain that wonderful passage about Christ's atoning death in Isaiah 53. "Then Philip opened his mouth, and began at the same scripture, and preached unto him Jesus."

We should remember that the only Scriptures available were Old Testament Scriptures, and that the plan of salvation is as clearly taught in Isaiah 53, in Numbers 21:5-9, in Exodus 12 concerning the passover lamb, and in many other passages, as it is in the New Testament. In hundreds of places in the Old Testament one may begin at the same Scripture and preach Jesus! And that Ethiopian eunuch saw that Christ died for sinners and rose again, and in his heart as they rode along in the chariot he trusted the Saviour.

VERSES 36–40:

36 And as they went on *their* way, they came unto a certain water: and the eunuch said, See, *here is* water; what doth hinder me to be baptized?

37 And Philip said, If thou believest with all thine heart, thou mayest. And he answered and said, I believe that Jesus Christ is the Son of God.

38 And he commanded the chariot to stand still: and they went down both into the water, both Philip and the eunuch; and he baptized him.

39 And when they were come up out of the water, the Spirit of the Lord caught away Philip, that the eunuch saw him no more: and he went on his way rejoicing.

40 But Philip was found at Azotus: and passing through he preached in all the cities, till he came to Cesarea.

The Eunuch Is Baptized

Philip's teaching had been thorough. No doubt he had preached the resurrection as did other New Testament preachers. Certainly he preached the atoning death of Jesus, His substitutionary death, as so clearly outlined in Isaiah 53. But always in New Testament times baptism immediately followed faith in Christ. The Great Commission specifically commanded baptism (Matt. 28:19, 20; Mark 16:15, 16). The converts of John were baptized. The converts of Jesus were baptized (John 4:1, 2). At Pentecost the new converts, some three thousand, were baptized (Acts

2:41). In fact, in preaching repentance Peter had clearly taught that baptism is a proper profession of repentance and faith (Acts 2:38), and that baptism normally should picture such an attitude of heart as preparing one for the gift of the Holy Ghost (Acts 2:38).

And since New Testament preachers make so much of the resurrection of Christ (which is part of the Gospel--I Cor. 15:3, 4), it is not surprising that they also made much of baptism as a picture of that resurrection and as picturing the identification of a Christian with Christ, His death and resurrection. "For if we have been planted together in the likeness of his death, we shall be also in the likeness of his resurrection" (Rom. 6:5). The Christian was buried in the likeness of Christ's death and so raised up to walk in newness of life, the Christ life (Rom. 6:4). So Philip had preached that converts ought to be baptized.

The best authorities and manuscripts omit verse 37. Philip may have asked such a question: it is quite certain that he insisted on a clear-cut faith in Christ as Saviour. The profession "that Jesus Christ is the Son of God" is not enough. However, one who had been seeking God and seeking salvation, who came to see that Jesus was the Son of God and Saviour, would trust Christ for salvation.

The baptism was clearly immersion. In the first place, the type picturing the burial and resurrection of Christ requires it (Rom. 6:4, 5). Then the meaning of the word to immerse, plunge, cover, to dip, requires it (so also the word in modern Greek and also the practice of Greek Christians). The inference of all the Scriptures about baptism indicated people from all Jerusalem went to John "and were baptized of him in Jordan, confessing their sins" (Matt. 3:6). "And Jesus, when he was baptized, went up straightway out of the water..." (Matt. 3:16). So "they went down both into the water, both Philip and the eunuch; and he baptized him. And when they were come up out of the water...." So baptism involved going down into the water, a burial in the water, resurrection from the water and coming up out of the water, just as it had been with Jesus and with others in the New Testament.

"The Spirit of the Lord caught away Philip...Philip was found at Azotus: and...preached in all the cities, till he came to Caesarea."

And the eunuch "went on his way rejoicing." Oh, thank God for hundreds of contacts where we have been able to win someone to Christ and they went away rejoicing while we went on to serve God somewhere else, and to meet in one glad day when Jesus comes to take away His own!

ACTS 9

VERSES 1, 2:

AND Saul, yet breathing out threatenings and slaughter against the disciples of the Lord, went unto the high priest,

2 And desired of him letters to Damascus to the synagogues, that if he found any of this way, whether they were men or women, he might bring them bound unto Jerusalem.

Saul, the Persecutor

Saul seems to have been the greatest persecutor of Christians thus far. The chief priest and the Sanhedrin were jealous for their official position and leadership over the people, but they were worldly, wicked men. They would stoop to bribing witnesses and other fraud to put down this religion and keep the power in their own hands (Matt. 26:59; Acts 6:11-14). On the other hand, young Saul was a dedicated Pharisee of the strictest sect (Acts 26:5). He was "taught according to the perfect manner of the law of the fathers, and was zealous toward God..." (Acts 22:3). Touching the righteousness of the law he was "blameless" (Phil. 3:6) as far as the unconverted man could be. Paul was not morally the wicked man that the high priest and Sadducees were, but he was a more ardent persecutor of Christians because of more heart loyalty to his Pharisee position.

He was a legalist, a moralist, and he was like his Jewish friends about whom he was inspired to write, "For they being ignorant of God's righteousness, and going about to establish their own righteousness, have not submitted themselves unto the righteousness of God" (Rom. 10:3). So with the fury of a fanatical religionist, Paul persecuted Christians. He "made havock of the church, entering into every house, and haling men and women committed them to prison" (Acts 8:3). He "persecuted this way unto the death, binding and delivering into prisons both men and women" (Acts 22:4). Sadly he says later, "I verily thought with myself, that I ought to do many things contrary to the name of Jesus of Nazareth. Which thing I also did in Jerusalem: and many of the saints did I shut up in prison, having received authority from the chief priests; and when they were put to death, I gave my voice against them. And I punished them oft in every synagogue, and compelled them to blaspheme; and being exceedingly mad against them..." (Acts 26:9-11).

Saul was consenting to the death of Stephen and felt himself guilty of that murder. And he always counted himself the chief of sinners, meant it that he "was before a blasphemer, and a persecutor, and injurious: but I obtained mercy, because I did it ignorantly in unbelief" (I Tim. 1:13). Notice Paul's persecution of others, that "I punished them oft in every synagogue...I persecuted them even unto strange cities" (Acts 26:11). So here in Acts 9:2 Saul took the aggressive, went to the high priest begging letters to Damascus for the synagogue there.

Note that Damascus is some two hundred miles away, and it is not in the province of Judaea. Evidently the Roman government allowed Jews in their own synagogues to maintain their normal government. The Roman government seemed to wisely succeed by making use of the local government setup in each province or country they conquered. So in most matters the Jews, through their synagogues, were allowed to rule their own people in matters of Jewish religion. It seems strange that in far-off cities like Damascus young Saul should want to hunt out Christians and have them arrested. But the high priest's authority is recognized in the synagogue, even in Damascus; so away he goes there to arrest Christians and "bring them bound unto Jerusalem."

———————

VERSES 3–8:

3 And as he journeyed, he came near Damascus: and suddenly there shined round about him a light from heaven:

4 And he fell to the earth, and heard a voice saying unto him, Saul, Saul, why persecutest thou me?

5 And he said, Who art thou, Lord? And the Lord said, I am Jesus whom thou persecutest: *it is* hard for thee to kick against the pricks.

6 And he trembling and astonished said, Lord, what wilt thou have me to do? And the Lord *said* unto him, Arise, and go into the city, and it shall be told thee what thou must do.

7 And the men which journeyed with him stood speechless, hearing a voice, but seeing no man.

8 And Saul arose from the earth; and when his eyes were opened, he saw no man: but they led him by the hand, and brought *him* into Damascus.

The Conversion of Saul

The conversion of Saul was dramatic. He tells the story of his conversion in Acts 22:1-16 and before Agrippa in Acts 26:9-18.

"Suddenly there shined round about him a light from heaven." It was "above the brightness of the sun, shining round about me and them which journeyed with me" (Acts 26:13). He was nearing Damascus and it was about noon (Acts 22:6). He and all with him fell to the earth (vs. 4; Acts 26:14). The men with him "saw indeed the light, and were afraid; but they heard not the voice of him that spake to me" (Acts 22:9). That is, they heard the sound, but only Paul understood the words. Dr. Scofield on this matter says, "Cf. Acts 22:9; 26:14. A contradiction has been imagined. The three statements should be taken together. The men heard the 'voice' as a sound (Gr. phone), but did not hear the 'voice' as articulating the words, 'Saul, Saul,' etc." That supernatural light blinded him for some three days. And when I could not see for the glory of that light, being led by the hand of them that were with me, I came into Damascus" (Acts 22:11). I wonder if after that Paul always had some weakness of the eyes as a reminder?

Then the voice from Heaven said, "Saul, Saul, why persecutest thou me?" Young Saul believed in the supernatural, he was a Pharisee. He was trying to serve the true God blamelessly. As soon as there was supernatural manifestation which he could not doubt, his heart was open. He said, "Who art thou, Lord?" And the answer came, "I am Jesus whom thou persecutest."

Had Saul had some agonizing doubts about all this persecution? Had he wondered if Jesus were truly the Messiah as claimed? Yes, he had! Ever since he had looked into the face of the dying Stephen there had been the nagging reminder of the glory of that innocent face, the testimony of that Spirit-filled man, dying so willingly for Jesus and saying that he could see Jesus standing at the right hand of God to receive him! Yes, like an oxgoad sticking him, a nagging conviction had been deepening, and young Saul could not get away from it. Although he was a fervent religionist reminding us of John Wesley and Luther before they were converted, there was some wicked pride, some selfwill, some glory in his own righteousness that had kept him away from Jesus. Now "he trembling and astonished said, Lord, what wilt thou have me to do?"

Here Paul was converted. The rebellion is over! He calls Jesus Lord. He willingly offers to do whatever the Lord Jesus commands! Paul is to go into the city of Damascus and there receive further instructions. Some of the Lord's instructions are not told here, but Paul did tell them before Agrippa in Acts 26:16-18:

> "But rise, and stand upon thy feet: for I have appeared unto thee for this purpose, to make thee a minister and a witness both of these things which thou hast seen, and of those things in the which I will appear unto thee; Delivering thee from the people, and from the Gentiles, un-

to whom now I send thee, To open their eyes, and to turn them from darkness to light, and from the power of Satan unto God, that they may receive forgiveness of sins, and inheritance among them which are sanctified by faith that is in me."

So blinded, humbled, but believing and surrendered, Saul of Tarsus becomes Paul the Christian. When Ananias comes to see him, he will call him "Brother Saul" (vs. 17), for he is now a Christian. He has trusted Christ.

So they led him by the hand to Damascus.

VERSES 9–17:

9 And he was three days without sight, and neither did eat nor drink.

10 ¶ And there was a certain disciple at Damascus, named Ananias; and to him said the Lord in a vision, Ananias. And he said, Behold, I *am here*, Lord.

11 And the Lord *said* unto him, Arise, and go into the street which is called Straight, and inquire in the house of Judas for *one* called Saul, of Tarsus: for, behold, he prayeth,

12 And hath seen in a vision a man named Ananias coming in, and putting *his* hand on him, that he might receive his sight.

13 Then Ananias answered, Lord, I have heard by many of this man, how much evil he hath done to thy saints at Jerusalem:

14 And here he hath authority from the chief priests to bind all that call on thy name.

15 But the Lord said unto him, Go thy way: for he is a chosen vessel unto me, to bear my name before the Gentiles, and kings, and the children of Israel:

16 For I will shew him how great things he must suffer for my name's sake.

17 And Ananias went his way, and entered into the house; and putting his hands on him said, Brother Saul, the Lord, *even* Jesus, that appeared unto thee in the way as thou camest, hath sent me, that thou mightest receive thy sight, and be filled with the Holy Ghost.

Saul Filled With the Spirit

Saul is now at peace with the Lord Jesus, but he will not eat. "He was three days without sight, and neither did eat nor drink." Ananias, a disciple at Damascus, is told, "Arise, and go into the street which is called Straight, and enquire in the house of Judas for one called Saul, of Tarsus: for, BEHOLD, HE PRAYETH." Paul was praying day and night for three days!

For what did he pray? It does not take three days and nights of praying to get saved. Paul had already surrendered to the Lord Jesus, he had already believed on Him and had surrendered his will and taken Him as Lord. He is "Brother Saul" when Ananias comes to him. But he is doubtless praying to have just what Stephen had. He wanted not only to be saved but as the Jews at Pentecost in Acts 2:38 were told not only the plan of salvation but how to receive the gift of the Spirit, as these New Testament Christians had, so Paul wanted what he had seen shining in the face of Stephen, what he had felt and heard in that Spirit-filled testimony of God's martyr! And when Ananias came to speak to him, he said, "The Lord, even Jesus, that appeared unto thee in the way as thou camest, hath sent me, that thou mightest receive thy sight, AND BE FILLED WITH THE HOLY GHOST." The three days and nights of fasting and prayer were the seeking of the new convert for the fullness of the Spirit.

In this Paul followed the plan clearly given by the Saviour in Luke 11:13--"...How much more shall your heavenly Father give the Holy Spirit to them that ask him?" And the word ask in the Greek is in the present tense, indicating continuous action. Jesus had commanded the apostles to "tarry ye in the city of Jerusalem, until ye be endued with power from on high" (Luke 24:49). And He had "commanded them that they should...wait for the promise of the Father, which, saith he, ye have heard of me. For John truly baptized with water; but ye shall be baptized with the Holy Ghost not many days hence" (Acts 1:4, 5).

John the Baptist had been filled with the Holy Ghost as a babe, after years of fervent prayer by his mother and father.

Jesus, after baptism, had prayed and the Holy Ghost came upon Him for His public ministry, but never a miracle or sermon before that!

Before Pentecost we are told of the twelve apostles, "these all continued with one accord in prayer and supplication, with the women, and Mary the mother of Jesus, and with his brethren" (Acts 1:14). And they were filled with the Spirit.

In Acts 4:31 we are told, "And when they had prayed, the place was shaken where they were assembled together; and they were all filled with the Holy Ghost...." And so here Saul, after three days and nights of prayer, has Ananias lay his hands upon him and he is filled with the Holy Spirit.

The narrow street called Straight is still in Damascus. Down under the accumulated layer of dirt and debris of nearly nineteen centuries is a house locally supposed to be the place where Ananias laid his hands upon Saul that he might receive his sight and be filled with the Holy Ghost.

Ananias was fearful at first. The tales of Saul's persecution of Christians had reached even to Damascus. But the Lord told Ananias, "For he is a chosen vessel unto me, to bear my name before the Gentiles, and kings, and the children of Israel: For I will shew him how great things he must suffer for my name's sake" (vss. 15, 16).

God has a way of telling other spiritually minded people when He calls a preacher so that often, when a man finds the call clear and surrenders to it, he finds that his mother or father or a godly preacher or others have already known for some time that he would be a minister of the Gospel! So God reveals to Ananias His plan for Paul. Paul is appointed to preach throughout the Roman Empire, to come before kings and to suffer greatly!

VERSES 18–25:

18 And immediately there fell from his eyes as it had been scales: and he received sight forthwith, and arose, and was baptized.

19 And when he had received meat, he was strengthened. Then was Saul certain days with the disciples which were at Damascus.

20 And straightway he preached Christ in the synagogues, that he is the Son of God.

21 But all that heard *him* were amazed, and said; Is not this he that destroyed them which called on this name in Jerusalem, and came hither for that intent, that he might bring them bound unto the chief priests?

22 But Saul increased the more in strength, and confounded the Jews which dwelt at Damascus, proving that this is very Christ.

23 ¶ And after that many days were fulfilled, the Jews took counsel to kill him:

24 But their laying wait was known of Saul. And they watched the gates day and night to kill him.

25 Then the disciples took him by night, and let *him* down by the wall in a basket.

The Spirit-Filled Paul Begins Preaching

Immediately Paul received his sight "and arose, and was baptized." Notice that baptism in the New Testament is a public profession of faith in Christ, and should follow one's conversion or salvation very soon. But properly baptism in New Testament times never came until one claimed to have trusted Christ and had forgiveness of sins. Then he ate after three days of fasting, and was strengthened.

And now "straightway he preached Christ in the synagogues, that he is the Son of God." It was inevitable that he should witness for Christ after being filled with the Holy Spirit.

It was foretold of John the Baptist that "he shall be filled with the Holy Ghost, even from his mother's womb. And many of the children of Israel shall he turn to the Lord their God" (Luke 1:15, 16). Witnessing and soul winning follow the fullness of the Spirit.

In Acts 2:4, "And they were all filled with the Holy Ghost, and began to speak..." and three thousand were saved! In Acts 4:8 "Peter, filled with the Holy Ghost, said...." Witnessing goes with the fullness of the Spirit.

In Acts 4:31, "And when they had prayed, the place was shaken where they were assembled together; and they were all filled with the Holy Ghost, and they spake the word of God with boldness." And many were saved. Stephen "full of the Holy Ghost, looked up...And said..." (Acts 7:55, 56). Later it is said about Barnabas, "For he was a good man, and full of the Holy Ghost and of faith: and much people was added unto the Lord" (Acts 11:24). It was even prophesied in Joel 2:28-30 about the Christians at Pentecost and following in these last days, and quoted by Peter at Pentecost, "I will pour out of my Spirit upon all flesh: and your sons and your daughters shall prophesy...And on my servants and on my handmaidens I will pour out in those days of my Spirit; and they shall prophesy" (Acts 2:17, 18). The fullness of the Spirit is given for witnessing, as Acts 1:8 plainly says. "Ye shall receive power, after that the Holy Ghost is come upon you: and ye shall be witnesses unto me...." So Paul, filled with the Spirit, must witness and does.

What a sensation! People were amazed that the persecutor has become a preacher! Speaking in the power of the Holy Spirit, this cultivated, scholarly, fervent young preacher filled with the Spirit "increased the more in strength, and confounded the Jews...proving that this is very Christ." Damascus was a Gentile city, but with many Jews, and Saul is still dealing only with Jews.

Note that being filled with the Spirit and the aggressive soul-winning witness which goes with that anointing leads to persecution. As with Jesus at Nazareth in Luke 4:16-29, as with Peter and John in Acts 4:1-4, and with all the apostles in Acts 5:17-33, and as with Deacon Stephen in Acts 7:54, the fullness of the Spirit and the burning, convicting testimony that followed led to persecution, so now they seek to kill Paul. The preacher raised such a commotion among the Jews that the Gentile governor under Aretas the king garrisoned the city with soldiers, trying to arrest Paul (II Cor. 11:32)! But he was let down through a window from the wall and escaped, and today in the ancient wall of Damascus a window is shown as a traditional place for this escape.

VERSES 26–29:

26 And when Saul was come to Jerusalem, he assayed to join himself to the disciples: but they were all afraid of him, and believed not that he was a disciple.

27 But Barnabas took him, and brought *him* to the apostles, and declared unto them how he had seen the Lord in the way, and that he had spoken to him, and how he had preached boldly at Damascus in the name of Jesus.

28 And he was with them coming in and going out at Jerusalem.

29 And he spake boldly in the name of the Lord Jesus, and disputed against the Grecians: but they went about to slay him.

New-convert Paul Back at Jerusalem

Saul left Jerusalem a fiery persecutor: he had returned a humble Christian seeking the fellowship of those whom he had hated. "He assayed to join himself to the disciples." Good old Barnabas, son of consolation, sought out the young man, learned the story of his conversion, recommended him to the apostles, and so Paul was received.

It seems that Saul sought and was received as a regular member of the congregation at Jerusalem.

Hear, too, the Spirit-filled Paul speak with such boldness that "they went about to slay him." That will be a regular pattern in the life of Paul. He will dispute, he will have controversy, he will be bold in his attack on sin and he will land in jail or have attempts on his life nearly everywhere he goes!

Oh, we preachers who never "dispute" and are never hated and persecuted, are not like the Apostle Paul!

VERSES 30, 31:

30 *Which* when the brethren knew, they brought him down to Cesarea, and sent him forth to Tarsus.

31 Then had the churches rest throughout all Judea and Galilee and Samaria, and were edified; and walking in the fear of the Lord, and in the comfort of the Holy Ghost, were multiplied.

Paul Returns to Tarsus

Here Paul returns to his old home town of Tarsus and there he will stay until Acts 11:25, "Then departed Barnabas to Tarsus, for to seek Saul," and helped to push the young preacher in the ministry.

But with Saul converted, the great persecution subsides. "Then had the churches rest throughout all Judaea and Galilee and Samaria...." Evidently those scattered abroad from Jerusalem (Acts 8:4) have won souls and made churches and gathered congregations of Christians, local churches throughout "all Judaea and Galilee and Samaria." Philip had the great revival in Samaria. Peter and John had preached in villages of Samaria (Acts 8:25). Paul had helped Ananias and others win souls in Damascus. Everywhere that the Gospel went, churches were springing up, and disciples, "walking in the fear of the Lord, and in the comfort of the Holy Ghost, were multiplied."

VERSES 32–35:

32 ¶ And it came to pass, as Peter passed throughout all *quarters*, he came down also to the saints which dwelt at Lydda.

33 And there he found a certain man named Eneas, which had kept his bed eight years, and was sick of the palsy.

34 And Peter said unto him, Eneas, Jesus Christ maketh thee whole: arise, and make thy bed. And he arose immediately.

35 And all that dwelt at Lydda and Saron saw him, and turned to the Lord.

Peter and the Healing of Aeneas

Peter is the outstanding figure in the book of Acts in the first six chapters. Even yet he is the principal voice among the apostles. Peter now goes among the Christians "throughout all quarters." The hand of God is upon Peter mightily, and he sees the man bedfast for eight years. I suppose this means he was paralyzed. This case is like that of the man brought to Jesus in Matthew 9:2. But Jesus had healed such a man. Peter has gone in the power of the same Spirit and is preaching the same Jesus. Jesus is raised from the dead and still has power on earth to heal and forgive sins. So "Peter said unto him, Aeneas, Jesus Christ maketh thee whole: arise, and make thy bed."

We have no doubt that Peter here perceived by the Spirit that the man would have faith. The man who could not rise, did arise. That which is impossible became possible.

Such a dramatic answer to prayer and evidence of the power of Jesus Christ resulted so that "all that dwelt at Lydda and Saron saw him, and turned to the Lord." Here, and in the case of the healing of the lame man at the temple in Acts 3, the healing was used to convince doubters and to turn many to the Lord.

VERSES 36–43:

36 ¶ Now there was at Joppa a certain disciple named Tabitha, which by interpretation is called Dorcas: this woman was full of

good works and almsdeeds which she did.

37 And it came to pass in those days, that she was sick, and died: whom when they had washed, they laid *her* in an upper chamber.

38 And forasmuch as Lydda was nigh to Joppa, and the disciples had heard that Peter was there, they sent unto him two men, desiring *him* that he would not delay to come to them.

39 Then Peter arose and went with them. When he was come, they brought him into the upper chamber: and all the widows stood by him weeping, and shewing the coats and garments which Dorcas made, while she was with them.

40 But Peter put them all forth, and kneeled down, and prayed; and turning *him* to the body said, Tabitha, arise. And she opened her eyes: and when she saw Peter, she sat up.

41 And he gave her *his* hand, and lifted her up; and when he had called the saints and widows, he presented her alive.

42 And it was known throughout all Joppa; and many believed in the Lord.

43 And it came to pass, that he tarried many days in Joppa with one Simon a tanner.

Tabitha Raised From the Dead

We would be thoughtless and unspiritual if we did not see in the healings and in this raising from the dead of Tabitha a mark of the deep compassion which God's people have for those in trouble. The compassion of the Lord Jesus is given to His prophets and people. As Jesus had "compassion on the multitude," so Peter saw the grief of all these people who were bereft by the death of Dorcas. I do not suppose that Dorcas would have preferred to come back from Heaven unless to be of more service to others. Certainly hundreds were comforted personally, and thousands of others were greatly encouraged at this evidence of God's blessing.

In the wonderful healing of the lame man in the temple, and in the healing of Aeneas, Peter seemed to have taken the initiative and he boldly announced to each one that they were to be made well. But in the case of Tabitha, the disciples sent two men "desiring him that he would not delay to come to them."

What wrestlings of soul must Peter have had as he shut

the door, and put everybody out! Then he kneeled down and prayed. Had these troubled people been right to send for Peter? Was it God's will to raise this good woman from the dead? God gave him faith and Peter turned to the body and said, "Tabitha, arise." So Peter had seen Jesus deal with the twelve-year-old daughter of Jairus, ruler of the synagogue, who had died. Jesus had "suffered no man to go in, save Peter, and James, and John, and the father and the mother of the maiden" (Luke 8:51), but had "put them all out." Then He took the maiden by the hand and called, "Maid, arise." So now Peter turned to the bed and bade Tabitha (or Dorcas) rise, and she did! The ministry of Jesus in the power of the Holy Spirit is reproduced in the ministry of Spirit-filled apostles and witnesses! As far as we know, no other apostle save Paul (Acts 20:9, 10) raised the dead, yet it was essential that the world should know that whenever there is need, we can have the power and do the work which Jesus did, as He promised in John 14:12, "He that believeth on me, the works that I do shall he do also; and greater works than these shall he do; because I go unto my Father." And again, "As my Father hath sent me, even so send I you" (John 20:21). And "as thou hast sent me into the world, even so have I also sent them into the world" (John 17:18).

What rejoicing when Peter lifted her up and called in the saints and widows and presented their saintly benefactress alive! "And it was known throughout all Joppa; and many believed in the Lord." Again, miraculous demonstration had been used of God to authenticate the Gospel and save souls. And now Peter stays with Simon the tanner at Joppa and is about to experience one of the high, great crises of his life and be sent to Gentiles.

ACTS 10

VERSES 1-6:

THERE was a certain man in Cesarea called Cornelius, a centurion of the band called the Italian *band,*

2 *A* devout *man,* and one that feared God with all his house, which gave much alms to the people, and prayed to God always.

3 He saw in a vision evidently, about the ninth hour of the day, an angel of God coming in to him, and saying unto him, Cornelius.

4 And when he looked on him, he was afraid, and said, What is it, Lord? And he said unto him, Thy prayers and thine alms are come up for a memorial before God.

5 And now send men to Joppa, and call for *one* Simon, whose surname is Peter:

6 He lodgeth with one Simon a tanner, whose house is by the sea side: he shall tell thee what thou oughtest to do.

Cornelius' Vision

Here is a remarkable event treated quite in detail in this chapter, of a heathen man who sought God, and of miraculous measures God took to see that he heard the Gospel and was saved.

Cornelius was a centurion (or officer, usually captain of a hundred men) in the group of Roman soldiers called the Italian band. He was "devout": not a Christian, but evidently prayerful, one whom we would call "God fearing." He gave much alms, he prayed continually. He wanted to do right, wanted to know God. To such a man God sent an angel. Cornelius was a righteous man by human standards, trying to do right, trying to please God, trying to help people. And it is evident that his was not simply a matter of outward religious conformity to certain rites and standards, like the Pharisees, but a heartfelt desire for God and the right. He "prayed to God always." And so he had turned "all his house" toward God and there was even "a devout soldier of them that waited on him continually" influenced by his prayerful seeking after God and righteousness.

It is probable that Cornelius knew nothing of the Old Testament. He was not a Jew, not a Jewish proselyte, like the Ethiopian eunuch in chapter 8. He was from Italy, probably spoke the Latin, possibly spoke also to some degree the Aramaic of the people about him. Or he may have spoken the common people's Greek which had become almost a world language, the language in which Paul preached in all his journeys and the language in which the New Testament was written. He was stationed at Caesarea, not Jerusalem. So probably he had no knowledge of God from the Old Testament Scriptures.

Whence then his morality, his prayerfulness, his God fearing, his devoutness? All men have some of God's law written in their hearts and consciences. "For when the Gentiles, which have not the law, do by nature the things contained in the law, these, having not the law, are a law unto themselves: Which shew the work of the law written in their hearts, their conscience also bearing witness, and their thoughts the mean while accusing or else excusing one another" (Rom. 2:14, 15). So in every heathen heart which does not intentionally stifle and pervert it, the conscience tells right from wrong: he knows it is wrong to steal, to cheat, to blaspheme God.

It is somewhat in this sense that Jesus Christ is "the true Light, which lighteth every man that cometh into the world" (John 1:9). Certainly Jesus promised that He, lifted up and dying on the cross, "will draw all men unto me" (John 12:32). And Jesus promised, "I am the Light of the world," not a light of only those who heard the Gospel, but of those who were given divine light through the conscience. And He said, "He that followeth me shall not walk in darkness, but shall have the light of life" (John 8:12). Evidently God has promised here that light will be given to all who seek it and follow it.

Jesus said, "Verily, verily, I say unto you, If a man keep my saying, he shall never see death" (John 8:51). That does not teach salvation by works nor by religious acts or rites. But it means that those who from the heart seek God and seek to please God with what light they have will be given the Gospel, will have opportunity to trust Christ and "shall never see death." There is no salvation without the Gospel, but God is committed that those who follow the light they have shall have more light, even the light of the Gospel, and salvation.

Here is a great principle of God's nature and God's dealing with men. In John 7:17 Jesus said, "If any man will do his will [or a better translation, if any man chooses and wills to do his will] , he shall know of the doctrine, whether it be of God, or whether I speak of myself." That promise was true of the Pharisees who denied Christ's deity. But it would also be true of the heathen who sought to know the true God and God's way of salvation.

Is not this truth beautifully given in James 4:6-10? "But he giveth more grace." Anywhere grace finds an open heart, God gives more grace (vs. 6). And "God resisteth the proud, but giveth grace to the humble." And again He promises, "Draw nigh to God, and he will draw nigh to you." There never was a heart that honestly sought God, wanted Him, wanted righteousness, longed for fellowship, but got it (vs. 8)! Again verse 10 says, "Humble yourselves in the sight of the Lord, and he shall lift you up." God could not, in view of these promises and in view of His righteous nature and infinite grace, ignore the prayers of Cornelius who sought Him sincerely and continually.

Again Hosea 6:3 says, "Then shall we know, if we follow on to know the Lord...." How well Proverbs 8:17 says, "Those that seek me early shall find me." And isn't this true, that God is available to all who seek Him, and that He will give more light to those who seek more light, promised in Matthew 7:7 and 8? "Ask, and it shall be given you; seek, and ye shall find; knock, and it shall be opened unto you: For every one that asketh receiveth; and he that seeketh findeth; and to him that knocketh it shall be opened."

Here the continuing meaning of the verbs is involved in the present tense. The honest, persistently seeking heart finds God! So God was under obligation to give him more light.

God then pays attention to thoughts and intents of the heart of unregenerate men everywhere, the heathen savage as well as the civilized man. He heard the prayer of those heathen sailors on the ship that Jonah took when the great storm arose (Jonah 1:14-16).

Probably God saw some seeking in the heart of Naaman the Syrian and brought it about that he should go to Israel and meet the Prophet Elisha and learn to trust the true God, as he did (II Kings 5:1-19). There are indications that possibly the Pharaoh who exalted Joseph and possibly King Nebuchadnezzar and Cyrus all may have sought and found the Lord, heathen men as they were, and that because of their seeking hearts, God sent to them someone who could tell them of the true God. Who knows but that Adoniram Judson was sent to Burma instead of India as he had intended because of some seeking heart to whom God must send the Gospel. Who knows all the circumstances controlled by God that leads one man to find a tract in a bus depot or by the roadside (as we have known again and again to take place) instead of another?

Why Are Heathen People, Without the Gospel, Lost?

What about the millions of heathen people who never heard the Gospel? It is clear that no one is ever saved but by the Gospel of Christ. "No man cometh unto the Father, but by me" (John 14:6), and that "there is none other name under heaven given among men, whereby we must be saved" (Acts 4:12). Possibly some of those lost heathen people could be won to Christ if the Gospel were powerfully preached to them, but certain it is that no man ever goes to Hell who seeks God, who wants God's mercy and forgiveness, whose heart calls on God for mercy. For He is "not willing that any should perish, but that all should come to repentance" (II Pet. 3:9). And "whosoever shall call upon the name of the Lord shall be saved" (Rom. 10:13).

Heathen men are lost, not because they did not hear the Gospel, but because they are sinners who deserve to be lost, just as others who do hear the Gospel and do not turn to Christ are lost because they are sinners.

The very fact of heathendom is itself an indication that men have turned away from what light they had. Once the whole race, Noah's sons and their families, knew God. But soon millions went into heathen darkness and idolatry, we are told in Romans, chapter 1. They went against many visible evidences of a true God, but "when they knew God, they glorified him not as God, neither were thankful; but became vain in their imaginations, and their foolish heart was darkened" (Rom. 1:21). They "are without excuse," we are told. And "they did not like to retain God in their knowledge." So we are told that "God gave them up to uncleanness," and "God gave them up unto vile affections," and "God gave them over to a reprobate mind." The heathen world deliberately went away from the light and became heathen. Generally men who stay in spiritual darkness stay in because of sin and the love of sin. God delights to reveal Himself to those who seek Him with honest hearts.

However, remember, there is no salvation without the Gospel. Though it take a miracle and a visit from an angel from Heaven, they must have someone to tell them how to be saved!

Perhaps the angel said to Cornelius, "I wish I could tell you how to be saved but I have never been a sinner, never been regenerated, and God has never given me the right to tell it. You must get God's man to tell you." And so Cor-

nelius was told where to send for Simon Peter, at the house
of Simon the tanner in Joppa! God makes circumstances and
revelation work together to save those who want mercy.
Those who hunger and thirst after righteousness shall be
filled.

VERSES 7, 8:

7 And when the angel which spake unto Cornelius was departed, he called two of his household servants, and a devout soldier of them that waited on him continually;

8 And when he had declared all *these* things unto them, he sent them to Joppa.

Cornelius Sends for Peter

Cornelius was not only "a devout man, and one that
feared God" (vs. 2), but he led all of his house, his kindred,
and evidently the servants and some of the soldiers under
him, to fear God and seek to know God and serve Him. For
these two household servants seem to understand the matter
and the soldier is "a devout soldier."

To these three, "he had declared all these things unto
them," and they departed for Joppa. Caesarea, where
Cornelius was stationed, is on the seacoast, on the coast
of the Mediterranean, and some thirty miles south on the
seacoast also was Joppa. Caesarea is now only a ruin, but
Joppa is modern Jaffa, immediately adjacent to the modern
Tel Aviv. Joppa was a seaport even in Jonah's day (Jonah
1:3). Caesarea had in New Testament times an important
man-made harbor.

The two servants and the soldier must have departed immediately after "the ninth hour" mentioned in verse 3, that
is, after midafternoon, after three p. m. They went speedily, for about noon the next day "the sixth hour" (vs. 9),
they drew near Joppa. They probably walked that distance
in eight or nine hours, spending the night somewhere en

route. A team of horses to a farm wagon can walk about thirty-five miles in a day; oxen or donkeys would be slower.

VERSES 9-16:

9 ¶ On the morrow, as they went on their journey, and drew nigh unto the city, Peter went up upon the housetop to pray about the sixth hour:

10 And he became very hungry, and would have eaten: but while they made ready, he fell into a trance,

11 And saw heaven opened, and a certain vessel descending unto him, as it had been a great sheet knit at the four corners, and let down to the earth:

12 Wherein were all manner of fourfooted beasts of the earth, and wild beasts, and creeping things, and fowls of the air.

13 And there came a voice to him, Rise, Peter; kill, and eat.

14 But Peter said, Not so, Lord; for I have never eaten any thing that is common or unclean.

15 And the voice *spake* unto him again the second time, What God hath cleansed, *that* call not thou common.

16 This was done thrice: and the vessel was received up again into heaven.

Peter's Remarkable Vision

With a remarkable vision three times repeated, the Lord must shake Peter loose from his Jewish background of ceremonial law. It seems strange that up till this time none of the apostles as far as we know, and perhaps no one else, had deliberately gone among the Gentiles to preach the Gospel. And there is no evidence that they had made any plans to do so!

This is strange for the following reasons.

1. In the Great Commission Jesus had been as plain as one possibly could be in the command to take the Gospel "to all the world" and "to every creature" and "to all nations" and to "the uttermost part of the earth" (Mark 16:15; Matt. 28:19, 20; Acts 1:8; Luke 24:47). The command, so often repeated and so emphasized as the one principal and central

instruction of the Saviour, included Gentiles as well as Jews, the whole world, every nation, every creature! They could hardly have misunderstood it! And yet their minds were held in a strait jacket of custom which was hard to break.

2. The Lord Jesus Himself had called particular attention to the Samaritans in His ministry. He preached at Sychar and won many, although "the Jews have no dealings with the Samaritans," the woman said, and although the apostles themselves were astonished that He should talk to her and they had no thought of speaking to the other Samaritans until Jesus reprimanded them that they should "lift up your eyes" to see a harvest already white. Jesus had told the parable of the good Samaritan (Luke 10:30-37). He called particular attention to the Samaritan leper healed, who of the ten was the only one to return to give thanks (Luke 17:11-19). Although Samaritans were mixed blood, part Jewish, and had some of the Jewish Scriptures and worshipped the true God, they had a somewhat perverted religion, they were despised by the Jews. But Jesus had put enough emphasis on evangelizing the Samaritans that Philip and then Peter and John had preached in Samaria and many had been saved (Acts 8:5-25).

3. Jesus' extended dealing with the Syrophenician woman in Mark 7:24-30 and Matthew 15:21-28 was evidently intended to show the disciples that the Gospel and the compassion of Christ were just as much meant for Gentiles as for Jews.

4. It has been plainly promised in the great covenant with Abraham that "in thee shall all families of the earth be blessed" (Gen. 12:3). That blessing was to come through Christ, Abraham's Seed. In the prophesied restoration of the Davidic kingdom under Christ the "Branch," Isaiah 11:10 had said, "To it shall the Gentiles seek: and his rest shall be glorious." See also Isaiah 42:1, "He shall bring forth judgment to the Gentiles," and 42:6, "...a light of the

Gentiles," and Isaiah 60:3, "And the Gentiles shall come to thy light."

5. Saul, at his conversion, had been announced to Ananias as "a chosen vessel unto me, to bear my name before the Gentiles" (Acts 9:15). Paul understood he was then and there called to preach to the Gentiles (Acts 26:17). But neither Paul nor others had yet gone to the Gentiles.

Philip had been led of the Spirit to win the Ethiopian eunuch, but that eunuch, we suppose, was a Jewish proselyte of Gentile blood, but already of Jewish faith, probably one who had some of the Scriptures and had come to the temple to worship. He was doubtless circumcised and so officially counted a Jew.

The Outward Forms of Worship Tend to Become More Important to Us Than Heart Worship and Obedience

Unsaved people often have "a form of godliness, but denying the power thereof" (II Tim. 3:5). So it was with many of the Pharisees in Christ's time whom He addressed again and again, "Woe unto you, scribes and Pharisees, hypocrites!" (Matt. 23:13-33). They made proselytes who were still children of Hell. Jesus twice in that chapter, called them "blind guides," and twice, "Ye fools and blind," and once, "Thou blind Pharisee." They paid tithe down to the slightest detail, but neglected the weightier matters, judgment, mercy and faith! They made clean the outside of the cup and platter, but left the inside full of extortion and excess. They outwardly appeared righteous, but inwardly they were full of hypocrisy and iniquity. Even today many a man goes through formal ceremonies in a church, ceremonies of confirmation, or prayer of general confession, or confession to a priest, or attending mass, who hope to obtain favor by the outward form but who have no heart for repentance and faith. So Cain offered sacrifices with a wicked, unrepentant heart.

But even in saved men, good men, spiritual men, there is a constant tendency to put too much emphasis on the externals of religion, on forms, ceremonies, buildings and organizations.

These Jews had been clearly taught in the Old Testament not to intermarry with heathen people and to avoid their idolatry (Josh. 23:12, 13; Deut. 7:1-4). They remembered how God had bidden them to destroy the Amorites and Canaanites when Joshua led them into conquering the land of Canaan (Josh. 11:19, 20). And God had commanded King Saul to utterly destroy the Amalekites who had gone so far into idolatry and sin (I Sam. 15:1-3). Most Gentiles were idolaters, so Jews had come to despise all Gentiles for thinking of themselves not only as the chosen race, but as inherently children of God. So there was a built-in antipathy to Gentiles which made even these good Christians loathe to go among them to preach the Gospel!

They knew the command of Jesus, but they had not in their own minds reconciled with that command their mores and customs, built in from childhood. It is often hard to differentiate between manners and morals; so instead of hating idolatry of itself, the Jews came to hate Gentiles. I knew a Jew trained as a rabbi, with eight years in the school of the Talmud, who was wonderfully converted. But long after he knew that Christ was the end of the law, he could not bring himself to eat pork or even beans which had been seasoned with pork, and instinctively reacted to seize his coat when it was laid on a bed on which a young mother, ceremonially unclean to a Jew, had reclined.

And so many a Christian who thinks of the Lord's Day, Sunday, as the Sabbath and measures it by ceremonial commands of the Old Testament, has just as deep convictions about this matter of his custom and resents what he calls "Sabbath breaking" by those who cook a meal on Sunday or travel or do work.

You say that he is thoroughly sincere in his conviction?

Yes, and so were these New Testament Jews, converted, born-again, godly, spiritual men, sincere in their instinctive feeling that they must keep the law of Moses. See how the Christian Jews at Jerusalem rebuked Peter saying, "Thou wentest in to men uncircumcised, and didst eat with them" (Acts 11:3).

See in Acts 15 how there must be a major conference of all the apostles and elders at Jerusalem to determine whether or not Gentile Christians must be circumcised and keep the law of Moses (Acts 15:1-29)! And even then, the Christian Jews were so sensitive that, to avoid offense, Gentile converts were commanded to "abstain from meats offered to idols, and from blood, and from things strangled..." (Acts 15:29).

And even Peter himself did not get this matter settled thoroughly in Acts 10. At least he had sympathy with the Judaizing Christians, and Paul had to rebuke him at Antioch. "For before that certain came from James, he did eat with the Gentiles: but when they were come, he withdrew and separated himself, fearing them which were of the circumcision" (Gal. 2:11, 12).

Nor was Paul the apostle at once freed from this Jewish prejudice, although he was from the day of his conversion sent to be an apostle to the Gentiles! In Acts 18:18 Paul "had a vow," a Jewish vow and he said, "I must by all means keep this feast that cometh in Jerusalem" (Acts 18:21). At Tyre, Paul en route to Jerusalem found some disciples "who said to Paul through the Spirit, that he should not go up to Jerusalem" (Acts 21:4). But Paul was determined. He was still in his heart a Jew, longed for the temple, the feasts, the ceremonies.

Agabus, God's prophet, bound Paul with his own girdle and said, "Thus saith the Holy Ghost, So shall the Jews at Jerusalem bind the man that owneth this girdle, and shall deliver him into the hands of the Gentiles" (Acts 21:10, 11). But Paul would not hear. So in Acts 21:18-26 Paul yielded to

these Judaizers, believers who were "all zealous of the
law" (Acts 21:20). And trying to counteract the fact that
they had heard that Paul taught people "that they ought not to
circumcise their children, neither to walk after the customs" (Acts 21:21), Paul was persuaded to enter with four
men who had a vow|, help pay the charges, shave their
heads, etc., in order to prove that he also walked orderly,
as they said, "and keepest the law" (vs. 24). Paul had gone
to the temple to pray and in a trance heard the Lord say,
"Make haste, and get thee quickly out of Jerusalem: for
they will not receive thy testimony concerning me" (Acts
22:18). But Paul protested and continued some seven days
and was arrested, imprisoned and sent to Rome!

Paul knew perfectly that the ceremonial law was finished,
that the ordinances of the ceremonies were nailed to the
cross and blotted out, and that they were simply "a shadow
of things to come; but the body is of Christ," as he himself
was inspired to write in Colossians 2:14-17. But the lifetime customs and preferences were so ingrained in his nature that he found it difficult to ignore them or leave them
alone.

This may remind us why it was necessary that the book of
Hebrews should be written, should be addressed to the Hebrews and before the destruction of Jerusalem, in order to
show them so emphatically that they did not need the priests
in the temple or the high priest since we had such a High
Priest in Jesus; that we did not need the temple at Jerusalem
since we have a temple in Heaven and since every Christian's body is a temple of the Holy Spirit; that we needed no
more sacrifices since Jesus Christ had been offered once
for all and had ended forever the offerings and sacrifices.

So Peter must be so thoroughly pressed to follow the
commands he had already received to carry the Gospel to
Gentiles. Even James, who was somewhat the occasion of
Peter's compromise in Galatians 2:11 and 12, knew that it

was prophesied that Gentiles should hear the Gospel as he said, quoting from the Old Testament in Acts 15:16-18.

And all of us should beware lest we likewise be sinful and blinded. Some call a church auditorium a "sanctuary." It is not. The only temple of God on earth is now the body of a Christian. God does not dwell in church houses. The home of any Christian may be as sacred as any church building. Church buildings, organs, stained glass windows, Gothic arches, statues, candles, chants, crucifixes--they had none of them in New Testament times! The place to worship God is "neither in this mountain, nor yet at Jerusalem," but those who worship God must worship Him in spirit and truth (John 4:21-24). The church house is not a temple, but simply a convenient meeting place. Where the preacher stands is not an altar, but simply a pulpit for preaching. The preacher is not a priest except in the same sense as every believer is a priest (I Pet. 2:5, 9). Baptism and the Lord's Supper are simply reminders, object lessons. They are not sacraments, they have no saving power. Your denomination may have been used of God, but it is not the bride of Christ, His body, including all the saved. Let us beware lest we think too much of outward incidentals and too little of the great spiritual essentials. Your denominational program is not necessarily the program of Christ or not exclusively that.

Jewish Dietary Laws Not Binding on New Testament Christians

When the voice came to Peter saying, "Rise, Peter; kill, and eat" of those four-footed beasts, wild beasts and creeping things and fowls of the air (vss. 12, 13), that command violated the dietary laws given the Jews in Leviticus, chapter 11. Of course a Jew, until the ceremonial law was fulfilled in the coming of Christ, should keep those ceremonies. But they were never a part of salvation nor the way to salvation. All the ceremonial laws were simply "a shadow of things to come; but the body is of Christ" (Col. 2:17).

Circumcision pictured circumcision of heart at the new birth. The Jewish weekly Sabbath pictured the rest in Heaven of one who would live perfectly and keep all the law blameless. But the passover Sabbath which began with eating the passover lamb whose blood had already been shed, pictured the blessed peace and Sabbath of heart which a Christian enters into when he trusts Christ. And then the Sabbath following the feast of unleaven bread pictures the eternal rest inherited by those who have taken Christ, the Passover. So the ceremonial dietary law was to ingrain in the Jewish people the idea of separation from evil and sin, just as in Deuteronomy 22:9-11 they were not to sow their vineyard with divers seeds, not to plough with an ox and ass together, not to wear a garment of divers sorts as of woolen and linen together. So every Jew knew that an idolatrous Gentile might eat pork but he, the Jew, should not, and so with other beasts.

However, that handwriting of ordinances was all nailed to the cross and so Paul could write to Christians, whether Gentiles or Jews, whether at Colosse or in our town, "Let no man therefore judge you in meat, or in drink, or in respect of an holyday, or of the new moon, or of the Sabbath days: Which are a shadow of things to come; but the body is of Christ" (Col. 2:16, 17). Now Paul could remind Peter that only seducing spirits and doctrines of devils would come "commanding to abstain from meats, which God hath created to be received with thanksgiving of them which believe and know the truth. For every creature of God is good, and nothing to be refused, if it be received with thanksgiving: For it is sanctified by the word of God and prayer" (I Tim. 4:3-5). Christians ought to be moderate in their eating and care for health. But there is no spiritual reason why beef roast is better than ham. And now no Christian should allow himself to be judged by the ceremonial law, whether about diet or Sabbath or other holy days.

Some intimation of the ceremonial meaning of animals used in sacrifices were given long before the Mosaic law. Abel and Noah knew to offer lambs for sacrifice. Noah knew the difference between clean and unclean beasts. Even God in killing innocent animals to make garments of skin for Adam and Eve, intimated some blessed lesson of the coming Lamb of God and the robe of His righteousness which would cover trusting sinners. But those ceremonies, which are never more than spiritual object lessons, are no longer fitting, no longer commanded.

It is noteworthy that this revelation to Peter came when he "went up upon the housetop to pray" (vs. 9). Such a revolutionary change in opinion and custom could not have been made with Peter had he not been earnestly seeking the Lord's will. How many wonderful things come as people wait upon God in prayer! So Peter and James and John, who were willing to trek up the stiff mountain trail to pray (Luke 9:28, 29), saw the marvelous transfiguration of Jesus which the other disciples who did not go to pray missed.

We wonder, did Peter after this marvelous revelation circumcise his own baby boy, or encourage other Christian Jews to circumcise their little sons? Did he keep the Jewish Sabbath? Probably as a way of life he did. It was attractive and familiar and dear, even after he was freed from the responsibility to do so. And this may have been one reason why he was susceptible to the temptation of compromise in Galatians 2:11-14.

VERSES 17–23:

17 Now while Peter doubted in himself what this vision which he had seen should mean, behold, the men which were sent from Cornelius had made inquiry for Simon's house, and stood before the gate,

18 And called, and asked whether Simon, which was surnamed Peter, were lodged there.

19 ¶ While Peter thought on the vision, the Spirit said unto him, Behold, three men seek thee.

20 Arise therefore, and get thee down, and go with them, doubting nothing: for I have sent them.

21 Then Peter went down to the men which were sent unto him from Cornelius; and said, Behold, I am he whom ye seek: what is the cause wherefore ye are come?

22 And they said, Cornelius the centurion, a just man, and one that feareth God, and of good report among all the nation of the Jews, was warned from God by a holy angel to send for thee into his house, and to hear words of thee.

23 Then called he them in, and lodged *them*. And on the morrow Peter went away with them, and certain brethren from Joppa accompanied him.

Peter Has Clear Revelation to Go to Cornelius With the Gospel

It is wonderful how God works at both ends of the line. He prepares Cornelius to hear Peter's preaching; he prepares Peter to go to a Gentile which he had never before done. So God had prepared the Ethiopian eunuch, had him reading Isaiah 53 when he brought Philip the evangelist to preach to him in Acts 8.

Christians can have clear leading as to duty. One of the dearest promises about the Holy Spirit is that He is to be our guide and teacher. "He shall teach you all things, and bring all things to your remembrance, whatsoever I have said unto you," Jesus said in John 14:26. "He shall testify of me," Jesus said in John 15:26. He will guide you into all truth, shall reveal the will of God and glorify Christ, Jesus said in John 16:13 and 14. Blessed is the Christian who waits on God for light and leading! How sad if Peter had not gone up on the housetop to pray, and so have found the clear leading of God! It may even be that Peter was asking God, "What is the next step?" Or, "Where now shall I go with the Gospel?" At any rate, the Holy Spirit led clearly.

So Jesus, filled with the Spirit, was led "and he must needs go through Samaria" (John 4:4). And there God had at the well where He sat at noon the woman of Sychar ready to receive the Gospel! So the Apostle Paul and his party, earnestly seeking leadership from God as to where they should minister, "were forbidden of the Holy Ghost to preach the word in Asia," and would have gone to Bithynia, "but the Spirit suffered them not." And then a vision appeared to Paul and a man calling, "Come over into Macedonia, and help us." And so they went "assuredly gathering that the Lord had called us for to preach the gospel unto them" (Acts 16:6-10).

Jesus had taught these disciples that they would be brought before governors and kings. "But when they deliver you up, take no thought how or what ye shall speak: for it shall be given you in that same hour what ye shall speak. For it is not ye that speak, but the Spirit of your Father which speaketh in you" (Matt. 10:19, 20). This depending upon God's leading and receiving such clear leading and following it, is one of the great distinctive marks of the Spirit-filled Christians in the book of Acts! So Peter had clear leading. His questions were answered, his scruples were dissolved, and he knew exactly what to do. And so may we, if we walk softly and wait before God and are eager always to give up our own plans for God's plans. A Christian may have clear leading for all he ought to do or say.

Peter called these three men in, the two servants and the devout soldier of Cornelius "and lodged them." I wonder if that is not the first time Peter ever sat at the same table for a pleasant meal with Gentiles? And was it not the first time he had slept in the same house with Gentiles and on the basis of close fellowship? But God had told him there were three men seeking him, that he must go with them, nothing doubting, and ever ringing in his ears was the message given him in the trance, "What God hath cleansed, that call not thou common" (vs. 15).

"On the morrow Peter went away with them." And certain brethren from Joppa accompanied him." These men came at noon or a little after noon. They were weary with some thirty miles traveled, probably on foot and in haste. They would need a few hours' rest. Besides, Peter must take with him "certain brethren," other saved Jews. There were six of them, as we see when Peter explained the matter in Acts 11:12. These brethren must go along for several reasons.

1. Not only Peter, but other Christians now must learn that the Gospel is to be taken to the Gentiles just the same as to the Jews. Others must be enlisted.

2. Besides, in every doubtful case, there ought to be more than one person, at least a quorum of Christians, to pass on converts ready for baptism. There might be some question: are these Gentiles really saved? There must be witnesses present who will be convinced of the genuineness of their conversion, and must endorse their baptism.

3. Then Peter, when he is to explain the matter to his Jewish Christian brethren, must have the testimony of others to back him up, to give witness that it was clearly of God. It will be hard enough for these Christian Jews to get away from the ceremonial law and from their ingrained antipathy to Gentiles. So substantial witnesses must be present when Peter preaches to Cornelius and his household, to bring the word back and safeguard Peter's testimony, and convince the doubting that the Gentiles are genuinely saved. And Peter was questioned sharply on the matter, and the witness of these six brethren helped him convince others, as we will see in chapter 11.

It has been the general custom among Baptists and others with local congregational self-government, autonomous local congregations, to vote to approve new converts for baptism, and to vote to approve people transferring membership from a distant congregation. That makes it unlikely that doubtful cases will be received until they give some evidence of genuine salvation.

Even when John baptized the multitude, he rejected the Pharisees and Sadducees who showed no evidence of repentance and personal saving faith. He said, "O generation of vipers, who hath warned you to flee from the wrath to come? Bring forth therefore fruits meet for repentance" (Matt. 3:7, 8). So it is generally regarded that the precept and spirit of the Scriptures indicate the wisdom of usually having others present approving those who came for baptism.

Thus these six brethren approved Cornelius and his household (Acts 10:46-48). So the disciples in Jerusalem as a group would not receive new-convert Saul until Barnabas told of his conversion and convinced them (Acts 9:26, 27). And so the brethren at Jerusalem wrote a letter to other disciples to receive in full fellowship and co-operation the preacher Apollos (Acts 18:27, 28). And so Paul wrote the brethren at Rome, urging them to receive and to approve Phebe, the servant of the church at Cenchrea (Rom. 16:1).

There were exceptions, of course, but there were exceptions to the general practice, for Philip baptized the Ethiopian eunuch after being convinced that he was saved (Acts 8:36-38). Paul and Silas baptized the Philippian jailer and his family with only those two to pass on their conversion (Acts 16:33). So we suppose as it was the general practice of Paul and Barnabas and later Paul and Silas on their missionary journey, so it is the practice today of missionaries on new mission fields with their first converts. But generally after there are other mature Christians, they, too, are invited to approve and pass on candidates for baptism and those who come for membership. That did not require any majority in Bible times nor do churches require any majority vote in general practice now. The one general rule is that we should try to see that people are genuinely trusting Christ for salvation before they are baptized and beyond that, spiritual wisdom and the circumstances may indicate the method.

Now these six brethren with Peter and the three messengers, a little party of ten, make the trek back to Caesarea to Cornelius and his household. We suppose they walked. And they went more slowly than the messengers had come. "On the morrow" Peter and the six brethren went with the messengers and then "the morrow after they entered into Caesarea" (vs. 24). They arrived, I suppose, on the second day "about the ninth hour" (vs. 30) or three o'clock in the afternoon. So they probably took a full day and a half or more for the thirty-mile journey and even that may have been strenuous walking for some of these Christians.

VERSES 24–35:

24 And the morrow after they entered into Cesarea. And Cornelius waited for them, and had called together his kinsmen and near friends.

25 And as Peter was coming in, Cornelius met him, and fell down at his feet, and worshipped *him*.

26 But Peter took him up, saying, Stand up; I myself also am a man.

27 And as he talked with him, he went in, and found many that were come together.

28 And he said unto them, Ye know how that it is an unlawful thing for a man that is a Jew to keep company, or come unto one of another nation; but God hath shewed me that I should not call any man common or unclean.

29 Therefore came I *unto you* without gainsaying, as soon as I was sent for: I ask therefore for what intent ye have sent for me?

30 And Cornelius said, Four days ago I was fasting until this hour; and at the ninth hour I prayed in my house, and, behold, a man stood before me in bright clothing,

31 And said, Cornelius, thy prayer is heard, and thine alms are had in remembrance in the sight of God.

32 Send therefore to Joppa, and call hither Simon, whose surname is Peter; he is lodged in the house of *one* Simon a tanner by the sea side: who, when he cometh, shall speak unto thee.

33 Immediately therefore I sent to thee; and thou hast well done that thou art come. Now therefore are we all here present before God, to hear all things that are commanded thee of God.

34 ¶ Then Peter opened *his*

mouth, and said, Of a truth I perceive that God is no respecter of persons:

35 But in every nation he that feareth him, and worketh right-eousness, is accepted with him.

Peter at Cornelius' House

1. Cornelius waited for them "and had called together his kinsmen and near friends." Already this good man, seeking to know God, had led others to have real confidence in his sincerity and character. Now with him is his house-hold, his kinsmen, servants, and some of the soldiers.

2. Cornelius was so eager to know the will of God that he fell down before Peter "and worshipped him." But Peter would not take that homage.

Note the term "worship." It is used in the Bible almost always for physical prostration, kneeling or perhaps even bending the forehead to the ground. The term generally re-fers to physical posture. In a few cases it refers to heart attitude, devotion, as in John 4:23, "When the true worship-pers shall worship the Father in spirit and in truth...." So Paul speaks of himself, "So worship I the God of my fa-thers" (Acts 24:14). So Philippians 3:3, "We...worship God in the spirit."

Some four Hebrew words and eleven Greek words are translated worship or worshiper in the New Testament, yet none of these ever refers to a public service. There were no "worship services" in the New Testament churches. That is an idea borrowed from Rome. It is the enemy of simple New Testament Christianity, the enemy of services with the kind of preaching and witnessing and teaching which they had in Bible times. The form, the ritualism, the ap-peal to the sensual, of robed choirs and ritualistic formal services, were totally unknown in the New Testament, and are a hurtful patterning after Romanism and after worldli-ness; an appeal to the flesh, and not the Spirit. Here when Cornelius "worshipped" Peter, he simply bowed down at his feet in veneration. It was a physical attitude.

Peter said, "Ye know how that it is an unlawful thing for a man that is a Jew to keep company, or come unto one of another nation..." (vs. 28). "Unlawful?" The adjective form of the same Greek word in I Peter 4:3 is translated "abominable." It was unlawful by custom and by the interpretation and traditions of the rabbis, not unlawful by the Old Testament Scriptures. Matthew Henry says:

> "It was not made so by the law of God, but by the decree of their wise men, which they looked upon to be no less binding. They did not forbid them to converse or traffic with Gentiles in the street or shop, or upon the exchange, but to eat with them....They might not come into the house of the Gentile, for they looked upon it to be ceremonially polluted. Thus scornfully did the Jews look upon the Gentiles, who were not behind hand with them in contempt, as appears by many passages in the Latin poets."

H. Porter in The International Standard Bible Encyclopedia, Vol. 2, page 1215, says:

> "The Gentiles were far less sharply differentiated from the Israelites in OT than in NT times. Under OT regulations they were simply non-Israelites, not from the stock of Abraham, but they were not hated or despised for that reason, and were to be treated almost on a plane of e- quality, except certain tribes in Canaan with regard to whom there were special regulations of non-intercourse. The Gentile stranger enjoyed the hospitality of the Israelite who was commanded to love him (Dt 10 19), to sympathize with him, 'For ye know the heart of the stranger, seeing ye were strangers in the land of Egypt'

(Ex 23 9 AV). The Kenites were treated almost
as brethren, esp. the children of Rechab (Jgs 1
16; 5 24; Jer 35). Uriah the Hittite was a trusted
warrior of David (2 S 11); Ittai the Gittite was
captain of David's guard (18 2); Araunah the Jeb-
usite was a respected resident of Jerus.   The
Gentiles had the right of asylum in the cities of
refuge, the same as the Israelites (Nu 35 15).
They might even possess Israelitish slaves (Lev
25 47), and a gentile servant must not be de-
frauded of his wage (Dt 24 15).   They could in-
herit in Israel even as late as the exile (Ezek 47
22.23). They were allowed to offer sacrifices in
the temple at Jerus, as is distinctly affirmed by
Jos (BJ, II, xvii, 2-4; Ant, XI, viii, 5; XIII, viii,
2; XVI, ii, 1; XVIII, v, 3; C Ap, II, 5), and it
is implied in the Levitical law (Lev 22 25).
Prayers and sacrifices were to be offered for
gentile rulers (Jer 29 7; Bar 1 10.11; Ezr 6 10;
Macc 7 33; Jos, BJ, II, x, 4). Gifts might be received from them (2 Macc 5 16; Jos, Ant, XIII,
iii, 4; XVI, vi, 4; BJ, V, xiii, 6; C Ap, II, 5).
But as we approach the Christian era the attitude
of the Jews toward the Gentiles changes, until we
find, in NT times, the most extreme aversion,
scorn and hatred. They were regarded as unclean, with whom it was unlawful to have any
friendly intercourse. They were the enemies of
God and His people, to whom the knowledge of
God was denied unless they became proselytes,
and even then they could not, as in ancient times,
be admitted to full fellowship. Jews were forbidden to counsel them, and if they asked about Divine things they were to be cursed.   All children
born of mixed marriages were bastards. That is
what caused the Jews to be so hated by Greeks

and Romans, as we have abundant evidence in the writings of Cicero, Seneca and Tacitus. Something of this is reflected in the NT (Jn 18 28; Acts 10 28; 11 3).

"If we inquire what the reason of this change was we shall find it in the conditions of the exiled Jews, who suffered the bitterest treatment at the hands of their gentile captors and who, after their return and establishment in Judaea, were in constant conflict with neighboring tribes and esp. with the Gr rulers of Syria. The fierce persecution of Antiochus IV, who attempted to blot out their religion and Hellenize the Jews, and the desperate struggle for independence, created in them a burning patriotism and zeal for their faith which culminated in the rigid exclusiveness we see in later times."

The Old Testament commands had been very plain that Jews were not to have fellowship with idolatry, were not to intermarry nor give their children in marriage to idolaters. They were not to hate nor avoid Gentiles as such. So Naaman the Syrian was healed and we believe soundly converted through Elisha (II Kings 5:1-19). So Ruth the Moabitess was well received when she returned with her mother-in-law Naomi.

Cornelius reports, "A man stood before me in bright clothing." The "man" was an angel (vs. 3). So the two angels of Genesis 19:1 looked like men and were called men in verses 5, 8, 10, 12, and then again called angels in verse 15.

Note, Cornelius carefully reports the words of the angel, "Thy prayer is heard, and thine alms are had in remembrance in the sight of God." Compare with verse 4. Good deeds do not save, but good deeds show good intentions and are pleasing to God. One who wants to do right is more susceptible to the Gospel than one who does not want to do right.

However, we must distinguish between the honest, God-fearing, seeking Cornelius and a self-righteous Pharisee whose goodness is only outward and pretentious and hypocritical. Cain brought an offering, representing good works, but he did not have a heart to seek nor to repent of his sins. That was not the case with Cornelius. So in verse 35 Peter will say, "But in every nation he that feareth him, and worketh righteousness, is accepted with him." So the teaching of Jesus in John 7:17 and so Romans 2:2, 7, 10, and 14, 15. Any man who wants to do right honestly from the heart will, when he hears the Gospel, run to Jesus Christ for salvation. The very fact that some moralists, lodge members and modernists do not turn in repentance to trust Christ as their only Saviour is proof positive that their hearts turn away from the light because their deeds are evil, as Jesus said (John 3:19). And so they hold on to their sin with outward morality and inward wickedness. But Cornelius honestly sought the truth, and such an one always finds Jesus. God is under obligation to bring further light to every sinner who seeks the light and follows what light he has, as did Cornelius.

VERSES 36-38:

36 The word which *God* sent unto the children of Israel, preaching peace by Jesus Christ: (he is Lord of all:)

37 That word, *I say*, ye know, which was published through-out all Judea, and began from Galilee, after the baptism which John preached;

38 How God anointed Jesus of Nazareth with the Holy Ghost and with power: who went about doing good, and healing all that were oppressed of the devil; for God was with him.

Peter Tells the Ministry of Jesus

Cornelius had certainly heard about Jesus. "That word, I say, ye know," because it "was published throughout all Judaea." Caesarea, where this Roman soldier was stationed was only some forty miles from Nazareth and Capernaum, perhaps fifty or fifty-five miles from Jerusalem. The multiplied thousands who assembled from time to time to hear Jesus (for example, five thousand men besides the women and children at one time) (Matt. 14:21), and the fact that the crowd around Jesus was called "the multitude" or "multitudes" more than twenty times in the Gospel of Matthew alone, shows that the people nationwide talked everywhere about Jesus. Again, He had sent the twelve and then the seventy "into every city and place, whither he himself would come" (Luke 10:1). All Judaea, all Jewish Palestine had been covered with reports about Jesus, His marvelous healings and His teaching.

But most likely he had heard the Gospel or had heard a lot about the Gospel and the preaching of Christ because of Philip the evangelist. After Philip won the Ethiopian eunuch in Acts, chapter 8, we read in verse 40: "But Philip was found at Azotus: and passing through he preached in all the cities, till he came to Caesarea." Azotus is the Greek form of the word Ashdod, a city of the Philistines to the west of Judaea. So Philip preached in that coastal area til' he came to Caesarea, and in Acts 21:8 we find that Paul and his company "came unto Caesarea: and we entered into the house of Philip the evangelist, which was one of the seven; and abode with him." Cornelius evidently did not know how to be saved. Even so, many people who hear about Christ do not know how to be saved. So Peter could say to Cornelius, "That word, I say, ye know, which was published throughout all Judaea...(vs. 37).

So Cornelius had heard that word though, we suppose, he had never heard the Gospel directly nor been told how to be saved. This Caesarea (different from Caesarea Philippi, another town north of the Sea of Galilee in northern Palestine) is not mentioned in the Gospels as having been visited by Jesus or the disciples. But the general public had all heard about Jesus.

Note that this word about Jesus "began from Galilee, after the baptism which John preached." Jesus worked no miracles, preached no sermons till after He was baptized of John in Jordan (Luke 3:21, 22).

Note here Peter is careful to say that the Gospel centers in "preaching peace by Jesus Christ." There is not now, and there never has been any way to approach God in peace and have peace with God but through Jesus Christ. So Abraham rejoiced to see Christ's day and he believed in God and it was counted to him for righteousness (John 8:56; Gen. 15:6; Rom. 4:3). Old Testament saints did not know in detail how God would provide a sacrifice to pay for sin, but spiritually minded saints in the Old Testament did trust in God's provision for their sins, the sacrifice, the Messiah who was to come. So when John the Baptist announced, "Behold the Lamb of God, which taketh away the sin of the world," he was announcing an expected person, long pictured in all the sacrifices and expected by spiritual Jews everywhere (John 1:29). Jesus is the only plan of salvation and always has been, as Peter states very clearly in verse 43.

Jesus Christ, "he is Lord of all" (vs. 36). Peter is here stressing the humanity of Jesus and His ministry as a Spirit-filled man (vs. 38). Even so, he first insists that Jesus is deity. He is not simply nor only a man. He is the God-Man. He is not simply a man upon whom the Spirit of the Christ came, as some unbelievers would say. No, Jesus personally is "the mighty God" (Isa. 9:6). God the Father said to the Son, "Thy throne, O God, is for ever and ever: a sceptre of righteousness is the sceptre of thy kingdom" (Heb. 1:8; Ps. 45:6, 7). He is the "I am" who met Moses in the wilderness and instructed him to deliver Israel (John 8:23, 24, 58; Exod. 3:14). After Jesus said, "Before Abraham was, I am. Then took they up stones to cast at him." They knew that Jesus was claiming to be Jehovah God of the Old Testament. John 5:17 and 18, "Jesus answered them, My Father worketh hitherto, and I work. Therefore the Jews sought the more to kill him, because he not only had broken the sabbath, but said also that God was his Father, making himself equal with God." No honest person can read the Gospels without seeing that Jesus claimed to be God, in person, equal with the Father.

John 1:1-3 says, "In the beginning was the Word, and the Word was with God, and the Word was God. The same was in the beginning with God. All things were made by him; and without him was not any thing made that was made." Jesus is God, the unique Son of God, the Creator of all things that are made. He is "the image of the invisible God" (Col. 1:15). And "by him were all things created... And he is before all things, and by him all things consist" (Col. 1:16, 17). Before Jesus was born, Mary, filled with the Spirit said, "My spirit hath rejoiced in God my Saviour" (Luke 1:47). Let us be solemnly warned by II John 9 and 10 that "whosoever transgresseth, and abideth not in the doctrine of Christ, hath not God," and that anyone who does not specifically bring this doctrine is not to be received as a Christian. The beautiful fact of the perfect humanity of Jesus should never lessen our conception of Him as the eternal God, one with the Father, whom we call the second person in the Trinity.

Jesus, Filled With the Spirit, Did All His Mighty Works as a Spirit-Filled, Perfect Man

Read again verse 38: "How God anointed Jesus of Nazareth with the Holy Ghost and with power: who went about doing good, and healing all that were oppressed of the devil; for God was with him."

This is one of the few times in the Bible where the three persons of the Trinity are mentioned in one verse. Notice the human name Jesus is used, given to Him by the angel before His birth (Matt. 1:21). So here we speak of Jesus as the perfect man, the model for all Christian work.

Jesus is, humanly speaking, "the son of David, the son of Abraham" (Matt. 1:1). He is "the son of Adam" (Luke 3:38). Seventy-nine times in the Gospels and once in the Acts of the Apostles He is called "the Son of man." He is the Second Adam (I Cor. 15:45). Carnally we are all patterned after the first Adam. Spiritually, born-again ones are patterned after the Second Adam. Christ is the perfect man, taking the place of and atoning for the sins and failures of all sinful, imperfect men.

Thus Christ is our pattern, our model, but only for born-again ones. Christ was conceived by the Holy Ghost (Luke 1:35). In our spiritual birth we are "born of the Spirit" (John 3:5, 6). So in baptism, Jesus started to set a pattern for the life and ministry of Christians. He said, "Thus it becometh us [Jesus and Christians] to fulfill all righteousness" (Matt. 3:15). It is foolish to suppose that anybody could walk the Jesus way without having the Jesus heart. Man must have a Saviour before an example will do him any good.

In India an educated Moslem said to me, "Oh yes, Jesus is a prophet, too, like Mohammed." I replied, "If you don't have more than a prophet, you are going to Hell. A prophet will not do a man any good who does not take Christ as Saviour."

Christ is an example to Christians in these ways.

1. In humility and self-surrender. "Let this mind be in you, which was also in Christ Jesus: Who, being in the form of God, thought it not robbery to be equal with God: But made himself of no reputation, and took upon him the form of a servant, and was made in the likeness of men: And being found in fashion as a man, he humbled himself,

and became obedient unto death, even the death of the cross" (Phil. 2:5-8).

2. We should be unselfish in pleasing others and not ourselves. "Even Christ pleased not himself" (Rom. 15:1-3).

3. We are to forgive others "even as Christ forgave you" (Col. 3:13).

4. Christ is our example in suffering. "Christ also suffered for us, leaving us an example, that ye should follow his steps" (I Pet. 2:21). (See also Colossians 2:14; Luke 9:22, 23; John 15:18-21).

5. It is clear that Jesus intended to lay upon His disciples the obligation to carry on the same kind of ministry that He Himself carried on. We are sent as He was sent. "The work that I do shall ye do also." Hence it was necessary for us to have the same kind of power, the anointing of the Holy Spirit which He had.

Jesus Did All His Miraculous Ministry as a Spirit-Filled Man

In verse 36 above, Peter made clear that Jesus "is Lord of all." He is the mighty God. Now in verse 38 he emphasizes that it was in His capacity as a perfect man, filled with the Spirit, that Jesus did all His mighty works, not in His own power as second person of the Trinity, the Creator, but in the power of the third person of the Trinity, the Holy Spirit, so He could be our pattern.

It is remarkable that Jesus, the perfect, sinless, blameless Son of God and Son of man, should wait until He was thirty years old to be baptized, to be filled with the Spirit, then begin His public ministry as told in Luke 3:21-23.

> "Now when all the people were baptized, it came to pass, that Jesus also being baptized, and praying, the heaven was opened, And the Holy Ghost descended in a bodily shape like a dove upon him, and a voice came from heaven,

which said, Thou art my beloved Son; in thee I
am well pleased. And Jesus himself began to be
about thirty years of age...."

The Gospel of John begins its narrative about the life of
Jesus with the ministry of John the Baptist and his baptism
of Jesus and his announcement that Jesus is "the Lamb of
God" (John 1:15-36). Then in chapter 2 we find the miracle
of the water turned to wine at the wedding in Cana of Galilee
and that "this beginning of miracles did Jesus in Cana of
Galilee" (John 2:11). So Jesus, thirty years old, sinless,
blameless, perfect, had never preached a sermon, had
never won a soul, had never worked a miracle. The foolish
traditions of Catholics that Jesus worked miracles as a
child are utterly contrary to the Scriptures. No, it is clear
from Luke 4:1-22, which follows immediately the narrative
of the baptism and the coming of the Holy Spirit upon Jesus,
that Jesus waited until Isaiah 61:1 was fulfilled--waited until
He was "anointed to preach the Gospel" before He preached
or did any of His public ministry. He was a fine student of
the Scriptures even as a boy (Luke 2:41-52). He regularly
attended the synagogue where He was the best student of the
Old Testament Scriptures, read them in public (Luke 4:16).
But He had never preached a sermon, never won a soul,
never worked a miracle, never opened blind eyes nor
cleansed a leper.

There are many scriptural proofs that all the ministry of
Jesus was in the power of a special anointing of the Holy
Spirit.

Several Scriptures Specifically Speak of
Christ as Filled With the Spirit or
With the Spirit of God Upon Him

1. Isaiah 42:1 says: "Behold my servant, whom I uphold;
mine elect, in whom my soul delighteth; I have put my
spirit upon him: he shall bring forth judgment to the Gen-

tiles." This is a clear prophecy about the Lord Jesus, "I have put my spirit upon him," for His ministry here on earth.

2. Isaiah 61:1 is a prophecy about Jesus, too: "The Spirit of the Lord God is upon me; because the Lord hath anointed me to preach good tidings unto the meek; he hath sent me to bind up the brokenhearted, to proclaim liberty to the captives, and the opening of the prison to them that are bound." Notice that Jesus quoted this verse and to the middle of verse 2 in Luke 4:18 and 19. That far it is about His first coming. After the middle of verse 2 it is about His Second Coming and the regathering and restoration of Israel. This Scripture specifically states that the fullness of the Spirit on Christ was for His ministry of preaching and comforting and healing.

3. Luke 3:21 and 22 tells us that "Jesus also being baptized, and praying, the heaven was opened, And the Holy Ghost descended in a bodily shape like a dove upon him, and a voice came from heaven which said, Thou art my beloved Son; in thee I am well pleased." This was a public manifestation of His anointing with the Holy Spirit to begin His public ministry. This was the outward sign that God had told John the Baptist to expect: this would prove that Jesus was "he which baptizeth with the Holy Ghost," that is, the Saviour (John 1:31-33). And John also explained later (John 3:34), "...For God giveth not the Spirit by measure unto him." Now the perfect man is perfectly filled with the Spirit.

And as the narrative takes up in Luke 4, it is evident that that anointing was a permanent enduement of power which never left Jesus. "And Jesus being full of the Holy Ghost returned from Jordan, and was led by the Spirit into the wilderness" (Luke 4:1). "And Jesus returned in the power of the Spirit into Galilee..." (Luke 4:14).

4. Then Jesus in the synagogue at Nazareth quoted Isaiah 61:1 and 2 and said to them, "This day is this scripture ful-

filled in your ears" (Luke 4:16-21). They had never heard Him speak like this, "And wondered at the gracious words which proceeded out of his mouth. And they said, Is not this Joseph's son?" (Luke 4:22). And now for the first time those who loved and honored the model young man began to hate and persecute this Spirit-filled Man and tried to kill Him.

5. In Hebrews 9:14 we read of "Christ, who through the eternal Spirit offered himself without spot to God...."

6. In Acts 1:2 we read that Jesus descended "after that he through the Holy Ghost had given commandments unto the apostles whom he had chosen." Even the resurrected Jesus was filled with the Spirit and did His work in the power and wisdom of the Spirit.

7. The reign of Christ on earth on David's throne at His return will be in the power of the Holy Spirit. Isaiah 11:1 and 2 says: "And there shall come forth a rod out of the stem of Jesse, and a Branch shall grow out of his roots: And the spirit of the Lord shall rest upon him, the spirit of wisdom and understanding, the spirit of counsel and might, the spirit of knowledge and of the fear of the Lord." So He will reign righteously, the greater David on David's throne.

So in Acts 10:38 Peter was inspired to say, "How God anointed Jesus of Nazareth with the Holy Ghost and with power: who went about doing good, and healing all that were oppressed of the devil; for God was with him."

Types in the Old Testament Pictured Jesus Would Do His Work in the Anointing of the Holy Spirit

1. The golden candlestick (or more exactly the golden lampstand) in the holy of holies on the left side as one entered, had seven lamps kept forever burning with olive oil (Exod. 39:37; Exod. 40:25). The seven lamps picture Jesus the perfect Saviour, the Light of the world, burning with the power of the Holy Spirit. On the other side of the holy of

holies was the table of shewbread picturing Christ the Bread of Life.

2. The sweet savor offerings and meat offerings (literally food offering) is described. "His offering shall be of fine flour; and he shall pour oil upon it, and put frankincense thereon" (Lev. 2:1). Christ, the Bread of Life, anointed with the Holy Spirit and so our interceding High Priest, is pictured as praying for us. Or there could be an "oblation of a meat-offering baken in the oven, it shall be unleavened cakes of fine flour mingled with oil, or unleavened wafers anointed with oil" (Lev. 2:4-7). Certainly the oil here and elsewhere pictures the fullness of the Spirit upon Christ.

3. The anointing of Aaron as high priest (Exod. 40:13) certainly pictured Christ our High Priest filled with the Spirit. The anointing of David in I Samuel 16:12 and 13 certainly pictured the anointing of Jesus. After David was anointed "the Spirit of the Lord came upon David from that day forward." Jesus is Son of David (Matt. 1:1). He is "King of the Jews." "The Lord God shall give unto him the throne of his father David" (Luke 1:32). And in Ezekiel 37:25 we read that Jesus, the second David, will reign over regathered Israel. So the anointing of David certainly typified the fullness of the Spirit which came upon Jesus for His ministry and for His reign on earth as described in Isaiah 11:1-4.

4. Even the Old Testament names of Jesus, Messiah in the Hebrew and Christ in the Greek, mean anointed, taken, I think, from Psalm 2:2 where we are told, "The kings of the earth set themselves, and the rulers take counsel together, against the Lord, and against his anointed, saying..." which certainly referred to Christ as the apostles knew (Acts 4:25, 26). And that Psalm about the Son calls Him God's "anointed." So for His ministry on earth and later for His reign, Christ has been filled with the Holy Spirit, anointed with the Spirit for service.

So all the ministry of Jesus was in the power of the Holy Spirit, and it will be so even in His reign on earth.

Thus, then, Christ could command His people that "he that believeth on me, the works that I do shall he do also; and greater works than these shall he do; because I go unto my Father" (John 14:12). And He could say, "As my Father hath sent me, even so send I you." "When he had said this, he breathed on them, and saith unto them, Receive ye the Holy Ghost" (John 20:21, 22). The indwelling of the Holy Spirit, received in their bodies on the day of the resurrection, meant that henceforth the dwelling place of the Holy Spirit would be in the bodies of Christians. And from this human headquarters will pour out "rivers of living water" (John 7:38). But the fullness for witnessing waited until they had prayed and Pentecost was come.

VERSES 39-42:

39 And we are witnesses of all things which he did both in the land of the Jews, and in Jerusalem; whom they slew and hanged on a tree:

40 Him God raised up the third day, and shewed him openly;

41 Not to all the people, but unto witnesses chosen before of God, *even* to us, who did eat and drink with him after he rose from the dead.

42 And he commanded us to preach unto the people, and to testify that it is he which was ordained of God *to be* the Judge of quick and dead.

The Apostles as Witnesses

The ministry of Jesus was "after the baptism which John preached" (vs. 37). All of the apostles must be "of these men which have companied with us all the time that the Lord Jesus went in and out among us, Beginning from the baptism of John, unto that same day that he was taken up from us, must one be ordained to be a witness with us of his resurrection" (Acts 1:21, 22). Jesus had told the disciples, "That repentance and remission of sins should be preached in his name among all nations, beginning at Jerusalem. And ye are witnesses of these things" (Luke 24:47, 48). So all through the book of Acts the preaching largely takes the form of witnessing. They must declare again and again that they were with Jesus, that they knew Him well, that He was risen from the dead, that they had talked with Him forty days, had handled Him, eaten with Him. So in Acts 2:32 Peter preached, "This Jesus hath God raised up, whereof we all are witnesses." And in Acts 4:20 Peter said, "For we cannot but speak the things which we have seen and heard." In Acts 4:33 we are told, "And with great power gave the apostles witness of the resurrection of the Lord Jesus...." In the second persecution Peter preached to the Sanhedrin, "And we are his witnesses of these things; and so is also the Holy Ghost, whom God hath given to them that obey him" (Acts 5:32). So now to Cornelius and his household in Acts 10:39-41 Peter properly says, "And we are witnesses of all things which he did both in the land of the Jews, and in Jerusalem; whom they slew and hanged on a tree: Him God raised up the third day, and shewed him openly; Not to all the people, but unto witnesses chosen before of God, even to us, who did eat and drink with him after he rose from the dead."

VERSE 43:

43 To him give all the prophets witness, that through his name whosoever believeth in him shall receive remission of sins.

All Prophets Preach the Same Saviour, the Same Plan of Salvation

Not only are the apostles witnesses of the life, death and resurrection of Jesus, and above five hundred other witnesses who saw Him after His resurrection, but "all the prophets," that is, every prophet in the Old Testament as well as the New Testament times, bears witness to the same Saviour and the same plan of salvation!

There are some who think that Old Testament saints were saved by animal sacrifices and the ceremonies of the law. They are utterly mistaken. The sacrifices and ceremonies of the Old Testament were simply object lessons pointing to Christ and salvation by faith in Him. Baptism now pictures that one is buried in the likeness of Christ's death and raised in the likeness of His resurrection (Rom. 6:4, 5), and those that take the Lord's Supper in the bread and the cup "do shew the Lord's death till he come" (I Cor. 11:26). So Old Testament sacrifices taught the same thing, that salvation is only through Christ. Every prophet in the Old Testament pictures Christ. So Jesus could preach to Nicodemus the Gospel from Numbers 21:5-9, about the serpents in the wilderness. So Philip could preach to the Ethiopian eunuch from Isaiah 53:4-6, preaching the same Saviour and the same Gospel. It was this Saviour whom Abraham saw and believed in (John 8:56; Rom. 4:3). It was by faith in this Jesus that "Abel offered unto God a more excellent sacrifice than Cain," the firstling of his flock which pictured an atoning Saviour. It is Christ and salvation by faith in His shed blood that is pictured in the passover.

There are those hyper-dispensationalists who think that John the Baptist preached a different Gospel from Christ when he commanded repentance (Matt. 3:2). But it is the same repentance Jesus commanded in Matthew 4:17, in Luke 13:3 and 5, and the same repentance that Paul preached in Athens that God "now commandeth all men every where to repent" (Acts 17:30, 31). Repentance is not a different plan of salvation from saving faith: it is a part of the same plan of salvation. Or rather repentance is simply another way of describing or looking at the plan of salvation. One who turns from sin to God has done so by trusting in Jesus Christ. A change of mind toward sin is necessarily involved in saving faith.

Everyone who genuinely repented under the preaching of John the Baptist put his trust in the Saviour John the Baptist preached, and was regenerated. There is no such thing as being "a disciple of John the Baptist" in any honest sense without being a disciple of Jesus, that is, without trusting Christ for salvation.

There are those who think that Peter in Acts 2:38 and 39 preached that baptism was essential to salvation when he said, "Repent and be baptized every one of you in the name of Jesus Christ for the remission of sins, and ye shall receive the gift of the Holy Ghost." But the phrase "for the remission of sins" could well be translated "referring to the remission of sins" for the indefinite preposition eis here translated for is really an indefinite preposition of reference and so used many, many times in the Bible. People are not baptized in order to be saved, but baptized with reference to the salvation they had when they repented. So it has always been among Bible-believing Christians who follow the Scriptures.

So here in Acts 10:43 we have the statement by Peter, "To him give all the prophets witness, that through his name whosoever believeth in him shall receive remission of sins." Get this great doctrinal matter settled: God has only one plan of salvation and that is all He ever had! He has only one Saviour, and that is Jesus Christ. Every Old and New Testament prophet agrees in this that "whosoever believeth in him shall have remission of sins."

VERSES 44–48:

44 ¶ While Peter yet spake these words, the Holy Ghost fell on all them which heard the word.

45 And they of the circumcision which believed were astonished, as many as came with Peter, because that on the Gentiles also was poured out the gift of the Holy Ghost.

46 For they heard them speak with tongues, and magnify God.

Then answered Peter,
47 Can any man forbid water, that these should not be baptized, which have received the Holy Ghost as well as we?

48 And he commanded them to be baptized in the name of the Lord. Then prayed they him to tarry certain days.

Cornelius' Household Saved and Filled With the Spirit

Here is an interesting and charming thing. Peter had no more than mentioned about Jesus, that "through his name whosoever believeth in him shall receive remission of sins" than the whole eager, awaiting family group trusted Christ, were wonderfully saved, and upon them God poured out the Holy Spirit. The interesting thing is that Peter had only given the introduction of the long sermon he had expected to preach. For, in explaining the matter later he said, "And as I began to speak, the Holy Ghost fell on them, as on us at the beginning" (Acts 11:15).

Note some important points.

1. The main thing is that these people were saved. Peter told the whole story to the protesting apostles and brethren in Judaea. "When they heard these things, they held their peace, and glorified God, saying, Then hath God also to the Gentiles granted repentance unto life" (Acts 11:18).

For these verses the Scofield Reference Bible puts a paragraph subhead, "The Holy Spirit given to Gentile believers." So He was given to Gentile believers, but that is not the principal point of these verses. They trusted Christ as soon as they learned that was the way to be saved. And they were saved.

2. Do not misunderstand verse 46. The circumcised Jews who came with Peter "heard them speak with tongues, and magnify God." The word tongues is a translation of the Greek word glossa, always meaning tongue or language. But to jump to the conclusion that this was a miraculous gift of tongues like Acts 2:4-11 is not justified by the statement

here. The Christian Jews literally "heard them speak with languages," I suppose not miraculous languages. Since Cornelius was of the Italian band (Acts 10:1), it is nearly certain that he and his soldiers regularly spoke Latin. Since they were in Palestine and we suppose they had been stationed here some time, probably some of them spoke Aramaic, the common tongue of the country and it is probable that the servants were natives of Palestine and spoke Aramaic. And since the general language of commerce throughout the whole Roman Empire was the Koine or commonplace Greek, in which Paul preached everywhere, in which the New Testament was written, and we suppose the language in which Peter spoke to these people. Then certainly some of them would speak Koine Greek. So in various languages in their happy excitement, these new converts praised God! Note that the reason Peter and others knew that these people were saved was that they heard them and understood their praises as "they magnified God."

When I preached in India, it was translated into the Tamil tongue or Telugu or another language, depending on the section I preached in. And some who came to claim Christ openly talked in broken English and others talked in their own language and their words were translated to me. Here in the land of Palestine where Aramaic was the common native language and Greek was a widely-known language of commerce and known everywhere and where the soldiers were themselves from Italy and naturally spoke Latin, these people simply praised God in several languages. We have no right to infer a miracle unless the Scriptures mention one, or the context indicates a miracle.

Some would like to say that these new converts talked in some heavenly tongue and that that was an evidence they were filled with the Holy Spirit. But if they had talked in some unknown language not understood by those present, the effect would have been as confusing to unlearned people as I Corinthians 14:23 indicates it would be. The gift of tongues in the Bible was the gift, as given at Pentecost, to speak in the language of some who would hear, and thus hear the Gospel. So in Acts 19:1-7 in the cosmopolitan city of Ephesus the "tongues" or languages in verse 6 were probably simply some of the various languages regularly spoken by the polyglot population.

In Chicago or Minneapolis I have heard a Swedish woman, greatly blessed, praise God in Swedish, and in Kaw City, Oklahoma, I heard a native Indian praise God in his own tongue, although the language regularly spoken in the congregations in each case was English.

3. These people were not only saved, but were "filled with the Holy Ghost." That was obvious in their Spirit-filled testimony (vs. 47). It is the "Holy Ghost" Himself who is the "like gift as he did unto us, who believed on the Lord Jesus Christ" in Acts 11:17. It is the same "gift of the Holy Ghost" which Jesus had promised at Pentecost in Acts 2:39. But the blessed testimonies made clear that these were saved, that they had the joy of the Lord, that they were moved by the Spirit of God.

Here a truth becomes evident: one may be saved and filled with the Holy Spirit at the same time. That was not the case with the original apostles who were saved before Pentecost and then at Pentecost were filled with the Holy Spirit. It was not true about the Samaritans to whom Philip preached and they were saved and then the apostles, Peter and John, "laid their hands on them, and they received the Holy Ghost" (Acts 8:17). And young Saul, later called Paul, was saved on the road to Damascus and after fasting and praying three days Ananias came "that thou mightest receive thy sight, and be filled with the Holy Ghost" (Acts 9:17). Salvation is one thing, the enduement of power or fullness of the Spirit is another thing. But in the case of Cornelius and his household, the salvation and the fullness of the Spirit or anointing for a testimony came at the same time.

Why? Probably because all the heart-searching, all the waiting on God that Cornelius' household had done before they were saved made them perfectly ready to be saved and not only ready to be saved, but ready to obey the Lord Jesus and follow Him. The waiting on God which the apostles did in the ten days before Pentecost (Acts 1:14) had already been done by Cornelius and his household, fasting and praying to know the will of God, to have salvation and the power of God.

4. Peter now asked the Jewish Christians who had come with him, "Can any man forbid water, that these should not be baptized, which have received the Holy Ghost as well as we?" There was no objection. That little quorum of Jews were convinced that Cornelius and his household were truly converted. It may be that to convince them God had arranged for the Spirit-filled testimony of the new converts so there could be no doubt. People are often truly saved without such a manifestation of joy and testimony. But their joyful praises and witnessing here gave evidence that they were truly saved and none could gainsay it! Therefore, they were fit subjects for baptism.

It is interesting to note that here, as throughout the New Testament, people who were saved were baptized at once. So was Lydia in Acts 16:15. So the jailer and his household at Philippi "the same hour of the night...was baptized, he and all his, straightway" (Acts 16:33). So Paul immediately, when he received his sight and as soon as Ananias laid his hands on him, "arose and was baptized" (Acts 9:18). Baptism is a public testimony that one has trusted Christ and so it should follow salvation as soon as possible. It should never precede salvation.

5. They were "baptized in the name of the Lord." So in Acts 8:16, "...They were baptized in the name of the Lord Jesus." So in Acts 19:5, "...They were baptized in the name of the Lord Jesus." This is not different from "baptizing them in the name of the Father, and of the Son, and

of the Holy Ghost" as commanded in Matthew 28:19. Jesus had said, "I and my Father are one." There is no jealousy between the persons of the Godhead. The Father, the Son and the Holy Spirit are all involved in the salvation of a soul. God gave His Son. Christ died. The Holy Spirit convicts and regenerates. So when I say that I have trusted Christ for salvation, I do not mean to leave out the Father nor the Holy Spirit. And when I baptize a convert "in the name of the Lord Jesus," I do not mean to leave out the Father and the Holy Spirit.

ACTS 11

VERSES 1-3:

AND the apostles and brethren that were in Judea heard that the Gentiles had also received the word of God.

2 And when Peter was come up to Jerusalem, they that were of the circumcision contended with him,

3 Saying, Thou wentest in to men uncircumcised, and didst eat with them.

"They Who Were of the Circumcision" Object

The news spread fast: "The apostles and brethren that were in Judaea" heard that over on the coast at Caesarea "Gentiles had also received the word of God." When Peter came back to Jerusalem, the center of New Testament Christianity, there "they that were of the circumcision" contended with him. That might have three shades of meaning.

First, it would mean generally simply circumcised Jews who were Christians. That meant all the Christians in the world perhaps except those saved at Cornelius' household. Even the Samaritans had been circumcised, we suppose, and so had all the Jewish proselytes coming from the Gentiles and so religiously and officially becoming Jews. So the term is, first of all, a general term for Jewish Christians. In that sense it may have included the apostles at Jerusalem or part of them.

Second, in a special sense those "of the circumcision" would refer to Jews who had been converted but were not well indoctrinated or well developed spiritually. Young Christians as they grow in grace and in the knowledge of the Lord Jesus come to more nearly the Christian standards. But first, they carry over the standards of the old life. So some Christians could own slaves and see no harm in it. So in early days in America Christians who would meet to raise the beams of a new church building, loyally volunteering, might see nothing wrong in serving hard cider or other alcoholic liquor. Even great Charles H. Spurgeon smoked cigars until a year or so before he died. So Christians who have been raised in pedobaptist groups may go for years and never see the spiritual meaning of immersion for baptism. Nearly all of us learn so slowly; so many Jews, truly born again, had yet been blind to the applications of the Great Commission, that they were to preach the Gospel "to every creature."

Third, even very serious, well-developed Christians were naturally shocked somewhat at the thought of associating with moral standards so low and idolatrous practices abhorrent as those to which Gentiles were accustomed. Since their captivity, Jews had turned entirely away from idolatry. Although in old times some Jews had had more than one wife, now it seems monogamy was the accepted custom, the moral standard of the whole community. It was still the recognized law among Jews that the adulterers were to be stoned, but fornication was very common among the Gentiles (Eph. 4:17-19). These people were not against Gentiles being saved, but they shrank from association with Gentiles. The complaint against Peter was, "Thou wentest in to men uncircumcised, and didst eat with them." He was not rebuked for preaching to them, but for intimate association with them.

Here is one of the very serious problems about integration of the races. All intelligent and spiritual Christians want colored people to have the Gospel, want them to have their proper rights under the law, want them to have opportunity for education, advancement and happiness. But when, as is true in many great centers, the incidence of venereal disease is ten times as great among Negroes as among whites, and the percentage of illegitimacy is correspondingly far greater, it is inevitable that cultured white Christians will not want their children to intermarry with Negroes, will not want them to have the dangers of intimate association with them on a social level. It is only fair to these circumcised Jewish Christians at Jerusalem to understand that there was a genuine moral risk in breaking down their inhibitions against association with Gentiles.

I do not think that any intelligent and warmhearted Christian objected to Gentiles being saved. However, since the moral and ethical standards were so different, spiritual and intelligent Jewish Christians may have felt uneasy still about intermarriage between Jewish Christians and Gentile Christians. Hearing the Gospel and turning so. thoroughly to Christ in saving faith makes a Christian; it does not immediately make a gentleman. One does not immediately attain to a new set of values. Neither good manners nor good morals make a Christian, but a good Christian ought to be sensitive about good manners and good morals, and so about his associations, the companions of his children, those among whom his own children will find their life partners. These Jewish Christians were good Christians, and they had to learn, as Peter did, that it was right to preach the Gospel to Gentiles and then, when they were saved, to count them Christian brethren.

VERSES 4-14:

4 But Peter rehearsed *the matter* from the beginning, and expounded *it* by order unto them, saying,

5 I was in the city of Joppa praying: and in a trance I saw a vision, A certain vessel descend, as it had been a great sheet, let down from heaven by four corners; and it came even to me:

6 Upon the which when I had fastened mine eyes, I considered, and saw fourfooted beasts of the earth, and wild beasts, and creeping things, and fowls of the air.

7 And I heard a voice saying unto me, Arise, Peter; slay and eat.

8 But I said, Not so, Lord: for nothing common or unclean hath at any time entered into my mouth.

9 But the voice answered me

again from heaven, What God hath cleansed, *that* call not thou common.

10 And this was done three times: and all were drawn up again into heaven.

11 And, behold, immediately there were three men already come unto the house where I was, sent from Cesarea unto me.

12 And the Spirit bade me go with them, nothing doubting.

Moreover these six brethren accompanied me, and we entered into the man's house:

13 And he shewed us how he had seen an angel in his house, which stood and said unto him, Send men to Joppa, and call for Simon, whose surname is Peter;

14 Who shall tell thee words, whereby thou and all thy house shall be saved.

The Amazing Revelation Reported

By an amazing series of events God had convinced Peter that he should go and preach to the Gentiles. Peter had needed this incontrovertible proof. So he gives them the story in detail.

First, there was a vision of a vessel "as it had been a great sheet, let down from heaven by four corners" containing beasts which, according to the Levitical laws, were not proper for a Jew to eat. But the voice plainly said, "Arise, Peter; slay and eat." Peter had protested to the Lord, "Not so, Lord: for nothing common or unclean hath at any time entered into my mouth." God had answered, "What God hath cleansed, that call not thou common." It was done three times.

The second impressive fact was that "immediately there were three men already come unto the house where I was, sent from Caesarea unto me." The vision and the facts fitted together.

Then there was direct leading of the Holy Spirit that he should "go with them, nothing doubting." And he went.

To guarantee further that the matter was not ill-considered or hasty or that Peter should not be misled in the matter, he had taken with him "these six brethren."

The further evidence that the whole cause was of God, was that Peter found the angel of God had come to Cornelius, bidding him send for Peter, "who shall tell thee words, whereby thou and all thy house shall be saved." That was proof enough for honest Christians. God had sent Peter to preach the Gospel to the Gentiles. In preaching the Gospel, he had necessarily been a guest in the house of Cornelius.

VERSES 15–18:

15 And as I began to speak, the Holy Ghost fell on them, as on us at the beginning.

16 Then remembered I the word of the Lord, how that he said, John indeed baptized with water; but ye shall be baptized with the Holy Ghost.

17 Forasmuch then as God gave them the like gift as *he* *did* unto us, who believed on the Lord Jesus Christ, what was I, that I could withstand God?

18 When they heard these things, they held their peace, and glorified God, saying, Then hath God also to the Gentiles granted repentance unto life.

The Conversion of the Cornelius Household Recounted

Peter had expected that it would take detailed exposition of the Old Testament Scriptures with which these Gentiles were not familiar, and perhaps urgent argument, to get them saved. It is a glad surprise that even as he began to speak, when he announced the theme of his message and thus revealed the plan of salvation, without further ado the whole household turned to Christ and were saved! He had summed up his proposed sermon in the words of Acts 10:43--"To him give all the prophets witness, that through his name whosoever believeth in him shall receive remission of sins."

Perhaps Peter had intended to quote the prophets and the Psalms about the coming of the Saviour, as he had done at Pentecost. His mind was freshly full of all those Old Testament Scriptures, for in the forty days before His ascension

He had taught them "that all things must be fulfilled, which were written in the law of Moses, and in the prophets, and in the psalms, concerning me," and had "opened...their understanding, that they might understand the scriptures" (Luke 24:44, 45). To some of the apostles, "beginning at Moses and all the prophets, he expounded unto them in all the scriptures the things concerning himself" (Luke 24:27).

Perhaps Peter had expected to find, as he had found with the Jewish leaders, such antipathy to the thought that Jesus was raised from the dead, that it must be forcibly argued. But not so: as soon as Cornelius and others, who for agonizing days, had sought the face of the Lord, heard that personal trust in Jesus Christ was the way to be saved, they believed on Him "while Peter yet spake these words" (Acts 10:44).

Oh, it never takes long for one to be saved who is tired of sin and wants the Lord. Those who seek Christ find Him.

Instantly Filled With the Holy Spirit When Saved!

The fullness of the Spirit or the gift of the Holy Spirit, the Holy Spirit coming upon one as an anointing for witnessing and soul winning, is an entirely separate matter from salvation.

It is true that the Holy Spirit Himself is the regenerator and so one who is saved is "born of the Spirit" (John 3:5, 6). And since that day when the resurrected Jesus breathed on the disciples and said, "Receive ye the Holy Ghost" (John 20:22), since Jesus was glorified (John 7:37-39), the Holy Spirit now dwells in the body of every saved person. The night before Jesus died, the Holy Spirit was with the disciples. But Jesus promised that "he dwelleth with you, and shall be in you" (John 14:17). Now every Christian has the Holy Spirit abiding in his body and that began simultaneous with conversion, with regeneration (I Cor. 3:16; I Cor. 6:19, 20; Rom. 8:9).

But the dwelling of the Holy Spirit in a Christian's body,

beginning the moment of regeneration, is one thing, and the enduement of power for witnessing is an entirely different thing. Although Jesus breathed on the disciples and said, "Receive ye the Holy Ghost" the day He rose from the dead, they were still commanded to "tarry ye in the city of Jerusalem, until ye be endued with power from on high" (Luke 24:49). Before Pentecost the disciples waited in the upper room, continued steadfastly in prayer (Acts 1:14) until the Holy Spirit came on them in power.

Philip had a great revival in Samaria and many were saved. But Peter and John came down from Jerusalem-- "who, when they were come down, prayed for them, that they might receive the Holy Ghost: (For as yet he was fallen upon none of them: only they were baptized in the name of the Lord Jesus)" says Acts 8:15, 16. The Apostle Paul trusted Christ and was saved on the road to Damascus. But it was not till after three days of fasting and prayer and the coming of Ananias to him that he was "filled with the Holy Ghost" (Acts 9:17). And the indwelling presence of the Spirit of God is a permanent part of the believer's salvation. But the enduement of power is necessary for a particular time, and one may seek again and have again when needed the fullness of the Spirit, even as the same disciples prayed again in Acts 4:31 and were filled again, and they witnessed again.

So salvation and the fullness of the Spirit are not the same event, and they do not usually occur at the same time. But in the case of Cornelius, his family and party, they were instantly saved and filled with the Holy Spirit.

Why were they filled with the Holy Spirit immediately? I think probably that all the heart searching, all the pleading and confession and forsaking of their known sin, all of the surrender of heart and the abandonment of self to Christ which were needed for the fullness of the Spirit, were already accomplished in these who had prayed for days and waited on God.

In the waters of baptism Jesus had prayed and so had been filled with the Spirit at once, with no delay (Luke 3:21, 22). In answer to many years of fervent prayer by his father and mother, John the Baptist was filled with the Holy Spirit even from his mother's womb (Luke 1:15).

There is no reason why any person who is saved may not be instantly filled with the Holy Spirit, provided his heart has paid the price one must pay to adequately witness for Christ and provided he is wholly committed to that blessed witnessing ministry which the fullness of the Spirit implies.

Again, it is interesting to note that in this case Cornelius and his household were filled with the Spirit before being baptized. Baptism pictures the heart surrender to God's soul-winning business, the identification of the surrendered Christian with Christ's burial, resurrection and newness of life (Luke 3:21, 22; Acts 2:38; Acts 1:5; Acts 19:3-6; Rom. 6:4-11). Thus one so thoroughly ready to bury the old man and to rise in newness of life, as pictured in baptism, was ready to be filled with the Spirit at once before baptism. Baptism is not essential to the fullness of the Spirit. But the heart surrender, the identification of self with Christ, His death, resurrection and soul-saving ministry, is essential to the fullness of the Spirit.

Notice carefully that Peter did not even mention that the Gentile converts had been heard to "speak with tongues." They only praised the Lord in natural languages , as far as we know, and that had no significance except that Peter and the Christian Jews with him could understand and heard them "magnify God" (Acts 10:46). They understood their praises. What Peter is reporting is that they were "baptized with the Holy Ghost" (vs. 16), that God had given them "the like gift as he did unto us" (vs. 17), the gift that Peter discussed at Pentecost in Acts 2:39.

You see, these Gentile converts were not only saved, but they would have every privilege, every blessing, every power, that the Jewish Christians were to have.

All this proved a certain matter to those of the circumcision, the apostles and elders at Jerusalem. "When they heard these things, they held their peace, and glorified God, saying, Then hath God also to the Gentiles granted repentance unto life." All the evidence follows that these Gentiles were really saved, saved just like Jews who trusted Christ were saved! And the Jerusalem Christians were glad and praised God.

VERSES 19–26:

19 ¶ Now they which were scattered abroad upon the persecution that arose about Stephen travelled as far as Phenice, and Cyprus, and Antioch, preaching the word to none but unto the Jews only.

20 And some of them were men of Cyprus and Cyrene, which, when they were come to Antioch, spake unto the Grecians, preaching the Lord Jesus.

21 And the hand of the Lord was with them: and a great number believed, and turned unto the Lord.

22 ¶ Then tidings of these things came unto the ears of the church which was in Jerusalem: and they sent forth Barnabas, that he should go as far as Antioch.

23 Who, when he came, and had seen the grace of God, was glad, and exhorted them all, that with purpose of heart they would cleave unto the Lord.

24 For he was a good man, and full of the Holy Ghost and of faith: and much people was added unto the Lord.

25 Then departed Barnabas to Tarsus, for to seek Saul:

26 And when he had found him, he brought him unto Antioch. And it came to pass, that a whole year they assembled themselves with the church, and taught much people. And the disciples were called Christians first in Antioch.

Antioch: Christians: Barnabas and Saul

The great boldness and power of Stephen's Spirit-filled preaching brought about great persecution and he was stoned (Acts 7:54-60). And that great revival of the power of God among the Christians led to further persecution.

"And at that time there was a great persecution against the church which was at Jerusalem; and they were all scattered abroad throughout the regions of Judaea and Samaria, except the apostles" (Acts 8:1). We are told that "they that were scattered abroad went every where preaching the word" (Acts 8:4).

Here we are told that they later went on beyond Judaea, up north, up the Mediterranean coast to Phenicia, then further on to Antioch of Syria, then out to Cyprus, an island in the Mediterranean Sea. It may be that some of these men originally from Cyprus and Cyrene (vs. 20) were at Jerusalem at the passover time when Jesus was crucified, stayed over for Pentecost and there were converted. Then at the great persecution they were scattered abroad. Now some of them came way north to Antioch and "spake unto the Grecians," that is, to Hellenist Jews, "preaching the Lord Jesus." Remember that these were "preaching the word to none but unto the Jews only" (vs. 19). Although Peter has now preached to Cornelius and his household, he went back to Jerusalem. The young Saul would become the apostle to the Gentiles and not until Paul's missionary journey would there be a great deal of preaching to the Gentiles. But these Spirit-filled disciples, going everywhere preaching, found that "a great number believed, and turned unto the Lord."

At Jerusalem the apostles and other disciples heard about the blessings of God at Antioch. They had sent Peter and John down to Samaria in Acts, chapter 8, to make sure of the proper teaching and to pray for the young disciples. But the Gospel is now spread so widely that there are not enough apostles to go everywhere. So they sent good Barnabas, "the son of consolation," who saw the good work of grace going on in the hearts of the people, the many new converts, and was glad.

"For he was a good man." That is not often said in the Bible about a man. But Barnabas deserved it. He was a Levite who had lived on the Island of Cyprus (Acts 4:36), but had moved to Jerusalem. He had land in that area and sold it all and gave it sacrificially for the feeding of the multitude (Acts 4:37). This is the generous and kindhearted man who took up with Saul when he came back from Damascus converted and when the apostles and others were afraid of him and did not believe he was a disciple. But Barnabas brought Saul to the apostles, explained how he had been converted and had Paul accepted by other disciples in Jerusalem.

It was just like this good man to go seek Saul in Tarsus and bring him to Antioch to preach the Gospel. These two men loved each other, they are both all-out for Christ and both are filled with the Spirit and so they gravitate together.

Note verse 24 again. Barnabas was a good man, "full of the Holy Ghost and of faith: and much people was added unto the Lord." The fullness of the Holy Spirit is not simply an experience to be enjoyed. It is an enduement of power for service and witnessing. So it was said of John the Baptist, "He shall be filled with the Holy Ghost, even from his mother's womb. And many of the children of Israel shall he turn to the Lord their God" (Luke 1:15, 16). So wherever in the Bible we find people filled with the Spirit, they witness for Christ and get people saved. So with this Barnabas, filled with the Holy Spirit, "much people was added unto the Lord."

All the talk of being filled with the Spirit simply as an experience of joy, or for a so-called "deeper life," or to eradicate the sin nature, is utterly foreign to the Bible teaching on this question. The fullness of the Holy Spirit is like a mighty railroad engine. It is not made to run up and down on a sidetrack ringing a bell and blowing a horn. It is made to couple on to a train and pull it to its destination. So wherever we find people in the Bible filled with the Holy Spirit, we find them witnessing for Jesus and people being saved. The fullness of the Spirit is an "enduement of power from on high" so people may witness for Christ.

Barnabas and young Saul worked together at Antioch a full year and the disciples there came to be called "Christians." Now it was "Barnabas and Saul." Soon it would be "Paul and Barnabas," since the younger disciple appointed of God as apostle to Gentiles would take the lead and Barnabas become his assistant.

VERSES 27-30:

27 ¶ And in these days came prophets from Jerusalem unto Antioch.

28 And there stood up one of them named Agabus, and signified by the Spirit that there should be great dearth throughout all the world: which came to pass in the days of Claudius Cesar.

29 Then the disciples, every man according to his ability, determined to send relief unto the brethren which dwelt in Judea:

30 Which also they did, and sent it to the elders by the hands of Barnabas and Saul.

Famine Coming: Antioch Christians Send Relief to Jerusalem Christians

Agabus was a prophet. A prophet is one who, filled with the Spirit, witnesses for God. Sometimes he foretells future events by revelation from God. Sometimes it is simply witnessing about salvation, as we see happening at Pentecost, foretold by Joel the prophet (Acts 2:17, 18). Prophecy is not necessarily preaching. Here Agabus seems to have prophesied in public (vs. 28). But the same man in Acts 21:10 and 11 came and revealed to Paul and his helpers the imprisonment he would suffer if he went on to Jerusalem. To prophesy is to speak for God in the power and moving of the Spirit of God. Prophets were sometimes preachers, as we see with Judas and Silas in Acts 15:32. But all Christians--whether preachers or not--should covet "that ye may prophesy" (I Cor. 14:1).

There was coming a "great dearth throughout all the

world," a famine. The "world" is a term used in the Greek, not of the whole planet but the "inhabited earth," perhaps a rather indefinite word referring to all the area with which the person speaking knew about. So the decree from Caesar Augustus "that all the world should be taxed" (Luke 2:1).

Already there was hardship among the Christians at Jerusalem, unemployed, great persecution and therefore poverty. A famine would make it worse. So the disciples "determined to send relief unto the brethren which dwelt in Judaea." They raised their collection and sent it to the elders at Jerusalem "by the hands of Barnabas and Saul."

Is this trip to Jerusalem the one Paul mentions later in Galatians 1:18 and 19?

Paul the apostle was greatly impressed with the need to care for the poor saints at Jerusalem. Besides, although God would not let him stay at Jerusalem but would send him far away and a little later would send him to the Gentiles, he never got away from his love for Jerusalem, his longing to help there. So we will find Paul later raising money among "the churches of Galatia" and "in Corinth" (I Cor. 16:1), and then over in the churches in Greece and Macedonia (II Cor. 8:1). So Paul raised money and was selected by the new churches to carry their gifts to Jerusalem (II Cor. 8:19-24).

It is noticeable that most of the teaching of the Scriptures about giving and most of the example, is not about giving to some far-off missions, but giving to the relief of other Christians and to the support of the minister.

ACTS 12

VERSES 1-4:

NOW about that time Herod the king stretched forth *his* hands to vex certain of the church.

2 And he killed James the brother of John with the sword.

3 And because he saw it pleased the Jews, he proceeded further to take Peter also. (Then were the days of unleavened bread.)

4 And when he had apprehended him, he put *him* in prison, and delivered *him* to four quaternions of soldiers to keep him; intending after Easter to bring him forth to the people.

Herod Kills James, Arrests Peter

Distinguish four Herods ruling at different times and places in New Testament times.

1. Herod the Great was king of Judaea when Christ was born; had the babies of Bethlehem slain; died a year or so later.

2. Herod Antipas was the son of Herod the Great and after his father's death was made ruler in the provinces of Galilee and Peraea. He is the Herod "that fox" mentioned by Christ in Luke 13:32. This Herod was visiting in Jerusalem at the time of Christ's crucifixion, and since Jesus was from Galilee, "Herod's jurisdiction," Pilate sent Christ before Herod where He was mocked, refused to work a miracle and was returned to Pilate (Luke 23:6-12). This is the Herod who had killed John the Baptist (Mark 6:14-28).

3. Herod Agrippa I is the Herod here discussed in Acts, chapter 12, who killed James, arrested Peter, and died by the curse of God (vs. 23).

4. Herod Agrippa II is the son of Agrippa I, is the "King Agrippa" of Acts, chapter 25 and 26, before whom the Apostle Paul witnessed.

James, the brother of John, seems to have been the first of the twelve original apostles to die as a martyr for Jesus.

Notice in the same chapter that James mentioned in verse 17 is another James, the brother of the Lord Jesus (His half brother, born of Mary and Joseph after the birth of Jesus). He seems to have been the principal pastor at Jerusalem, as we see from Acts 15:13-21 where James said in verse 19, "Wherefore my sentence is..." as if he had a deciding voice.

Note "the days of unleavened bread," the seven days which had begun with the eating of the passover lamb (Exod. 12:15-20). The word Easter in verse 4 is a mistranslation--it should be "the passover." Note that the feast of unleavened bread and the passover feast were now called, the whole seven days, the passover. Actually, since it was forbidden to have any leaven in the house, the night of the passover time (Exod. 12:19), the Jews customarily had unleavened bread the day that the passover lamb was killed in the afternoon, which would really make eight days of unleavened bread. So, we think that the term "the passover" in the Gospels generally refers to the whole extended period of time. I do not believe that Jesus ate of the passover lamb with His disciples, but ate of a preliminary meal of the passover season (Matt. 26:17-25). In all the Gospels telling of that occasion, no mention is made of a passover lamb killed or eaten by the apostles and Jesus. Also it is clear from John 19:14 and 31 that when Jesus was tried and crucified, "it was the preparation of the passover." That is the day when the passover lamb was to be killed, and so Jesus was crucified and died at the time passover lambs were being killed. Jesus did not eat of the passover lamb, and the meal He had with His disciples the preceding night was a preliminary meal of the passover season.

This Herod tried to please the Jews (vs. 3). So he would not kill Peter during this passover season but intended to do so afterward. So Peter lay in jail awaiting death when the feast of unleavened bread should be ended as the Jews did not want Jesus' body to remain on the cross on the annual

Sabbath day, which began the passover at sundown the day of the crucifixion (John 19:31). So the Jewish leaders would not want Peter killed during the time of the feast of unleavened bread.

VERSES 5–12:

5 Peter therefore was kept in prison: but prayer was made without ceasing of the church unto God for him.

6 And when Herod would have brought him forth, the same night Peter was sleeping between two soldiers, bound with two chains: and the keepers before the door kept the prison.

7 And, behold, the angel of the Lord came upon *him*, and a light shined in the prison: and he smote Peter on the side, and raised him up, saying, Arise up quickly. And his chains fell off from *his* hands.

8 And the angel said unto him, Gird thyself, and bind on thy sandals: and so he did. And he saith unto him, Cast thy garment about thee, and follow me.

9 And he went out, and followed him; and wist not that it was true which was done by the angel; but thought he saw a vision.

10 When they were past the first and the second ward, they came unto the iron gate that leadeth unto the city; which opened to them of his own accord: and they went out, and passed on through one street; and forthwith the angel departed from him.

11 And when Peter was come to himself, he said, Now I know of a surety, that the Lord hath sent his angel, and hath delivered me out of the hand of Herod, and *from* all the expectation of the people of the Jews.

12 And when he had considered *the thing*, he came to the house of Mary the mother of John, whose surname was Mark; where many were gathered together praying.

Unceasing Prayer Answered: An Angel Delivers Peter From Jail

Note here the strange contrast. God allowed King Herod to kill the Apostle James with a sword. In answer to prevailing prayer, He sent an angel to deliver Peter from prison and from death. God surely means to teach us here two great lessons which balance each other.

First, God does not always keep His people from suffering. Down through the centuries it has been true, "Yea, and all that will live godly in Christ Jesus shall suffer persecution" (II Tim. 3:12). Note how Paul approved himself as the minister of God, "In much patience, in afflictions, in necessities, in distresses, In stripes, in imprisonments, in tumults, in labours, in watchings, in fastings" (II Cor. 6:4, 5). So Peter taught people to rejoice, "Though now for a season, if need be, ye are in heaviness through manifold temptations: That the trial of your faith, being much more precious than of gold that perisheth, though it be tried with fire, might be found unto praise and honour and glory at the appearing of Jesus Christ" (I Pet. 1:6, 7). And he was inspired to teach people, "For even hereunto were ye called: because Christ also suffered for us, leaving us an example, that ye should follow his steps" (I Pet. 2:21). And again, "Forasmuch then as Christ hath suffered for us in the flesh, arm yourselves likewise with the same mind: for he that hath suffered in the flesh hath ceased from sin" (I Pet. 4:1).

Christ suffered and His servants are no better than their Lord. Stephen was stoned to death. Since Pentecost Peter and John had been imprisoned (Acts 4:3). And all of the apostles had been imprisoned and delivered by night by the angel of the Lord (Acts 5:17-20), and then after preaching again were severely beaten and put to shame (Acts 5:40, 41). Stephen had been stoned to death (Acts 7:54-60). Then the young zealot, Saul, had brought on a great wave of persecution so that Christians, except the apostles, were scattered everywhere (Acts 8:1-4). The Jews at Damascus had tried to kill young Saul after he was converted (Acts 9:22-25), but he was delivered. Then in Jerusalem Pau' preached so boldly that "they went about to slay him" (Act 9:29).

Now we need not be shocked that James the apostle died

glorious martyr's death. Later Paul the apostle will be imprisoned for years, was often in prison.

"Thrice was I beaten with rods, once was I stoned, thrice I suffered shipwreck, a night and a day I have been in the deep; In journeyings often, in perils of waters, in perils of robbers, in perils by mine own countrymen, in perils by the heathen, in perils in the city, in perils in the wilderness, in perils in the sea, in perils among false brethren; In weariness and painfulness, in watchings often, in hunger and thirst, in fastings often, in cold and nakedness."--II Cor. 11:25-27.

And at last Paul would be beheaded at Rome.

In this world Christ is despised and rejected. For God's people who are true, it is now an age for crosses, not for crowns.

The other lesson is that all the wicked kings cannot put to death God's servant until it is God's will. Here God spared Peter in answer to persistent prayer. God had work for Peter to do. No man of God, in the will of God, can die until God wants him to die.

In the case of Peter, "Prayer was made without ceasing of the church unto God for him" (vs. 5). Was not the same prayer for James? Perhaps not. I think that the Holy Spirit led people to pray for Peter's deliverance, encouraged them to pray, although all the outward circumstances made it seem improbable. It may be that had they prayed as persistently for James, he would have been spared. But it seems likely that God did not give them faith for the deliverance of James. On such a matter, faith is a gift of God, although when prayer was answered, they had not expected such an answer at once. Their faith seemed very small and uncertain, yet there was some faith in their persistent praying, and they must have had some urge of the Spirit of God to pray.

First Corinthians 12:9 says that to some it is given by the Spirit, various gifts, "To another faith by the same Spirit...." And everyone is commanded to think soberly, not proudly, "according as God hath dealt to every man the measure of faith" (Rom. 12:3). On matters where the Scripture does not clearly make known the will of God, then one cannot pray in the will of God unless that will is revealed by the Holy Spirit. And one cannot have faith unless faith is given. You see, faith is depending upon God to do what He promised to do or what He is obligated to do by His Word or by His nature and character.

There are some matters clearly revealed in the Word of God about which it would be a sin not to believe. If God said it, we ought to believe it. If He promised, we ought to expect it. So it is clearly promised that God will save everyone who comes to Him through Christ and depending on Christ. One who thus does not trust Christ for salvation, sins. Faith in such settled matters promised in the Word of God comes "by hearing, and hearing by the word of God" (Rom. 10:17). But on other matters not clearly revealed in the Bible, on matters where we cannot definitely know what is the will of God except as He reveals it by His Spirit, the Holy Spirit must help us pray, and give us faith. Doubtless He did help these Christians at Jerusalem pray for Peter's deliverance, although they had little expectation. Their persistent prayer at least was a matter of faith, however imperfect.

It is wonderful to remember that no prison can hold the man whom God would release. He had brought the apostles out of jail before. Now the angel brings Peter out again. In Acts 16 Paul and Silas are delivered by an earthquake. And whether by miraculous means or by influencing the will of men or by controlling circumstances not miraculous, God has His way. Oh, we should remember that Christ has said

I am "he that openeth, and no man shutteth; and shutteth, and no man openeth" (Rev. 3:7). Before kings and governors and judges, the Saviour had instructed the disciples they should "take no thought how or what ye shall speak; for it shall be given you in that same hour what ye shall speak. For it is not ye that speak, but the Spirit of your Father which speaketh in you" (Matt. 10:19, 20). When Jesus was before Pilate, "Then saith Pilate unto him, Speakest thou not unto me? knowest thou not that I have power to crucify thee, and have power to release thee? Jesus answered, Thou couldest have no power at all against me, except it were given thee from above: therefore he that delivered me unto thee hath the greater sin" (John 19:10, 11). In some sense that is true of every Christian who does the will of God. Peter could not be imprisoned by Herod except it was given to Herod from above.

It is interesting that Peter himself was sleeping soundly while others in the city were awake in the night praying for his deliverance! We believe that God had given Peter sweet peace so that he had no fret. As Paul could say in prison at Rome, "I have learned, in whatsoever state I am, therewith to be content" (Phil. 4:11), so Peter had surely learned to have peace. He could sleep when he knew Herod intended to kill him tomorrow morning!

The chains of Peter fell off. God is master of all the chains. The doors opened before Peter and the angel. God has keys for all the locks! The guarding soldiers and guards did not even see Peter and the angel! God is master of all the faculties of men. Man has invented "an electric eye" so that when a beam of light is broken by one standing before the door, the door opens. But man has never made an invention to do an intricate and marvelous thing but that God has done it before him.

Peter "came to the house of Mary the mother of John, whose surname was Mark." It is this same John Mark in whose home the prayer meeting for Peter's deliverance was held, who in verse 25 went from Jerusalem with Paul and Barnabas to Antioch and then on the missionary journey. This same John Mark was young and unstable, who on the first missionary journey "departed from them from Pamphylia, and went not with them to the work" (Acts 15:37-39). And over Mark, Paul and Barnabas broke up their long partnership in travel and missionary soul winning. Why was Barnabas so attached to John Mark? Because Mary, John's mother, was sister to Barnabas! He was concerned about his nephew. Colossians 4:10 speaks of "Marcus, sister's son to Barnabas."

Barnabas was a devoted, good man called "the son of consolation" by the apostles (Acts 11:24; Acts 4:36, 37). Evidently his sister, too, was a devoted Christian woman in whose home the people having no church building met for prayer, and perhaps for other services of the church.

VERSES 13–17:

13 And as Peter knocked at the door of the gate, a damsel came to hearken, named Rhoda.

14 And when she knew Peter's voice, she opened not the gate for gladness, but ran in, and told how Peter stood before the gate.

15 And they said unto her, Thou art mad. But she constantly affirmed that it was even so. Then said they, It is his angel.

16 But Peter continued knocking: and when they had opened *the door*, and saw him, they were astonished.

17 But he, beckoning unto them with the hand to hold their peace, declared unto them how the Lord had brought him out of the prison. And he said, Go shew these things unto James, and to the brethren. And he departed, and went into another place.

Surprise at Answered Prayer!

Peter knocked at the door of the street gate which shut Mary's home off from the city. There "many were gathered together praying" so earnestly that others paid no attention, but "a damsel came to hearken, named Rhoda." She knew

Peter's voice! Excited, she neglected to open the gate, but ran to tell the good news that Peter was delivered and stood before the gate!

How strange that they did not believe it! They said she was crazy! "Thou art mad." And when she insisted that she had heard his voice and knew him, "Then said they, It is his angel," that is, his spirit or his ghost. They thought perhaps Peter was already slain and this was his spirit speaking outside the gate! As Peter continued knocking they at last opened the door and "were astonished."

How slow we are to believe the good things God has in mind for us!

It is well here to note that faith is not the only condition of answered prayer. Consider that on any one of these grounds God has promised to answer prayer.

1. On faith (Matt. 21:22; Mark 9:23; Mark 11:24, etc.)

2. Asking in Jesus' name (John 14:13, 14).

3. When the Holy Spirit has united two or more in prayer for the same object (Matt. 18:19).

4. Keeping God's commandments and doing the things that are pleasing in His sight (I John 3:22, 23). This would involve, of course, wanting the will of God and thus learning to pray acceptably.

5. Persistence in prayer (Matt. 7:7, 8; Luke 11:9, 10. See also Luke 18:8 where faith seems to be equated with persistence). In "ask, and it shall be given you," the word ask and similar verbs in the same passage are in the present tense, implying continued, persistent action. And so with James 4:2.

God is so anxious to answer our prayers that He opens many doors for us and makes many promises to us. And any one of His promises, honestly claimed, is enough to receive the blessing. So these people who prayed so persistently, but perhaps not with very strong faith, yet got the answer to their prayers. How many times we have prayed and then were surprised when God gave the answer!

And thus we should remember that the throne of prayer is "the throne of grace," and that we should come boldly "to obtain mercy," not justice and not according to our deserts (Heb. 4:16). God gave His Son, in loving grace, and how then will He not also freely give us all things as a matter of mercy and grace (Rom. 8:32). So we should pray whether we have all the faith we should like to have or not. We should continue praying even when we are conscious of little expectancy. God delights to have us call upon Him. He is ready to give more than we can ask or think (Eph. 3:20).

What a chatter in the room at Mary's house! But Peter "beckoning unto them with the hand to hold their peace" told how he had been delivered. He said, "Go shew these things unto James, and to the brethren." James, the brother of the Lord Jesus, the author of the Epistle James, was now evidently one of the most influential of the apostles in Jerusalem.

But Mary's house was so well known as a center for worship and fellowship among Christians: perhaps the soldiers tomorrow morning will come here inquiring for Peter. So he went to another place for safety.

VERSES 18–23:

18 Now as soon as it was day, there was no small stir among the soldiers, what was become of Peter.

19 And when Herod had sought for him, and found him not, he examined the keepers, and commanded that *they* should be put to death. And he went down from Judea to Cesarea, and *there* abode.

20 ¶ And Herod was highly displeased with them of Tyre and Sidon: but they came with one accord to him, and, having made Blastus the king's chamberlain their friend, desired peace; because their country was nourished by the king's *country*.

21 And upon a set day Herod, arrayed in royal apparel, sat upon his throne, and made an oration unto them.

22 And the people gave a shout, *saying, It is* the voice of a god, and not of a man.

23 And immediately the angel of the Lord smote him, because he gave not God the glory: and he was eaten of worms, and gave up the ghost.

Herod's Anger, Pride and Death

What a stir among the soldiers--"What was become of Peter?" (vs. 18). Herod would not believe in a miracle. He believed that some of the keepers of the prison had conspired to release Peter. He commanded them to be put to death. Then he went down from Judaea to Caesarea on the Mediterranean coast, "and there abode."

I wonder what conviction, what unrest was stirring in his wicked heart. Why had Jerusalem become distasteful to him? Since he is about to die in his sins, it seems likely that God was straightly warning him.

At Caesarea, some officials or leading citizens of Tyre and Sidon, two cities perhaps fifty and seventy miles north on the coast, had sued for peace. All the imports from Egypt, from the rich Jordan valley and from India tended to come through King Herod's country to Tyre and Sidon, so they sought the favor of the king's chamberlain and set out to have the favor of King Herod.

Herod was a proud man of the dynasty of Herod the Great. He had been educated in Rome, had the favor of Caesar. Now flattering men waited on him to gain his favor. When he made an oration the crowd of flatterers about, such as always follow a king or man of great power, cried out, "It is the voice of a god, and not of a man."

Did they believe it? I doubt it. Possibly some of them did. Greek mythology spoke often of gods coming among men. In Acts 14:11-13, when Paul healed a man at Lystra, the people thought, "The gods are come down to us in the likeness of men. And they called Barnabas, Jupiter; and Paul, Mercurius..." and the priests of Jupiter would have sacrificed oxen to them.

So since idolatry was the way of the most of the world at

that time, a jealous God would not let Herod get by in claiming to be God.

And so "immediately the angel of the Lord smote him." He "was eaten of worms" and died a horrible death. It is noteworthy that the Caesars at Rome wanted to be worshipped as God. Daniel was put in the lions' den because he would not agree to follow the law that for thirty days he would pray to no one but to the king of Babylon (Dan. 6:7-24). In godless, communistic Russia, Stalin and Lenin have been put in song and prayer as gods.

VERSES 24, 25:

24 ¶ But the word of God grew and multiplied.

25 And Barnabas and Saul returned from Jerusalem, when they had fulfilled *their* ministry, and took with them John, whose surname was Mark.

Getting Ready for the Great Missionary Journeys

The shocking death of King Herod so soon following his slaughter of James and the deliverance of Peter, gave a greater audience for the Gospel, and so "the word of God grew and multiplied."

Here we see that "Barnabas and Saul returned from Jerusalem when they had fulfilled their ministry." Their ministry had been to deliver the money that had been sent, "relief unto the brethren which dwelt in Judaea." Barnabas and Saul delivered the goods to the Christians, to the elders of the church at Jerusalem and the nearby area (Acts 11:29, 30). And it was "now about that time" that Herod persecuted the church, killed James and imprisoned Peter. So Barnabas and Saul were in Jerusalem at the time of Peter's deliverance.

Weren't they in the prayer meeting at the house of Mary, the mother of John Mark? We doubt it, because James, the brother of Jesus, was not there, as we see from verse 17. James is one of the "pillars" of the church mentioned at Jerusalem in Galatians 2:9, when the other James, the apostle, the brother of John, had been slain. And this James seems to have been the chief pastor in Jerusalem, as we learn from Acts 15:13-19. But if Barnabas and Saul were in Jerusalem, they may have been hiding out since the principle apostles were all in danger of death. And then they have not even seen Peter and James on this trip. But they very likely did see Mary, the mother of John Mark, because he would have probably been with his mother, and they took John Mark with them when they returned from Jerusalem to Antioch.

Barnabas was a native of Cyprus (Acts 4:36). Saul was a native of Tarsus and son of a prominent native there, a Roman citizen (Acts 9:30; Acts 11:25; Acts 21:39). So Barnabas and Saul "returned from Jerusalem" when they felt led that their ministry there was finished, taking with them John Mark. No doubt they had some urging, some leading toward what God was going to do with them in the future. Whether they knew it or not, they were getting ready for the great missionary journeys that would spread the Gospel in power to Asia Minor and into Greece and then to Rome, the center of the known world at that time.

ACTS 13

VERSES 1–5:

NOW there were in the church that was at Antioch certain prophets and teachers; as Barnabas, and Simeon that was called Niger, and Lucius of Cyrene, and Manaen, which had been brought up with Herod the tetrarch, and Saul.

2 As they ministered to the Lord, and fasted, the Holy Ghost said, Separate me Barnabas and Saul for the work whereunto I have called them.

3 And when they had fasted and prayed, and laid *their* hands on them, they sent *them* away.

4 ¶ So they, being sent forth by the Holy Ghost, departed unto Seleucia; and from thence they sailed to Cyprus.

5 And when they were at Salamis, they preached the word of God in the synagogues of the Jews: and they had also John to *their* minister.

Paul and Barnabas Called and Set Apart for a Particular Work

God often tells favored saints what He will do. So "the Lord said, Shall I hide from Abraham that thing which I do; Seeing that Abraham shall surely become a great and mighty nation...For I know him, that he will command his children and his household after him, and they shall keep the way of the Lord..." (Gen. 18:17-19). God told the prophet Samuel about His plans for David (I Sam. 16). God told Simeon and Anna about the baby Jesus (Luke 2:25-36). God had told Ananias about His plans for Saul (Acts 9:10-16). Now God put it on the heart of "certain prophets and teachers" at Antioch to set apart Barnabas and Saul for the work to which He had called them.

In nearly every case when God calls some man to preach the Gospel, He has impressed someone else of His will also.

When God calls a man to preach, He calls others to pray and to support him and help him and He also calls people to hear. So every missionary goes out, not representing himself alone, but representing some church or churches that love him, pray for him, support him. So every preacher should have those who pray for God's anointing upon him and should count him their representative in preaching the Gospel.

Five men are here named, three others besides Barnabas and Saul. There may have been some others, but it was not the church congregation as a whole. A church by a vote cannot make a preacher. They may vote to encourage his preaching and to endorse his preaching or vote to support him, but a church cannot call a preacher to preach or cannot stop him from preaching. As a sinner comes directly to Jesus Christ to be saved, so a preacher must have his call directly from God and his enduement of power directly through the Spirit of God. The preacher is not a hireling. Paul and Barnabas here are "sent forth by the Holy Ghost" (vs. 4). Doubtless there were many immature Christians or carnal and worldly Christians who knew nothing about the plan of God. God's Spirit did not talk to them about the ministry He would have Barnabas and Saul undertake. Here these two are sent out by the Holy Spirit. And the Spirit talked to a few select Christians about it that all might pray together and all might unite in the task ahead.

Notice that the divine revelation came "as they ministered to the Lord, and fasted." God speaks to people who wait on Him in prayer. And the fasting indicated a great concern to know the will of God and to have His power. It seems likely that God had been dealing with Barnabas and Saul in bringing them from Jerusalem (Acts 12:25) and that He had been dealing with these other prophets and teachers, pressing upon their hearts the command of the Great Commission. Where should they start? Who should take the lead? What form should their soul-winning activities take? So they "ministered to the Lord, and fasted."

When the Holy Spirit made clear that He would send forth

Barnabas and Saul, then "when they had fasted and prayed," again they laid their hands upon them and sent them away.

Fasting is as suitable in New Testament times as in Old Testament times. There is no special virtue in fasting as a form. But for one to have such concern of heart to find the will of God and do it, and to have the power and blessing of God that his mind withdraws from food and other pleasures and needs for the time, is perfectly proper. Even should one determine that he will deliberately put aside food or sleep or other duties for a time in order to more thoroughly seek the will and power of God, is perfectly legitimate and proper. We have no doubt that the disciples, waiting on God before Pentecost, fasted as "these all continued with one accord in prayer and supplication" (Acts 1:14). Jesus had promised that "when the bridegroom shall be taken from them, then shall they fast" (Matt. 9:15). Paul, after his conversion and waiting upon God for the power of the Holy Spirit, went three days and nights without food, praying (Acts 9:9, 11). We have often seen a mother so concerned about a sick baby that she could not eat. Would it not be proper, then, for one to become so concerned about soul winning and finding God's will and having the power of the Holy Spirit upon our witness, that we should sometimes go without food? So these Christians fasted before they knew the will of God, then fasted as they prayed for power and blessing after they knew the will of God.

These other prophets and teachers "laid their hands on them"--on Barnabas and Saul--and "sent them away." This, like the ordination of deacons in Acts, chapter 6, is part of the background for our present-day ordination services. It is obviously intended that as brethren pray over one whom God has called, God will give power, spiritual discernment, faith and perhaps other gifts such as he would not have given without prayer. Paul was inspired to write Timothy, "Neglect not the gift that is in thee, which was given thee by prophecy, with the laying on of the hands of the presbytery"

(I Tim. 4:14). Ordination does not give a man authority to preach: he has that authority from God, if he is truly called. But ordination ought to mean the endorsement of other good Christians and their earnest prayer for God's blessing upon the one for whom they pray and upon whom they lay their hands.

So they, "being sent forth by the Holy Ghost, departed...." They knew they were called: they knew where to go. They had the power of the Holy Spirit and the leading of the Holy Spirit. They were backed up by the prayers of godly men. Oh, any preacher who is really "sent forth by the Holy Ghost" may have great blessings of God upon his ministry. And every man called of God should wait on God till he is truly "sent forth by the Holy Ghost." They went to Seleucia, then sailed to the Island of Cyprus which was Barnabas' old home. John Mark, who had come from Jerusalem with them, started with them on this first missionary journey as helper and servant.

Missionary Work Starts at Cyprus

Verse 4 tells us, "So they, being sent forth by the Holy Ghost, departed unto Seleucia; and from thence they sailed to Cyprus." They went to the seacoast and took a boat immediately for Cyprus. Their missionary journeys began with that island in the Mediterranean.

Why? Evidently because that was the old home of Barnabas. Acts 4:36 tells us, "And Joses, who by the apostles was surnamed Barnabas, (which is, being interpreted, The son of consolation,) a Levite, and of the country of Cyprus."

When Barnabas felt the holy fire in his soul, an urgency to win people to Christ, he wanted to go to his old home country, the island of Cyprus, and there preach the Gospel in the areas where he had relatives and friends perhaps, and where he knew so well the spiritual needs of the people!

The next place these two missionaries are to go would be

in the provinces in the peninsula of what we now call Asia Minor. They will be preaching in Pamphylia, in the cities of Perga, Antioch, Lystra, Iconium, etc. (vs. 13). That was Paul's native country and Tarsus was a city of Cilicia where Paul had been brought up. Immediately after Paul's conversion and after going to Jerusalem and meeting the apostles, he had returned to Tarsus (Acts 9:30). Barnabas had gone there to bring Paul back to Antioch (Acts 11:25, 26). And now Paul felt that he must carry the Gospel back to that whole needy area.

This illustrates a clear principle of the Bible, that one is first accountable to those who are near him. The Lord Jesus told the disciples, "That repentance and remission of sins should be preached in his name among all nations, beginning at Jerusalem" (Luke 24:47). He had told them, "But tarry ye in the city of Jerusalem, until ye be endued with power from on high" (Luke 24:49). They were in Jerusalem, so that was the place to begin preaching.

A familiar phrase is "to the Jew first," from Romans 2:9, 10. But that does not mean that every Christian has a duty to preach the Gospel to Jews first. No, the Gospel started with the Jews and they should first preach to their own relatives and neighbors. In the same context where the Lord has just said twice, "to the Jew first," He adds, "For there is no respect of persons with God" (Rom. 2:11). Chronologically the Gospel came to the Jew first, that is all. And one who is a Jew and lives among Jews should probably start preaching among them. One who is a Gentile and lives among Gentiles should probably begin witnessing to Gentiles.

We know that Christians are commanded to take the Gospel "to all the world" and "to every creature." But foreign missions have no priority with God for individual Christians and for every individual Christian his own town or city is more important than some far-off town or city. His own lost loved ones are more important than some lost ones with whom he has no contacts nor opportunity, and for whom he is not directly responsible.

When Jesus healed the Gadarene demoniac, the wild man was tamed, the naked man is clothed, the insane wretch is now a sweet tempered, comforted believer. But the citizens cared more for their pigs than for the man out of whom Jesus had cast a legion of devils and they besought Jesus to depart. So the healed and cleansed and saved demoniac now wanted to go with Jesus. "Now the man out of whom the devils were departed besought him that he might be with him: but Jesus sent him away, saying, Return to thine own house, and shew how great things God hath done unto thee. And he went his way, and published throughout the whole city how great things Jesus had done unto him" (Luke 8:38, 39).

It is always right and proper to begin where you are. So Barnabas and Paul went first to Cyprus and then to Paul's old home area.

It is strange that we do not have a detailed account of the ministry of other apostles, after Paul comes into the picture. Peter and John are mentioned as going to Samaria, in Acts 8. Peter went to Cornelius' household to win these Gentiles in Acts 10. Later, we suppose, Peter went to Babylon where he wrote his epistles (I Pet. 5:13). Thomas, we understand, went to India and the Mar Thoma body of thousands of Christians there claim to be descended from those who heard Thomas preach. We know from Revelation 1:1-9 that John was later exiled to the Island of Patmos in the Aegean Sea for preaching. But now the rest of the book of Acts is taken up principally with the story of Paul's ministry and his associates.

VERSES 6–13:

6 And when they had gone through the isle unto Paphos, they found a certain sorcerer, a false prophet, a Jew, whose name *was* Bar-jesus:

7 Which was with the deputy of the country, Sergius Paulus, a prudent man; who called for Barnabas and Saul, and desired to hear the word of God.

8 But Elymas the sorcerer (for so is his name by interpretation) withstood them, seeking to turn away the deputy from the faith.

9 Then Saul, (who also *is called* Paul,) filled with the Holy Ghost, set his eyes on him,

10 And said, O full of all sub-tilty and all mischief, *thou* child of the devil, *thou* enemy of all righteousness, wilt thou not cease to pervert the right ways of the Lord?

11 And now, behold, the hand of the Lord *is* upon thee, and thou shalt be blind, not seeing the sun for a season. And immediately there fell on him a mist and a darkness; and he went about seeking some to lead him by the hand.

12 Then the deputy, when he saw what was done, believed, being astonished at the doctrine of the Lord.

13 Now when Paul and his company loosed from Paphos, they came to Perga in Pamphylia: and John departing from them returned to Jerusalem.

A Sorcerer Blinded; an Official, Sergius Paulus, Converted

Jesus had warned the disciples and warns us, "Beware of false prophets, which come to you in sheep's clothing, but inwardly they are ravening wolves" (Matt. 7:15). It is a part of any faithful ministry for Christ that we meet false doctrine, wicked men who pretend to serve God, and that we oppose them. Here in the town of Paphos the false prophet was a Jew with the strange name of Bar-jesus, that is, son of Jesus or son of the Saviour. He was a Jew and knew about the true God in the Old Testament Scriptures. He evidently knew about Jesus also, though he himself was not a Christian. He sought "to turn away the deputy," Sergius Paulus, from the faith. Sergius Paulus, a wise man, had "called for Barnabas and Saul, and desired to hear the word of God."

What should a Christian do in such a case? Withstand the evil one openly and strongly!

Once in a Texas city, a worldly mother tried to prevent her grown daughter from coming forward to claim Christ. The weeping daughter pleaded; the mother threatened and forbade the seventeen-year-old young woman. I felt led to publicly call the attention of the congregation to the sin of this woman and rebuke her from the pulpit. She stood shocked, humiliated and convicted. The daughter came weeping to trust Christ and claim Him openly. God got great honor in the occasion. But notice that here Paul was "filled with the Holy Ghost." So one must be if he witnesses for Jesus with power, if he rebukes sin openly, if he expects victory over false prophets.

Note the sharp, plain words of the rebuke in verse 10. It reminds us of the words of Stephen to the Jewish leaders in Acts 7:51-53, and the words of Jesus to the Pharisees in Matthew 23. As Ananias and Sapphira were struck dead at the words of Spirit-filled Peter in Acts 5:1-11, so this false prophet, sorcerer, was struck blind for a season (vs. 11).

The earnest inquirer, official of the country, was greatly convicted and now was saved (vs. 12).

Note the turning point in Acts 13:9. Up to this time the fervent young preacher has been called Saul. Now we have in parenthesis "who also is called Paul." And hereafter throughout the book of Acts he will be called Paul.

Note also that up until this verse, it has been "Barnabas and Saul," as you see in Acts 9:27; Acts 11:25, 30; and Acts 13:1 and 2. From now on it will be Paul and Barnabas. Verse 13 says, "Paul and his company." Paul seems to have been pressed out by the Holy Spirit to take the leadership, and Barnabas, the older, milder man, is second to Paul.

Notice in verse 13 that "John departing from them returned to Jerusalem." This is not John the apostle, but John Mark, as we see from Acts 15:37. The work, the dangers he thought too hard; perhaps he was homesick, discouraged, so he returned to Jerusalem.

VERSES 14, 15:

14 ¶ But when they departed from Perga, they came to Antioch in Pisidia, and went into the synagogue on the sabbath day, and sat down.

15 And after the reading of the law and the prophets, the rulers of the synagogue sent unto them, saying, Ye men *and* brethren, if ye have any word of exhortation for the people, say on.

Paul Preaches in the Synagogue at Antioch

Paul was the apostle to the Gentiles, (Gal. 2:7, 8; Rom. 15:16; Eph. 3:8; II Tim. 1:11), so-called even from the time of his salvation (Acts 9:15; Acts 22:21). But everywhere Paul went he started at the natural place for a Jewish leader to start--among the Jews. So at Antioch "they went into the synagogue on the sabbath day." And there as a man of culture and training in the Old Testament law and the traditions according to the stricter sect the Pharisee (Phil. 3:5, 6), he was asked to speak. In every Jewish synagogue were some or all of the Old Testament Scriptures carefully copied out by hand. It had pleased God that through the Jews should come the prophets, the Old Testament and the Saviour. So Jesus had said to the woman at Samaria, "Ye worship ye know not what: we know what we worship: for salvation is of the Jews" (John 4:22). So the Lord Jesus had commanded that the Gospel be preached "in his name among all nations, beginning at Jerusalem" (Luke 24:47). And now Paul preached the Gospel "to the Jew first, and also to the Greek" (Rom. 1:16; Rom. 2:10).

Note the regular habit of Paul preaching in the synagogue everywhere he went--in Damascus (Acts 9:20, here in Antioch of Pisidia (Acts 13:14), in Iconium (Acts 14:1), in Thessalonica (Acts 17:1), at Berea (Acts 17:10), in Corinth (Acts 18:4), in Ephesus (Acts 18:19; Acts 19:8).

There are some important observations here.

1. The fact that Jewish Christians went to their Jewish brethren does not mean that God is more concerned about a Jew hearing the Gospel than a Gentile. But God has promised, "Tribulation and anguish, upon every soul of man that doeth evil, of the Jew first, and also of the Gentile; But glory, honour, and peace, to every man that worketh good, to the Jew first, and also to the Gentile: For there is no respect of persons with God" (Rom. 2:9-11).

Andrew was to win his brother Peter, not because Peter was a Jew, but because he was his brother and near at hand. The apostles were to begin in Jerusalem because they were in Jerusalem and Christ was crucified there and it was the center of Jewish worship. After the maniac of Gadara was freed of his devils, healed and saved, he besought Jesus "that he might be with him: but Jesus sent him away, saying, Return to thine own house, and shew how great things God hath done unto thee..." (Luke 8:38, 39). The claim of some Jewish mission agencies that now Jewish missions should have priority is not based on a true understanding of the Scriptures. "There is no respect of persons with God." Paul and Barnabas went to synagogues because there they found the people most susceptible to the Gospel and most interested in God and the Scriptures.

2. The synagogues regularly met on the Jewish Sabbath, Saturday. Paul and his associates went to the synagogue on that day because that was the day of meeting, the day there would be a crowd to whom they might preach the Gospel. Attending the synagogue services were not a part of the Sabbath command. The Jewish observance of the Sabbath was simply that they did not work on the Sabbath. "In it thou shalt not do any work, thou, nor thy son, nor thy daughter, thy manservant, nor thy maidservant, nor thy cattle, nor thy stranger that is within thy gates" (Exod.

20:10). There was no command to assemble and no provision made for assembly on the Sabbath in the Old Testament law. Even the synagogue worship did not develop until the captivity. So when Paul attended the synagogue on the Sabbath so that he might preach to the crowd there, or when Jesus preached in the synagogue, they were not keeping the Sabbath.

When Christians met together, we suppose they followed the same pattern of those at Troas. "And upon the first day of the week, when the disciples came together to break bread, Paul preached unto them..." (Acts 20:7).

Note there is not a single New Testament command to keep the Sabbath. "Sabbath breaking" is never mentioned as a sin. Jesus Himself broke the Sabbath. "Therefore the Jews sought the more to kill him, because he not only had broken the sabbath, but said also that God was his Father, making himself equal with God" (John 5:18). And in Colossians 2:14-17, Paul was inspired to teach that the handwriting and ceremonial laws were nailed to the cross and "let no man therefore judge you in meat, or in drink, or in respect of an holyday, or of the new moon, or of the sabbath days: Which are a shadow of things to come; but the body is of Christ" (vss. 16, 17). Preaching in the synagogue on the Sabbath day did not mean that New Testament Christians kept the Jewish Sabbath. They did not. The Sabbath was particularly given as a sign between God and Israel as a separated people (Exod. 31:12-17; Ezek. 20:20). The Sabbath was never "made known" until God revealed it to Israel after they were in the wilderness near Mount Sinai (Neh. 9:12-14).

3. It seems probable that some of these Jews who had the Old Testament were godly, trusting Jews and therefore saved. Probably others were earnestly seeking light and were glad to know about salvation through Christ. Judaism, when it took to heart the Scriptures of the Old Testament

and feared God and sought His will, would find Christ, as did Abraham, David and other Old Testament saints.

VERSES 16–39:

16 Then Paul stood up, and beckoning with *his* hand said, Men of Israel, and ye that fear God, give audience.

17 The God of this people of Israel chose our fathers, and exalted the people when they dwelt as strangers in the land of Egypt, and with a high arm brought he them out of it.

18 And about the time of forty years suffered he their manners in the wilderness.

19 And when he had destroyed seven nations in the land of Chanaan, he divided their land to them by lot.

20 And after that he gave *unto them* judges about the space of four hundred and fifty years, until Samuel the prophet.

21 And afterward they desired a king: and God gave unto them Saul the son of Cis, a man of the tribe of Benjamin, by the space of forty years.

22 And when he had removed him, he raised up unto them David to be their king; to whom also he gave testimony, and said, I have found David the *son* of Jesse, a man after mine own heart, which shall fulfil all my will.

23 Of this man's seed hath God, according to *his* promise, raised unto Israel a Saviour, Jesus:

24 When John had first preached before his coming the baptism of repentance to all the people of Israel.

25 And as John fulfilled his course, he said, Whom think ye that I am? I am not *he*. But, behold, there cometh one after me, whose shoes of *his* feet I am not worthy to loose.

26 Men *and* brethren, children of the stock of Abraham, and whosoever among you feareth God, to you is the word of this salvation sent.

27 For they that dwell at Jerusalem, and their rulers, because they knew him not, nor yet the voices of the prophets which are read every sabbath day, they have fulfilled *them* in condemning *him*.

28 And though they found no cause of death *in him*, yet desired they Pilate that he should be slain.

29 And when they had fulfilled all that was written of him, they took *him* down from the tree, and laid *him* in a sepulchre.

30 But God raised him from the dead:

31 And he was seen many days of them which came up with him from Galilee to Jerusalem, who are his witnesses unto the people.

32 And we declare unto you glad tidings, how that the promise which was made unto the fathers,

33 God hath fulfilled the same unto us their children, in that he hath raised up Jesus again; as it is also written in the second psalm, Thou art my Son, this day have I begotten thee.

34 And as concerning that he raised him up from the dead, *now* no more to return to corruption, he said on this wise, I will give you the sure mercies of David.

35 Wherefore he saith also in another *psalm*, Thou shalt not suffer thine Holy One to see corruption.

36 For David, after he had served his own generation by the will of God, fell on sleep, and was laid unto his fathers, and saw corruption:

37 But he, whom God raised again, saw no corruption.

38 ¶ Be it known unto you therefore, men *and* brethren, that through this man is preached unto you the forgiveness of sins:

39 And by him all that believe are justified from all things, from which ye could not be justified by the law of Moses.

Paul's Sermon at Antioch of Pisidia

Let us follow the outline of this sermon.

1. Paul addressed the people as, "Men of Israel, and ye that fear God." And then in verses 17 to 21 he tells how God raised up the nation Israel through whom He was to bless the world. He had multiplied them in Egypt, brought them out "with an high arm...suffered...their manners in the wilderness" forty years, gave them the land of Canaan, then the period of judges, then the king. He is starting to prove that when God raised up the nation Israel, He was preparing to bring a Saviour through Israel.

2 David had been raised up as a king (vss. 22 and 23). Note the contrast between David and King Saul. Note that other great Old Testament heroes--Abraham, Isaac, Jacob, Moses--are not mentioned, nor are other kings. The reason is that David was king after God's heart, the ancestor

of the Lord Jesus. David was a "man after mine own heart," that is, evidently a type of Jesus Christ as well as the ancestor. He has in mind the Davidic covenant given in II Samuel 7:10-16, that eventually David's house and kingdom should be established forever through David's seed. And he did not mean Solomon, but Jesus. That covenant is also given in I Chronicles 17:4-15. So the angel Gabriel, announcing to Mary that Jesus would be born, said, "...The Lord God shall give unto him the throne of his father David: And he shall reign over the house of Jacob for ever; and of his kingdom there shall be no end" (Luke 1:32, 33). And Isaiah 11:1 speaks of the rod or sprout from the stump of Jesse and the Branch that shall grow out of his roots. Jesus is of the house of David.

In fact, even as Jesus is the Second Adam, so He is the second and greater David and in His reign we are told, "And David my servant shall be king over them," over Israel (Ezek. 37:24). So here to these Jews in the synagogue Paul could preach "of this man's seed hath God according to his promise raised unto Israel a Saviour, Jesus" (vs. 23). Note that Solomon is not mentioned. Jesus is not descended through Solomon, but through David's other son Nathan who did not reign (Luke 3:31, the genealogy through Mary. We think the genealogy in Matthew 1:1-16 is the genealogy of "Joseph, the husband of Mary...").

3. Jesus was announced to Israel by John the Baptist (vss. 24, 25). John had been the only great prophet of Israel for several hundred years, impressing the whole nation. His ministry was widely known, but John had plainly testified that Jesus was much greater than he, and that he was not worthy to loose His shoes from His feet. That testimony of John was intended for the whole nation of Israel in introducing Jesus, and so it was proper to use his testimony here.

Summing up thus far, Paul seemed to say, "I brought you God's dealing down to the rise of the nation, the rise of David's kingdom and the covenants, then through the ministry of John the Baptist and now to Jesus: and 'to you is the word of this salvation sent.' "

4. The Jewish leaders had crucified Jesus, as Paul explains in verses 26-29, "Because they knew him not, nor yet the voice of the prophets." Yet they "fulfilled them in condemning him." Jesus was innocent but died for the sins of all. 'According to the Gospel Christ died for our sins and was buried....'

5. And now comes the great theme of the New Testament preachers--the resurrection of Christ! In verses 30 to 37 notice these themes. First, God raised Christ from the dead. Second, many living witnesses saw Him and proved His resurrection. Third, good news; all the promises of God about Jesus were fulfilled (vss. 30-33)! Fourth, then quoting the second Psalm, Christ is God's Son or as Romans 1:4 says it, "Declared to be the Son of God with power, according to the spirit of holiness, by the resurrection from the dead."

"The sure mercies of David" quoted in verse 34 from Isaiah 55:3, refers to the plan of salvation as you will see from Isaiah 55:1-7.

Again, he quotes Psalm 16:8-11, which prophesied the resurrection of Christ. And Paul uses the same argument here that Peter used at Pentecost in Acts 2:25-34. In Psalm 16, David could not be speaking about himself because his body was buried and decayed. So David was speaking about Christ, the Messiah who would come, Jesus the Saviour.

This emphasis on the resurrection was necessary and it indicates why there must be the twelve official witnesses who had been with Jesus all the time from His baptism to His ascension (Acts 1:21, 22). For all honest men believing the Old Testament and seeking the true God, needed but to know that Jesus was risen from the dead according to the Scriptures to accept Him as their Saviour.

So in Romans 10:9, to one who believed in his heart "that God hath raised him from the dead" and claimed such a

Saviour, it is promised, "Thou shalt be saved." The resurrection of Jesus Christ cannot be overestimated in importance. It is part of the saving Gospel (I Cor. 15:3, 4). That is one reason it should be pictured in every convert by baptism, going down into the water and coming out of the water (Rom. 6:4, 5).

6. Salvation is offered with a clear, simple statement in verses 38 and 39. Jesus is here mentioned as "this man." The perfect Man, the perfect God presented to them as having humbled Himself and become a man. Now here is a great matter, the end for which Christ came and died, the aim of the Gospel, the great benefit and blessing offered. They may have sins all forgiven and thus with forgiveness have peace with God. This is the "abundant pardon" offered in Isaiah 55:7. Man cannot be right with God by simply starting to do better or reforming or by offering sacrifices. Man must have his sins forgiven to face God in peace.

"Justified" here in verse 39 is a synonym of forgiveness in verse 38. But justification goes further. Not only can sins be forgiven through Christ, but they can be so blotted out of the record, that one is counted just. Valentine Burke, a notorious criminal, was saved in prison by reading one of D. L. Moody's sermons. His life was wonderfully transformed and he was so active in Christian work and became so trusted and honored that the governor of Illinois had his picture and record removed from the rogue's gallery.

Thus when Abraham believed God, "it was counted unto him for righteousness" (Rom. 4:3; Gen. 15:6). And so we are told, "But to him that worketh not, but believeth on him that justifieth the ungodly, his faith is counted for righteousness" (Rom. 4:5). And thus as Psalm 32:1 and 2 and Romans 4:6-8 tell of "the blessedness of a man, unto whom God imputeth righteousness without works," his sins are not only forgiven, but covered, and to him God will not impute sin!

This justification could not come by the law of Moses,

whether moral law or ceremonial law. In Romans 3:9-18 are fourteen indictments of the whole human race and these indictments are based on violation of the moral law. And what is the law for? Romans 3:19 and 20 say: "Now we know that what things soever the law saith, it saith to them who are under the law: that every mouth may be stopped, and all the world may become guilty before God. Therefore by the deeds of the law there shall no flesh be justified in his sight: for by the law is the knowledge of sin." The law is simply a "schoolmaster to bring us unto Christ" (Gal. 3:24). It does not save, but it stops the excuses, stops the claims of self-righteousness, stops all the hopes of any man that by his deeds he may become acceptable to God.

No, what God wants of a sinner is for him to shut his mouth, stop all boasting and all claims and excuses as a guilty sinner. For "by the deeds of the law there shall no flesh be justified in his sight for by the law is the knowledge of sin" (Rom. 3:20). The Ten Commandments and other commands of God were never meant as a plan of salvation. They were intended to bring "the knowledge of sin." The righteousness described in the law is "that the man which doeth those things shall live by them" (Rom. 10:5). One who did everything right, never left undone a single thing God commanded, never did a thing wrong, never fell short of perfection and holiness, would have the righteousness described by the law. But no man ever lived except Jesus Christ who was thus righteous.

Why did Jesus tell the rich young ruler, "But if thou wilt enter into life, keep the commandments"? (Matt. 19:17). Because the young ruler had inquired for a way of salvation by good works saying, "What good thing shall I do, that I may have eternal life?" He wanted to be saved by good deeds. The only way to be saved by good deeds is absolute perfection.

So when the rich young ruler called Jesus, "Good Master," or "Good Rabbi," Jesus answered rather indignantly,

"Why callest thou me good? there is none good but one, that is, God." Unless Jesus is God, as He claimed to be, He is not good, and unless that young ruler was God, he was not good either. And no one can be saved by keeping the commandments because he starts already as a sinner. One who has already broken the law cannot be saved by keeping the law. The Lord Jesus called the attention of the young ruler to these commandments as a 'schoolmaster to bring him to Christ,' for "by the law is the knowledge of sin" (Rom. 3:20). Then He showed the young ruler that he had not kept the very first commandment, to love the Lord with all his heart, mind and soul, nor had he kept the other commandments because he was not willing to give up his wealth for the poor. Giving money to the poor does not save a soul. In this case the command to give to the poor was to reveal his selfishness. It only showed the natural wicked heart of a lost man, to show him he needed the Saviour.

As is plainly stated here, believing in Christ brings salvation and justification as one cannot and never could be justified by the law of Moses! This contrast between the ideas of whether everyone should be justified by keeping the law or justified by faith, is the great theme of the epistles of Romans and of Galatians. Now Galatians 5:4 says, "Christ is become of no effect unto you, whosoever of you are justified by the law; ye are fallen from grace," that is, fallen from the doctrine of salvation by grace. And Galatians 3:10 says, "For as many as are of the works of the law are under the curse: for it is written, Cursed is every one that continueth not in all things which are written in the book of the law to do them." Ah, all the people who try to be saved by doing good--from Cain who brought of the fruit of the ground and of his toil, down to the Jews who went about to establish their own righteousness but did not submit themselves to the righteousness of God (Rom. 10:3), down to the present-day moralist--are all under a curse, for sin has brought death; now it is too late for anybody to be justified by the law. So the conclusion of the next verse in Galatians 3:11 is "but that no man is justified by the law in the sight of God, it is evident: for, The just shall live by faith." That is, the just shall have life, everlasting life, by faith. So both the Old Testament and the New Testament teach salvation by grace, through faith, not of works. (And this quotation, "The just shall live by faith," is from Habakkuk 2:4 in the Old Testament).

Note that phrase in Galatians 3:11--"That no man is justified by the law in the sight of God...." Good works make a man appear just to men. They do not make him appear just to God. Salvation depends on what Christ has done for us and our faith in Him, and so being justified in the sight of God.

Being justified in the sight of man is another matter. Discussed in James 2:17-26, there verses 17 and 18 say, "Even so faith, if it hath not works, is dead, being alone. Yea, a man may say, Thou hast faith, and I have works: shew me thy faith without thy works, and I will shew thee my faith by my works." To show others that I am a Christian takes works as well as grace. So one can be justified in the sight of men only as he lives outwardly, something that shows what has happened inwardly.

Of course, the implication properly is that salvation makes a change in the heart which ought to be manifest openly. And all that is called faith is not genuine saving faith, for in the same passage James 2:19 says, "Thou believest that there is one God; thou doest well: the devils also believe, and tremble." So a faith which simply means an acceptance of certain Bible truth mentally is not the same as heart trust. Any faith which does not bring some change in the heart and motives is, of course, not honest dependence on Jesus Christ.

However, in James remember the emphasis is on "I will shew thee my faith by my works" (vs. 18), that is, to be justified in the sight of men. And Jesus commanded, "Let your light so shine before men, that they may see your good works, and glorify your Father which is in heaven" (Matt. 5:16). In that sense, good works justify one before men. However, we must remember "that no man is justified by the law IN THE SIGHT OF GOD, it is evident: for, The just shall live by faith" (Gal. 3:11). James 2:17-26 does not contradict Galatians 3:11 and Romans 3:20.

We should remember that "if Abraham were justified by works, he hath whereof to glory; but not before God" (Rom. 4:2). Anybody who is saved by his good works may praise himself. He need not praise Christ or God. Don't bring God into it, nor Christ, nor Calvary, nor the blood, nor faith, if you are saving yourself by your good works! If you do the saving, then you get the glory. If Jesus Christ does the saving, He gets the glory. There is no way to reconcile being justified before God by your good deeds, on the one hand, with being justified by faith, on the other hand, so that one has to his credit the imputed righteousness of Christ and so that God does not charge up his sins to him.

An Instant, Once-for-All Salvation by Faith

Here in Acts 13:38 and 39 Paul is giving the same teaching of salvation by faith in Christ as is given in John 1:12; John 3:15, 16, 18, 36; John 5:24; John 6:40, 47; and Acts 16:31. In those Scriptures, when one believes, he is promised that he is born of God, has everlasting life, is not condemned, does not come to judgment. And all that means the same as forgiveness and justification promised here.

Note also that here the salvation promised is instant, once-for-all salvation. "All that believe ARE justified...." The promise is not that one will bit by bit be justified as he daily believes and daily gets more nearly justified. No! Those who believe "ARE" already justified! So one who trusts in Christ "hath everlasting life" (John 3:36; John 5:24; John 6:47). And one who is condemned is condemned "because he hath not believed in the name of the only begotten

Son of God" (John 3:18). Faith here is an act of instant committal. So Paul was inspired to write, "...For I know whom I have believed, and am persuaded that he is able to keep that which I have committed unto him against that day" (II Tim. 1:12). Paul had already believed and that simply means that he had already committed himself and his salvation to Christ! So a one-time committal, an act of the will which trusts Christ once for all for salvation, brings forgiveness and justification from all things! So then the Christian may boldly and happily claim, "Therefore being justified by faith, we have peace with God through our Lord Jesus Christ" (Rom. 5:1).

VERSES 40–43:

40 Beware therefore, lest that come upon you, which is spoken of in the prophets;

41 Behold, ye despisers, and wonder, and perish: for I work a work in your days, a work which ye shall in no wise believe, though a man declare it unto you.

42 And when the Jews were gone out of the synagogue, the Gentiles besought that these words might be preached to them the next sabbath.

43 Now when the congregation was broken up, many of the Jews and religious proselytes followed Paul and Barnabas; who, speaking to them, persuaded them to continue in the grace of God.

Such Preaching Demands Response

A man plants an orchard for fruit, and a preacher should preach a sermon for results. In this message Paul has alluded to many Scriptures, going through the story of Israel in Egypt, the forty years in the wilderness, the time of the judges, King Saul, then David. He has referred to the Davidic covenant and referred generally to many prophecies and promises of the Old Testament. He has referred to the second Psalm (vs. 33), to Isaiah 55:3 (vs. 34), to Psalm 16:8-11 (vs. 36). Now he refers in verse 41 to Habakkuk 1:5. Dr. Scofield's notes on that passage say:

"Verse 5 anticipates the dispersion 'among the nations' (cf. Deut. 28:64-67). While Israel as a nation is thus dispersed, Jehovah will 'work a work' which Israel 'will not believe.' Acts 13:37-41 interprets this prediction of the redemptive work of Christ. It is significant that Paul quotes this to Jews of the dispersion in the synagogue at Antioch."

We should remember that Paul did not expound Scripture for its own sake. There was about him none of the popular way of "gathering around the Scriptures" to enjoy it or even to learn it for its own sake. No, Bible preachers used the Scriptures to get definite results. So, although there is a reason for expository preaching in many cases, and there are some advantages to expository preaching in teaching the Word of God consecutively, yet preachers of the New Testament nearly always preached topical sermons and used many Scriptures bearing on one point or more. I do not know of any sermon by any Bible preacher recorded in the Bible which was only a detailed exposition of a single passage. So Paul here has been driving toward a definite decision to get men to turn to Christ and trust Him and be forgiven. Now he closes with a solemn warning. They should beware lest their unbelief become permanent, lest they should lose the light given them and should perish unsaved.

We believe that every preacher ought always to expect some definite decisions, some repentance for sin, some new acceptance of duty, some new venture of faith. And in the case of unsaved people, preaching should always be intended to turn them to Christ and should press upon them the duty of repenting and trusting, with plain, sharp words, as did Paul.

So after the warning the crowd dispersed. Some Gentiles had heard a bit of the message, and now they pressed upon

Paul: will he preach to them the same thing the next Sabbath?

I suppose as Paul and Barnabas left the synagogue they found many "Jews and religious proselytes" who "followed Paul and Barnabas." It is indicated that some of these surely believed in Christ, and so Paul and Barnabas "persuaded them to continue in the grace of God."

VERSES 44–49:

44 ¶ And the next sabbath day came almost the whole city together to hear the word of God.

45 But when the Jews saw the multitudes, they were filled with envy, and spake against those things which were spoken by Paul, contradicting and blaspheming.

46 Then Paul and Barnabas waxed bold, and said, It was necessary that the word of God should first have been spoken to you: but seeing ye put it from you, and judge yourselves unworthy of everlasting life, lo, we turn to the Gentiles.

47 For so hath the Lord commanded us, *saying,* I have set thee to be a light of the Gentiles, that thou shouldest be for salvation unto the ends of the earth.

48 And when the Gentiles heard this, they were glad, and glorified the word of the Lord: and as many as were ordained to eternal life believed.

49 And the word of the Lord was published throughout all the region.

A Great Revival, Opposition of Jews

"The next sabbath day": Jews did not work on the Sabbath and so that was the proper time to reach them. And that day the synagogue was open. "Almost the whole city came together to hear the word of God." It seems likely that some Gentiles had been in the synagogue the preceding Sabbath (vs. 42) and had heard Paul: now they, I suppose, wanted to use the synagogue. But if "almost the whole city" came to hear Paul, they could not get in the synagogue, so doubtless in some open place the great multitude heard Paul preach.

We should remember that nearly all the preaching of Jesus and New Testament preachers was wherever they could find a crowd. Usually Paul started in a synagogue, and usually he was soon expelled to preach outside. Paul preached to the women at the women's prayer meeting by the riverside (Acts 16:13). Peter preached in the street or in the porch of the temple when a crowd came rushing to see the man healed at the Beautiful Gate of the temple (Acts 3:11). Jesus preached by the seaside or on a mountain or in a desert place. John the Baptist preached by the River Jordan. Every great revival means that the Gospel is taken outside the church buildings, to larger crowds at any convenient place. So it was with Whitefield and Wesley. John Wesley in his Journal said, "I preached near the hospital to twice the people we should have had at the church house. What a marvel that the Devil does not like the field-preaching! Neither do I! I like a commodious room, a soft cushion, a handsome pulpit. But where is my zeal if I do not trample all these underfoot in order to save one more soul?"

I have preached to about six thousand in the Chicago Arena, to great crowds in the open air, under southwestern stars, and in big tents, in a tobacco warehouse, and in theaters many times. I have preached from the back end of a truck to the great crowds in country towns and in public auditoriums in many cities. To take the Gospel "to every creature" must involve more than just preaching in church houses. So Paul preached to "almost the whole city."

The Jews were envious and jealous when they saw the multitudes, "for the Jews have no dealings with the Samaritans" (John 4:9). When the Canaanitish woman came crying after Jesus, "His disciples came and besought him, saying, Send her away; for she crieth after us" (Matt. 15:23). Any religion that was offered to the Gentiles was abhorrent to

the proud, haughty Jews. So they contradicted and blasphemed, interrupting Paul's speaking!

This is far different from the quiet form of dignity in
many of our churches. The preacher who comes to grips
with the rough and wicked everywhere must expect opposition, but it is only in such a crowd and with such plainness
of speech that he can expect many to be saved.

How boldly Paul and Barnabas took hold of the situation!
They said, "It was necessary that the word of God should
first have been spoken to you...." The Jews were a point
of contact for the whole city. The message in the synagogue
opened doors to Gentiles and the great multitudes. Those
who had the law and knew of the true God were the starting
place. But now that strong opposition, contradiction, blaspheming comes from the Jews. Paul said, "Lo, we turn to
the Gentiles." But Paul makes sure they understand that
they are rejecting everlasting life.

Paul and Barnabas Turn to the Gentiles

Notice that term, "We turn to the Gentiles" in verse 46.
Some hyper-dispensationalists (Bullinger in England, O'Hair
in Chicago, and others) have thought that Acts 28:28, when
Paul said, "Be it known therefore unto you, that the salvation of God is sent unto the Gentiles, and that they will hear
it" was a turning point in doctrine, the beginning of, perhaps we should say, a new dispensation. Some of them
think that John the Baptist and Peter in Acts 2:38 required
people to be baptized in order to be saved. They think that
the preaching of John the Baptist about repentance is not now
in order, and that baptism is not now proper. Some of them
say that the Sermon on the Mount, the Lord's Prayer, and
some even say the Great Commission, are not for us. They
seem to teach that God has one plan for Israel and now when
the Jews have definitely rejected Christ and the Gospel, God
turns to the Gentiles with a modified Gospel. Such people
talk of Paul's Gospel and kingdom Gospel as different. For
all such I suggest they read in my book, Twelve Tremen-

dous <u>Themes</u>, the chapter on " 'Paul's Gospel' or 'Kingdom Gospel.' "

However, Acts 28:28 is only saying at Rome what here Acts 13:46 says to Antioch of Pisidia. Everywhere Paul and Barnabas went, they went first to the Jews. They preached first in the Jewish synagogue, if there was a synagogue. And almost in every case they had to leave the synagogue and soon when many Jews rejected the Gospel (and some were saved) they turned to preach also to the Gentiles. So it is here in Antioch of Pisidia. So it is in Acts 14:1 and 5 at Iconium. They preached first in the synagogue of the Jews and "a great multitude both of the Jews and also of the Greeks believed."

So in Acts 17:1-4 at Thessalonica Paul began preaching to the Jews. "And some of them believed, and consorted with Paul and Silas; and of the devout Greeks a great multitude, and of the chief women not a few." Note he preached first to Jews, then to Greeks and more Greeks were converted than Jews.

In Acts 18:1-6 we find Paul preaching for eighteen months at Corinth. First, he "reasoned in the synagogue every sabbath, and persuaded the Jews and the Greeks" (Acts 18:4). Paul "was pressed in the spirit, and testified to the Jews that Jesus was Christ. And when they opposed themselves, and blasphemed, he shook his raiment, and said unto them, Your blood be upon your own heads; I am clean: from henceforth I will go unto the Gentiles" (Acts 18:5, 6). So Paul left the synagogue and in the home of Justus next door he continued preaching and many were saved.

Now consider Acts 13:46; Acts 18:6 and Acts 28:28. All say the same thing. In every city and town where Paul went, he preached first to the Jews, then to the Gentiles. He is simply following the outline Jesus gave in the Great Commission in Acts 1:8, "...And ye shall be witnesses unto me both in Jerusalem, and in all Judaea, and in Samaria, and unto the uttermost part of the earth." It is the plan of God that they should preach "beginning in Jerusalem" when they were in Jerusalem. The plan of God was "to the Jew first and also to the Greek." There is no dispensational meaning to these terms. There has never been but one plan of salvation (Acts 10:43) for Jews or Gentiles. The plan of salvation preached by John the Baptist and that of Jesus was the same.

We should expect to find this pattern carried out everywhere Paul and Barnabas, and later Paul and Silas, go on their missionary journeys. They will preach first to the people of their own blood and language and religious background, the Jews: afterwards they will turn to all the others they can find who will listen. That is just as Andrew did, who first won his brother Simon and then won others.

Note in verse 47 the quotation from Isaiah 42:6 and 7. Everytime Paul found it impossible to preach to the Jews, he remembered the promises of God to the Gentiles! Note that the quotation in verse 47 is that Jesus "shouldest be for salvation unto the ends of the earth."

Here many Gentiles heard and were glad and believed and were saved! And throughout the whole region people heard the Word of the Lord by the testimony of those who were saved as well as the multitudes who came to hear Paul themselves.

VERSES 50–52:

50 But the Jews stirred up the devout and honourable women, and the chief men of the city, and raised persecution against Paul and Barnabas, and expelled them out of their coasts.

51 But they shook off the dust of their feet against them, and came unto Iconium.

52 And the disciples were filled with joy, and with the Holy Ghost.

Trouble, Opposition to Plain Preaching

Paul and Barnabas were not popular preachers. Everywhere they had opposition. New Testament preachers preaching in the power of God had opposition and they expected and received persecution. The preaching that gets nobody saved may make no one angry. But Spirit-filled preaching that condemns sin and turns many to God will also arouse opposition. It will bring Paul jail and beatings and poverty and slander and imprisonment and eventual death as a martyr.

My home-town newspaper editorially praised a famous evangelist who was preaching to great crowds in Chicago, praised the evangelist that nothing he said offended Catholics or Protestants, modernists or fundamentalists, because he taught them all to identify themselves as Christians. How different that is from the ministry of the New Testament preachers like the Apostle Paul!

"But they shook off the dust of their feet against them, and came unto Iconium." Here Paul and Barnabas followed the exact instructions of Jesus. When He sent the twelve forth to preach He told them in Luke 9:5, "And whosoever will not receive you, when ye go out of that city, shake off the very dust from your feet for a testimony against them." One who preaches in the power of God has some of the authority of God. One who preaches boldly the grace of God sometimes has a right to pronounce the judgment of God. So it was with Peter in the case of Ananias and Sapphira in Acts 5:1-11. So it was with Paul concerning Elymas the sorcerer when Elymas was struck blind in Acts 13:9-11.

Once I preached boldly for nearly six weeks in a fine American city. Hundreds were saved. Six or eight churches sponsored the meetings in a downtown theater seating two thousand. But the modernistic and worldly ministers in the ministerial association fought the meeting, openly protested the plain preaching, objected about the denunciation of sin. Terrible corruption in the city was exposed during the meeting, but the religious leaders voiced their opposition to our services boldly. So the morning I left, after hundreds had been saved and after a solemn warning, I shook the dust from my feet and lifted my hat and prayed that God would vindicate the preaching of His servant. That day a warm March sun and warm air had begun to melt nineteen inches of packed snow. In two days a great flood plagued the city with more than a million dollars' loss and with one or two lives lost. God backs up the preaching of those who are faithful and who suffer persecution for Him.

Elijah, the faithful prophet of God, was allowed to shut up Heaven for three and a half years that it would not rain except at his word (I Kings 17:1).

And this passage closes with this sweet word. "And the disciples were filled with joy, and with the Holy Ghost." Salvation, persecution and soul-winning witnessing make God's people glad! And their joy was the joy of the Holy Ghost! Oh, the joy of His comfort, His leading, His reminding, His prayer help and, most of all, the joy of His mighty power for soul winning!

ACTS 14
VERSES 1–5:

AND it came to pass in Iconium, that they went both together into the synagogue of the Jews, and so spake, that a great multitude both of the Jews and also of the Greeks believed.

2 But the unbelieving Jews stirred up the Gentiles, and made their minds evil affected against the brethren.

3 Long time therefore abode they speaking boldly in the Lord, which gave testimony unto the word of his grace, and granted signs and wonders to be done by their hands.

4 But the multitude of the city was divided: and part held with the Jews, and part with the apostles.

5 And when there was an assault made both of the Gentiles, and also of the Jews with their rulers, to use *them* despitefully, and to stone them,

Iconium: Great Blessing, Souls Saved, Persecution

Unbelieving Jews and others in Antioch persecuted Paul and Barnabas "and expelled them out of their coast." So they came to Iconium, and as usual, began to preach in the synagogue. Many were saved. "A great multitude both of the Jews and also of the Greeks believed." The miraculous healings and miracles: God "granted signs and wonders to be done by their hands" (vs. 3). The "multitude of the city was divided." So it always is when there is plain, sharp, Bible preaching, hewing to the line as closely as one ought. Again, there was persecution and they fled.

Paul and Barnabas "So Spake, That a Great Multitude . . .Believed"

Not only the message they gave was of God, but their manner of speaking was also of God. There is a foolish idea abroad that if the Word of God is preached, it will bring the same results, whether preached fervently or lukewarmly, whether preached with strong personal application or not, whether preached in the power of the Holy Ghost or in the wisdom of men. That simply is not true. The Word of God is "the sword of the Spirit" (Eph. 6:17). The Holy Spirit must use His sword. Speaking on this matter in II Corinthians 3:5 and 6, Paul was inspired to say, "Not that we are sufficient of ourselves to think any thing as of ourselves; but our sufficiency is of God: Who also hath made us able ministers of the new testament; not of the letter, but of the spirit: for the letter killeth, but the spirit giveth life." There is no sufficiency in man for preaching the Gospel. Paul had divine "sufficiency" to make him an able minister of the New Testament, "Not of the letter, but of the spirit: for the letter killeth, but the spirit giveth life." Note carefully that the letter, even of the Word of God, kills. The Pharisees and Sadducees read the Scriptures in the synagogues, and went on in their unbelief. Churches which never teach people to be born again have regularly assigned Scriptures to read in the services. I have known preachers who knew nothing about salvation by grace and the new birth, who could quote many passages of Scripture. The two divine elements in regeneration of a sinner are mentioned in Titus 3:5, the "washing of regeneration" and "the renewing of the Holy Ghost." Those in Christ's church are cleansed "with the washing of water by the word" (Eph. 5:26), but the Holy Spirit must empower the Word. Orthodox preaching is not enough: we need Spirit-filled preaching. One might outline this great truth as follows:

1. They spoke in the power of the Holy Spirit.

2. Therefore, there was great boldness (vs. 3) to denounce sin, and demand decision.

3. They so spake because of a holy abandon that continually they risked death, persecution, abuse, misrepresentation.

Some misapply Isaiah 55:11 about the Word of God that "it shall not return unto me void...." But that does not mean that the Word of God whether preached in power or not, preached fervently or not, will get people saved. The context makes it clear that God means when He makes a promise, that guarantees the future. Every promise He makes will be fulfilled, every event He prophesies will take place. But that does not mean that the Word alone, preached without the power of God, will do as much as with Spirit-filled preachers.

The apostles spoke boldly. That is what the apostles at Jerusalem had prayed for in Acts 4:29. "And now, Lord, behold their threatenings: and grant unto thy servants, that with all boldness they may speak thy word." Immediately they were filled with the Holy Ghost "and they spake the word of God with boldness" (Acts 4:31).

That boldness here is connected with miraculous evidence of God's favor mentioned in verse 3. God here "gave testimony unto the word of his grace, and granted signs and wonders to be done by their hands." It was that kind of signs and wonders that the disciples at Jerusalem had asked for when they prayed for boldness. They asked for boldness "by stretching forth thine hand to heal; and that signs and wonders may be done by the name of thy holy child Jesus" (Acts 4:30). If God clearly shows His power, one may speak boldly for God with a full assurance of His presence and blessing. God's answer to prayer for a three and a half year's drought emboldened Elijah to pray as he did on Mount Carmel in I Kings 18. God's answer from Heaven encouraged miraculous descent of the fire that burned up the sacrifice and the altar, encouraged him to slay the 450 prophets of Baal there!

We mentioned before the preaching of an evangelist which was approved by a newspaper editor as pleasing Catholics and Protestants and offending no one. Not so with the preaching of Paul and Barnabas. The line of division between belief and unbelief, between Christ and idols, was made so strong and plain that "the multitude of the city was divided." So it ought to be nearly always when the Word of God is preached in power. It was with Paul all the way through his ministry. So here again organized opposition turned into vigorous persecution and Paul and Barnabas, knowing of it, fled into Lystra and Derbe in Lycaonia.

VERSES 6, 7:

6 They were ware of *it*, and fled unto Lystra and Derbe, cities of Lycaonia, and unto the region that lieth round about: 7 And there they preached the gospel.

Paul and Barnabas Flee Into Lycaonia

Paul and Barnabas were not surprised at the effort of mobs of Gentiles and Jews with their rulers, that is, with the leaders of the synagogues, "to use them despitefully, and to stone them." That opposition had been brewing (vs. 2) all the time they had been in Iconium and knowing that "long time therefore abode they speaking boldly in the Lord..." (vs. 3). Now the opposition had crystalized; great numbers are intent on harming or killing these apostles. It is amazing and blessed how these men took it as a regularly expected matter that they should be attacked, and run for their lives! That is an exciting kind of a life. To one not wholly committed or not trusting, it would be a life of tension, torment and fret, discouragement and dispair! This may help us to see why John Mark quit the team of Paul and Barnabas in Acts 13:13 and whom Paul would not allow to go with them again (Acts 15:37, 38). We must have in mind the violent hatred which Jewish leaders had for the Gospel, particularly if people were encouraged to leave off circumcision and the ceremonial law. In this case they stirred up the Gentiles, too, but most of the opposition seemed to have originated by the Jews. It was strict Jewish Christians who insisted that the new converts were to be circumcised (Acts

15:1, 5). It was "Jews which believed not" which caused trouble in Thessalonica and in Berea (Acts 17:5, 13). It was the Jews which made insurrection against Paul at Corinth (Acts 18:2). It was the Jews who tried to kill Paul at Jerusalem, which resulted in his imprisonment and trip to Rome (Acts 21:27-40).

The Gentiles became violent and persecuted Paul in particular instances when the Gospel interfered with their ungodly income, as with the masters of the unconverted slave girl in Acts 16:19, and the idol makers in Ephesus (Acts 19:23-29).

This is an illustration of the fact that plain, sharp, Spirit-filled Bible preaching in the boldness of the Holy Ghost will have opposition from two sources. The first from denominational leaders who are interested in "the program" and do not want the people disturbed with any talk of liberal unbelief, and are more concerned about the institutions, and the program from which come their salaries and their prestige and security, rather than being concerned about souls being saved. The other opposition will come from those who make money out of the liquor traffic or gambling or other wicked ways which are interrupted by the power of God in great revivals and in Spirit-filled preaching.

So Paul and Barnabas Fled, Undiscouraged, to Lystra and Derbe and Started Again

Jesus commanded in Matthew 10:23, when He sent His twelve out to go two and two over Israel, "But when they persecute you in this city, flee ye into another: for verily I say unto you, Ye shall not have gone over the cities of Israel, till the Son of man be come." They were not intentionally to stay and get killed. They were not necessarily to try to defend themselves. They were not to quit preaching! But they were to simply go somewhere else and start over!

So throughout the book of Acts we find when the apostles were persecuted in one city, they went to another.

Here is a picture of New Testament Christianity that every man of God should get in his heart. This world is against Jesus Christ, but He loves sinners still. Preaching the Gospel in the power of the Holy Spirit will bring opposition and trouble if we are to go on preaching! We are not to be discouraged, for this, the Scriptures foretold, would happen. We are not to quit, because the Lord Jesus still loves sinners and the Great Commission command still presses on the conscience of every true Christian.

The personal soul winner will have doors slammed in his face. He will tend to be discouraged. He will be abused. He will often seem to fail. But still God intends that he shall press on in getting out the Gospel. Jesus came into a world that would crucify Him; and so He sends us forth into the same world to tell sinners how He loves them, tell them of the judgment of God on sin. Some will be saved. Some will ignore us. Some will oppose us. And if we preach in power and interfere with ungodly lives, some will hate us and try to kill us!

The holy resolution in the hearts of Paul and Barnabas seemed to be summed up about as follows: "Don't be surprised at persecution! Don't get killed. Don't be discouraged. Better to run away and preach again somewhere else. Don't delay. Go to the next open door."

Thank God, He allows persecution to go only as far as it will honor Him. And that is the business of God to control and not ours.

It is remarkable that in all these cases in the New Testament there was no physical resistance to persecution by the apostles and others, as far as the Bible records. In the first place, the opposition was nearly always by mobs or by armed soldiers when bodily resistance or fighting would be useless as well as wrong. So the apostles would try to evade the mobs which sought to kill them and go somewhere else to preach again, and sometimes they returned to the same city. In Acts 14:21 they returned to Lystra where Paul had been stoned and later Paul returned even to Jerusalem.

VERSES 8–10:

8 ¶ And there sat a certain man at Lystra, impotent in his feet, being a cripple from his mother's womb, who never had walked:

9 The same heard Paul speak: who steadfastly beholding him, and perceiving that he had faith to be healed,

10 Said with a loud voice, Stand upright on thy feet. And he leaped and walked.

The Impotent Man Healed at Lystra

Another miracle! Too long most of God's preachers and writers have ignored the fact that all the way through the book of Acts is a story of supernatural intervention by the hand of God. The sound of a rushing mighty wind at Pentecost, the visible tongues like as of fire resting on the disciples, the supernatural gift of tongues so that others might hear the Gospel "in our own tongue, wherein we were born" started the ministry of these who set out to obey the Great Commission and take the Gospel to every creature. In chapter 3 there is the wonderful miracle of the lame man healed at the Beautiful Gate of the temple, a case almost identical with this miracle in Lystra at the hands of Paul and Silas. That man was "lame from his mother's womb" (Acts 3:2). This one was "being a cripple from his mother's womb, who never had walked." At the temple Peter had said, "In the name of Jesus Christ of Nazareth rise up and walk" (Acts 3:6). Here Paul "said with a loud voice, Stand upright on thy feet"--immediate, complete, supernatural. In each case a tremendous impact was made upon the gathering throng, and Peter preached in Jerusalem as Paul preached here.

But on through the book of Acts follow the trail of miracles. In chapter 4 the disciples prayed that God would give them boldness "by stretching forth thine hand to heal; and that signs and wonders may be done by the name of thy holy child Jesus. And when they had prayed, the place was shaken where they were assembled together..." (Acts 4:30, 31).

In Acts, chapter 5, Ananias and Sapphira, lying to the Holy Ghost, were stricken dead and the angel of the Lord opened the prison doors and brought forth James and John. We read in Acts 6:8, "And Stephen, full of faith and power, did great wonders and miracles among the people." In Acts 7:55 and 56, Stephen, being stoned, saw the heavens opened and Jesus standing on the right hand of God.

In chapter 8 with Philip in Samaria, verse 7 tells us, "For unclean spirits, crying with loud voice, came out of many that were possessed with them: and many taken with palsies, and that were lame, were healed." There also the angel of the Lord gave miraculous instructions to Philip as to finding and winning the Ethiopian eunuch and "the Spirit of the Lord caught away Philip, that the eunuch saw him no more" (Acts 8:39).

In chapter 9 we have the miraculous appearing of Jesus Christ to Saul on the road to Damascus. He was blinded but after three days miraculously regained his sight. Also in Acts 9:34 Peter healed Aeneas sick of palsy eight years and Tabitha was raised from the dead at Joppa (vss. 36-43).

Chapter 10 tells of the miraculous appearance of an angel to Cornelius and of Peter's miraculous vision and instruction from the housetop and the conversion of this Gentile household through a series of miracles so he could hear the Gospel.

Chapter 11, verse 28, records the miraculous revelation to the prophet Agabus. In chapter 12 Peter is miraculously delivered from prison. Chapter 13 tells how Elymas the sorcerer was blinded at Paul's word; now in chapter 14 we find a miraculous, instantaneous healing of a man crippled from birth.

In Acts, chapter 15, verse 32, we find that "Judas and Silas, being prophets also themselves, exhorted the brethren with many words, and confirmed them." But the term prophets in the New Testament involves a supernatural gift from God.

Acts 16 is full of miracles. The Spirit's supernatural guidance; the vision of the man over in Macedonia; the casting out of the soothsaying demon in the slave girl in verse 18; the earthquake that nearly shook the jail apart. No miracle is mentioned in chapter 17, but in 18:9 a miraculous vision came to Paul in the night. In chapter 19, "God wrought special miracles by the hands of Paul: So that from his body were brought unto the sick handkerchiefs or aprons, and the diseases departed from them, and the evil spirits went out of them" (vss. 11, 12). In chapter 20 Paul raised from the dead Eutychus who fell out of a third story window (vs. 9). In chapter 21 supernatural prophecy is given to the prophet Agabus about Paul's imprisonment (vss. 10, 11). Chapter 22 is principally a speech of Paul's in which he recounts many miracles. In chapter 23, "The Lord stood by him, and said, Be of good cheer, Paul: for as thou hast testified of me in Jerusalem, so must thou bear witness also at Rome" (vs. 11). During Paul's imprisonment, he had no chance to preach except to the rulers, as far as we know. And no miracles are mentioned. But in chapter 27 during the terrible storm at sea, Paul had a heavenly visitor in the night and reassurance.

Chapter 28 tells of Paul's being healed after a venomous snake bite, and of the healing of the father of Publius of a fever and bloody flux, and of the arrival in Rome.

The book of Acts is a book of miracles. New Testament Christianity is a supernatural religion. The message is of a supernatural atonement, a supernatural resurrection of Christ and of a supernatural change of heart, a divine birth

for those who trust Christ. The Bible we preach is a supernatural book. The power needed for preaching is the miraculous power of the Holy Spirit. And God answers prayer
miraculously for those who are given faith to trust Him for
miracles.

VERSES 11–18:

11 And when the people saw what Paul had done, they lifted up their voices, saying in the speech of Lycaonia, The gods are come down to us in the likeness of men.

12 And they called Barnabas, Jupiter; and Paul, Mercurius, because he was the chief speaker.

13 Then the priest of Jupiter, which was before their city, brought oxen and garlands unto the gates, and would have done sacrifice with the people.

14 *Which* when the apostles, Barnabas and Paul, heard *of*, they rent their clothes, and ran in among the people, crying out,

15 And saying, Sirs, why do ye these things? We also are men of like passions with you, and preach unto you that ye should turn from these vanities unto the living God, which made heaven, and earth, and the sea, and all things that are therein:

16 Who in times past suffered all nations to walk in their own ways.

17 Nevertheless he left not himself without witness, in that he did good, and gave us rain from heaven, and fruitful sea-sons, filling our hearts with food and gladness.

18 And with these sayings scarce restrained they the people, that they had not done sacrifice unto them.

Paul and Barnabas Are Thought to Be Greek Gods

The miraculous healing of the impotent man was supernatural. It was an act of God, intervening in human affairs.
Also the people cried out, "The gods are come down to us
in the likeness of men."

We must bear in mind that Lystra, in the Province of
Lycaonia, is on the peninsula across the strait from Greece
and that Greece had shortly before this ruled the whole

known world and the Greek culture and language were spread throughout what is now the Roman Empire, which took over world rule from the Greeks after the death of Alexander. The Greek mythology (and religion) had a number of gods, and the tales of Homer, the Greek poet, tell how Greeks believed that their gods often came down to visit the earth. Jupiter here is the Latin word for the chief national god of the Greeks, Zeus. Mercurius represents the Greek god Hermes. They are here called by Roman names. Matthew Henry supposes that because Barnabas was probably older, perhaps more portly and distinguished than Paul, he is thought to be the chief god, Jupiter. Paul, although perhaps younger and not as handsome and distinguished looking but active and fiery, is called Mercurius or Hermes. In mythology these two gods were thought often to go together. Mercurius was the god of the merchants, the god of trade, while Jupiter (Zeus) was the sky god, the chief god. So these people, accustomed to the myths and legends of their religion, saw the miracle and supposed that "the gods are come down to us in the likeness of men."

Thus the priests of Jupiter brought oxen and garlands and would have done sacrifice to these two.

Think for a moment about those sacrifices. The world had largely gone into heathendom after the tower of Babel and the confusion of tongues told in Genesis 11. Everybody in the world is descended from Noah's three sons, and so the ancestors of all the heathen people in the world knew about God's dealing with men, knew originally about bloody sacrifices which pointed to the coming Saviour. Even yet in the legends and records of nearly all the heathen people in the world is some perverted recollection of the flood kept alive by oral tradition, distorted but recognizable. So these heathen people would have sacrificed oxen, although their ancestors had turned away from the true God.

Romans 1:21 tells us, "Because that, when they knew God, they glorified him not as God, neither were thankful;

but became vain in their imaginations, and their foolish heart was darkened." We learn that "their foolish heart was darkened" and "wherefore God also gave them up to uncleanness," and "God gave them up unto vile affections," and "God gave them over to a reprobate mind" (Rom. 1:21, 24, 26, 28). That is the origin of all the heathen races. They were not climbing up from a beast ancestory. They had fallen into the darkness of heathendom by the rejection of Christ and the truth. But still everywhere, even among the heathen, there is some understanding still that there needs to be a sacrifice for sin. My brother, Dr. Bill Rice, saw a heathen witch doctor in Africa sacrifice a chicken. Early American Aztecs offered human sacrifices. God has not forsaken the heathen race entirely, but has kept them reminded by conscience that they need forgiveness, need some redemption, need some atonement for their sin.

Of course, no sacrifice to heathen gods would make peace with our God, even as for a Jew it would do no good to offer a lamb for a sacrifice without recognizing that God had a lamb who would take away the sin of the world. The bloody sacrifice would do him no good, so no sacrifice would do anybody any good except as it was an object lesson pointing to the Saviour.

Paul and Barnabas were shocked and horrified. They explained, "We also are men of like passions with you" (vs. 15). They explained that they came to preach to these heathen people that they should "turn from these vanities unto the living God, which made heaven, and earth, and the sea, and all things that are therein."

Note the twofold appeal to these heathen people. There was a God who made the heaven and the earth. This God had given witness of His benevolent care in rain and fruitful seasons and food and care of mankind!

We are reminded of Psalm 19 which declares that all the starry heavens give witness that there is a living God, a Creator. The lustful, warring, erring gods of Greek mythology are not sufficient to explain this marvelous universe! Note that Paul used a similar argument when he preached at Athens, reminding Athenians of "God that made the world and all things therein, seeing that he is Lord of heaven and earth," and that an idol god could not be the answer to an orderly creation which shows an all-powerful, benevolent God (Acts 17:21-31).

Here again is an inspired reminder that "the fool hath said in his heart, There is no God" (Ps. 14:1). Only a fool can say that here is a universe with no creator, here is mankind and with no one greater than man to make man. There is a God of greater wisdom, greater power, and greater duration than man or things.

The Scriptures about the healing of this lame man do not tell how many were saved and how many turned to trust the Lord in response to these teachings of Paul and Barnabas, but some were, because when Paul was dragged out of the city later, and thought dead, "The disciples stood round about him." So God did save souls and raise up disciples through the ministry in wicked Lystra.

VERSES 19, 20:

19 ¶ And there came thither *certain* Jews from Antioch and Iconium, who persuaded the people, and, having stoned Paul, drew *him* out of the city, supposing he had been dead.

20 Howbeit, as the disciples stood round about him, he rose up, and came into the city: and the next day he departed with Barnabas to Derbe.

Paul Stoned at Lystra

What a shocking transition! From being worshiped as God, Paul and Barnabas fell from popular favor and Paul was stoned and literally dragged out of the city as dead!

Those two contradictory receptions were familiar to Jesus. Multitudes thronged about Him to hear Him preach, to see Him heal their sick, but the same multitude soon forsook Him and were crying, "Crucify Him." Paul later was inspired to write the Philippians, "Not that I speak in respect of want: for I have learned, in whatsoever state I am, therewith to be content. I know both how to be abased, and I know how to abound: every where and in all things I am instructed both to be full and to be hungry, both to abound and to suffer need" (Phil. 4:11, 12). That is a part of the same paradox: the Christian messenger is to be loved and hated, exalted and abased. Sometimes, like Jesus, the servant of God is to have poured upon him the alabaster box of precious ointment; sometimes, like Jesus, he is to be hated, scourged and crucified. To borrow a phrase from Rudyard Kipling's If, the apostles learned and we should learn "to treat those two impostors just the same." The preacher must not be too much impressed with the adulation and praise of men, with success and numbers; he must not be too much downcast by persecution, hate and abuse. They are together the proper lot of the true minister of God!

Note this contrast Paul was inspired to write in II Corinthians 6:8-10:

> "By honour and dishonour, by evil report and good report: as deceivers, and yet true; As unknown, and yet well known; as dying, and behold, we live; as chastened, and not killed; As sorrowful, yet alway rejoicing; as poor, yet making many rich; as having nothing, and yet possessing all things."

They "stoned Paul, drew him out of the city, supposing he had been dead." Was Paul dead? The Scripture does not say. The inference is that he was not, but there is no clear statement here. The indefinite statement was certainly intended.

Was this the occasion Paul refers to in II Corinthians 12:2-4? Probably so. <u>Ussher's Chronology</u> gives this occasion when Paul was stoned as A. D. 45 and the writing of II Corinthians as A. D. 60. So since Paul says it was "above fourteen years ago" when the event happened, it probably refers to the same thing.

There Paul says:

> "I know a man in Christ above fourteen years ago, (whether in the body, I cannot tell; or whether out of the body, I cannot tell: God knoweth;) such an one caught up to the third heaven. And I knew such a man, (whether in the body, or out of the body, I cannot tell: God knoweth;) How that he was caught up into paradise, and heard unspeakable words, which it is not lawful for a man to utter."--II Cor. 12:2-4.

The word "knew" here ought to be "know." We think Paul is speaking of himself. Notice Paul says, "Whether in the body, or out of the body, I cannot tell: God knoweth." So was Paul still alive, and did God, while he was unconscious, give wonderful revelation to him, transported in spirit to paradise? Or did Paul really die? Did his spirit leave the body dead for a bit, then was he raised from the dead? We will have to answer with Paul, "I cannot tell: God knoweth." It does not matter. At any rate, he was caught up to Paradise and heard unspeakable words and had such glorious revelations that only a thorn in the flesh could keep him from being proud and "exalted above measure" (II Cor. 12:7).

Do not pity Paul. Only to a man abused, beaten and suffering terribly could God reveal the things He wanted to reveal to Paul. Paul ever afterward looked back on that occasion, no doubt, not as a time when he was stoned and when he suffered, but as a time when he heard unspeakable words and was caught up to Paradise and the greatest time of exaltation spiritually he had ever known! Oh, those of us who would escape persecution and who would seek always to please men instead of God, we who shun the self-crucifixion which ought to be the part of God's faithful witnesses, miss also the glory that goes with such persecution!

Now God's blessed work is done. Wicked men thought to kill Paul and stop the Gospel. God had a hedge about Paul (see Job 1:10). Satan and evil men could go only as far as God permitted for His own glory; so now Paul rose up and came into the city. A few hours of rest and recuperation and he was ready the next day to go to Derbe and start again.

They had preached at Derbe before (see vs. 6).

VERSES 21-23:

21 And when they had preached the gospel to that city, and had taught many, they returned again to Lystra, and *to* Iconium, and Antioch,

22 Confirming the souls of the disciples, *and* exhorting them to continue in the faith, and that we must through much tribulation enter into the kingdom of God.

23 And when they had ordained them elders in every church, and had prayed with fasting, they commended them to the Lord, on whom they believed.

Paul and Barnabas Return to the Fields They Have Visited

Those unquenchable apostles! They spent the night in Lystra where Paul had been stoned. The next day they went back to Derbe. And after preaching the Gospel there and teaching many "they returned again to Lystra!" Then they returned "to Iconium" to where, verse 5 tells us, there had been "an assault made both of the Gentiles, and also of the Jews with their rulers, to use them despitefully, and to stone them." They also returned to Antioch. There are two Antiochs--Antioch of Syria from which Paul and Barnabas started (Acts 13:1-3), and Antioch of Pisidia, where they ministered on this journey in Acts 13:14-52. There the Jews had contradicted and blasphemed (Acts 13:45). There "the Jews stirred up the devout and honourable women, and the chief men of the city, and raised persecution against Paul and Barnabas, and expelled them out of their coasts" (Acts 13:50). Paul and Barnabas had shaken the dust off their feet against them, but now they returned to the same city from whence they had been expelled--Antioch of Pisidia! But there were precious new converts there, and so they "confirming the souls of the disciples, and exhorting them to continue in the faith, and that we must through much tribulation enter into the kingdom of God."

Isn't it strange that many of us have never learned this lesson that Paul and Barnabas taught their converts: "We must through much tribulation enter into the kingdom of God"? Ah, alas, I fear we are not very good Christians by the standard of the book of Acts! Small wonder that our kind of Christianity does not flourish like the Christianity Paul and Barnabas preached and lived!

In every church "they ordained elders." The word "ordained" here seems to be "to point out" or to appoint men who were fitted for leadership, more mature Christians, to take leadership. The word "elder" in New Testament churches generally refers to a preacher, at least to a mature and trusted leader. An elder might become a bishop, a pastor or overseer of a church, or he might not. The terms are not interchangeable. Peter was inspired to write, "The elders which are among you I exhort, who am also an elder..." (I Pet. 5:1). Timothy was commanded, "Rebuke not an elder, but intreat him as a father..." (I Tim. 5:1). And again, "Let the elders that rule well be counted worthy of double honour, especially they who labour in the word and doctrine" (I Tim. 5:17). And "against an elder receive not an accusation, but before two or three witnesses" (I Tim. 5:19). The second and third Epistles of John start out, "The elder unto the elect lady" and "the elder unto the wellbeloved Gaius." So John was an elder, that is, a preacher, though not a pastor or bishop of any church, as was also true of Peter.

Some of these elders Paul and Barnabas appointed may have become pastors.

Note the wise provision, that these elders were "appointed." The Greek word means "to designate by stretching out the hand." Should all things be settled by majority rule in a local congregation? Well, let us say that all things should be settled by the clear leading of the Holy Spirit. Later when many mature Christians are in the churches and when the Bible is completed and the apostles not present, a Spirit-led pastor or pastors and other Spirit-led people will come to the same conclusion about the will of God in all important matters, if the Holy Spirit has His way. But with a young church it is often wise for young Christians to defer to some spiritual guidance of an older Christian at first.

I have had the great privilege of organizing eight or ten independent local congregations of Christians as churches. In such cases I found it spiritually wise to ask the people to let me, at first, appoint someone to act as treasurer, someone to lead the song service, those to act as a building committee, etc., until the church should be settled down and until mature Christians grew in spiritual wisdom. That was the policy Paul and Barnabas followed here.

VERSES 24–28:

24 And after they had passed throughout Pisidia, they came to Pamphylia.

25 And when they had preached the word in Perga, they went down into Attalia:

26 And thence sailed to An-tioch, from whence they had been recommended to the grace of God for the work which they fulfilled.

27 And when they were come, and had gathered the church together, they rehearsed all that

God had done with them, and how he had opened the door of faith unto the Gentiles.

28 And there they abode long time with the disciples.

They Return to Antioch, Completing the First Missionary Journey

Wherever Paul and Barnabas had preached there had been converts and new congregations established. Now they went through Pisidia to Pamphylia, their second stop on their missionary journey (Acts 13:13), and to Perga and into Attalia, then they took a ship down the coast back to Antioch in Syria.

They gathered the church together and "rehearsed all that God had done with them, and how he had opened the door of faith unto the Gentiles." So they settled down to praise and rest and to help the congregation of Christians at Antioch for a season.

Peter had first gone to preach to the Gentile household of Cornelius and his family in Acts 10. And the principle was established: "then hath God also to the Gentiles granted repentance unto life" (Acts 11:18). But there had been little actual soul-winning work among the Gentiles until Paul and Barnabas, in each place, after preaching to the Jews, turned to the Gentiles. The whole thing is still to be worked out and God's will made clear that He is done with the ceremonial law. Jerusalem will soon be destroyed and Jews will be scattered all over the Roman Empire. God has already forsaken the temple at Jerusalem. The Jews must become acquainted with this mystery, "As it is now revealed unto his holy apostles and prophets by the Spirit; That the Gentiles should be fellowheirs, and of the same body, and partakers of his promise in Christ by the gospel" (Eph. 3:5, 6). So in the next chapter the question must be settled: Are the Gentiles to be circumcised? Must they obey the Jewish dietary laws?

Here the question comes up: Who authorized Paul and

Barnabas to go on the missionary journey? On what authority did they baptize converts and establish new churches? They were not sent out by any denomination or headquarters, certainly. And from Acts 13:1 it seems clear that a small prayer meeting band of "certain prophets and teachers" met to pray, and to them God revealed that He wanted Paul and Barnabas sent on the journey. "So they, being sent forth by the Holy Ghost, departed unto Seleucia..." (Acts 13:4). On any great missionary work it is proper to have the backing, the support, the spiritual wisdom of Christian people. But in this case it is clear that good men were moved by the Holy Spirit to urge Paul and Barnabas to go, and they were sent forth by the Holy Ghost.

So although they had the prayers, we trust, of the church at Antioch, we are not told that they had any financial support from that church. Perhaps they did, though it is not revealed.

The one essential thing about all missionary work, all preaching work, all witnessing work, is that one must go sent by the Holy Spirit.

That is what Jesus urged us all to pray about. "Pray ye therefore the Lord of the harvest, that he will send forth labourers into his harvest" (Matt. 9:38, Luke 10:2). Where the Holy Spirit sends a preacher, he will have someone to hear. Where His preacher needs support, God will have somebody to help support him.

Thus ends the first missionary journey of Paul and Barnabas.

ACTS 15

VERSES 1–6:

AND certain men which came down from Judea taught the brethren, *and said,* Except ye be circumcised after the manner of Moses, ye cannot be saved.

2 When therefore Paul and Barnabas had no small dissension and disputation with them, they determined that Paul and Barnabas, and certain other of them, should go up to Jerusalem unto the apostles and elders about this question.

3 And being brought on their way by the church, they passed through Phenice and Samaria declaring the conversion of the Gentiles: and they caused great joy unto all the brethren.

4 And when they were come to Jerusalem, they were received of the church, and *of* the apostles and elders, and they declared all things that God had done with them.

5 But there rose up certain of the sect of the Pharisees which believed, saying, That it was needful to circumcise them, and to command *them* to keep the law of Moses.

6 ¶ And the apostles and elders came together for to consider of this matter.

The Great Question: Must Christians Be Circumcised?

This is one of the most important councils ever called among Christians. They are to decide the nature of Christianity itself and verify the plan of salvation. Is the Jewish ceremonial law part of the requirement for salvation? Are people to be saved by works or by grace? Are they to be saved by rites and ceremonies, or by personal faith in Christ? Must one be circumcised and really become a Jew in order to be saved?

The question involved not only circumcision but the whole Jewish economy. Is the temple worship a part of Christianity? Must they continue animal sacrifices? When this council gathered, the temple still stood at Jerusalem, the sacrifices were still offered, the Jewish priesthood went on its fruitless way. God had already forsaken the temple. But the priesthood, sacrifices, temple worship, dietary laws, were all still a part of Jewish life. They still observed the Jewish Sabbath weekly and yearly. Tithes still went to the temple at Jerusalem. The Levites and priests got their income from the ceremonies, sacrifices, and requirements of the Mosaic law. Are all these things to be changed in a moment? Yes, all the handwriting of ordinances are nailed to the cross and now the command to the Christian is, "Let no man therefore judge you in meat, or in drink, or in respect of an holyday, or of the new moon, or of the sabbath days: Which are a shadow of things to come; but the body is of Christ" (Col. 2:16, 17). So circumcision stood for the whole setup of the ceremonial law. If the new converts are not to be circumcised and to keep the law of Moses, what a cataclysmic change that will be!

That means that the Jewish people will no longer, simply because they are Jews, have the favored place as God's people! God has future plans for the nation Israel: to restore David's throne, restore Jews to Palestine and for Christ's millennial kingdom to be set up to fulfill prophecies. But now since Jesus died on the cross there is a revelation that was shocking to the Jews! In Christ "there is neither Jew nor Greek, there is neither bond nor free, there is neither male nor female: for ye are all one in Christ Jesus" (Gal. 3:28). Not only is the mystery now made known, that the middle wall of partition between Jews and Gentiles is to be broken down (Eph. 2:14), but this is to be brought about by "having abolished in his flesh the enmity, even the law of commandments contained in ordinances..." (Eph. 2:15). Now the mystery is known "that the Gentiles should be fellowheirs, and of the same body, and partakers of his promise in Christ by the gospel" (Eph. 3:6), but all the preferential standing Jews have had is gone. God has not cast away his people, the Jews. He still has plans for the Jewish nation as such. But individual Jews and individual

Gentiles are just the same and the separation marks of circumcision and ceremonial laws are now gone forever!

Jerusalem is soon to be destroyed. Soon there will be no temple and no priesthood, and Jews themselves will be scattered all over the Roman Empire. And it must be settled that Christianity does not have the trappings of Judaism; not the circumcision nor the sacrifices nor priesthoods nor dietary laws nor Sabbaths.

This Is the Great Theme of the Epistles to Hebrews and Galatians

In the book of Hebrews in great detail it is made clear that Christ is better than the angels (chapters 1 and 2). Jesus is greater than Moses. Moses was a servant and Christ the Son (Heb. 3:5, 6). He is the great High Priest (Heb. 4:14-16; Heb. 5). He is a priest typified by Melchisedec, greater than the Aaronic order of priests. The new covenant is better than the old covenant. The ordinances and sanctuary of the old covenant were merely types, shadows, promising greater to come. Christ Himself is the one great Sacrifice pictured in all the sacrifices and thus is the end of sacrifices.

In Galatians it is made clear that "to Abraham and his seed were the promises made" (Gal. 3:16). And that the law, four hundred and thirty years later, could not annul that covenant. Abraham believed God and it was counted to him for righteousness.

There we are told in Galatians 3:19, "Wherefore then serveth the law? It was added because of transgressions, till the seed should come to whom the promise was made; and it was ordained by angels in the hand of a mediator."

And again Galatians 3:24 and 25 says, "Wherefore the law was our schoolmaster to bring us unto Christ, that we might be justified by faith. But after that faith is come, we are no longer under a schoolmaster."

It is clear, then, that the spiritual mind ought to have seen all along that all the ceremonies of the Mosaic law were intended as object lessons, illustrations, pointing to Jesus Christ. They are "a shadow of things to come; but the body is of Christ" (Col. 2:17). Circumcision in the flesh pictured the circumcision of heart, regeneration. The Sabbath day's rest after six days of labor showed that by the law Heaven could be reached only by perfection, which all have missed. So in the passover and the feast of unleavened bread, they were taught that after one meal of the passover lamb, with the blood on the door, this seven days' feast of unleavened bread was started with a Sabbath picturing the sweet rest and the peace of God which a born-again Christian has now, and ends with the Sabbath, a rest picturing Heaven (Exod. 12:14-16). So in Hebrews 4:9 and 10, "There remaineth therefore a rest to the people of God. For he that is entered into his rest, he also hath ceased from his own works, as God did from his."

All the animal sacrifices picture Jesus. That was made clear surely in the preaching of John the Baptist when he cried out, "Behold the Lamb of God, which taketh away the sin of the world" (John 1:29). And even in the Old Testament the plan of salvation was made clear, that it did not depend on the ceremonies or works of the law. "And he believed in the Lord; and he counted it to him for righteousness" (Gen. 15:6).

> "Behold, his soul which is lifted up is not upright in him: but the just shall live by his faith."
> --Hab. 2:4.

> "...Whosoever shall call on the name of the Lord shall be delivered."--Joel 2:32.

How clear the Lord Jesus had made this matter in talking to the woman at Sychar of Samaria. It is true that He said that salvation is of the Jews, that is, came through the Jewish Scriptures and the Jewish Saviour:

"Jesus saith unto her, Woman, believe me, the hour cometh, when ye shall neither in this mountain, nor yet at Jerusalem, worship the Father. Ye worship ye know not what: we know what we worship: for salvation is of the Jews. But the hour cometh, and now is, when the true worshippers shall worship the Father in spirit and in truth: for the Father seeketh such to worship him. God is a Spirit: and they that worship him must worship him in spirit and in truth."--John 4:21-24.

But such a deep-seated, fundamental change in all the outward forms of religion required a big council to settle the matter officially among the apostles and brethren and the great congregation of thousands at Jerusalem. So "the apostles and elders came together for to consider of this matter."

VERSES 7–11:

7 And when there had been much disputing, Peter rose up, and said unto them, Men *and* brethren, ye know how that a good while ago God made choice among us, that the Gentiles by my mouth should hear the word of the gospel, and believe.

8 And God, which knoweth the hearts, bare them witness, giving them the Holy Ghost, even as *he did* unto us;

9 And put no difference between us and them, purifying their hearts by faith.

10 Now therefore why tempt ye God, to put a yoke upon the neck of the disciples, which neither our fathers nor we were able to bear?

11 But we believe that through the grace of the Lord Jesus Christ we shall be saved, even as they.

Peter's Argument Against Requiring Circumcision and the Ceremonial Law for Christians

It was proper, after many had disputed and stared the

case pro and con, for Peter, the chief of the twelve apostles and the one whom God had chosen to preach the Gospel first to the Gentiles, to speak. And he did. If God had directly led Peter to preach to the household of Cornelius and if Peter had personally seen the converts and the evidence of their salvation, he would be a proper witness in this matter. Notice his argument.

1. God showed evidence that these in Cornelius' household had truly been converted by faith; they had never been circumcised, they had not kept Jewish dietary laws, did not worship in the temple, nor bring sacrifices and yet they had been saved and filled with the Spirit of God, had praised the Lord. There was abundant evidence that the Spirit of God had come into these converts and upon them. These converts who were from Italy had spoken in languages that Peter and his six Jewish companions could understand, praising God.

2. There was much evidence that these people had been saved exactly as Jews had been saved who trusted Christ. Their hearts were "purified by faith." They were turned from sin, their conversion was genuine. In fact, the outward evidence was in some ways like that at Pentecost.

3. But Peter sought deeper than this. Jews had never been saved by keeping the law. The law demanded perfect obedience. "For as many as are of the works of the law are under the curse: for it is written, Cursed is every one that continueth not in all things which are written in the book of the law to do them" (Gal. 3:10). No Jew had ever been saved by the ceremonies of the law, nor even by the moral precepts of the law. Why tempt God to put such a burden on Gentiles which no Jew had ever been able to bear? This is the heart of the whole matter. People were never saved by works, by ceremonies, by rites. All these were vain for salvation. They were given only as pictures and pointers toward Christ.

4. So Peter concludes that since people are to be saved

"through the grace of our Lord Jesus Christ," then Jews and Gentiles alike must be saved by faith without the deeds of the law (vs. 11).

VERSE 12:

12 ¶ Then all the multitude kept silence, and gave audience to Barnabas and Paul, declaring what miracles and wonders God had wrought among the Gentiles by them.

Paul and Barnabas Now Testify of Their Ministry Among the Gentiles

Paul and Barnabas had recently returned from a great missionary journey. Many thousands had been saved. In scores of towns and cities new groups of converts were organized into local churches. Again and again, after starting to preach to Jews, Paul and Barnabas had turned to the Gentiles and there had been a blessed reaping in the white harvest. These in Jerusalem had heard rumors and second-hand reports, so now these two stood and the rapt multitude heard them tell of God's blessings as Paul and Barnabas spoke "declaring what miracles and wonders God had wrought among the Gentiles by them."

Before them Peter had called attention to the fact that God had obviously given the Holy Spirit in saving and witnessing power to the converts in Cornelius' house. Now Paul and Barnabas surely must have used the same argument. Writing a little later to the Galatians who had been led off in this same Judaistic heresy wanting to keep the law and be circumcised instead of trusting in Christ alone, Paul challenged, "This only would I learn of you, Received ye the Spirit by the works of the law, or by the hearing of faith? Are ye so foolish? having begun in the Spirit, are ye now made perfect by the flesh?" (Gal. 3:2, 3). And again he said, "Christ hath redeemed us from the curse of the law...That the blessing of Abraham might come on the Gentiles through Jesus Christ; THAT WE MIGHT RECEIVE THE PROMISE OF THE SPIRIT THROUGH FAITH" (Gal. 3:13, 14). So as Paul and Barnabas told of wonderful conversions, of transformed lives, of the power of the Holy Ghost on these Gentile converts, the people listened spellbound.

Christianity meant the regeneration by the Spirit, the indwelling of the Spirit, and that Christians should witness in the fullness of the Spirit. This was the evidence, and surely Paul and Barnabas must have made clear, as Paul was inspired to make clear to the Galatians later, that to go back to any plan of salvation depending on human works or ceremonies was to fall from the doctrine of salvation by grace. "Christ is become of no effect unto you, whosoever of you are justified by the law; ye are fallen from grace" (Gal. 5:4).

No honest man who knew of the marvelous, spiritual revolution that went with Paul and Barnabas on their missionary journey could deny that God's mighty power had been with them, that there had been genuine conversions to Christ, marvelous work of the Holy Spirit. And that was good evidence that people did not need to keep the ceremonies of the law in order to be saved.

VERSES 13–18:

13 ¶ And after they had held their peace, James answered, saying, Men *and* brethren, hearken unto me:

14 Simeon hath declared how God at the first did visit the Gentiles, to take out of them a people for his name.

15 And to this agree the words of the prophets; as it is written,

16 After this I will return, and will build again the tabernacle of David, which is fallen down; and I will build again the ruins thereof, and I will set it up:

17 That the residue of men might seek after the Lord, and all the Gentiles, upon whom my name is called, saith the Lord, who doeth all these things.

18 Known unto God are all his works from the beginning of the world.

James Reasons That the Outcalling
of the Gentiles Agrees With the
Promises to Israel

Remember, this is not James, the brother of John, whose death is recorded in chapter 12. This is "James the Lord's brother" (Gal. 1:19) who was inspired to write the book of James. He seems to have been the leading elder in the church at Jerusalem and he, not Peter, had the last say here. Here James refers to Amos 9:11 and 12. The remaining verses of Amos 9 tell of the time when God will bring back the captivity of Israel and build the waste cities and plant Israel again in their land. So James is correct in saying that the Lord has promised through the prophets, "After this I will return, and will build again the tabernacle of David." There are hundreds of Old Testament Scriptures which he may have had in mind. Doubtless such Scriptures as Deuteronomy 30:1-6; Jeremiah 23:3-8; Ezekiel 34:11-31; 36:24-28; Ezekiel 37.

"Moreover I will appoint a place for my people Israel, and will plant them, that they may dwell in a place of their own, and move no more; neither shall the children of wickedness afflict them any more, as beforetime, And as since the time that I commanded judges to be over my people Israel, and have caused thee to rest from all thine enemies. Also the Lord telleth thee that he will make thee an house. And when thy days be fulfilled, and thou shalt sleep with thy fathers, I will set up thy seed after thee, which shall proceed out of thy bowels, and I will establish his kingdom. He shall build an house for my name, and I will establish the throne of his kingdom for ever. I will be his father, and he shall be my son. If he commit iniquity, I will chasten him with the rod of men, and with the stripes of the children of men: But my mercy shall not depart away from him, as I took it from Saul, whom I put away before thee. And thine house and thy kingdom shall be established for ever before thee: thy throne shall be established for ever."

That covenant is described also in I Chronicles 7:4-15. God will build again the house of David through Jesus Christ, at His return.

That is what the angel Gabriel told Mary, prophesying the birth of Jesus, "And, behold, thou shalt conceive in thy womb, and bring forth a son, and shalt call his name JESUS. He shall be great, and shall be called the Son of the Highest: and the Lord God shall give unto him the throne of his father David: And he shall reign over the house of Jacob for ever; and of his kingdom there shall be no end" (Luke 1:31-33).

During this age, then, the Lord will "visit the Gentiles, to take out of them a people for his name" (Acts 15:14). So before Christ's kingdom on earth the Gospel must be preached to the Gentiles everywhere.

VERSES 19–35:

19 Wherefore my sentence is, that we trouble not them, which from among the Gentiles are turned to God:

20 But that we write unto them, that they abstain from pollutions of idols, and *from* fornication, and *from* things strangled, and *from* blood.

21 For Moses of old time hath in every city them that preach him, being read in the syna-gogues every sabbath day.

22 Then pleased it the apostles and elders, with the whole church, to send chosen men of their own company to Antioch with Paul and Barnabas; *namely,* Judas surnamed Barsabas, and Silas, chief men among the brethren:

23 And they wrote *letters* by them after this manner; The apostles and elders and brethren

send greeting unto the brethren which are of the Gentiles in Antioch and Syria and Cilicia:

24 Forasmuch as we have heard, that certain which went out from us have troubled you with words, subverting your souls, saying, *Ye must* be circumcised, and keep the law; to whom we gave no *such* commandment:

25 It seemed good unto us, being assembled with one accord, to send chosen men unto you with our beloved Barnabas and Paul,

26 Men that have hazarded their lives for the name of our Lord Jesus Christ.

27 We have sent therefore Judas and Silas, who shall also tell *you* the same things by mouth.

28 For it seemed good to the Holy Ghost, and to us, to lay upon you no greater burden than these necessary things;

29 That ye abstain from meats offered to idols, and from blood, and from things strangled, and from fornication: from which if ye keep yourselves, ye shall do well. Fare ye well.

30 So when they were dismissed, they came to Antioch: and when they had gathered the multitude together, they delivered the epistle:

31 *Which* when they had read, they rejoiced for the consolation.

32 And Judas and Silas, being prophets also themselves, exhorted the brethren with many words, and confirmed *them.*

33 And after they had tarried *there* a space, they were let go in peace from the brethren unto the apostles.

34 Notwithstanding it pleased Silas to abide there still.

35 Paul also and Barnabas continued in Antioch, teaching and preaching the word of the Lord, with many others also.

The Council Unanimously Agrees: Christians Are Not Under the Ceremonial Law

James pronounced his judgment and all were convinced, as they should have been. The laws of Moses would be read in the synagogues wherever Jews gathered. They would not be discrediting the Word of God given through Moses. But it was decided "that we trouble not them, which from among the Gentiles are turned to God." They were already saved without the works of the law. The works of the law need not be added to the plan of salvation. Neither circumcision nor any other part of the ceremonies were to be required, and, of course, even the moral law was not the plan of salvation. In the New Testament all the moral requirements of the law would be restated, rather "for Christ is the end of the law for righteousness to every one that believeth" (Rom. 10:4). But Christ died for us "that the righteousness of the law might be fulfilled in us, who walk not after the flesh, but after the Spirit" (Rom. 8:4).

But Gentile Converts Were Not to Be Offensive to Godly Jews

However, these Gentile converts needed special instruction and warning, as new converts always do. The heathen people did not have the strict standards of morality that the Jews had, inculcated by the Mosaic law, so it was necessary to warn them about four things.

1. They were to "abstain from pollutions of idols" (vs. 20). Since the captivity Jews had been cured of idolatry. That was not so among the heathen saved under the ministry of Paul and Barnabas. So these Gentile converts were to make sure of a clear-cut separation, not only from idol worship but from any reverance toward idols and any tolerance toward idol worship.

2. They were to abstain "from fornication." Sex sin, immorality, polygamous marriages were common among the heathen people. So new converts needed special warning on this matter.

3. They were to abstain "from things strangled, and from blood." These two things had the same warning. All the Jews had been taught not to eat things strangled, and even to this day the blood must be carefully drained from kosher meats, acceptable to orthodox Jews. They had been taught, "For the life of the flesh is in the blood: and I have given it to you upon the altar to make an atonement for your souls: for it is the blood that maketh an atonement for the soul," and also, "For it is the life of all flesh; the blood of it is for the life thereof: therefore I said unto the children

of Israel, Ye shall eat of the blood of no manner of flesh: for the life of all flesh is the blood thereof: whosoever eateth it shall be cut off" (Lev. 17:11, 14). The great stress on animal sacrifices, and the insistence on the importance of the blood, the sprinkling of blood before the altar and before the veil of the temple, the blood on the doorposts on the passover night--all these had given a reverence for the blood which pictured and pointed toward the blood of Christ.

Gentiles would not naturally have this reverence for the blood. If they were careless about it, it would greatly offend godly Jews. They would be counted crude and coarse. Besides, they themselves needed to grow in a constant reminder of the blood of Christ. The Lord's Supper is intended for that purpose, and one who was accustomed to careless bloodshed ought to learn that reverence. If the new converts were to be blessed and helped by Jewish leaders and if they were to have fellowship with Jewish Christians in the same churches, then they must grow in appreciation of the Jewish ethics and morals, and not be offensive to godly Jews.

So these instructions were given to the Gentile converts in verse 29 and they are not given as part of the plan of salvation but wise counsel as to how to live now acceptably to God and in good fellowship with Jewish Christians.

Two trusted men, specially representing the apostles at Jerusalem, were sent with Paul and Barnabas. They were Judas, surnamed Barsabas, and Silas, chief men among the brethren. They sent the nice letter quoted in verses 23 to 29 "unto the brethren which are of the Gentiles in Antioch and Syria and Cilicia."

Note the comments on these two good men, Judas and Silas. They are "men that have hazarded their lives for the name of our Lord Jesus Christ." And these men were to tell by mouth the same message included in the letter. Jewish Christians, leaders, apostles and elders at Jerusalem did not believe that Gentile converts needed to be circum-

cised or keep the law of Moses. That was not required of
Gentiles.

Notice verse 28. "For it seemed good to the Holy Ghost,
and to us." They were sure they had the clear leading of
God. The Holy Spirit had made these elders and the multitude at Jerusalem of one mind. The real administrator of
the local church is the Holy Spirit. Pastors are to "rule,"
as we see from Hebrews 13:7, 17, 24; I Timothy 3:4 and 5.
But pastors can only rule properly as they are led of the
Spirit of God and when people are prayerful, patient, con-
siderate and wait upon God for His will to be known. Then
the will of the church will be united and the blessed Holy
Spirit can have His way as He had in this assembly at Jerusalem.

Earnestly Contending for the Faith
Is Sometimes Necessary

Let us go back to consider that council at Jerusalem. We
are told that "Paul and Barnabas had no small dissension
and disputation with them" who said you must be circumcised and keep the law of Moses to be saved (vs. 2). Notice
in verse 7, "And when there had been much disputing...."
Earnest debate, marshaling of Scriptures, persuading the
people, is oftentimes necessary to make the truth of the
Gospel clear.

Notice how sharply Paul spoke about these same kind of
Judaizers in his letter to the Christians at Galatia. He said
he wished that anyone who would bring another gospel
should be accursed (Gal. 1:8, 9). He said, "I would they
were even cut off which trouble you" (Gal. 5:12). On this
same matter of the influence of the Judaizers in the church,
Paul faced Peter who had compromised. And Galatians
2:11-14 tells how publicly Paul rebuked Peter for this sin
which had led Barnabas and others in that same dissimula-
tion.

How deadly is the carnal mind which wants to be saved by

works instead of by grace! How "prone to wander" is the poor human heart even of saved people.

No wonder Paul was inspired to write Titus, "For there are many unruly and vain talkers and deceivers, specially they of the circumcision: Whose mouths must be stopped, who subvert whole houses, teaching things which they ought not, for filthy lucre's sake" (Titus 1:10, 11). Wherefore, Titus was commanded to "rebuke them sharply, that they may be sound in the faith" (Titus 1:13).

And Paul was inspired to write people at Rome a solemn warning: "Now I beseech you, brethren, mark them which cause divisions and offenses contrary to the doctrine which ye have learned; and avoid them. For they that are such serve not our Lord Jesus Christ, but their own belly; and by good works and fair speeches deceive the hearts of the simple" (Rom. 16:17, 18). And Timothy was commanded, in a letter suitable for all preachers, "Preach the word; be instant in season, out of season; reprove, rebuke, exhort with all longsuffering and doctrine" (II Tim. 4:2). And Jude 3 and 4 gives us a solemn warning that we "should earnestly contend for the faith" because of false teachers.

Dispute, argument, contending for the faith, are necessary parts of preaching the Gospel, and no preacher is true to God who does not take heed to the command, "Beware of false prophets, which come to you in sheep's clothing, but inwardly they are ravening wolves" (Matt. 7:15), and who does not even rebuke brethren who lead people astray in false doctrine.

Purity in doctrine is so important that with love and patience and humility we should "earnestly contend for the faith" (Jude 3).

Paul and Barnabas took the messengers and went to Antioch of Pisidia. Judas and Silas exhorted the brethren also. Judas, whose surname was Barsabas, went back to the apostles at Jerusalem, but Silas stayed in Antioch of Syria, and Paul and Barnabas continued there, preaching and teaching.

VERSES 36–41:

36 ¶ And some days after, Paul said unto Barnabas, Let us go again and visit our brethren in every city where we have preached the word of the Lord, *and see* how they do.

37 And Barnabas determined to take with them John, whose surname was Mark.

38 But Paul thought not good to take him with them, who departed from them from Pamphylia, and went not with them to the work.

39 And the contention was so sharp between them, that they departed asunder one from the other: and so Barnabas took Mark, and sailed unto Cyprus;

40 And Paul chose Silas, and departed, being recommended by the brethren unto the grace of God.

41 And he went through Syria and Cilicia, confirming the churches.

Paul's Second Missionary Journey

But Paul has a call to be the apostle to the Gentiles and a dispensation of the Gospel is committed unto him. Even the apostles could see that "the gospel of the uncircumcision was committed unto me, as the gospel of the circumcision was unto Peter; (For he that wrought effectually in Peter to the apostleship of the circumcision, the same was mighty in me toward the Gentiles:)" as Paul said in Galatians 2:7 and 8. In II Timothy 1:11 he says, "I am appointed...a teacher of the Gentiles." In Romans 11:13 he said, "I am the apostle of the Gentiles." And God would not let Paul forget that, and in Jerusalem as he prayed in the temple, the Lord said to him, "For I will send thee far hence unto the Gentiles" (Acts 22:21).

So Paul planned again a missionary journey. And this time he felt a burden to go back again "and visit our brethren in every city where we have preached the word of the Lord, and see how they do."

Barnabas agreed to go, but he wanted to take with him John Mark, his nephew, who had left the party at Pamphylia in the preceding journey (13:13). There was sharp contention between them. So Barnabas took Mark and sailed unto

Cyprus and passes out of the New Testament story and is never mentioned again except as Paul recalls his compromise at Antioch, following Peter's example, as rebuked in Galatians 2:11-14.

"Paul chose Silas," a good, Spirit-filled man and departed, "being recommended by the brethren unto the grace of God." And so back through the provinces of Syria and Cilicia they went confirming the churches. But that is not all of the second missionary journey as we will see. Soon the Holy Spirit leads them out into new regions and over into Europe and the country of Greece.

Paul's three missionary journeys might be distinguished thus: his companion on the first journey was Barnabas and continued through the thirteenth and fourteenth chapter and the first four verses of the fifteenth chapter. It includes Cyprus and some provinces in the peninsula generally called Asia Minor. On the second missionary journey his companion was Silas and part of the time at least Timothy, although they did not stay with Paul all the time (Acts 18:5). And the second journey included a trip through the provinces of Greece as well as through the provinces formerly visited. It is described from the last of the fifteenth chapter down to 18:22. The third missionary journey begins, I suppose, with Acts 18:23 down to Acts 20:17 and perhaps included various companions in travel, including Gaius and Aristarchus (Acts 19:29).

It is probable that there was at least another missionary journey coming between Paul's first and second imprisonment at Rome. Since Paul had been inspired to write to those at Rome, "Whensoever I take my journey into Spain, I will come to you" (Rom. 15:24). And he was inspired to write to the Philippians from prison in Rome, "Nevertheless to abide in the flesh is more needful for you. And having this confidence, I know that I shall abide and continue with you all for your furtherance and joy of faith; That your rejoicing may be more abundant in Jesus Christ for me by my coming to you again" (Phil. 1:24-26). Also he was inspired to write Philemon at Colosse, "But withal prepare me also a lodging: for I trust that through your prayers I shall be given unto you" (Philem. 22).

ACTS 16

VERSES 1–3:

THEN came he to Derbe and Lystra: and, behold, a certain disciple was there, named Timotheus, the son of a certain woman, which was a Jewess, and believed; but his father *was* a Greek:

2 Which was well reported of by the brethren that were at Lystra and Iconium.

3 Him would Paul have to go forth with him; and took and circumcised him because of the Jews which were in those quarters: for they knew all that his father was a Greek.

Paul Finds a Worthy Assistant, Timothy

On the map of the eastern Mediterranean, Antioch of Syria is some three hundred miles from Jerusalem. That was a starting place of Paul and Barnabas for the first missionary journey, and the starting place of the second journey with Silas as partner. Beginning where they were in Syria, they visited the churches, then on north into Cilicia, and northwest through Galatia, now generally called Asia Minor, though in Bible times the term Asia referred only to the western part of that peninsula. As they turned westward, (being north of the east end of the Mediterranean Sea) they would probably pass through Tarsus, Paul's native city. Now they had set out to visit the churches established in the first missionary journey and the groups of Christians throughout Cilicia and Galatia.

But as he came to Derbe and Lystra, towns some fifty or sixty miles apart but usually named together, he found a young convert, Timothy (Timotheus in the Greek). Possibly he had been converted since Paul's visit here before, or possibly he had only recently developed as a strong, young Christian, feeling the call of God. His mother was a Jewess and had been saved; his father was a Greek. Young Timothy's character, devotion and promise of usefulness commended him to the brethren and to Paul. "Him would Paul have to go forth with him...." Paul took this young man with him on the missionary journey. No doubt Timothy will come nearer than anybody else to carrying on Paul's great ministry after Paul, the apostle, shall die a martyr at Rome. Timothy is mentioned five times more in the book of Acts--in 17:14, 17:15, 18:5, 19:22, and in 20:4. Several times he sent Timothy to churches to help and teach them, as at Corinth in I Corinthians 4:17, and 16:10; to Philippi, as in Philippians 2:19; to Thessalonica, in I Thessalonians 3:2, 6. Paul wrote Timothy, "As I besought thee to abide still at Ephesus, when I went into Macedonia, that thou mightest charge some that they teach no other doctrine" (I Tim. 1:3). Paul loved and trusted Timothy greatly, calling him, "My own son in the faith" (I Tim. 1:2). When Paul determined to take Timothy with him, evidently they had a season of prayer together and possibly fasting, and doubtless Timothy felt the call of God and was set apart for this soul-winning ministry, as Paul and Barnabas had been set apart in Antioch of Syria, in Acts 13:1-4. So Paul later wrote Timothy, "Neglect not the gift that is in thee, which was given thee by prophecy, with the laying on of the hands of the presbytery" (I Tim. 4:14). Again, he was inspired to write Timothy, "Wherefore I put thee in remembrance that thou stir up the gift of God, which is in thee by the putting on of my hands" (II Tim. 1:6).

How carefully the apostle trained the young preacher Timothy! And what holy exhortation in the two epistles to Timothy, inspired, of course, from God. In a particular sense he was Paul's best representative. Paul wrote the people of Corinth, "For this cause have I sent unto you Timotheus, who is my beloved son, and faithful in the Lord, who shall bring you into remembrance of my ways which be in Christ, as I teach every where in every church" (I Cor. 4:17). And he was inspired of God to write the church at Philippi, "But I trust in the Lord Jesus to send Timotheus shortly unto you, that I also may be of good comfort, when I know your state. For I have no man likeminded, who will naturally care for your state" (Phil. 2:19, 20).

So Timothy was Paul's most trusted lieutenant. It was to Timothy that he wrote the farewell letter of II Timothy, just before he was beheaded in prison in Rome.

Why Did Paul Circumcise Timothy?

Paul "took and circumcised him because of the Jews which were in those quarters: for they knew all that his father was a Greek."

1. Paul certainly did not have Timothy circumcised to insure his salvation. He and Timothy went on their journey together, telling Gentile Christians everywhere the decrees of the council at Jerusalem, that circumcision and the Mosaic law were not required for salvation, in fact, not required at all of Gentile converts.

No, it was evidently a matter of expediency. Timothy's father was a Greek. So "because of the Jews" and because "they all knew that his father was a Greek," Paul circumcised Timothy, evidently to make him acceptable to the Jews. After all, as Jesus said, "salvation is of the Jews," and if Timothy were to preach Christ to the Jews, he must preach from the Jewish Old Testament and from Jewish sacrifices and about the God of the Jewish Old Testament, not the god of the idol worshipers among the Gentiles. It is inferred that the Jews would not listen well to a half-breed Jew who was not circumcised.

It may be of things like this that Paul was inspired to write:

> "For though I be free from all men, yet have I made myself servant unto all, that I might gain the more. And unto the Jews I became as a Jew, that I might gain the Jews; to them that are under the law, as under the law, that I might gain them that are under the law; To them that are without

> law, as without law, (being not without law to
> God, but under the law to Christ,) that I might
> gain them that are without law. To the weak be-
> came I as weak, that I might gain the weak: I
> am made all things to all men, that I might by
> all means save some. And this I do for the gos-
> pel's sake, that I might be partaker thereof with
> you."--I Cor. 9:19-23.

So "unto the Jews I became as a Jew, that I might gain the
Jews; to them that are under the law, as under the law, that
I might gain them that are under the law."

Hudson Taylor, when going to China, dressed in native
Chinese costume, lived in a Chinese house, and ate Chinese
food.

2. Did Paul do wrong to circumcise Timothy? I do not
know; this Scripture does not say. We know that later Paul
shaved his head and had a vow (Acts 18:18). We know that
he said, "I must by all means keep this feast that cometh in
Jerusalem" (Acts 18:21). In Jerusalem he joined four men
who had a vow, purified himself according to the ceremonial law, and helped pay the expenses of these men to show
the Jews at Jerusalem "that those things, whereof they were
informed concerning thee, are nothing; but that thou thyself
also walkest orderly, and KEEPEST THE LAW!" (Acts
21:24, 26). So Paul and four others entered into the temple
"to signify the accomplishment of the days of purification,
until that an offering should be offered for every one of
them." Paul the apostle having animal sacrifices and "purifying" himself according to the Mosaic law in the temple at
Jerusalem!

I think we must conclude that Paul was more influenced
than he should have been by his love for his own people, the
Jews. He insisted on coming back to Jerusalem, though
warned against it. Even in the temple praying he was in a
trance and God said to him, "Make haste, and get thee

quickly out of Jerusalem: for they will not receive thy testimony concerning me" (Acts 22:18).

You see, even after Paul knew that circumcision, the sacrifices and the customs of the ceremonial law were not required, that they were all fulfilled in Christ, he could not immediately divorce himself from the habits, diet, friendships, and the manner of thinking of a lifetime. The Jewish way of life was not only morals but manners. It was not only types pointing to Jesus Christ, but it was a way of life that influenced what people wore, what they ate, how they talked, and every idea of right and wrong.

In my home a beloved Jewish brother, who studied ten years in the Talmud to be a rabbi, then was wonderfully converted and became well-taught in the things of the Lord, still found himself bound by the habits and customs of a lifetime. He could not bring himself to eat beans with a bit of pork fat in them! I started to lay his coat across the bed where my wife lay with a new baby, and he snatched it up quickly, so ingrained was the idea of purification and the uncleanness of everything that a woman might touch within weeks after childbirth!

This must help us to see the terrific pressure which came upon Peter and caused his compromise at Antioch, as reported in Galatians 2:11-14, where he was rebuked by Paul. It must remind us of the enormous pressure of the Judaizers on the Christians in Galatia, which led them into heresy and sin. Paul had Timothy circumcised! Whether it was wrong or not, at least Paul was intent on making Timothy a Jew!

VERSES 4-11:

4 And as they went through the cities, they delivered them the decrees for to keep, that were ordained of the apostles and elders which were at Jerusalem.

5 And so were the churches established in the faith, and

increased in number daily.

6 Now when they had gone throughout Phrygia and the region of Galatia, and were forbidden of the Holy Ghost to preach the word in Asia,

7 After they were come to Mysia, they assayed to go into Bithynia: but the Spirit suffered them not.

8 And they passing by Mysia came down to Troas.

9 And a vision appeared to Paul in the night; There stood a man of Macedonia, and prayed him, saying, Come over into Macedonia, and help us.

10 And after he had seen the vision, immediately we endeavoured to go into Macedonia, assuredly gathering that the Lord had called us for to preach the gospel unto them.

11 Therefore loosing from Troas, we came with a straight course to Samothracia, and the next *day* to Neapolis;

Paul, Silas and Timothy Visit the Churches and Are Halted

The little party "went through the cities," evidently spending some time in each city of the province in order. They read publicly the written letter from the apostles and elders at Jerusalem, declaring that circumcision and the law of Moses were not required of Gentile converts. And everywhere not only were the churches "established in the faith," but souls were saved day after day and the Christians "increased in number daily."

The one big thing in New Testament churches was soul winning. After Pentecost at Jerusalem, "the Lord added to the church daily such as should be saved" (Acts 2:47). And again, despite persecutions and beatings, we are told, "And daily in the temple, and in every house, they ceased not to teach and preach Jesus Christ" (Acts 5:42). Later after Paul had preached at Ephesus for three years and then returned, he called the elders to Miletus, the little seaport nearby, and reminded them "...how I kept back nothing that was profitable unto you, but have shewed you, and have taught you publickly, and from house to house." And again, "Therefore watch, and remember, that by the space of three years I ceased not to warn every one night and day with tears" (Acts 20:20, 31). To follow in the train of New Testament churches, groups of Christians everywhere should "increase in number daily."

They went "throughout Phrygia and the region of Galatia," and I suppose visiting every principal town in those provinces. Next on the west, toward the end of the peninsula, was the province of Asia, and they would have gone there but "were forbidden of the Holy Ghost to preach the word in Asia." So they went on by to Mysia, the point nearest Greece, and they would have turned northwest again into the province of Bithynia, "but the Spirit suffered them not." So they came back and bypassed the province of Mysia, not preaching in the towns and cities there, on to Troas on the most western seacoast of the peninsula now called Asia Minor. There in the little town of Troas on the Agean Sea a vision appeared to Paul with further detailed leading; they were to go into Macedonia.

Note how clearly the Spirit guided. One can feel in his heart a check, a warning, a sense of unrest if a proposed course is displeasing to God. Oh, blessed Holy Spirit, make us sensitive to listen! The tender, earnest heart that has no will of its own except to find the Lord's will, can know the will of God, can have the sweet, clear leading of the Holy Spirit. So Philip was led from Samaria out to the highway where he met the Ethiopian eunuch in Acts 8. And Peter was led to the house of Cornelius in Acts 10. So Jesus "must needs go through Samaria" (John 4:4).

We spend too much time trying to get God to put His approval and blessing upon our plans. How much better if we would make sure that we know and follow His plans! The Holy Spirit dwells within every believer. He is to be teacher, reminder, guide, comforter, as Jesus taught in John, chapters 14, 15, and 16. He is our prayer helper (Rom. 8:26).

From Asia Into Europe, and
Luke Joins the Party

Paul and his party had been earnestly waiting on God, so in the night a vision came. "There stood a man of Macedonia, and prayed him, saying, Come over into Macedonia, and help us." Paul and all were convinced alike that "the Lord had called us for to preach the gospel unto them" in Macedonia.

Note in verse 10 Luke, who is writing the book of Acts, says, "Immediately WE endeavoured to go into Macedonia." In verse 4 he had written, "As THEY went through the cities." In verse 6, "Now when THEY had gone throughout Phrygia." In verse 7, "After THEY were come to Mysia, THEY assayed to go into Bithynia." In verse 8, "And THEY passing by Mysia came down to Troas." But in verse 10 the writer says, "Immediately WE endeavoured to go into Macedonia." So here Luke joined the party and hereafter, as you see in verses 13, 16, it is "we." However, after they came to Philippi the narrative returns to the third person, as we see in verses 39 and 40. Timothy and Silas stay, as we see in 17:14. Luke evidently had left the party for a time but comes into the story again, using the first person plural in Acts 20:5, 6, 13, 14, 15, and again in Acts 21. There Luke went with the party from Troas back to Jerusalem.

So the Gospel has come into continental Europe; now into Greece, the center of learning, and eventually after a rest, Paul will go on to Rome, the capital city of the world empire! They sailed to the island of Samothracia and then to the seaport town of Neapolis in Macedonia, and Philippi close by.

VERSES 12–15:

12 And from thence to Philippi, which is the chief city of that part of Macedonia, *and* a colony: and we were in that city abiding certain days.

13 And on the sabbath we went out of the city by a river side, where prayer was wont to be made; and we sat down, and spake unto the women which resorted *thither*.

14 ¶ And a certain woman named Lydia, a seller of purple, of the city of Thyatira, which worshipped God, heard *us:* whose heart the Lord opened, that she attended unto the things which were spoken of Paul.

15 And when she was baptized, and her household, she besought *us,* saying, If ye have judged me to be faithful to the Lord, come into my house, and abide *there.* And she constrained us.

The First Convert in Europe

Paul went to the center of things. He felt that the Gospel ought to go to the big cities and that whole nations ought to be covered with the Gospel. So it is mentioned, "Philippi, which is the chief city of that part of Macedonia, and a colony." A "colony" meant that it had been settled by certain Roman citizens from Italy. They were privileged people, had special honor in the Roman Empire. Paul Himself was a Roman citizen from birth. Such an influential city would be the place to start.

On the Sabbath they went to a prayer meeting by the riverside. Since it was on the Sabbath, that indicates that these were Jewish women who met there for prayer. Paul usually began with Jews. They would understand him better. So here at the riverside he preached the Gospel to these women. Among them was Lydia, a seller of purple. She was a native of Thyatira back in the province of Asia. Perhaps she traveled to sell her fine goods dyed with the coloring matter taken from shelfish. More likely she had moved her business to Philippi where it is probable there was more wealth. At least she had a household here. We are not told that she had a husband or children; her household may have been her servants and helpers.

Lydia "worshipped God." Possibly she had in her heart trusted God as Abraham did and as a good many other Jews did, seeing through the sacrifices and through the ceremonies of the law a picture of the Saviour who should come. Perhaps she knew of the prophecies in Isaiah 53 and other Old Testament promises about the Saviour. At any rate, she worshiped God. So had the Ethiopian eunuch worshiped God, though as far as we know he was not saved until Philip preached the Gospel to him. At least her heart was hungry and was seeking the Lord, so when she listened to Paul her heart was opened; she claimed the Saviour openly and was baptized.

Perhaps she was well-to-do. Likely she had a good business and several helpers. So she invited the entire party-- Paul, Silas, Timothy, Luke--to stay in her home and there they came to abide in answer to her entreaty.

Trying to prove infant baptism, some people have supposed that Lydia had babies and that they were baptized! But nothing like that is mentioned either in this case or anywhere else in the Bible. Those who believed and claimed the Lord as Saviour were baptized. None in Bible times were ever taught to be baptized unless they claimed an honest heart-turning to Christ for forgiveness and salvation.

VERSES 16–24:

16 ¶ And it came to pass, as we went to prayer, a certain damsel possessed with a spirit of divination met us, which brought her masters much gain by soothsaying:

17 The same followed Paul and us, and cried, saying, These men are the servants of the most high God, which shew unto us the way of salvation.

18 And this did she many days. But Paul, being grieved, turned and said to the spirit, I command thee in the name of Jesus Christ to come out of her. And he came out the same hour.

19 ¶ And when her masters

saw that the hope of their gains was gone, they caught Paul and Silas, and drew *them* into the marketplace unto the rulers,

20 And brought them to the magistrates, saying, These men, being Jews, do exceedingly trouble our city,

21 And teach customs, which are not lawful for us to receive, neither to observe, being Romans.

22 And the multitude rose up together against them; and the magistrates rent off their clothes, and commanded to beat *them*.

23 And when they had laid many stripes upon them, they cast *them* into prison, charging the jailer to keep them safely:

24 Who, having received such a charge, thrust them into the inner prison, and made their feet fast in the stocks.

A Devil-Possessed Girl Saved and Healed: Persecution

A damsel or young woman "possessed with a spirit of divination," that is, possessed of a demon who helped her to tell fortunes and to foretell events, "brought her masters much gain by her soothsaying." Four times in Daniel "the soothsayers" are mentioned along with the astrologers, the magicians, or the Chaldeans. This kind of soothsaying or prophesying by the power of an evil spirit was common in the land of Canaan among the wicked nations which Israel was to cast out. Deuteronomy 18:9-14 says:

"When thou art come into the land which the Lord thy God giveth thee, thou shalt not learn to do after the abominations of those nations. There shall not be found among you any one that maketh his son or his daughter to pass through the fire, or that useth divination, or an observer of times, or an enchanter, or a witch, Or a charmer, or a consulter with familiar spirits, or a wizard, or a necromancer. For all that do these things are an abomination unto the Lord: and because of these abominations the Lord thy God doth drive them out from before thee. Thou shalt be perfect with the Lord thy God. For

these nations, which thou shalt possess, hearkened unto observers of times, and unto diviners:
but as for thee, the Lord thy God hath not suffered thee so to do."

They were not allowed to have among them one "that uses
divination," or "a consulter with familiar spirits," or "diviners." It was a similar sin for which King Saul died:

"So Saul died for his transgression which he
committed against the Lord, even against the
word of the Lord, which he kept not, and also
for asking counsel of one that had a familiar
spirit, to enquire of it; And enquired not of the
Lord: therefore he slew him, and turned the
kingdom unto David the son of Jesse."--I Chron.
10:13, 14.

Devil possession actually occurred in Bible times. And
wise missionaries in China and in Africa and elsewhere
have often found among the heathen, people literally demon
possessed. Sometimes demons help people foretell the
future. No demon would tell the truth enough to be a blessing. He would tell the truth only enough to mislead people.
Most fortunetellers are frauds and cheats, of course.
Sometimes those who are in any sense genuine are possessed of devils, as was this slave girl.

It is a strange thing that demons have an awareness of
Christ and God and a Spirit-filled Christian. Two men were
possessed of devils in the country of the Gergesenes and
they met Jesus and these demons cried out, "What have we
to do with thee, Jesus, thou Son of God? art thou come
hither to torment us before the time?" (Matt. 8:29). They
knew Jesus. They also knew that they eventually must be
tormented in Hell. Jesus sent His disciples to cast out de-

vils, and they often did. It is interesting to read the true story of Pastor Hsi in China, published by the China Inland Mission. He had a lifetime calling to cast out devils and to cure Chinese people from addiction to opium. It is an amazing, true story.

Here this slave girl cried out a strange thing: "These men are the servants of the most high God, which shew unto us the way of salvation." And she continued soothsaying through the influence of demons many days!

Paul was grieved. At first, perhaps, he did not have enough faith to cast out the demon. But God laid a burden on his heart and gave him faith, so boldly he demanded that evil spirit, "I command thee in the name of Jesus Christ to come out of her." We are told that "he came out the same hour."

Well, the fortunetelling girl has been healed, the devils cast out. And I can have no doubt she trusted the Lord and was wonderfully saved. Who knows but maybe her poor tortured soul sought and hungered for the Lord Jesus and salvation, in the midst of the possession and oppression of the evil spirit that was upon her! No more fortunetelling! No more fees collected from the passers-by! The young woman was a slave girl. She was business property, owned by "her masters"--more than one. Probably the girl had brought in great gain for these men; now they are angered and so "they caught Paul and Silas, and drew them into the marketplace unto the rulers." Here is the lying charge they made: "These men, being Jews, do exceedingly trouble our city, And teach customs, which are not lawful for us to receive, neither to observe, being Romans."

There was no truth in it, of course: The preachers were not lawless. And there was no truth in the lies told on Jesus when they tried Him and sentenced Him to death.

But the multitude turned against these two at the hated word, "They are Jews." The magistrates tore off their clothes and commanded to beat them. Then they put them in the dungeon in the inner prison, and made their feet fast in stocks!

The preacher who preaches as he ought to will come in contact with wicked men who make a profit out of sin. If he is bold and successful in getting people saved and delivering them from the clutches of wicked men who make merchandise of their folly, the preacher will be hated and slandered. So in Acts 19 the men who made the idol images of Diana had Paul's companions arrested at Ephesus. So those who sold liquor hated Billy Sunday whose preaching won so many thousands of drunkards and closed up so many bars! And I, too, have been hated, slandered and threatened because hundreds of drunkards have turned from their sin to trust Christ. When my preaching has turned people away from supporting modernism and infidelity in the churches, then denominational leaders have hated me and slandered me and have thought that it would be God's blessing if I should die. Communists and socialists hate the preachers whose Bible preaching hinder their exploitation of the masses of common people. The Jewish leaders hated Paul because he freed converts from the bondage of the law and thus interfered with the support and prestige and authority of the priesthood and Sanhedrin. Blessed is the preacher who is true to God and so arouses the enmity of wicked men. Blessed Paul and Silas who freed a slave girl from demon possession and then, beaten and mistreated, sit painfully cramped with feet in stocks on a stone floor in the dungeon!

The jailer had received the command from the magistrates "to keep them safely." There was quite naturally some heathen fear of these men who could cast out devils. So in the dungeon their feet were made fast in stocks. In its crudest form, perhaps they had consisted of a heavy beam with notches cut in it to fit human ankles. Then another beam was spiked or locked down on top of that, holding the prisoners securely, sitting uncomfortably on the stone floor!

VERSES 25-29:

25 ¶ And at midnight Paul and Silas prayed, and sang praises unto God: and the prisoners heard them.

26 And suddenly there was a great earthquake, so that the foundations of the prison were shaken: and immediately all the doors were opened, and every one's bands were loosed.

27 And the keeper of the prison awaking out of his sleep, and seeing the prison doors open, he drew out his sword, and would have killed himself, supposing that the prisoners had been fled.

28 But Paul cried with a loud voice, saying, Do thyself no harm: for we are all here.

29 Then he called for a light, and sprang in, and came trembling, and fell down before Paul and Silas,

Songs at Midnight and an Earthquake

I fear this Scripture is so familiar to us that the glory of it, the wonder and joy of it, has escaped us! Here are two of God's men beaten and in pain and disgrace, with a threatening tomorrow! They are among strangers, far away from home. Yet instead of despair there is joy and gladness. So "at midnight Paul and Silas prayed, and sang praises unto God...."

What did they do before midnight? They suffered, of course, with stripes on their back that later needed the blood washed away. After a great triump such as the casting out of the demon from the fortunetelling girl, it would be normal to have a spiritual letdown. God's people need always to beware of Satan after some great victory and when abuse, false charges, slander, public disgrace and painful beating followed, we may suppose that Paul and Silas took stock very seriously of their situation. At least, we are not told that they prayed and sang praises to God until midnight. I suspect that during those painful hours they had again the counting of the cost; they made again their holy decisions. Paul, along with his partner, Silas, had doubtless formed in his mind the holy resolution which he expressed later in Acts 20:22-24.

> "And now, behold, I go bound in the spirit unto Jerusalem, not knowing the things that shall befall me there: Save that the Holy Ghost witnesseth in every city, saying that bonds and afflictions abide me. But none of these things move me, neither count I my life dear unto myself, so that I might finish my course with joy, and the ministry, which I have received of the Lord Jesus, to testify the gospel of the grace of God."

Remember that the Lord Jesus had given instructions, "...If any man will come after me, let him deny himself, and take up his cross DAILY, and follow me" (Luke 9:23). Let us not suppose that any man, by one time of resolution settles his consecration forever. No, he needs again, day after day, to offer himself a living sacrifice. So Paul could say, "I die daily," meaning surely that he gave himself up to die every day.

And in those quiet hours before midnight I have no doubt that Paul and Silas reviewed again their sufferings, their holy calling, and the eternal rewards that await all who suffer for Jesus. And so they rejoiced and began to pray and then to praise God in song!

David had been inspired to write, "I call to remembrance my song in the night" (Ps. 77:6). So in the nighttime sweet songs of praise that Paul had memorized came flooding to his soul, and he sang and so did Silas.

It was a song God puts in the heart of the redeemed who trust Him. "And he hath put a new song in my mouth, even praise unto our God: many shall see it, and fear, and shall trust in the Lord" (Ps. 40:3).

And in Psalm 119:62 the inspired pen of the psalmist says, "At midnight I will rise to give thanks unto thee because of thy righteous judgments."

Here is the "peace like a river" of Isaiah 48:18. Here is the "peace that passeth understanding" of Philippians 4:6

and 7. They had the promise here fulfilled, "Thou wilt keep him in perfect peace, whose mind is stayed on thee: because he trusteth in thee" (Isa. 26:3). How many song writers of a past generation have written of the peace which God gives in trouble. And in the song, "Jesus, I My Cross Have Taken," one verse says:

> "Let the world despise and leave me,
> They have left my Saviour, too;
> Human hearts and looks deceive me;
> Thou art not, like man, untrue;
> And, while Thou shalt smile upon me,
> God of wisdom, love, and might,
> Foes may hate, and friends may shun me;
> Show Thy face, and all is bright."

No wonder the Lord Jesus taught His disciples to "rejoice, and be exceeding glad" over persecution (Matt. 5:12). And so the suffering Christian may learn the sweet truth that "we glory in tribulations also: knowing that tribulation worketh patience" (Rom. 5:3). And again like Paul with his thorn in the flesh when God's all-sufficient grace is promised, "Most gladly therefore will I rather glory in my infirmities, that the power of Christ may rest upon me. Therefore I take pleasure in infirmities, in reproaches, in necessities, in persecutions, in distresses for Christ's sake: for when I am weak, then am I strong" (II Cor. 12:9, 10). Oh, here is sweet and wonderful truth almost too good to be true, truth that contradicts all the precepts of this world, that the Christian can glory in tribulation, can be strong in weakness, can take pleasure in infirmities, reproaches, necessities, persecutions and distresses for Christ's sake!

In my song, "His Yoke Is Easy," I have said:

> "A slave to Jesus, Oh gladly would I ever be;
> His labor joyful, Reproach for Him is sweet to me;
> Ten thousand blessings repay all pain I'll ever see."

But Paul and Silas "prayed, and sang praises unto God." They prayed first. And that is the order instructed for us in Philippians 4:6 and 7. We are to "be careful for nothing; but in every thing by prayer and supplication with thanksgiving let your requests be made known unto God. And the peace of God, which passeth all understanding, shall keep your hearts and minds through Christ Jesus."

It may be that the praying of Paul and Silas was through the long hours of darkness before midnight. It may be that then all fret and worry were taken away and they had perfect peace and a sense of certainty that God had heard and would answer. It may be that they had pleaded, and now they began to believe and expect their deliverance and the victory which God soon gave! There is no way to have that peace of God beyond all understanding except as we commit everything to the Lord with prayer and supplication and thanksgiving. Then we can have that peace which Jesus promised in John 14:27.

Suddenly there was a great earthquake. Every locked door in the prison was thrown open. Every chain broke off the hands of prisoners. The stocks which bound the feet of Paul and Silas ripped open. Here God is saying that when praying men enlist God's power, all human restraint is vain!

God had silently delivered Peter from prison in Acts, chapter 12, with the loosening of bonds, the temporary blinding of the guard and the automatic opening of the doors. Not until the next morning was it known that Peter had escaped. And again in Acts 5:19 when the "apostles," possibly all of them which were in Jerusalem, were put in prison "the angel of the Lord by night opened the prison doors, and brought them forth" with instructions to go on preaching. That deliverance, too, we suppose was quiet. But heathen men who had resisted the power of God in saving and in casting out the devil from the fortunetelling slave girl must be shown openly that God's power is above that of Roman courts and prisons. So God with a mighty earthquake ripped off the chains, broke open the doors and freed the prisoners.

The "keeper of the prison awaking out of his sleep, and seeing the prison doors open, drew out his sword, and would have killed himself, supposing that the prisoners had been fled." Note again the attitude of the magistrates when they had torn off the clothes of these two prisoners, commanded to beat them, and cast them into the prison "charging the jailer to keep them safely." These are notable prisoners. Special care was taken to keep them bound. If they had escaped, the jailer's life might be forfeited. So King Herod, when Peter had been delivered from jail by an angel, "examined the keepers, and commanded that they should be put to death" (Acts 12:19). So the despairing jailer would have killed himself, "but Paul cried with a loud voice, saying, Do thyself no harm: for we are all here."

Wise, Spirit-led Paul! One can not only be filled with the Spirit, but can "walk in the Spirit" (Gal. 5:16, 25), and so know moment by moment what ought to be said or done.

So it was with Joseph down in Egypt. "And the Lord was with Joseph, and he was a prosperous man..." (Gen. 39:2). In prison "whatsoever they did there, he was the doer of it...And that which he did, the Lord made it to prosper" (Gen. 39:22, 23). When he suddenly faced Pharaoh he could say, "It is not in me: God shall give Pharaoh an answer of peace" (Gen. 41:16). We are told about the boy David, when he was anointed by Samuel under the Lord's orders to be king, "...And the Spirit of the Lord came upon David from that day forward..." (1 Sam. 16:13).

Paul, filled with the Spirit, sees in the jailer a lost soul who needs saving and in the occasion he sees an open door for preaching the Gospel.

So the jailer "called for a light, and sprang in, and came trembling, and fell down before Paul and Silas." These men cast out a devil from a slave girl who quit her fortunetelling. Now they have prayed until an earthquake shakes open every door, breaks every chain in prison. With fear and trembling the jailer is aware of his sins, aware that these men are from God.

Let us remember that always conscience is on the side of the plain Bible preacher. Men may argue that they do not believe this or that about the Bible or about Christ, but always God speaks to the conscience of men that they are sinners who need a Saviour. Blessed is the preacher who so deals with sin and who so expects God's intervention to show His power that conscience and the Word of God together may be used to win men.

VERSES 30–34:

30 And brought them out, and said, Sirs, what must I do to be saved?

31 And they said, Believe on the Lord Jesus Christ, and thou shalt be saved, and thy house.

32 And they spake unto him the word of the Lord, and to all that were in his house.

33 And he took them the same hour of the night, and washed *their* stripes; and was baptized, he and all his, straightway.

34 And when he had brought them into his house, he set meat before them, and rejoiced, believing in God with all his house.

The One Simple Plan of Salvation: the Jailer and Family Saved

Now they are out of jail, Paul and Silas, possibly in the jailer's home where they will return later after the baptizing (vs. 34).

Here is the clear-cut question, the only time that in these plain words it is asked in the Bible, "Sirs, what must I do to be saved?" In Acts 2:37, those who were pricked in their hearts, who had seen the mighty power of God at Pentecost and the miraculous gift of languages and had seen, no doubt, the tongues like as of fire resting on the disciples, asked

Peter and the rest of the apostles, "Men and brethren, what shall we do?" There the question is not the same. They want to be saved, no doubt, but they want more than that: they want what these Spirit-filled apostles have, that fullness of the Spirit promised in Joel, chapter 2, here expounded so clearly by the Apostle Peter (Acts 2:15-21). So, thinking not only of individual salvation but of Israel when Peter said, "Therefore let all the house of Israel know assuredly, that God hath made that same Jesus, whom ye have crucified, both Lord and Christ," they asked the question, "Men and brethren, what shall we do?" So the answer involves not only the plan of salvation but how to be filled with the Spirit, as were these. They were to repent and then they were to be baptized in obedience to Christ's command and showing openly their understanding and the meaning of Christ's burial and resurrection pictured in baptism. And then they were promised, "Ye shall receive the gift of the Holy Ghost" (Acts 2:38).

Here the simple question by this Gentile jailer is, "What must I do to be saved?" The answer here is given, "Believe on the Lord Jesus Christ, and thou shalt be saved, and thy house." Notice that the plan of salvation pictured here is not only good for the jailer; it is good for his family. This is no special private plan for one person or a few. This is the only plan God ever has had for saving sinners! That is why in Acts 10:43 Peter was inspired to say, "To him give all the prophets witness, that through his name whosoever believeth in him shall receive remission of sins."

What a list of Scriptures say the same thing!

Genesis 15:6 says Abraham "believed in the Lord; and he counted it to him for righteousness" (quoted in Romans 4:3 also).

John 1:12--"But as many as received him, to them gave he power to become the sons of God, even to them that believe on his name."

John 3:14, 15--"And as Moses lifted up the serpent in the

wilderness, even so must the Son of man be lifted up: That whosoever believeth in him should not perish, but have eternal life."

John 3:16--"For God so loved the world, that he gave his only begotten Son, that whosoever believeth in him should not perish, but have everlasting life."

John 3:18--"He that believeth on him is not condemned: but he that believeth not is condemned already, because he hath not believed in the name of the only begotten Son of God."

John 3:36--"He that believeth on the Son hath everlasting life: and he that believeth not the Son shall not see life; but the wrath of God abideth on him."

John 5:24--"Verily, verily, I say unto you, He that heareth my word, and believeth on him that sent me, hath everlasting life, and shall not come into condemnation; but is passed from death unto life."

John 6:40--"And this is the will of him that sent me, that every one which seeth the Son, and believeth on him, may have everlasting life: and I will raise him up at the last day."

John 6:47--"Verily, verily, I say unto you, He that believeth on me hath everlasting life."

Acts 13:38, 39--"Be it known unto you therefore, men and brethren, that through this man is preached unto you the forgiveness of sins: And by him all that believe are justified from all things, from which ye could not be justified by the law of Moses."

Romans 4:5--"But to him that worketh not, but believeth on him that justifieth the ungodly, his faith is counted for righteousness."

Romans 5:1--"Therefore being justified by faith, we have peace with God through our Lord Jesus Christ."

First John 5:13--"These things have I written unto you that believe on the name of the Son of God; that ye may know that ye have eternal life, and that ye may believe on the name of the Son of God."

Again, we remind you that God has several ways of saying the same thing so that the wayfaring man, though a fool, may not err therein. When God says, "Draw nigh to God, and he will draw nigh to you" (Jas. 4:8), He means that the approaching to God is with a trusting heart which receives salvation.

When He said in John 6:37, "All that the Father giveth me shall come to me; and him that cometh to me I will in no wise cast out," He means coming by a simple act of faith.

One who, in his heart, believes that Christ can save and will save, comes to Him; no one else ever does.

When the Scripture says, quoting from Joel 2:32, in Romans 10:13, "For whosoever shall call upon the name of the Lord shall be saved," the calling upon God for mercy is the simple outward expression of faith in the heart, for the next verse explains, "How then shall they call on him in whom they have not believed?" The heart calling on Christ for mercy is simply an outward expression of heart faith.

So with repentance. The heart that really turns from sin in heart repentance, an honest change of mind and heart toward sin, trusts in Jesus for mercy. One cannot separate faith and repentance. They are different ways of expressing the same truth. The heart that comes to Jesus, turning from sin, trusts Him for salvation and is saved.

Some people speak scornfully of "simple believism" as if we were wrong to take at face value what God has said. Once I preached to a great crowd of high school students. I went through the Gospel of John and had each one mark with me all the verses that told the simple plan of salvation by trusting Jesus. Then fifteen or twenty of these young people turned to Christ and claimed Him openly there. As we went away a preacher said, "Brother Rice, I am afraid you have made it too easy." And I replied then, as I do here, that Jesus Christ died to make it easy and any one who is tired of sin and wants mercy and forgiveness may have it the moment he depends on Jesus Christ.

It is true that as far as simply accepting a fact or doctrine, "devils also believe, and tremble" (Jas. 2:19). But that Scripture does not mean and the Bible never hints that such demons trusted Christ for salvation, and the Bible does not mean that anyone can honestly trust Christ without being saved. Oh, we sin greatly against the Lord and against His Word by trying to make man's part of salvation complex and difficult. Anyone who wants to be saved can be saved instantly, the moment he is ready to turn himself and his sins over to Jesus Christ for forgiveness and cleansing and a new heart. "Believe on the Lord Jesus Christ, and thou shalt be saved."

Some people have taken verse 31 as a promise that if the jailer himself would believe, his family would be saved also. It is true that a godly father ought to be able to influence his family and win all of them to Christ. But this promise does not say and does not mean, surely, that anyone can be saved on the faith of his father. No, each one for himself must personally trust in Jesus Christ. What Paul told the jailer is the simple truth, that if he, the jailer, should believe in Christ, he would be saved, and that just as truly, when wife or child should believe in Christ, they, too, should be saved. It is a universal plan of salvation. How sweet and true!

Here let me say that the little 24-page pamphlet of mine entitled "What Must I Do to Be Saved?" has been spread in more than thirty languages around the world in perhaps fifteen million copies and we have letters from over 12,000 people who trusted Christ as Saviour, most of them through this booklet in the English language and other thousands have claimed Christ and have written missionaries' committees to say so through this same simple message in other languages. Oh, we should preach it. "Believe on the Lord Jesus Christ, and thou shalt be saved!"

And the jailer was saved at once. Paul and Silas "spake unto him the word of the Lord, and to all that were in his house." The penitence of this man was genuine. He took Paul and Silas the same hour of the night and washed their stripes. He is ashamed and sorry for his part in the persecution of these men of God. He reminds us of Zacchaeus sliding down the sycamore tree, saved, to tell Jesus, "Behold, Lord, the half of my goods I give to the poor; and if I have taken any thing from any man by false accusation, I restore him fourfold" (Luke 19:8). Faith in Christ works a change in the heart. The man who enjoyed sin now wants to please God. He who was an enemy of God's preachers now washes their stripes tenderly and feeds them in his home past the midnight hour!

And we learn that the whole family was saved also. "They spake unto him the word of the Lord, and to all that were in his house," and he "was baptized, he and all his, straightway." And then after they had fed the hungry preachers in the wee hours of the morning the jailer "rejoiced, believing in God with all his house." All heard the Gospel; all believed in Christ, all were baptized, all rejoiced.

"The Same Hour of the Night . . . and Was Baptized"

The jailer was baptized the same hour of the night and so were other members of his household.

There are those who teach that one, after conversion, ought to go on probation before being baptized. That was not the plan in the New Testament. In the Great Commission the disciples were commanded to go make disciples, to baptize them and then "teaching them to observe all things whatsoever I have commanded you" (Matt. 28:19, 20). So the Ethiopian eunuch, in the midst of Philip's explanation of the Scriptures, stopped the chariot and asked to be baptized and was (Acts 8:36-39)! Paul was converted. Then Ananias came to him "that thou mightest receive thy sight, and be filled with the Holy Ghost. And immediately there fell from his eyes as it had been scales: and he received sight forthwith, and arose, and was baptized" (Acts 9:17, 18). So at Pentecost "they that gladly received his word were baptized: and the same day there were added unto them about three thousand souls" (Acts 2:41). Here at Philippi Lydia found her heart open and she was baptized at once and begged Paul and Silas and Timothy and Luke to stay in her home (Acts 16:14, 15). The Bible plan is that when people are saved they ought soon to be baptized and thus publicly profess their faith in the Saviour. Baptism does not proclaim, "I am now a mature Christian, well-taught in the Word. I have learned my catechism." No, baptism proclaims, "I have trusted Christ; I count this old sinner dead and now publicly bury him and raise up to live a new life." So says Romans 6:3-5. When the jailer and his household were saved and baptized the same hour of the night, they were following the regular pattern of the New Testament preachers and churches. The plan was that only those who trust Christ for salvation are to be baptized. They are to be baptized by immersion and publicly, as a public testimony that they have taken Christ as Saviour.

Great Rejoicing for This Believing, Obedient Family

We are told that the jailer took Paul and Silas the "same hour of the night and washed their stripes; and was baptized, he and all his, straightway. And when he had brought them into his house, he set meat before them, and rejoiced, believing in God with all his house." Rejoicing properly and usually follows the baptism of a new convert. So the Ethiopian eunuch, after he was baptized and Philip was caught away, "went on his way rejoicing" (Acts 8:39). Gladness in salvation and baptism are connected following Pentecost in Acts 2:41.

Often a convert has much greater assurance of salvation

after baptism. When I was baptized, a twelve-year-old boy in West Texas, I came out of the water with a November chill upon it in the pond or reservoir and all the people sang:

> **"O happy day that fixed my choice**
> **On Thee, my Saviour and my God!**
> **Well may this glowing heart rejoice,**
> **And tell its raptures all abroad."**

We who stood at the water's edge with dripping clothes were glad. I remember that I was so warm inside I did not notice the cold wind until my father wrapped me in a quilt for the two-mile journey home in an open carriage.

In Decatur, Texas, in a blessed revival campaign that lasted ten weeks, out of which grew a strong, new congregation, a woman was baptized in the new tabernacle we built. I heard her whispering to herself, "Oh, praise the Lord!"

And I said, "Say it aloud, sister, if you wish." And to all the congregation she cried out, "Oh, praise the Lord! I have been wanting to do this for nineteen years!" And weeping for joy she rose dripping from the water of baptism, and down in the dressing room I heard her further softly praising the Lord!

In hundreds of cases I have seen the joy that baptism brings to a new convert. And why? I think it is proper and understandable. The Lord Jesus made a promise, "Whosoever therefore shall confess me before men, him will I confess also before my Father which is in heaven" (Matt. 10:32). So when one in baptism openly claims that he has trusted Christ, that now he counts the old sinner dead and he plans to be raised up to live a new life for Christ, he has confessed Christ before men. Up in Heaven the Lord Jesus claims him and the blessed Spirit of God comes to whisper in the heart the assurance.

Several times in the Bible the fullness of the Spirit is

connected with baptism. So it was when Jesus was baptized and the Holy Spirit descended in bodily shape like a dove upon Him (Luke 3:21, 22). The two are involved in the same promise in Acts 2:38 and 39. What should these Jews do, not only to be saved but to have the same power of the Holy Spirit which was upon Peter and others at Pentecost? "Then Peter said unto them, Repent, and be baptized every one of you in the name of Jesus Christ for the remission of sins, and ye shall receive the gift of the Holy Ghost" (Acts 2:38). And from the case of the twelve disciples at Ephesus described in Acts 19:1-7, it seems evident that those who were baptized should know the joy and power of the Holy Spirit.

So when the Philippian jailer and his family, after being saved and baptized, rejoiced, they followed the very usual New Testament pattern.

No doubt the straightforward sincerity and forthrightness of the jailer is one reason the other members of his family and household turned to Christ in their hearts also. What repentance! How tenderly he washed the disciples stripes! How eagerly they prepared a meal for these who had had no supper! And he was quick to go the whole route of open profession, being baptized and thus branding himself as a Christian. I do not wonder that the household went gladly with such an outright stand for the Lord Jesus.

VERSES 35–40:

35 And when it was day, the magistrates sent the serjeants, saying, Let those men go.

36 And the keeper of the prison told this saying to Paul, The magistrates have sent to let you go: now therefore depart, and go in peace.

37 But Paul said unto them, They have beaten us openly uncondemned, being Romans, and have cast *us* into prison; and now do they thrust us out privily? nay verily; but let them come themselves and fetch us out.

38 And the serjeants told these words unto the magistrates: and they feared, when they heard that they were Romans.

39 And they came and besought them, and brought *them* out, and desired *them* to depart out of the city.

40 And they went out of the prison, and entered into *the house of* Lydia: and when they had seen the brethren, they comforted them, and departed.

Out of Jail With Honor

The morning came. After all the Roman Empire had been built on law. And the beating of Paul and Silas and putting them into the prison without a trial, without them having committed any crime, was not according to the just system of laws that the Romans were trying to install everywhere. So the judges sent the sergeants saying, "Let those men go."

But Paul had no inferiority complex about this matter of preaching the Gospel. He did not mean to slip out of town like a vagrant subject to arrest on any pretext. No, Paul reminded the sergeants that he and Silas were a part of the elite group known as Roman citizens who had rights beyond other men. Yet they had been beaten openly and without a trial. So Paul indignantly said, "And now do they thrust us out privily? nay verily; but let them come themselves and fetch us out!" So the judges were informed and now, embarrassed because they had overstepped authority and wronged men who might influence some at Rome and cause them trouble, they came politely and apologetically to escort them publicly out of the jail in the presence of prisoners and people and then "desired them to depart out of the city."

No doubt they feared there might be other riots. And Paul was quick to see that possibility, and as he did in most cases when riots occurred and when his life was endangered, he departed to another city to preach the Gospel.

A few hours at the home of Lydia--the new converts crowded in to see them, to rejoice that they are free, to mourn over their bruises, and to praise the Lord together. And then instead of Paul and Silas being comforted by these Christians, they, who had been persecuted and beaten, comforted the brethren! And they departed.

We can sense here only little of the sweetness that this whole incident left in the mind of Paul. We can see it in the epistle to the Philippians. There we find that Paul thanked God every time he thought of them! That he remembered them in every prayer! And always "making request with joy" (Phil. 1:3, 4). And there he tells them tenderly, "Because I have you in my heart; inasmuch as both in my bonds, and in the defence and confirmation of the gospel, ye all are partakers of my grace" (Phil. 1:7). Great was his longing for them, he says (Phil. 1:8). And how gladly he looks forward to being with them again, "that your rejoicing may be more abundant in Jesus Christ for me by my coming to you again" (Phil. 1:26). How tenderly he addresses them, "My beloved" (Phil. 2:12). He said, "Therefore, my brethren dearly beloved and longed for, my joy and crown..." (Phil. 4:1). And these converts in Philippi loved Paul, too. They were the only church when Paul should leave Macedonia who would send him offerings (Phil. 4:15). And they did send him offerings in Thessalonica (Phil. 4:16), and when he was in jail at Rome (Phil. 4:18).

So there are many fragrant flowers that bloom in the soil of persecution, and to suffer for Christ binds Christians together like nothing else in the world.

ACTS 17

VERSES 1–4:

NOW when they had passed through Amphipolis and Apollonia, they came to Thessalonica, where was a synagogue of the Jews:

2 And Paul, as his manner was, went in unto them, and three sabbath days reasoned with them out of the Scriptures,

3 Opening and alleging, that Christ must needs have suffered, and risen again from the dead; and that this Jesus, whom I preach unto you, is Christ.

4 And some of hem believed, and consorted with Paul and Silas; and of the devout Greeks a great multitude, and of the chief women not a few.

The Gospel Comes to Thessalonica

We remember that Paul, Silas and Timothy are in Macedonia and if you have a map of Paul's missionary journeys, you will see that he entered by the Island of Samothracia, landed in Macedonia at Neapolis and then went the short distance to Philippi.

Now they went west, on through Amphipolis and Apollonia to the city of Thessalonica, "where was a synagogue of the Jews." It is likely that only a few special cities in Greece had enough Jews assembled to have a synagogue for regular worship. These synagogues were the best open doors for the preaching of the Gospel. Here people would have some Old Testament Scriptures, would know about the sacrifices, the priesthood, the prophecies about the coming Messiah or Saviour. So as the apostles were to begin in Jerusalem (Luke 24:47), Paul would naturally go first to those who knew about the true God, knew something of the Old Testament Scriptures. So through other towns they came to Thessalonica, probably eighty miles or more from Philippi. And Paul, "as his manner was," when he hit the synagogue and as a learned Jew, trained under Gamaliel at Jerusalem

in all the law and the Old Testament (Acts 22:3), would always be allowed to speak. So in the synagogue for three
sabbath days he "reasoned with them out of the Scriptures."
He showed them "that Christ must needs have suffered, and
risen again from the dead." He would prove this by Isaiah
50:3, by Psalm 16:9, 10, as Peter did at Pentecost (Acts
2:25-31), by the promises to David about the Messiah, by
the types and shadows and the priesthood and offerings, by
the passover lamb. Jesus is the one, Paul told them.

There was varied reaction. "Some of them believed, and
consorted with Paul and Silas," that is, some of the Jews,
but "of the devout Greeks a great multitude." "Devout
Greeks" must refer to hungry-hearted people who prayed,
who sought God, even as the Ethiopian eunuch went up to
Jerusalem to worship in Acts 7, even as Cornelius earnestly
prayed and sought God and gave alms, in Acts 10 before he
heard the Gospel. It was a blessed experience in preaching
the Gospel even to great masses of heathen people, as I
have done in India, Japan and Korea, to find some heart so
hungry and so open for the Gospel. So Paul found it here.
And even of the very influential "chief women," not a few
were saved. But there was opposition, too, and persecution.

VERSES 5-9:

5 ¶ But the Jews which believed not, moved with envy,
took unto them certain lewd
fellows of the baser sort, and
gathered a company, and set
all the city on an uproar, and
assaulted the house of Jason,
and sought to bring them out
to the people.

6 And when they found them
not, they drew Jason and certain brethren unto the rulers of
the city, crying, These that have
turned the world upside down
are come hither also;

7 Whom Jason hath received;
and these all do contrary to the
decrees of Cesar, saying that
there is another king, *one* Jesus.

8 And they troubled the people
and the rulers of the city, when
they heard these things.

9 And when they had taken
security of Jason, and of the
others, they let them go.

Unconverted Jews Cause Riots: Threaten Paul and Silas

God had given greater light to the Jews. By His grace He had chosen the Jewish nation Israel from the time of Abraham. All the prophets had risen among the Jews. The Old Testament Scriptures were written by Jews. So Jesus could tell the woman of Samaria, "we know what we worship: for salvation is of the Jews" (John 4:22). So the Gospel would be taken first to the Jews who would be better prepared to receive it by having some acquaintance with the Old Testament Scriptures and with the true God. But by the same token, the Jews who did not turn to Christ, Jews who had a rabid adherence to the outward forms of Judaism but had never turned in heart to God for saving mercy, these Jews would be the most radical opponents of the Gospel everywhere Paul went. So the unconverted Jews in Thessalonica "moved with envy, took unto them certain lewd fellows of the baser sort," gathered a mob and started a riot.

There is an almost inevitable kinship between spiritual unbelief, and lewdness and immorality. These Jews who hated Paul because they thought the Gospel would interfere with the carrying on of the Old Testament rites and ceremonies and so would say that they opposed Paul from religious convictions, yet "took unto them certain lewd fellows of the baser sort" to help them abuse and persecute God's preachers!

So Christians everywhere marvel at the way religious liberals, who deny the inspiration of the Bible, the blood atonement, the deity, virgin birth and bodily resurrection of Christ, gravitate to the same camp as socialists and communists. A preacher who does not believe the Bible and a Marxist communist who is an avowed atheist are really of the same general sort. They gravitate together. The followers of Bob Ingersoll, of Voltaire and Tom Paine have been usually the most profane and drunken and lawless segments of society. So whatever excuse men may give for rejecting Jesus Christ as Saviour and Lord, the fundamental reason is wickedness of heart. "And this is the condemnation, that light is come into the world, and men loved darkness rather than light, because their deeds were evil. For every one that doeth evil hateth the light, neither cometh to the light, lest his deeds should be reproved. But he that doeth truth cometh to the light, that his deeds may be made manifest, that they are wrought in God" (John 3:19-21). There is a moral wickedness in unbelief. Unbelief and crime go together.

Unbelief in Germany, the higher criticism, the liberalism in Germany, was the primary factor in bringing on two great World Wars. Where personal devotion and trust in Christ as Saviour, along with acceptance and reverent effort to follow the Bible, give way to unbelief, then morality gives way to crime, lewdness and wickedness. So it was in Thessalonica.

Remember it was religious unbelievers who took the principal part in crucifying Jesus Christ.

The mob "assaulted the house of Jason, and sought to bring them out [that is, Paul and Silas] to the people." But Paul and Silas were not in the house, so Jason and certain brethren were seized and the mob dragged them ("drew" here literally means dragged) unto the rulers of the city. The public riots here at Thessalonica were like that at Iconium (Acts 14:5), like the mob that stoned Paul at Lystra (Acts 14:19), like the mob at Corinth in Acts 18:12 that brought Paul before Gallio, like the idol makers at Ephesus who abused Paul's companions (Acts 19:23-41), and the mob that seized Paul in the temple at Jerusalem (Acts 21:27-32). So Paul learned to count such riots a part of the price for serving God. So as part of the price of "approving ourselves as the ministers of God," he puts, "In stripes, in imprisonments, in tumults..." (II Cor. 6:4, 5). Oh, how little we know of what it ought to cost a preacher to be a good minister of Jesus Christ!

The charges against these Christians at Thessalonica are at once foolish and glorious. "These that have turned the world upside down are come hither also," they said! It was an earth-shaking business when the Apostle Paul came to town!

At Jerusalem the chief priests and elders complained, "Ye have filled Jerusalem with your doctrine" (Acts 5:28)! Surely all the riots which had occurred wherever Paul and Silas preached had been reported by word of mouth across this country. The devils cast out, and the slave girl healed, the jail nearly shaken down, the embarrassment of the judges at Philippi--all this had been carried by word of mouth.

What a pity that most preachers do not "turn the world upside down." They go in an orderly routine. They offend few and help few. Where are the preachers like Sam Jones and Billy Sunday who got so many drunkards converted (and saloonkeepers, too), that often the saloons closed after their meetings? We are reminded somewhat of the travels by John Wesley on horseback throughout England winning many, and of the abuse and insults he received. Oh, for preaching that would make Felix tremble, that would awake the guilty conscience of Herod, that would keep Darius awake at night while Daniel was in the lions' den! God, give us men who will, in the language of these accusers, "turn the world upside down" as Paul and Silas.

The charges were foolish. They say that Jason had received Paul and Silas and that all these Christians "do contrary to the decrees of Caesar, saying that there is another king, one Jesus." Men who hate Christians habitually lie, part of the reason being that their hearts are so blinded that they do not even know the truth. They did not know that the Christian religion would make the best citizens; that to a Christian "the powers that be are ordained of God" (Rom. 13:1), and that Paul would teach people everywhere to pay taxes to Caesar, to obey the Roman laws, although he himself would be beheaded by Nero!

The founders of the United States understood that morality and law-abiding citizenship would be promoted largely by churches and preachers. So churches are usually tax free. So there are chaplains of the House of Congress and the Senate and state legislative bodies, and chaplains in the armed services. And our presidents are sworn in with a Bible, and men take oaths before God in court. There is no way to have the morality of the Bible without having Christianity. And the charge could not be more foolish than that to love and honor Jesus Christ would be against Caesar, that is, against the civil government.

Those men who do not want prayer or Bible reading in the public schools are no friends of morality and righteousness and good government, whatever their intentions.

The slander "troubled the people and the rulers." So Jason was put under peace bond. If they could have gotten Paul and Silas, they would have probably beaten them, perhaps killed them. But since Paul and Silas were not found, Jason and other brethren were taken to the council and then released under bond to keep the peace.

VERSES 10-14:

10 ¶ And the brethren immediately sent away Paul and Silas by night unto Berea: who coming *thither* went into the synagogue of the Jews.

11 These were more noble than those in Thessalonica, in that they received the word with all readiness of mind, and searched the Scriptures daily, whether those things were so.

12 Therefore many of them believed; also of honourable women which were Greeks, and of men, not a few.

13 But when the Jews of Thessalonica had knowledge that the word of God was preached of Paul at Berea, they came thither also, and stirred up the people.

14 And then immediately the brethren sent away Paul to go as it were to the sea: but Silas and Timotheus abode there still.

Paul and Silas at Berea

When the mob at Thessalonica had dispersed, the brethren in the night sought out Paul and Silas. They must get away. So in the night they started to Berea, still forty or fifty miles further west.

Nothing daunted by the abuse and persecution, which they should certainly expect by this time, they went into the synagogue with the Jews at Berea and there they preached. "These were more noble than those in Thessalonica." How? In that they "received the word with all readiness of mind, and searched the scriptures daily, whether those things were so." This must refer to Jewish leaders. They would have in the synagogue some copies of the Pentateuch and scrolls of some of the prophets and perhaps of the Psalms. And so it became a daily business that crowds would gather in the synagogue asking questions, having some of the leaders look up this Scripture and that to see whether Paul and Silas told the truth. So it is not remarkable that "many of them believed" (vs. 12), Greeks as well as Jews.

Oh, for the nobility of spirit that searches the Scriptures to see whether these things are so, and insists that every preacher prove his message by the Word of God!

But fifty miles away, back at Thessalonica, these same indignant Jews, with the same misguided zeal and anger that pressed Saul on the road to Damascus to persecute Christians there in Acts 9, now come to arouse the people against Paul and Silas in Berea! Doubtless there were caravans going back and forth daily, and wherever Paul and Silas went, there would be happenings soon to be reported. So the unbelieving Jews "came thither also" to Berea from Thessalonica "and stirred up the people."

Another riot was expected. So "immediately the brethren sent away Paul to go as it were to the sea." He did go to the sea, that is, far south to Athens. But Silas and Timothy stayed for the time at Berea. They were quieter men, not so much hated by the Jews and perhaps not so bold in their preaching, perhaps not so filled with God's power.

VERSES 15–21:

15 And they that conducted Paul brought him unto Athens: and receiving a commandment unto Silas and Timotheus for to come to him with all speed, they departed.

16 ¶ Now while Paul waited for them at Athens, his spirit was stirred in him, when he saw the city wholly given to idolatry.

17 Therefore disputed he in the synagogue with the Jews, and with the devout persons, and in the market daily with them that met with him.

18 Then certain philosophers of the Epicureans, and of the Stoics, encountered him. And some said, What will this babbler say? other some, He seemeth to be a setter forth of strange gods: because he preached unto them Jesus, and the resurrection.

19 And they took him, and brought him unto Areopagus, saying, May we know what this new doctrine, whereof thou speakest, is?

20 For thou bringest certain strange things to our ears: we would know therefore what these things mean.

21 (For all the Athenians, and strangers which were there, spent their time in nothing else, but either to tell or to hear some new thing.)

Paul at Athens, the Seat of Culture

Athens was two hundred miles south and beside the Mediterranean Sea. Athens was then, as now, the greatest city in Greece or what was then called Macedonia. Greece had ruled the world before Rome, but culture had reached its peak, not in Rome but in Greece. The Greek language was spoken throughout the Roman Empire. All the New Testament is written in Koine Greek. It was the Koine Greek or common people's Greek which Paul used in preaching. And Paul could say, "I thank my God, I speak with tongues more than ye all" or literally, with a tongue (or language) (I Cor.

14:18). Philosophers Socrates, Plato and Aristotle made tremendous impact on the culture of the world. So did the writings of Homer and Xenophon and the great Greek sculptors. So Athens was at this time the seat of the world's culture, as Rome was the seat of world government.

Paul at once sent "a commandment unto Silas and Timotheus for to come to him with all speed" (vs. 15). Paul has earned a leadership that could command his fellow workers.

But Paul, waiting for Silas and Timothy, found "his spirit was stirred in him, when he saw the city wholly given to idolatry." Paul felt as he did when day after day he had heard the slave girl at Philippi (Acts 16:17, 18). He was like Jeremiah who said, "Then I said, I will not make mention of him, nor speak any more in his name. But his word was in mine heart as a burning fire shut up in my bones, and I was weary with forbearing, and I could not stay" (Jer. 20:9). Paul felt here that same urgency that he felt, as he said in I Corinthians 9:16, "Woe is unto me, if I preach not the gospel!"

Is not this what we are taught to pray for when the Saviour says, "Pray ye therefore the Lord of the harvest, that he will send forth labourers into his harvest" (Matt. 9:38; Luke 10:2)? Oh, for a burning heart! Oh, for a holy stirring over people who are lost and need salvation. The Saviour looked on the multitude and "he was moved with compassion on them, because they fainted, and were scattered abroad, as sheep having no shepherd" (Matt. 9:36). I pray that each one who reads this may seek some of that holy urgency, that fire of God that presses us to seek the lost.

This must be part of the explanation why Paul would leave beatings and jail and mobs in one place and go to another to face the same experiences and opposition again!

He saw the city "wholly given to idolatry." This was shocking to Paul as a Christian. But even as a Jew it would be shocking. Since the return from Babylonian captivity, there had been no idolatry among the Jews of which we have any record. They seemed to have been cured of running after heathen gods by that captivity. In the time of Christ there were Sadducees who did not believe in the resurrection and miracles (Mark 12:18), the rationalists of the day, which unbelief involved the high priest and many of the leaders (Acts 5:17). But they were not idolaters. There were Pharisees, very strict about the letter and routine of the ceremonial law, but unconverted. There were Herodians who were worldly and followed the influence of the corrupt court. But among the Jews there were no idolaters serving heathen gods like those in Athens. So Paul was shocked and properly grieved.

Oh, these blind, lost people like sheep with no shepherd, rushing on to eternal ruin! So Paul, stirred to his depths, "disputed...in the synagogue with the Jews, and with the devout persons, and in the market daily with them that met with him." He followed his usual and obvious plan of beginning with Jews and in the synagogue, but there were "devout persons" hungry for the true God, and many began to meet him daily in the market.

We should remember that Christianity grew in the days of impromptu debates, fervent defense of the faith, open attack on unbelief and sin, Paul "disputed" in Athens. He "reasoned" and "persuaded" at Corinth (Acts 18:4). At Ephesus Paul "spake boldly for the space of three months, disputing and persuading..." (Acts 19:8). Apollos "mightily convinced the Jews" at Achaia (Acts 18:28). The Gospel deserves the boldest presentation, the sharpest disputing, the mightiest lodging, the tenderest persuasion, the holiest enthusiasm! We should not forget that about Jesus it was prophesied, "The zeal of thine house hath eaten me up..." (Ps. 69:9; John 2:17).

Athens had more philosophers, more teachers, more cultivated, thinking men than any other city in the world.

The Epicureans, we are told, were "disciples of Epicurus, B.C. 342-271, who abandoned as hopeless the search by reason for pure truth...seeking instead true pleasure through experience." The Stoicks were "disciples of Zeno, B.C. 280, and Chrysippus, B.C. 240. This philosophy was founded on human self-sufficiency, inculcated stern self-repression, the solidarity of the race, and the unity of Deity. Epicureans and Stoics divided the apostolic world," says Dr. Scofield.

So Paul had a ready audience, not necessarily of contrite sinners, but of inquiring philosophical minds, interested intellectually if not spiritually. They took him to Areopagus, Mars' hill, halfway up the Acropolis at Athens. There recently I saw a big bronze plaque with Paul's Athenian sermon openly displayed in the English language. So Paul preached unto them Jesus and the resurrection, as all New Testament preachers did, the resurrection being the evidence for Christ's deity and an essential part of the Gospel.

VERSES 22-31:

22 ¶ Then Paul stood in the midst of Mars' hill, and said, Ye men of Athens, I perceive that in all things ye are too superstitious.

23 For as I passed by, and beheld your devotions, I found an altar with this inscription, TO THE UNKNOWN GOD. Whom therefore ye ignorantly worship, him declare I unto you.

24 God that made the world and all things therein, seeing that he is Lord of heaven and earth, dwelleth not in temples made with hands;

25 Neither is worshipped with men's hands, as though he needed any thing, seeing he giveth to all life, and breath, and all things;

26 And hath made of one blood all nations of men for to dwell on all the face of the earth, and hath determined the times before appointed, and the bounds of their habitation;

27 That they should seek the Lord, if haply they might feel after him, and find him, though he be not far from every one of us:

28 For in him we live, and move, and have our being; as

certain also of your own poets have said, For we are also his offspring.

29 Forasmuch then as we are the offspring of God, we ought not to think that the Godhead is like unto gold, or silver, or stone, graven by art and man's device.

30 And the times of this ignorance God winked at; but now commandeth all men every where to repent:

31 Because he hath appointed a day, in the which he will judge the world in righteousness by *that* man whom he hath ordained; *whereof* he hath given assurance unto all *men*, in that he hath raised him from the dead.

Paul's Sermon From Mars' Hill

Paul immediately accused the Athenians, "Ye are too superstitious." The word may better mean "much given to reverence." And some have said, "too religious." They had altars to many gods and tried to worship them all, had even an altar "to the unknown God." People can be very religious and not know the true God, not be born again, not know Christ as Saviour. Ardent advocates of a false religion are hard to win. The sated, sophisticated person who knows about all religions and thinks all of them very good, who says, "We are all going to the same place; we just travel different roads," may be harder to win. In India I found that the cultivated student of the philosophy of religion who approached the matter on an intellectual basis was harder to win than the Hindu who felt a need of forgiveness of his sins and had some conscience and fear of judgment.

But Paul began at this part of common interest and preached to them about "the unknown God." At least many of them knew there was a god with whom they were not well-acquainted. There must be some deity more righteous and more powerful than the sinful, imperfect gods and goddesses of Greek mythology! As Psalm 19:1 says, "The heavens declare the glory of God." As Paul was inspired to write in Romans 2:14-16, heathen Gentiles "shew the work of the law written in their hearts, their conscience also bearing witness, and their thoughts the mean while accusing or else excusing one another." It could not be said that the vilest sinner or the most ignorant heathen in the world has not had some light which he did not follow, some drawing of heart and conscience toward God, some fear of meeting judgment, some sense of need of forgiveness. And so in Athens there were "devout persons" (vs. 17). And so the worst heathen has an altar "to the unknown God."

Remember that Paul is greatly stirred because "he saw the city wholly given to idolatry" (vs. 16). So his argument is that the God, the Creator, does not dwell in temples (vs. 24), and is not worshiped by outward observances. God does not need our money, our food, our animals. And in verse 26 Paul shows that all races in the world were made by the same God. This verse gives a reason why patriotism, love of country and love of race is proper. God who caused the confusion of tongues and separated people at the tower of Babel (Gen. 11:5-9) evidently meant for different races to live in different areas. All men are "of one blood." Eve is "the mother of all living" (Gen. 3:20). Every person in the world is descended from Noah and his three sons. But God has chosen certain races for certain purposes and "hath determined...the bounds of their habitation." Efforts to mix the races are not wise. There are good reasons why in marriage, in religion, in government, people fare better who mingle and deal with their own race.

In verses 27 and 28 Paul says that God is "not far from every one of us." And the statement in verse 28, "In him we live, and move, and have our being," reminds us of Colossians 1:16 and 17: "For by him were all things created, that are in heaven, and that are in earth, visible and invisible, whether they be thrones, or dominions, or principalities, or powers: all things were created by him, and for him: And he is before all things, and by him all things consist." In Jesus Christ everything holds together. He is the Creator and Sustainer of all life and, as Lord Tennyson said, "Closer is He than breathing and nearer than hands and feet."

Paul was an educated man and here he quotes one of the Grecian poets. "For we are also his offspring." Probably he referred to Aratus or Cleanthes. But he uses the word "offspring" in the sense that we are made by God, that we and everything in the universe came from God and thus it is foolish to think "that the Godhead is like unto gold or silver, or stone, graven by art and man's device." God as a Creator proves how vain are idols.

It is true that mankind is made in the likeness of God (Gen. 1:26, 27). But that does not mean and the Bible never teaches that all men are spiritually children of God. In Galatians 3:26 Paul wrote to the Christians saying, "For ye are all the children of God by faith in Christ Jesus." But Jesus was wonderfully clear in teaching Nicodemus that "except a man be born again, he cannot see the kingdom of God" (John 3:3), and that that which is born of the flesh is only flesh, and not born of the Spirit, but that which is born of the Spirit is Spirit (John 3:6). Jesus discussed this plainly with the Pharisees in John 8:41-47:

> "Ye do the deeds of your father. Then said they to him, We be not born of fornication; we have one Father, even God. Jesus said unto them, If God were your Father, ye would love me: for I proceeded forth and came from God; neither came I of myself, but he sent me. Why do ye not understand my speech? even because ye cannot hear my word. Ye are of your father the devil, and the lusts of your father ye will do. He was a murderer from the beginning, and abode not in the truth, because there is no truth in him. When he speaketh a lie, he speaketh of his own: for he is a liar, and the father of it. And because I tell you the truth, ye believe me not. Which of you convinceth me of sin? And if I say the truth, why do ye not believe me? He

> that is of God heareth God's words: ye therefore
> hear them not, because ye are not of God."

Jesus plainly tells these people that they are not children of God but "ye are of your father the devil." All humankind is made in the image of God, and in the sense of the Greek poet quoted, is the offspring of God, the work of His hands, but men are not spiritually children of God until they are born again spiritually. And we all "were by nature the children of wrath, even as others" (Eph. 2:3). But Paul's argument here is good that the Creator of mankind could not be wood and stone or graven images.

The Long—Suffering God Now Commands Repentance

Verse 30 tells us that "the times of this ignorance God winked at...." That does not mean that God ever made light of sin. Rather, the word "winked at" might be translated that God overlooked sin. In other words, God is a long-suffering, merciful God. He sends the rain on the just and on the unjust. He showers a thousand blessings on the unconverted, the irreverent, the wicked. The mercy of the Lord endures forever. God had already shed some light into every heathen heart, had already pricked the conscience of every sinning person. Now the Gospel is come and God demands repentance.

Repentance and faith in the Lord Jesus Christ are different ways of speaking of the same changed attitude of heart and mind which God requires. But to the unconcerned, the term "repentance" puts more stress on the sin question. To the jailer, already deeply convicted and falling down before Paul and Silas and begging to be saved, they said, "Believe on the Lord Jesus Christ, and thou shalt be saved..." (Acts 16:30, 31). And that was the same plan of salvation offered here to the Athenians. It is true that anyone who trusts in Jesus Christ is instantly forgiven and saved, as many Scriptures say (John 3:14, 16, 18, 36; Acts 13:38, 39; Acts 16:30, 31). But one cannot have saving faith unless there is an honest heart-turning away from sin.

Then Paul brings solemn warning. A day of judgment is coming. Jesus Christ Himself will be the Judge. And the resurrection of Christ is the assurance that God has given all judgment into His hand (vs. 31).

The resurrection of Jesus means that "the hour is coming, and now is, when the dead shall hear the voice of the Son of God: and they that hear shall live," and God "hath given him authority to execute judgment also, because he is the Son of man" (John 5:25, 27). Jesus continues to say, "Marvel not at this: for the hour is coming, in the which all that are in the graves shall hear his voice, And shall come forth; they that have done good, unto the resurrection of life; and they that have done evil, unto the resurrection of damnation" (John 5:28, 29). John 5:22 says that the Father "hath committed all judgment unto the Son." So Paul warns the Athenians and we must warn men everywhere that they must face Jesus Christ as Saviour or face Him, despairing, as Judge, at the great white throne judgment. The resurrection of Christ points toward judgment time.

VERSES 32–34:

32 ¶ And when they heard of the resurrection of the dead, some mocked: and others said, We will hear thee again of this *matter.*

33 So Paul departed from among them.

34 Howbeit certain men clave unto him, and believed: among the which *was* Dionysius the Areopagite, and a woman named Damaris, and others with them.

Very Few Saved, Paul Departs

Here at Athens there seems to have been fewer results than at other places where Paul preached. At Philippi a church was founded. At Thessalonica some of the Jews "and of the devout Greeks a great multitude" were saved (vs. 4). At Berea "many of them believed" (vs. 12). Later at Colosse and Ephesus great churches are founded, but there is no later reference to a church at Athens. Paul wrote no epistle to the Athenians as he did to the Thessalonians, Philippians, Galatians, Ephesians and Corinthians.

There is some evidence that Paul may have felt later that he had been too scholarly, too polished in his approach at Athens. He reasoned, he quoted their poets, he was logical and eloquent. But few were saved. We find that when Paul went to Corinth, his next stop, he came "in weakness, and in fear, and in much trembling," and that he "came not with excellency of speech or of wisdom," but instead said, "For I determined not to know any thing among you, save Jesus Christ, and him crucified" (I Cor. 2:1-5). Paul may have been heartsick over the few results at Athens. He may have pledged himself to go back to more simple speech and preach more about Christ and His crucifixion. Certainly he was in fear and trembling as he went to Corinth. Perhaps that is why at Corinth the Lord spoke to Paul at night by a vision and said, "Be not afraid, but speak, and hold not thy peace: For I am with thee..." (Acts 18:9, 10).

I do not know whether Paul's experience at Athens with few results was the reason for his fear and trembling as he went to Corinth, the reason for his re-examining his message and making new vows, determined to know only Christ and Him crucified, but "certain men clave unto him, and believed." Two are named in verse 34 and there were a few others. He would have better results at Corinth!

ACTS 18

VERSES 1–3:

AFTER these things Paul departed from Athens, and came to Corinth;

2 And found a certain Jew named Aquila, born in Pontus, lately come from Italy, with his wife Priscilla, (because that Claudius had commanded all Jews to depart from Rome,) and came unto them.

3 And because he was of the same craft, he abode with them, and wrought: (for by their occupation they were tentmakers.)

Paul Goes to Corinth

Corinth is some sixty miles west of Greece. Corinth was on the isthmus which joins the peninsula on which was Sparta and the lower part of Greece to the mainland. Corinth was well placed, with a port in the Gulf of Corinth and also with ports receiving shipping from the east, the Aegean Sea. Then sometimes small ships were dragged across the isthmus. Now a great canal is cut which takes big ships through, saving much time. But in those days when the sea was the best means of communication and transportation, Corinth became a great city. It was second only to Athens, and as Athens was the center of culture, Corinth was the center of commerce, wealth and wickedness. The ruins of much of Corinth have now been excavated, and in February 1962, I walked along the street where Paul walked, stood before the Bema judgment seat where he was brought before Gallio.

Since Corinth was a great commercial city, many Jews were there. For the same reason many languages were common there, and there a "tongues heresy" arose which Paul had to rebuke in I Corinthians 14, not a supernatural gift of tongues but the use of foreign languages in worldly wisdom, languages unknown by many of those who heard.

Here Paul met Aquila and his wife Priscilla, both of whom

had a great part in the life of Paul. A year and a half later or more, these two left Greece with Paul and he left them at Ephesus (vss. 18, 19). At Corinth Aquila and Priscilla had "lately come from Italy," since all Jews were required to depart from Rome. But in Romans 16:3, some five or six years later, they are back in Rome and Paul writes greetings to them (Rom. 16:3, 4). There he tells how they "for my life laid down their own necks," and how they were a blessing to "all the churches of the Gentiles."

When Apollos came to Ephesus, Aquila and Priscilla "took him unto them, and expounded unto him the way of God more perfectly" (Acts 18:26).

Three years after Paul took Aquila and Priscilla to Ephesus with him, he wrote his first epistle to the Corinthians saying, "...Aquila and Priscilla salute you much in the Lord, with the church that is in their house" (I Cor. 16:19). Years later when Paul was a prisoner in Rome, he wrote to Timothy back in the province of Asia and where Priscilla and Aquila were again, and said, "Salute Prisca and Aquila, and the household of Onesiphorus" (II Tim. 4:19).

It was with these busy commercial tentmakers that Paul made his home. And we learn that Paul had also learned the tentmaking trade. "He was of the same craft." And so he worked with them day by day, during the week, preaching in the synagogue on the Sabbath.

VERSES 4–11:

4 And he reasoned in the synagogue every sabbath, and persuaded the Jews and the Greeks.

5 And when Silas and Timotheus were come from Macedonia, Paul was pressed in the spirit, and testified to the Jews *that* Jesus *was* Christ.

6 And when they opposed themselves, and blasphemed, he shook *his* raiment, and said unto them, Your blood *be* upon your own heads; I *am* clean: from henceforth I will go unto the Gentiles.

7 ¶ And he departed thence, and entered into a certain *man's* house, named Justus, *one* that worshipped God, whose house joined hard to the synagogue.

8 And Crispus, the chief ruler of the synagogue, believed on the Lord with all his house; and many of the Corinthians hearing believed, and were baptized.

9 Then spake the Lord to Paul in the night by a vision, Be not afraid, but speak, and hold not thy peace:

10 For I am with thee, and no man shall set on thee to hurt thee: for I have much people in this city.

11 And he continued *there* a year and six months, teaching the word of God among them.

Paul's Eighteen Months' Ministry at Corinth

Again, Paul began at his usual and obvious point--preaching to Jews primarily in the synagogue, but it had come to pass that now Greeks also flocked to hear him in each city where he ministered.

Silas and Timothy do not appear with Paul in Athens. They had been commanded "for to come to him with all speed" (Acts 17:15). But as he waited in Athens he preached and his stay there was short. So they followed from Macedonia, then came on and caught up with Paul at Corinth.

Here is a very interesting thing: Before the coming of Silas and Timothy, Paul worked daily in tentmaking to earn his living and preached in the synagogue every Sabbath. Now when Silas and Timothy arrive, Paul "was pressed in the spirit" and evidently began a much more active ministry. But in his second letter to these Christians at Corinth, he said:

> "Have I committed an offence in abasing myself that ye might be exalted, because I have preached to you the gospel of God freely? I robbed other churches, taking wages of them, to do you service. And when I was present with you, and wanted, I was chargeable to no man: for that

which was lacking to me the brethren which
came from Macedonia supplied: and in all things
I have kept myself from being burdensome unto
you, and so will I keep myself."--II Cor. 11:7-9.

In this rich city Paul "was chargeable to no man." He
worked with his own hands until "the brethren which came
from Macedonia," Silas and Timothy, supplied him with
offerings they had brought from the upper part of Greece,
that is, Philippi, Thessalonica, and Berea. And he writes
in Philippians 4:15, "Now ye Philippians know also, that in
the beginning of the gospel, when I departed from Macedonia, no church communicated with me as concerning giving and receiving, but ye only."

Thus we learn that if a preacher does not have enough
support to preach day and night, he may work for a living
until means are supplied so he may preach all the time. So
it was with Paul. It was God's plan, he said, "Even so hath
the Lord ordained that they which preach the gospel should
live of the gospel" (I Cor. 9:14). But Paul would preach
even if he must labor at tentmaking through the week to get
to preach on the Jewish Sabbath in the synagogue!

Later Paul boasted to the Corinthians that "in all things I
have kept myself from being burdensome unto you, and so
will I keep myself" (II Cor. 11:9). But it is also proper that
to these at Corinth, who did not do right in supporting Paul,
he was inspired to write extended passages to them teaching
the grace of giving (I Cor. 9:1-18; II Cor., chapters 8
and 9).

Here again "Paul was pressed in the spirit." He felt that
same holy urgency and burden to speak for God as he had
had at Athens (Acts 17:16) and at Philippi (Acts 16:18) the
deep moving of the Holy Spirit on his soul. How vigorously
and boldly he preached is indicated when we are told in
verse 6 that "they opposed themselves, and blasphemed.
With holy indignation "he shook his raiment, and said unto

them, Your blood be upon your own heads; I am clean: from henceforth I will go unto the Gentiles."

In a sense that was the same policy he had followed all through his missionary journeys. First, he would go to his own people, the Jews, in synagogues where the Word of God was read. But when Jews turned down the Gospel, he would go to Gentiles in the same area. So it was at Antioch of Pisidia in Acts 13:46 where Paul and Barnabas said, "But seeing ye put it from you, and judge yourselves unworthy of everlasting life, lo, we turn to the Gentiles." So we will find Paul's attitude in Rome in Acts 28:28.

In other cities there had been opposition. Here there was also blasphemy (vs. 6). So Paul left preaching in the synagogue and went next door to a large home of Justus, a Christian man. There he preached. Crispus, the chief ruler of the synagogue, came to hear him and was saved and all his family "and many of the Corinthians hearing believed, and were baptized." And thus the large church to whom Paul later wrote I and II Corinthians came into being.

What comfort that Paul, after so many mobs, after so often fleeing for his life, after abuse and persecution, should have the Lord come to him in a night vision and promise him success and say, "No man shall set on thee to hurt thee: for I have much people in this city." So boldly Paul continued preaching a year and six months.

This Crispus, the ruler of the synagogue, Paul himself baptized with his own hands. He also baptized Gaius in the household of Stephanas (I Cor. 1:14-16). No doubt Silas and Timothy did more of the actual baptizing, as Paul did more of the preaching. The family of Stephanas is called "the firstfruits of Achaia" (a province of which Corinth is a city), as we learn in I Corinthians 16:15. Later when Paul returned to Corinth, he wrote the letter to the Romans and said, "Gaius mine host, and of the whole church, saluteth you" (Rom. 16:23). So we know that Crispus, Gaius, and the household of Stephanas were specially dear to Paul and thus no doubt he baptized them personally by his choice, but he reminds the Corinthians that he came not to baptize but to preach, and that one baptized by Paul is no better than one baptized by any other gospel preacher (I Cor. 1:17). Paul did not baptize individuals to make them his followers, but only as a public profession of their faith in Christ.

VERSES 12-17:

12 ¶ And when Gallio was the deputy of Achaia, the Jews made insurrection with one accord against Paul, and brought him to the judgment seat,

13 Saying, This *fellow* persuadeth men to worship God contrary to the law.

14 And when Paul was now about to open *his* mouth, Gallio said unto the Jews, If it were a matter of wrong or wicked lewdness, O *ye* Jews, reason would that I should bear with you:

15 But if it be a question of words and names, and *of* your law, look ye *to it;* for I will be no judge of such *matters.*

16 And he drave them from the judgment seat.

17 Then all the Greeks took Sosthenes, the chief ruler of the synagogue, and beat *him* before the judgment seat. And Gallio cared for none of those things.

Paul Brought by a Mob Before Gallio

A mob again! Resentment had been building up for a year and a half among the unconverted Jews in this great commercial city of Corinth. So at last somebody brought matters to a head and "the Jews made insurrection with one accord against Paul, and brought him to the judgment seat." It was a tremendous mob, but here is something wonderfully sweet and good. God had promised him that "no man shall set on thee to hurt thee" (vs. 10). And so the mob simply brought Paul before the Roman deputy Gallio, the deputy governor or proconsul of the province. No beating, no jail for Paul this time! The mob of Jews brought their foolish charge, "This fellow persuadeth men to worship God contrary to the law." Their real grievance was that the

Gospel was replacing the law of Moses. So Paul was an offence to the great Jewish population of the city, some of them the leading merchants, no doubt. But they would leave the impression perhaps that the worship Paul taught was also contrary to the worship of Caesar at Rome and the worship of Grecian gods.

Notice the forthrightness of this Roman proconsul. "If it were a matter of wrong or wicked lewdness, O ye Jews, reason would that I should bear with you: But if it be a question of words and names, and of your law, look ye to it; for I will be no judge of such matters."

Our party walked last February through the ruins of old Corinth. Yonder on a hill was the great fort, the easily defended Acropolis. Not far away the ports on the sea. There were streets; palaces of the gods. Here were shops and stores. And there was the Bema, the judgment seat. I stood on the stone paving, looked on Corinthian columns still standing, and imagined that mob bringing Paul here before Gallio. Then I preached to the party assembled in the big bus, reminding them of the sacrificial, burning heart of Paul and what he suffered to spread the Gospel.

So Paul was released. The angry Greeks beat Sosthenes, and the Roman proconsul, Gallio seemed not to mind. He had stirred up a mob; he was lawless, let him take the results of it!

We are reminded that although the Roman government was a heathen government which, though King Herod at Jerusalem, killed James the brother of John with a sword, imprisoned Paul and eventually beheaded him, yet on the whole it was the best government on a large scale that the world had yet seen. There was a just and wise code of laws. The rule was not so much by the whim of a monarch as by due processes of law written down. Not everybody had the right to vote, slavery was permitted, but yet in a remarkable way the rights of free speech and free assembly and free worship were maintained. There was the right of proper trial by law and at least for Roman citizens the right of appeal (Acts 25:10, 11).

Business was carried on across the boundary lines of all the provinces and countries now united in the Roman Empire. And this Roman Empire was not only united by Roman law but by Greek culture and more particularly by the Greek language. Paul could go all over the Roman Empire and preach in the common people's koine Greek and be understood. I have no doubt that God in loving mercy got the world somewhat ready for the coming of the Saviour so that in thirty years after Christ died, the Gospel was preached throughout the Roman Empire and beyond! The relative world-wide peace and law and freedom of passage from country to country and the very widespread use of the same language made the world ripe for the spreading of the Gospel in the first century.

Here is an interesting sidelight. This man Sosthenes, who took the place as chief ruler of the synagogue at Corinth after Crispus was converted, may himself have become a Christian. When Paul, at the close of his three years at Ephesus, writes the epistle of I Corinthians, he greets the people thus: "Paul, called to be an apostle of Jesus Christ through the will of God, and Sosthenes our brother, Unto the church of God which is at Corinth..." (I Cor. 1:1, 2). Did Sosthenes get converted and then go with Paul? He was a prominent man. It seems the church at Corinth would know him. No other Sosthenes is mentioned. So as Paul remained after this riot, it is possible that Sosthenes, like the chief ruler of the synagogue Crispus, who preceded him, may have been converted, too, and gone with Paul!

VERSES 18–23:

18 ¶ And Paul *after this* tarried *there* yet a good while, and then took his leave of the brethren, and sailed thence into Syria, and with him Priscilla and Aquila; having shorn *his* head in Cenchrea: for he had a vow.

19 And he came to Ephesus, and left them there: but he himself entered into the synagogue, and reasoned with the Jews.

20 When they desired *him* to tarry longer time with them, he consented not;

21 But bade them farewell, saying, I must by all means keep this feast that cometh in Jerusalem: but I will return again unto you, if God will. And he sailed from Ephesus.

22 And when he had landed at Cesarea, and gone up, and saluted the church, he went down to Antioch.

23 And after he had spent some time *there*, he departed, and went over *all* the country of Galatia and Phrygia in order, strengthening all the disciples.

Paul the Apostle Takes Jewish Vow

Paul remained at Corinth "yet a good while," how long, we do not know. When he left Corinth he took with him Priscilla and Aquila who had become dear to his heart and very valuable in the Lord's work. Cenchrea was a small seaport town near Corinth, and at Cenchrea he had shorn his head in connection with a vow he had taken.

It seems certain that Paul's vow was the vow of a Nazarite for which provision is made in Numbers 6:1-21. It was a vow of the special consecration or devotion, and was required:

> "He shall separate himself from wine and strong drink, and shall drink no vinegar of wine, or vinegar of strong drink, neither shall he drink any liquor of grapes, nor eat moist grapes, or dried. All the days of his separation shall he eat nothing that is made of the vine tree, from the kernels even to the husk. All the days of the vow of his separation there shall no razor come upon his head: until the days be fulfilled,

in the which he separateth himself unto the Lord, he shall be holy, and shall let the locks of the hair of his head grow. All the days that he separateth himself unto the Lord he shall come at no dead body."--Num. 6:3-6.

Note that the Nazarite was not to touch wine, grape juice, raisins, or grapes, nor eat anything made from grapes, nor drink any alcoholic liquor: he was to let his hair grow during that time, entirely. He was not to touch any dead body nor otherwise allow himself to become ceremonially unclean. The Nazarite could be "either man or woman" (Num. 6:2), and his vow could be for a certain period of time or for a lifetime. The lifetime vow would be initiated by the parents under divine instruction, we suppose, as in the case of Samson (Judg. 13:2-14), and the case of John the Baptist (Luke 1:13-17). At least we suppose that John the Baptist's consecration and separation was like that of the Nazarites because of the pledge that he "shall drink neither wine nor strong drink," because he is set apart for a lifetime of service for the Lord, and because he kept himself separate in the wilderness and different in habit and diet.

The vow of the Rechabites, the sons of Jonadab, is described in Jeremiah 35:1-10. It is kin also to the devoted vow of Daniel in Daniel 1:8.

Note that at the close of the set time the Nazarite had devoted himself to God: "And the Nazarite shall shave the head of his separation at the door of the tabernacle of the congregation, and shall take the hair of the head of his separation, and put it in the fire which is under the sacrifice of the peace-offerings" (Num. 6:18). And there were certain offerings to be made also--a he lamb, an ewe lamb, a ram, a basket of unleavened bread, a case of fine flour mingled with oil and wafers of unleavened bread anointed with oil and meat offerings and drink offerings (Num. 6:14, 15). But if the Nazarite should become defiled by touching a dead body before his days of separation were over, "then he shall shave his head in the day of his cleansing, on the seventh day shall he shave it" (Num. 6:9), and he should then bring two turtledoves or young pigeons and start over and fulfill all the time he originally pledged.

The hair was all cut at the close of the period of separation and if he had to start over, it was cut. Then, we suppose, it was customary and proper to cut the hair completely at the beginning of the vow, and then when the period was fulfilled, to cut the hair again. So Paul had "shorn his head in Cenchrea: for he had a vow." And we suppose that he set himself the extended period until he should come to Jerusalem later, as described in Acts 21:21-26, which led to Paul's arrest in the temple.

Was Paul Right to Take This Jewish Vow of a Nazarite?

At once we are faced with the problem: Was it proper for Paul to take such a Jewish vow? We know that the council at Jerusalem in Acts 15 had decided, as Paul had already decided, that Gentiles need not keep the law of Moses nor be circumcised. In Paul's letters, particularly in Romans and Galatians, he was inspired to make it abundantly clear that those who looked to the law for salvation were frustrating the grace of God and falling from the doctrine of grace and under a curse.

However, we should remember that the Nazarite vow was a voluntary matter, it was not commanded for all of Israel, and no one looked to the Nazarite vow as a plan of salvation. Even the Pharisees, strict legalists in the time of Christ, and the Judaizers, who caused so much trouble to Paul on his missionary journeys, did not teach that the Nazarite vow was necessary or a part of the plan of salvation. It was a vow of special dedication for service. Samson was dedicated to be filled with the Holy Spirit and be a mighty judge in Israel, to deliver the nation and was chosen of God; so it was not only a ceremonial matter. And his mother, the only woman we know of who was set apart for a season as a Nazarite (Judg. 13:2-14), was thus in some way dedicating herself to be the mother of such a son. And with John the Baptist it was surely not simply nor primarily a ceremonial matter. He was set apart as a forerunner of Christ, and the pledge that "he should drink neither wine nor strong drink" was certainly what any proper mother would want to hear about her son. And John the Baptist was to be after the pattern and to go "in the spirit and power of Elias" to win souls, we are told (Luke 1:16, 17).

Some people believe that Samuel, so dedicated to the Lord by his mother, was a Nazarite (I Sam. 1:11, 28). Surely it was not wrong for Paul to make a holy vow to be more wholly given over to the Lord. And if he wished to have a sign between him and God, one with which he was very familiar, that is, he would let his hair grow until the completion of a certain period of service, that would not be necessarily wrong, if it did not imply to others that it was proper to keep the ceremonial law, and if Paul and others did not expect to get any credit or that there would be any virtue in the ceremonial part of it. You see, the ceremonial law was a way of life, it was manners as well as morals, and if Paul, who had never eaten pork before, now found no taste for it, it would not be sinful. And just so if, before his conversion he had been accustomed to make holy vows and to wear his hair long for a season until the vow was completed, it would not be amiss now if his vow were a holy one, to have some set sign between him and God.

I knew a young man who vowed that he would neither eat nor drink until his brother was saved. In two days his brother was wonderfully converted. I knew a woman, an important executive in a department store, who vowed to God with tears that she would never sell another bit of goods nor go back to the store until her husband was converted. He was saved very soon. It is not wrong to make vows to God. It would be wrong to leave an impression that there was some special virtue in the outward forms of the ceremonial law.

However, this vow may have been a snare to Paul, well intentioned, but leading to some compromise of truth which he did not intend. Paul loved Israel so much that he was never content not to preach to the Jews. When, after his conversion, he first went back to Jerusalem, "they went about to slay him" (Acts 9:29). And there in Jerusalem as he prayed in the temple in a trance, God said to him, "Make haste, and get thee quickly out of Jerusalem: for they will not receive thy testimony concerning me." And again, "Depart: for I will send thee far hence unto the Gentiles" (Acts 22:18, 21). And in every city where Paul went, he naturally, and I think, properly, went to the synagogues to preach first, but generally most of the Jews would not hear him. And now, perhaps in connection with this vow and certainly in connection with that unsatisfied yearning to preach to Israelites, he said, "I must by all means keep this feast that cometh in Jerusalem" (vs. 21). So Paul was biased and somewhat blinded on this matter.

Later when he would return to Jerusalem Paul came to Tyre. Acts 21:4 tells us, "And finding disciples, we tarried there seven days: who said to Paul through the Spirit, that he should not go up to Jerusalem," but he went anyway. He came to Caesarea and there in the house of Philip, a prophet, Agabus, "took Paul's girdle, and bound his own hands and feet, and said, Thus saith the Holy Ghost, So shall the Jews at Jerusalem bind the man that owneth this girdle, and shall deliver him into the hands of the Gentiles" (Acts 21:11). That was of God but Paul did not heed the pleading and weeping of his friends there. So when Paul got to Jerusalem, he was enticed to go into the temple and there make a public ceremony of purifying himself, shaving his head, burning the hair at the altar, offering a lamb, and joining in with four other men, strict Judaizers, with the same ceremony!

Since his love for Israel was Paul's weakness, his vow may have been a mistake. And he could have made any vow for pure life and self-discipline and prayer and devotion without going through the Jewish ceremonies. The ceremonial part was a trap, it seems, which led Paul wrong, although I have no doubt that the purpose of his vow was holy and good.

What feast was it at Jerusalem? Was it the Passover or the feast of unleavened bread connected with the Passover? Was it the feast of the firstfruits, Pentecost, or feast of trumpets or of tabernacles? The Bible does not say and it is of no importance to us here. "He sailed from Ephesus" and in two short verses, 22 and 23, we are told of the trip to Caesarea, then to Jerusalem, the greetings with the church, the trip back to Antioch, and then a tour through Galatia and Phrygia strengthening the disciples where he had been on his missionary journeys. So the nature of the trip to Jerusalem and the feast does not matter, but the Spirit of God wanted us to know that Paul sought and felt he must go there.

VERSES 24–28:

24 ¶ And a certain Jew named Apollos, born at Alexandria, an eloquent man, *and* mighty in the Scriptures, came to Ephesus.

25 This man was instructed in the way of the Lord; and being fervent in the spirit, he spake and taught diligently the things of the Lord, knowing only the baptism of John.

26 And he began to speak boldly in the synagogue: whom when Aquila and Priscilla had heard, they took him unto *them*, and expounded unto him the way of God more perfectly.

27 And when he was disposed to pass into Achaia, the brethren wrote, exhorting the disciples to receive him: who, when he was come, helped them much which had believed through grace:

28 For he mightily convinced the Jews, *and that* publicly, shewing by the Scriptures that Jesus was Christ.

Apollos at Ephesus

After Paul left Ephesus and left Priscilla and Aquila there, and possibly Silas and Timothy (or were Silas and Timothy left at Corinth?), Apollos came to Ephesus. He was a converted Jew, "an eloquent man, and mighty in the scriptures." He was "instructed in the way of the Lord; and being fervent in the spirit." What wonderful equipment for a man of God! He was mighty in the Old Testament Scriptures. He knew clearly the plan of salvation. He was "fervent in the spirit," that is, fervent in the power of the Holy Spirit, we think. His impact on the people at Corinth was tremendous, as we see from I Corinthians 1:11 and 12. I think our brethren with some overemphasis on dispensations have wronged Apollos. A note in that very greatly used and blessed Scofield Reference Bible says, "Apollos' ministry seems to have gone no further; Jesus was the long expected Messiah. Of Paul's doctrine of justification through the blood, and sanctification through the Spirit, he seems at that time to have known nothing." But that is not the description of a man "instructed in the way of the Lord," "mighty in the scriptures," and "fervent in the spirit."

It is true that Aquila and Priscilla "took him unto them, and expounded unto him the way of God more perfectly." They help fill in some gaps in his knowledge. He was from Alexandria, Egypt. He had evidently heard John the Baptist in Judaea, but the crucifixion and Pentecost and the revelations about the fullness of the Spirit he evidently did not fully understand. But he knew the way of the Lord, so he preached the plan of salvation and he "helped them much which had believed through grace" (vs. 27). And again, "he mightily convinced the Jews, and that publickly, shewing by the scriptures that Jesus was Christ." That is exactly what Peter had done at Pentecost and what Paul has done throughout his missionary journey. As far as we can tell from

Acts 19:1-7, he had not instructed the new converts fully in the matter of the fullness of the Spirit, and he had not been near Jerusalem at the time of Pentecost and following. But his preaching was true to the Scriptures and powerful; he got people saved; he helped Christians, and his converts were genuine converts, no doubt.

Apollos later "was disposed to pass into Achaia," that is, the lower provinces of Greece including Corinth, etc., and "the brethren wrote, exhorting the disciples to receive him." But more about Apollos in the next chapter.

ACTS 19

VERSES 1-7:

AND it came to pass, that, while Apollos was at Corinth, Paul having passed through the upper coasts came to Ephesus; and finding certain disciples,

2 He said unto them, Have ye received the Holy Ghost since ye believed? And they said unto him, We have not so much as heard whether there be any Holy Ghost.

3 And he said unto them, Unto what then were ye baptized? And they said, Unto John's baptism.

4 Then said Paul, John verily baptized with the baptism of repentance, saying unto the people, that they should believe on him which should come after him, that is, on Christ Jesus.

5 When they heard *this*, they were baptized in the name of the Lord Jesus.

6 And when Paul had laid *his* hands upon them, the Holy Ghost came on them; and they spake with tongues, and prophesied.

7 And all the men were about twelve.

Converts of Apollos Learn of the Fullness of the Spirit

Now Paul, going back through Galatia and Phrygia, has returned at last to the great city of Ephesus and there he finds certain disciples to whom he asked the plain question, "Have ye received the Holy Ghost since ye believed?"

Consider that in New Testament times one who was saved was supposed to know about the fullness of the Spirit and it was a simple matter, without confusion, in the minds of the people.

It is unfortunate and sad that there has been great and unnecessary confusion and false teaching about the fullness of the Holy Spirit in these modern times. The confusion has been brought about by certain misunderstandings of Pentecost.

1. Some people think that Pentecost meant the origin of the church. Because I Corinthians 12:13 says, "For by one

Spirit are we all baptized into one body...," and since Jesus in Acts 1:5 promised the disciples, "For John truly baptized with water; but ye shall be baptized with the Holy Ghost not many days hence," they leap far across probabilities and the inherent meaning of Pentecost to the conclusion that the baptism of the Holy Spirit was simply some official dispensational matter in which the church was originated and the disciples welded together into one body. However, it is certain that the people at Corinth, addressed in I Corinthians 12:13, were not at Pentecost and were not even saved. And we miss the point entirely by supposing that it was some routine and official matter or ceremonial matter or dispensational matter at Pentecost.

No, the Scripture plainly says that Jesus commanded the disciples to "tarry ye in the city of Jerusalem, until ye be endued with power from on high" (Luke 24:49). And again, "But ye shall receive power, after that the Holy Ghost is come upon you: and ye shall be witnesses unto me..." (Acts 1:8). No, the Bible never mentions nor hints that the church originated at Pentecost. As far as we can see from Hebrews 12:23, in I Peter 2:5 and Ephesians 2:20-22, it seems clear that every individual was put into the body of Christ at the time of salvation, that this body or spiritual building is continually growing as each member is buried into the body or made a part of it by regeneration, and that this will include all the "spirits of just men made perfect" who will be caught out at the rapture, to be the called-out assembly or ekklesia of Christ in the air. At any rate, God says nothing about Pentecost being the birthday of the church and we ought not to miss what God does say by insisting on what He does not say.

Some have supposed that Pentecost meant a second work of grace, the burning out of the old carnal nature, the dying of the sinful disposition in those already saved. But the Bible mentions nothing of the kind. There is a Bible doctrine of sanctification, but it is not taught in connection with Pentecost.

Others stress that tongues or miraculous languages were the evidence of the fullness of the Spirit, and are not impressed with the fact that God had promised soul-winning power, and that on the day of Pentecost there were added to them some three thousand souls.

The confusion about Pentecost is sinful and wicked. But perhaps most wicked is the neglect of the great Bible doctrine of the fullness of the Spirit. Christians need not sneer at these disciples at Ephesus who said, "We have not so much as heard whether there be any Holy Ghost." The average preacher could cause consternation among good Christians by going among them and insisting on an answer to the same question, "Have ye received the Holy Ghost since ye believed?" Many would answer that they did not know what was meant by receiving the Holy Ghost, and others would offer various signs and answers, not intended in the Scriptures, and many could say they had never heard an earnest sermon on the command to be filled with the Spirit! In New Testament times Christians were much more familiar with this question of the fullness of the Spirit than church members are today.

Again, the Scofield Bible, the most useful reference Bible in the world, is wrong and hurtful, it seems to me, in discussing these disciples of Acts 19:1-7. The Scofield note says, "Paul was evidently impressed by the absence of spirituality and power in these so-called disciples. Their answer brought out the fact that they were Jewish proselytes, disciples of John the Baptist, looking forward to a coming King, not Christians looking backward to an accomplished redemption."

May I suggest that Dr. Scofield, too much influenced by Plymouth Brethren, allowed himself to make a very foolish statement here. The Bible calls these twelve men "certain disciples." Dr. Scofield calls them "these so-called dis-

ciples." Paul asked them about what had happened "since ye
believed." They were believers and Dr. Scofield has no
right to call them Jewish proselytes and "not Christians."
One who has believed in Christ, one who is sincerely a
disciple, is a Christian, if we hold to New Testament language.

The misunderstanding here comes because many Plymouth Brethren and other ultradispensationalists tried to
make John the Baptist in a different dispensation and have
even suggested that John the Baptist offered a different plan
of salvation from that of Jesus. That is shortsighted and
foolish. In Acts 10:43 Peter said to Cornelius, "To him
give all the prophets witness, that through his name whosoever believeth in him shall receive remission of sins." So
the Old Testament plan of salvation was exactly the same as
the New Testament plan, and if John the Baptist had been
counted in the Old Testament, he would still not have
preached a different plan of salvation.

In fact, we have a discussion by John the Baptist in John
3:27-36. And there John the Baptist says in verse 36, "He
that believeth on the Son hath everlasting life: and he that
believeth not the Son shall not see life; but the wrath of God
abideth on him." That is exactly the same plan of salvation
Jesus gave in the same chapter, verses 14, 16, 18, and
many other places. Oh, some will say, "But John preached
repentance!" And so did Jesus, announcing word for word
the same command, "Repent ye: for the kingdom of heaven
is at hand" (compare Matt. 3:2 with Matt. 4:17). And Jesus
preached repentance in Luke 13:1-5, just as Paul preached
repentance at Athens in Acts 17:30, and II Peter 3:9 says
that "the Lord is...not willing that any should perish, but
that all should come to repentance." It is interesting that
the Gospel of Mark, before starting to tell of the ministry
of John the Baptist, announces, "The beginning of the gospel
of Jesus Christ, the Son of God."

So there was nothing wrong with the Gospel as preached

by John the Baptist. There was nothing wrong with the baptism he administered. It was exactly what Jesus and all the twelve apostles had. And when Apollos had heard John the Baptist preach, he was "instructed in the way of the Lord," and "mighty in the scriptures." No doubt he needed to instruct disciples more on the fullness of the Spirit, just as many good preachers need to do today. But these were disciples, they had believed, they had been baptized on their profession of faith. The Bible does not hint that they are not Christians and no one else has a right to infer that.

But Paul asked them, "Unto what then were ye baptized?" It is obvious that new converts should be taught to expect to be filled with the Holy Spirit, and the devotion and surrender, which is properly involved in baptism, ought to lead people to the fullness of the Spirit. So Peter taught in Acts 2:38. And Jesus was filled with the Holy Spirit when He was baptized (Luke 3:22). If, immediately, young converts should be taught to claim the Lord openly and be baptized, also they should immediately be taught that there is a blessed anointing of God which every Christian ought to have, "For the promise is unto you, and to your children, and to all that are afar off, even as many as the Lord our God shall call" (Acts 2:39).

Paul was accustomed to new converts being filled with the Spirit and accustomed to having them know it. So he could write to his Galatian converts, "Received ye the Spirit by the works of the law, or by the hearing of faith? Are ye so foolish? having begun in the Spirit, are ye now made perfect by the flesh?" (Gal. 3:2, 3). He could chide them, "Where is then the blessedness ye spake of?" (Gal. 4:15).

So these converts had been taught to believe on Christ as Saviour, and they had. But after further instruction, either on the assurance of salvation or on the blessedness of the fullness of the Spirit available for every Christian, they were baptized in the name of the Lord Jesus, then Paul laid his hands upon them and the Holy Ghost came on them.

Let us note, first, that if one did not fully understand the meaning of baptism, it is perfectly proper to be baptized again when the meaning is clear. Baptism is not a means of grace in the sense that one by baptism receives some favor with God. However, baptism is a public profession; it is a figure of salvation. If the picture was not a true picture, let us make it again. If the testimony was not clear, let us restate it. So those who were not baptized properly or those who were baptized unconverted or those who were saved but did not understand the meaning of baptism and got no joy and blessing from it, might be baptized again sincerely, in some circumstances.

These disciples now "spake with tongues." That simply means plural languages. Were these languages supernaturally given, as at Pentecost, to people who were not otherwise able to speak in the language of others who heard and understood? The Bible does not say and we have no right to infer a miracle, I think, when it is neither stated nor needed. Evidently these men were greatly blessed and praised the Lord. In the great cosmopolitan city of Ephesus, people spoke many languages.

The International Standard Bible Encyclopedia tells us that Ephesus was a great commercial city "with an artificial harbor accessible to the largest ships...connected by highways with the chief cities of the province. Ephesus was the most easily accessible city in Asia both by land and sea ....Because of its wealth and situation it gradually became a chief city of the province....Not only did the temple (of Diana) bring vast numbers of pilgrims to the city...but it employed hosts of people apart from the priests and priestesses." In such a great commercial center, with trade coming from all over the Roman Empire, it is not surprising that these twelve disciples may have been of different nationalities. At any rate, they simply spoke in different languages, whether those languages were miraculously given or not.

Paul laid his hands on them to pray that they might receive the Holy Ghost. Paul had laid his hands on Timothy, we suppose, at an ordination (I Tim. 4:14 and II Tim. 1:6). And surely that is the intention of the ordination service, that good men representing the churches should lay hands on those who are called of God and pray that God will give them the gifts for the ministry and the power of the Holy Spirit.

VERSES 8–10:

8 And he went into the synagogue, and spake boldly for the space of three months, disputing and persuading the things concerning the kingdom of God.

9 But when divers were hardened, and believed not, but spake evil of that way before the multitude, he departed from them, and separated the disciples, disputing daily in the school of one Tyrannus.

10 And this continued by the space of two years; so that all they which dwelt in Asia heard the word of the Lord Jesus, both Jews and Greeks.

In Synagogue and School of Tyrannus at Ephesus

Paul was in Ephesus. He met certain disciples here and prayed with them that they might receive the Holy Ghost. Then he went into the synagogue "and spake boldly for the space of three months, disputing and persuading...." He came to Jews first because they were of the same background, because they had the Scriptures, because they knew of the true God. And doubtless some of them were saved just as Abraham was saved (Gen. 15:6), just as old Simeon, who lived to see the baby Jesus (Luke 2:25-35), was saved, and as were other Old Testament Jews who trusted in the coming Saviour.

Paul "spake boldly." That was a great characteristic of Spirit-filled New Testament preachers (see Acts 4:13, 30,

31). Preaching the Gospel is a warfare against evil, against Satan, against wicked-hearted men, against evil spirits, against false doctrine.

With Spirit-filled, bold preaching, one of two reactions is inevitable: some would believe, and others would be hardened and oppose the Gospel. The preaching that makes no one angry and makes no one very glad, the preaching that does not offend some, does not bless others with saving power.

So when there was a reaction unfavorable to Paul and the Gospel, he "departed from them, and separated the disciples" and moved his preaching place to the school of one Tyrannus. Here they followed the Greek custom of collecting in groups for discussion of philosophy, as it was at Athens (Acts 17:18-21). A philosopher like Socrates or Aristotle or Plato would gather disciples and teach them his philosophy. These "schools" were often open forums of discussion for intelligent people. And it was the fashion for cultured and well-to-do people who had slaves to do their work, to gather and study philosophy and religion. New Testament churches at first had no church buildings, so Christians gathered where they could, in a synagogue or in some other public meeting place, like the school of Tyrannus, and this was a daily matter and "continued by the space of two years."

Notice that "all they which dwelt in Asia heard the word of the Lord Jesus, both Jews and Greeks." The word Asia here refers to that province in part of what we now call Asia Minor, and is now in Asiatic Turkey. Remember that the book of Revelation is addressed to "the seven churches in Asia" and most of Paul's missionary work was done in this peninsula and over in Macedonia (the northern part of Greece) and Achaia (southern Greece).

But since this was a busy commercial center with people going and coming, soon all that populace province heard the Word of God, Jews and Greeks!

Paul was in Ephesus three months, preaching in the synagogue (vs. 8). Then two years he continued in the school of Tyrannus and perhaps elsewhere (vs. 10). But after the events in verses 11 to 22, "he himself stayed in Asia for a season" more. So his entire ministry in Ephesus was three years (Acts 20:31).

VERSES 11–16:

11 And God wrought special miracles by the hands of Paul:

12 So that from his body were brought unto the sick handkerchiefs or aprons, and the diseases departed from them, and the evil spirits went out of them.

13 ¶ Then certain of the vagabond Jews, exorcists, took upon them to call over them which had evil spirits the name of the Lord Jesus, saying, We adjure you by Jesus whom Paul preacheth.

14 And there were seven sons of one Sceva, a Jew, and chief of the priests, which did so.

15 And the evil spirit answered and said, Jesus I know, and Paul I know; but who are ye?

16 And the man in whom the evil spirit was leaped on them, and overcame them, and prevailed against them, so that they fled out of that house naked and wounded.

Miraculous Healings and Demons Cast Out

We read here "God wrought special miracles by the hands of Paul." Special simply means not ordinary but unusual. Handkerchiefs or aprons were brought from his body and God used these to heal the sick and cast out evil spirits! But actually a miracle is a miracle. The Scripture does not command anyone else to send out handkerchiefs or aprons for the healing of sick, but neither does the Scripture forbid it. The simple truth is that this was a special miracle and miracles are gifts of God, are extraordinary, not ordinary. If God saw fit to heal many by "the shadow of Peter passing by" (Acts 5:15), or to raise a man from the dead by touching the bones of Elisha (II Kings 18:20, 21), or to cast out a demon by a word, or to heal the sick by the touch of the hand, it is still all miraculous, the work of God. And the Christian religion is a religion of the supernatural.

The Bible is full of miracles and the ministries of God's preachers in the book of Acts show as wonderful results of God's power as the personal ministry of Jesus in the Gospels. And these miracles were not confined to the apostles. For "Stephen, full of faith and power, did great wonders and miracles among the people" (Acts 6:8). And when Deacon Philip was in Samaria, "...the people with one accord gave heed unto those things which Philip spake, hearing and seeing the miracles which he did. For unclean spirits, crying with loud voice, came out of many that were possessed with them: and many taken with palsies, and that were lame, were healed" (Acts 8:6, 7). Healing the sick and casting out the unclean spirits were named as miraculous healings alike (Acts 5:16). We had as well face the clear teaching of the Bible that as the Father sent Jesus into the world, so Jesus has sent us, His people (John 17:18; John 20:21; John 14:12).

The diversities of gifts by the Holy Spirit are named in I Corinthians 12:4-11, and those gifts include wisdom, the word of knowledge, faith, gifts of healing, working miracles, prophecy, discerning of spirits, and gifts of languages or interpretation. But in the same chapter, verses 29 and 30 tell us, "...are all workers of miracles? Have all the gifts of healing?..." And we are reminded from the Great Commission as given in Mark 16:17 and 18, that certain signs or miracles "shall follow them that believe," that is, those who have faith for these signs or miracles, and that includes "In my name shall they cast out devils...they shall lay hands on the sick, and they shall recover." Where God gives faith for miracles, God gives the miracles.

The modern "healing movement" has had some fanaticism and some false doctrine. It is certainly not always God's will to heal the sick now, as it was not in Bible times. Sometimes it is God's will for people to be sick and so

learn some lesson or receive some blessing or give some
gracious testimony to God's help in trouble. Sometimes
Christians ought to die. And the doctors and medicines are
not wrong. God more usually uses means to heal people,
just as He even uses human means and testimony in getting
out the Gospel and in saving souls. But making allowance
for heresies and fanaticism, which we do not endorse, it is
still true that God today sometimes miraculously intervenes
to heal the sick.

Many would say that there are no miraculous healings today. I answer first that I know from personal experience
that God has wonderfully intervened miraculously in healing
those who were given up to die, and healing instantly those
where medical help had failed. But my own testimony is
buttressed by many reliable witnesses. I do not here give
the testimony of any of the healing evangelists or of any
fanatics. The Ministry of Healing by A. J. Gordon tells of
"miracles of cure in all ages." Gordon was the founder of
Gordon College, a Baptist. Henry W. Frost wrote the book
Miraculous Healing, a personal testimony and biblical
study, published by Revell. He was the American secretary
for the China Inland Mission, as I recall, intimate friend of
Hudson Taylor. A. B. Simpson, a Presbyterian minister
who founded the Christian and Missionary Alliance, wrote
the Gospel of Healing, with one chapter of personal testimony of healings. The immortal Andrew Murray wrote the
book Divine Healing, Its Scriptural Basis and My Personal
Testimony. The book, Modern Miracles of Healing, edited
by David J. Fant, gives the testimony of Dr. P. W. Philpott,
Mr. Robert G. LeTourneau, President V. Raymond Edman
of Wheaton, and many, many others. Dr. John Roach
Straton, pastor of Calvary Baptist Church, New York,
wrote Divine Healing in Scripture and Life, with his own
testimony and many others. Dr. W. B. Riley wrote a
strong pamphlet on Divine Healing or Does God Hear Prayer
for the Sick? with unusual testimony. In the literature of

the China Inland Mission and the literature of the Sudan Interior Mission, and articles in The Sunday School Times and elsewhere, are many accounts of demons cast out.

The book, Biblical Demonology, by Merrill F. Unger, has a tremendous bibliography on the subject of demonology. No doubt in America spiritism and fortunetelling are sometimes manifestations of evil spirits and sometimes dope and alcohol habits and mental illness represent the work of evil spirits.

Miracles are not playthings. Not everyone is given the gift of miracles or gifts of healing. But God's compassion for the sick and suffering is as great as ever it was, and God's answer to the prayer of faith is as willing and blessed now as it ever was!

John Wesley in his Journal tells of some amazing healings in answer to prayer and of demons cast out, although that practical and voluminous mind seems to have had no special doctrine about healing and made no issue of it.

Mrs. Jonathan Goforth, Presbyterian missionary, tells of wonderful healings in answer to prayer. The book, Pastor Hsi, of the China Inland Mission, tells of many demons cast out.

Is healing in the atonement? Yes, no doubt, in the sense of our glorified and resurrection bodies which are paid for as a part of our redemption but not yet given us. So all healing is, this side of the resurrection and rapture, only relative and temporary. Those healed and even those raised from the dead in Bible times eventually sickened and died, as do those whom God in loving mercy heals today. (See chapters on healing and miracles in the author's book, Prayer--Asking and Receiving.)

VERSES 17–20:

17 And this was known to all the Jews and Greeks also dwelling at Ephesus; and fear fell on them all, and the name of the Lord Jesus was magnified.

18 And many that believed came, and confessed, and shewed their deeds.

19 Many of them also which used curious arts brought their books together, and burned them before all *men:* and they counted the price of them, and found *it* fifty thousand *pieces* of silver.

20 So mightily grew the word of God and prevailed.

Repentance and Book Burning at Ephesus

In most of the cities where he had preached, Paul had found his principal opposition from unconverted Jews, who held steadfastly to the outward ceremonies of the law, though being far from God in their hearts. But in Ephesus he runs up strongly against this world center of idolatry. Here the Greek civilization had supplanted the oriental, and Greek language was spoken and "the Asiatic goddess of the temple assumed more or less the character of the Greek Artemis." Here was the home of the goddess Diana with its statue and great temple and wealth.

So here Paul came up against the demon world, unseen evil spirits. Many were delivered from evil spirits (vs. 12), so much so that certain "vagabond Jews, exorcists," tried to do the same thing, using Jesus' name. God allowed the evil spirit to answer, "Jesus I know, and Paul I know; but who are ye?" And the demon-possessed man leaped on them, stripped off their clothes and wounded them. And that tale widely told became great publicity for Paul and his Gospel. So that among the unconverted, "fear fell on them all, and the name of the Lord Jesus was magnified" (vs. 17).

Evil spirits knew Jesus and felt compelled to recognize Him, acknowledging His authority as we see in Matthew 8:29; Mark 5:7 and Luke 8:28; so the evil spirit of divination in the slave girl in Acts 16:16 felt compelled to cry out about Paul and Silas, "These men are the servants of the most high God, which shew unto us the way of salvation." Evidently evil spirits are subject also to Christians filled with the Holy Spirit, for here the evil spirit had cried out, "Jesus I know, and Paul I know; but who are ye?" (vs. 15).

Evil spirits, we suppose, were in many people in this area and so "fear fell on them all." And a deep-seated penitence for their sins and turning from sin resulted as the mighty power of God, conquering demons, casting them out, made people conscious of their frailty and wickedness and their danger.

Those who used "curious arts," that is, literally magical arts, or those who dealt with evil spirits, as spiritists and sometimes fortunetellers do, now brought their books and burned them. They were hand-copied books, expensive and often kept secret within certain groups, and the market value of all these books burned was "fifty thousand pieces of silver."

Many preachers and churches fear the spectacular. Paul's services were not "formal worship services." There was no soft organ music, no light filtered through stained glass windows, no robed choirs, no practiced responses, no rhythmic march of choir or ushers. In Paul's ministry the mighty power of God clashed with demonic forces and sin. The scene here at Ephesus, the public confession and renouncing of sin and burning of their evil books, would remind us of a Billy Sunday campaign when there was a closing of saloons, the smashing of beer barrels, the pouring of liquor down the drain. We are reminded of thieves who come forward to confess and make restitution for their theft, of Christians publicly renouncing evil habits.

Here Satan helped to publicize Paul's Gospel. And let us learn the lesson that sharp, plain condemnation of sin, holy boldness in preaching, boldness in prayer, will be used of God to get crowds to hear the Gospel. Your services are not likely to be more sensational than these of Paul in Ephesus.

"So mightily grew the word of God and prevailed," we are told. Praise the Lord!

VERSES 21, 22:

21 ¶ After these things were ended, Paul purposed in the spirit, when he had passed through Macedonia and Achaia, to go to Jerusalem, saying, After I have been there, I must also see Rome.

22 So he sent into Macedonia two of them that ministered unto him, Timotheus and Erastus; but he himself stayed in Asia for a season.

Paul Plans Other Missionary Journeys to Include Rome

Paul "purposed in the spirit" to go through Macedonia and Achaia (what is now northern and southern Greece), where he had preached and founded churches at Philippi, Thessalonica, Berea, and Corinth, and possibly elsewhere. "In the spirit" some think means "in his own mind." But Matthew Henry well says that it might have been "in the Holy Spirit" or led by the Spirit of God, as we think it was. He would strengthen those churches, correct any mistakes, encourage the Christian workers. Then he would go again to Jerusalem. Probably he intended there at the completion of his Nazarite vow to cut his hair and be released from it, at least, so he did, as we read in Acts 21:23-27.

And then after Jerusalem Paul purposed to go to Rome. I think that very probably it was his own intention to go to Jerusalem, being pressed by his love for Israel and his longing to preach the Gospel to them, and to be received of his own people. But I think that God's Spirit was moving him towards Rome, when he insisted on going to Jerusalem and in spite of the warnings given (Acts 20:22; Acts 21:4, 10-13; Acts 22:17-21). So we do not think he was led of the

Spirit to go back to Jerusalem, but Paul was called to be an apostle to the Gentiles. He had been to Antioch in Syria and Antioch of Pisidia, Ephesus, Athens, Corinth, great popular centers, and the Gospel had been spread through all those areas. Now to get the Gospel to the Gentile centers meant that Paul should go to Rome, the center of world government at that time.

A little later, in Corinth (Acts 20:1-3), he will write his epistle to the church at Rome and he says:

> "And they wrote letters by them after this manner; The apostles and elders and brethren send greeting unto the brethren which are of the Gentiles in Antioch and Syria and Cilicia: Forasmuch as we have heard, that certain which went out from us have troubled you with words, subverting your souls, saying, Ye must be circumcised, and keep the law: to whom we gave no such commandment: It seemed good unto us, being assembled with one accord, to send chosen men unto you with our beloved Barnabas and Paul."--Acts 15:23-25.

He has pretty well covered provinces of Syria, Asia, Macedonia and Achaia. He has had "a great desire these many years to come unto you" at Rome. He planned not only to go to Rome but on to Spain, for the Gentile part of the Roman Empire must be evangelized.

We think it clear that the Spirit of God had put it in his heart to go to Rome. And Romans 15:24 is not simply Paul writing but is the Spirit of God. So God had determined that Paul would go to Rome. Also we can take this as divine prophecy that Paul would go to Spain and that means that Paul would be released after a season of imprisonment, and between the two imprisonments he would visit the Philippians (Phil. 1:25), he would visit Philemon at Colosse

(Philem. 22), and he would take that long-promised and prophesied journey to Spain (Rom. 15:24).

The clear leading of the Spirit on to Rome and regions beyond is inferred also. He was led to say to the Ephesian elders in Acts 20:25, "And now, behold, I know that ye all, among whom I have gone preaching the kingdom of God, shall see my face no more." God had given Paul some understanding of where his future ministry would be, although God would have to use his imprisonment to get him to Rome, since he did not go directly from Ephesus but insisted on going to Jerusalem!

Now he sent across the Aegean Sea into Macedonia two of his helpers, Timothy and Erastus. He will stay for some season yet in the province of Asia, around Ephesus. This Erastus, now going up into Macedonia and later down into Achaia, is called in Romans 16:23 the chamberlain of the city of Corinth.

VERSES 23–34:

23 And the same time there arose no small stir about that way.

24 For a certain *man* named Demetrius, a silversmith, which made silver shrines for Diana, brought no small gain unto the craftsmen;

25 Whom he called together with the workmen of like occupation, and said, Sirs, ye know that by this craft we have our wealth.

26 Moreover ye see and hear, that not alone at Ephesus, but almost throughout all Asia, this Paul hath persuaded and turned away much people, saying that they be no gods, which are made with hands:

27 So that not only this our craft is in danger to be set at nought; but also that the temple of the great goddess Diana should be despised, and her magnificence should be destroyed, whom all Asia and the world worshippeth.

28 And when they heard *these sayings*, they were full of wrath, and cried out, saying, Great *is* Diana of the Ephesians.

29 And the whole city was filled with confusion: and having

caught Gaius and Aristarchus, men of Macedonia, Paul's companions in travel, they rushed with one accord into the theatre.

30 And when Paul would have entered in unto the people, the disciples suffered him not.

31 And certain of the chief of Asia, which were his friends, sent unto him, desiring *him* that he would not adventure himself into the theatre.

32 Some therefore cried one thing, and some another: for the assembly was confused; and the more part knew not wherefore they were come together.

33 And they drew Alexander out of the multitude, the Jews putting him forward. And Alexander beckoned with the hand, and would have made his defence unto the people.

34 But when they knew that he was a Jew, all with one voice about the space of two hours cried out, Great *is* Diana of the Ephesians.

The Mob of Idol Makers at Ephesus

Heretofore Paul has often been abused and beaten or slandered by Jews. At Ephesus, more than other places perhaps, he has dealt with evil spirits. But now comes conflict with those whose attack is for financial reasons. In Acts 16:19-21 the masters of the fortunetelling slave girl possessed of demons whom Paul healed, had Paul and Silas arrested and beaten because "the hope of their gains was gone." They slandered God's preachers, making other untrue charges, but the real motive was they had made a gain of the devil-possessed girl and did not want her saved. Now at Ephesus idolatry was a big business and the silversmiths, which made much gain by making silver shrines for Diana (vs. 24), organized a mob on this basis. To the "workmen of like occupation," Demetrius said, "Sirs, ye know that by this craft we have our wealth." But "this Paul hath persuaded and turned away much people, saying that they be no gods, which are made with hands." So they were to lose money and be out of work.

However, they must make their attack on Paul seemingly on religious grounds so they would say that "the temple of the great goddess Diana should be despised, and her magnificence should be destroyed," if Paul and these Christians were allowed to stay! How often it is that the cry, "Great is Diana of the Ephesians" or "Our beloved denomination" or "Our great denominational program" is the cry, when in truth, what men work for is to retain their own place and prestige and income!

There is always sin in unbelief. And unbelief is always hypocritical. Those who reject Christ pretend they have some good reason. Those who reject the authenticity of the Bible or deny the virgin birth and deity of Christ make some plea of scholarship or reason. But actually they reject New Testament Christianity because it condemns their sins, and they reject Christ because they are not willing to bow to Him and accord Him that which He claims, "All power is given unto me in heaven and in earth" (Matt. 28:18).

By this time Paul has many friends who realize the danger to the bold apostle. Some important people of the province, his friends, sent him word not to go before the mob in the public meeting place called "the theatre." Since they could not get Paul, the mob caught Gaius and Aristarchus, Christian workers who have followed Paul from Macedonia to help him. Paul's companions, Gaius and Aristarchus, men of Macedonia, were seized. They would go back into Macedonia and then would return with him again to Asia (Acts 20:4). Aristarchus, a native of Thessalonica in Macedonia, will later go with Paul to Rome (Acts 27:2). The Jews push out Alexander, another companion of Paul, for these Gentile idol makers to abuse and charge. Is this the same Alexander of whom Paul speaks later as having made shipwreck of the faith (I Tim. 1:19, 20)? He is not named here as one of Paul's "companions in travel" as are Gaius and Aristarchus (vs. 29), but one selected by the Jews. And here he "would have made his defence unto the people," but they shouted him down because he was a Jew. Perhaps this is the same Alexander the coppersmith who did Paul much evil, later, as he wrote from Rome (II Tim. 4:14). He was probably a Christian or a professed Christian who fell into sin and broke with Paul. What a roaring for two hours!

VERSES 35–41:

35 And when the townclerk had appeased the people, he said, Ye men of Ephesus, what man is there that knoweth not how that the city of the Ephesians is a worshipper of the great goddess Diana, and of the *image* which fell down from Jupiter?

36 Seeing then that these things cannot be spoken against, ye ought to be quiet, and to do nothing rashly.

37 For ye have brought hither these men, which are neither robbers of churches, nor yet blasphemers of your goddess.

38 Wherefore if Demetrius, and the craftsmen which are with him, have a matter against any man, the law is open, and there are deputies: let them implead one another.

39 But if ye inquire any thing concerning other matters, it shall be determined in a lawful assembly.

40 For we are in danger to be called in question for this day's uproar, there being no cause whereby we may give an account of this concourse.

41 And when he had thus spoken, he dismissed the assembly.

The Town Clerk Quiets and Dismisses the Mob

It is significant that in this chapter we find the only cases in the New Testament when the Greek word ekklesia is translated into any other word but church. In verses 32, 39 and 41, the word assembly is a translation of the word ekklesia, everywhere else in the New Testament translated church.

The word ekklesia means a called-out assembly. And it is used in four different kinds of assemblies in the Bible.

1. In Acts 7:38, Israel, called out of Egypt and assembled at mount Sinai, is called "the church in the wilderness." It was a called-out assembly.

2. Here at Ephesus this mob is called a church. It was a

group called together by the idol makers, so a called-out assembly, and the Greek word <u>ekklesia</u> is used for it. Whether it is an unlawful assembly as in verses 32 and 41, or a lawful assembly as in verse 39, a general group of people called out for some purpose and assembled together fulfills the literal meaning of the word <u>ekklesia</u> as used in the Bible.

3. The word <u>ekklesia</u> is used about the body of Christ, including all the Christians who will be called out at the rapture, when Christ comes for His own. In Hebrews 12:23 this group is called "the general assembly and church of the firstborn, which are written in heaven." And they will be assembled, we are told, at "the heavenly Jerusalem" (Heb. 12:22). This is the church which Christ loved and for which He gave Himself, the "glorious church, not having spot, or wrinkle...or blemish" mentioned in Ephesians 5:25, 27, 32. This is "the body, the church" of which Christ is the head (Col. 1:18, 24).

4. Then the word is used most often in the New Testament, about ninety times, about local congregations or called-out assemblies of Christians, as "the church of God which is at Corinth" (I Cor. 1:2), as "the churches of Galatia" (Gal. 1:2), as "the care of all the churches" (II Cor. 11:28) and as "the seven churches which are in Asia" (Rev. 1:4). A called-out assembly is a church. The church that will be called out at the rapture includes all the saved of all ages. But the principal use of the term in the New Testament is for local congregations of Christians, and for these certain patterns and instructions are laid down in the Bible.

It is also interesting that in this same nineteenth chapter of Acts is the only place in which the King James Version of the Bible uses the word <u>church</u> as a translation for any other Greek word. The term "robbers of churches" in verse 37 should be "robbers of temples." The town clerk is saying that these Christians had not robbed any of the heathen temples. This is the only place in the Bible when the word church refers to a building, and it is a mistranslation. The word church in the Bible never means a denomination, never means a building, but always a called-out assembly or a congregation.

Note again and admire the orderly processes of Roman law. The town clerk "appeased the people." Sure he said all the city of Ephesus worshiped the great goddess Diana, so why have a riot? "Ye ought to be quiet, and to do nothing rashly." These men could not be convicted of any crime. If they have a case against these men, bring it to court; there are lawyers (deputies), let them sue one another. But every public assembly ought to be lawful. The Roman government might punish the city for riots. Roman law was generally just and fairly strict, the best the world had seen up to that time.

So the people, appeased and somewhat cowed, dismissed and went about their business!

ACTS 20

VERSES 1–5:

AND after the uproar was ceased, Paul called unto him the disciples, and embraced them, and departed for to go into Macedonia.

2 And when he had gone over those parts, and had given them much exhortation, he came into Greece,

3 And *there* abode three months. And when the Jews laid wait for him, as he was about to sail into Syria, he purposed to return through Macedonia.

4 And there accompanied him into Asia Sopater of Berea; and of the Thessalonians, Aristarchus and Secundus; and Gaius of Derbe, and Timotheus; and of Asia, Tychicus and Trophimus,

5 These going before tarried for us at Troas.

Another Tour of Macedonia and Greece

About three years Paul has been at Ephesus and in that area, as we see from verse 31. As he had gone more than once to the churches founded in his first missionary journey (Acts 14:21-25; Acts 15:40, 41; Acts 16:4, 5), so now he would go through Macedonia and Achaia, or Greece. Again, he went first to Macedonia, the northern part of what is now Greece, and then south. "Greece" here must refer to Achaia, perhaps particularly to Corinth.

The work must have been very extensive, visiting all the communities where he had preached before, churches he had founded, and other churches, no doubt, founded by the new converts through all the area. And so either going or coming to help him besides Timothy and Erastus whom he had sent on ahead (Acts 19:22) were Sopater of Berea, Aristarchus and Secundus of Thessalonica, Gaius of Derbe, Tychicus and Trophimus. Note that Aristarchus and Gaius had been with him at Ephesus before; now they come back in the province of Asia with him. We suppose, during this trip Paul wrote his epistle to the Romans and there he mentions this Gaius of Derbe, who was with him in Corinth and evidently had wealth, for he was host to Paul and of the church (Rom. 16:23). And Erastus is named as "chamberlain of the city." So evidently Erastus had been converted when Paul was in Corinth before, had come over across the Aegean Sea to help him in the province of Asia, and now returns to his important position in Corinth.

Paul has heard sad things about the worldliness and division at Corinth, as one can tell from I and II Corinthians. In I Corinthians 4:17 Paul had written the people at Corinth, "For this cause have I sent unto you Timotheus, who is my beloved son, and faithful in the Lord, who shall bring you into remembrance of my ways which be in Christ, as I teach every where in every church." And again he had said unto them in I Corinthians 16:10 and 11, "Now if Timotheus come, see that he may be with you without fear: for he worketh the work of the Lord, as I also do. Let no man therefore despise him: but conduct him forth in peace, that he may come unto me: for I look for him with the brethren." Thus Paul explains why he had sent Timothy and Erastus ahead of him into Macedonia and Greece (Acts 19:22) and after he got into Macedonia on this trip he found such a blessed blossoming of the grace of Christian giving in the churches in Macedonia, the northern part of Greece (II Cor. 8:1-6). So he then sent Titus down to Corinth to develop this wonderful grace in them. He had already instructed them in I Corinthians 16:1 and 2 about laying by for the poor saints at Jerusalem, the money which he would collect upon his arrival and take with him to Jerusalem. But he sends Titus ahead to teach and encourage them to give. And so with chapters 8 and 9 of II Corinthians.

Eventually his journey through these provinces and his contact with the churches is finished. He had collected money for the poor saints at Jerusalem and longed to go there. So his helpers went ahead of him across the Aegean Sea into Asia Minor and waited for Paul at the seaport town of Troas.

VERSES 6–12:

6 And we sailed away from Philippi after the days of unleavened bread, and came unto them to Troas in five days; where we abode seven days.

7 And upon the first *day* of the week, when the disciples came together to break bread, Paul preached unto them, ready to depart on the morrow; and continued his speech until midnight.

8 And there were many lights in the upper chamber, where they were gathered together.

9 And there sat in a window a certain young man named Eutychus, being fallen into a deep sleep: and as Paul was long preaching, he sunk down with sleep, and fell down from the third loft, and was taken up dead.

10 And Paul went down, and fell on him, and embracing *him* said, Trouble not yourselves; for his life is in him.

11 When he therefore was come up again, and had broken bread, and eaten, and talked a long while, even till break of day, so he departed.

12 And they brought the young man alive, and were not a little comforted.

Paul at Troas

It was springtime, "after the days of unleavened bread," when "we sailed away from Philippi...." Notice the "we." Evidently Luke, the beloved physician, is again with Paul! Where is Silas? He has not been mentioned since he met Paul at Corinth (Acts 18:5). Notice the "we," including Luke, in verses 6, 13, 15; the word "us" in verse 14. Notice "we" in Acts 21:1 and through the chapter, to Jerusalem.

It evidently took five days in a sailing ship across that Aegean Sea.

Note, "upon the first day of the week" it was, the disciples "came together to break bread." That indicates that in Troas, at least, it was a custom to meet together to break bread, to take the Lord's Supper every Sunday. That was on the first day of every week. This is the only such reference in the New Testament. If the church at Troas took the Lord's Supper the first day of every week, it still may not have been the general custom. The frequency is left undetermined in every command about the Lord's Supper.

In giving the Lord's Supper the most Jesus said was, "This do in remembrance of me" (Luke 22:19). And in the discussion of the Lord's Supper in I Corinthians 11:25-27, the instruction is, "This do ye, as oft as ye drink it, in remembrance of me. For as often as ye eat this bread, and drink this cup, ye do shew the Lord's death till he come." Where the Bible is silent, we should be silent. There are no rules about how often we should take the Lord's Supper. Certainly it should never be treated as an insignificant routine, and Christians should not go through the form without feeling the blessed teaching and reminder of the sufferings of Christ for us. And certainly we should not neglect and go too long without remembering His death and marking it for each other by this simple ceremony. Doubtless the church at Troas was a good example, and the mention of their meeting on the first day of the week to break bread may be a hint that when we enter into the matter heartily and with sweet gratitude, such a frequent observance is pleasing to God. But there is no command that the Lord's Supper is to be taken Sunday morning or Sunday night or that it need be on the first day of the week at all.

Paul preached, "and continued his speech until midnight." There were many lights and possibly that used up much of the oxygen and made people sleepy. Or possibly the lights hurt the young man's eyes. So in a window of this upper chamber crowded with people where Paul preached till midnight, sat Eutychus and he fell fast asleep. He "fell down from the third loft, and was taken up dead." Paul brought him back to life. Or perhaps the Scripture means that he was apparently dead or insensible to things around him, for Paul said "his life is in him." So at midnight when they came back into the upper chamber and "had broken bread, and eaten," they talked even to daybreak and Paul departed.

A man with a burning heart may be excused if he talks

long. A man without a burning heart ought not to afflict others. The indication is that physical conditions led the young man to fall asleep, not boredom. We think it a sin for a preacher not to be interesting and not to speak with zeal and joy or indignation, or other holy emotion!

VERSES 13–16:

13 ¶ And we went before to ship, and sailed unto Assos, there intending to take in Paul: for so had he appointed, minding himself to go afoot.

14 And when he met with us at Assos, we took him in, and came to Mitylene.

15 And we sailed thence, and came the next *day* over against Chios; and the next *day* we arrived at Samos, and tarried at Trogyllium; and the next *day* we came to Miletus.

16 For Paul had determined to sail by Ephesus, because he would not spend the time in Asia: for he hasted, if it were possible for him, to be at Jerusalem the day of Pentecost.

From Troas to Miletus

Paul had preached till midnight, had brought the young man Eutychus to life again, had talked on to daylight. Now with a burning in his soul he needs to be alone. So Paul's companions went to the ship and sailed on to Assos while Paul walked across the peninsula, perhaps twenty-five miles, and met the ship there and they took him in! Then they stopped at Mitylene on the island of Lesbos in the Aegean Sea, then by the island of Chios and to Samos and they passed by the gulf on which Ephesus was built and stopped at the town of Trogylium. Paul "had determined to sail by Ephesus." There were too many demands on his time. He was intent on being at Jerusalem by Pentecost. Yet he had a great concern to speak again to the elders of the church at Ephesus. So they stopped at Miletus and sent word for the Ephesian elders to come there to meet him, perhaps seventy-five or eighty miles away by boat and further by land. There he could talk to these assembled elders without going to any homes or spending further time among the multitude who loved him in the great city of Ephesus.

VERSES 17–31:

17 ¶ And from Miletus he sent to Ephesus, and called the elders of the church.

18 And when they were come to him, he said unto them, Ye know, from the first day that I came into Asia, after what manner I have been with you at all seasons,

19 Serving the Lord with all humility of mind, and with many tears, and temptations, which befell me by the lying in wait of the Jews:

20 *And* how I kept back nothing that was profitable *unto you*, but have shewed you, and have taught you publicly, and from house to house,

21 Testifying both to the Jews, and also to the Greeks, repentance toward God, and faith toward our Lord Jesus Christ.

22 And now, behold, I go bound in the spirit unto Jerusalem, not knowing the things that shall befall me there:

23 Save that the Holy Ghost witnesseth in every city, saying that bonds and afflictions abide me.

24 But none of these things move me, neither count I my life dear unto myself, so that I might finish my course with joy, and the ministry, which I have received of the Lord Jesus, to testify the gospel of the grace of God.

25 And now, behold, I know that ye all, among whom I have gone preaching the kingdom of God, shall see my face no more.

26 Wherefore I take you to record this day, that I *am* pure from the blood of all *men*.

27 For I have not shunned to declare unto you all the counsel of God.

28 ¶ Take heed therefore unto yourselves, and to all the flock, over the which the Holy Ghost hath made you overseers, to feed the church of God, which he hath purchased with his own blood.

29 For I know this, that after my departing shall grievous wolves enter in among you, not sparing the flock.

30 Also of your own selves shall men arise, speaking perverse things, to draw away disciples after them.

31 Therefore watch, and remember, that by the space of three years I ceased not to warn every one night and day with tears.

Paul Addresses the Ephesian Elders

When the elders of the church at Ephesus came to him, he reviewed his three years' stay with them. He reminded them of his tears and trials (vs. 19). He had kept back nothing that was profitable from them. The thoroughness of his teaching is indicated by the letter to the Ephesians which goes into deep and rich things of God.

He had taught them "publickly, and from house to house." He had followed the plan of the disciples at Jerusalem, "And daily in the temple, and in every house, they ceased not to teach and preach Jesus Christ" (Acts 5:42). He did not follow the plan of so many preachers--to spend the morning in his comfortable study and the afternoon visiting the saints.

His work had been complicated because he must take the Gospel to the divergent groups, "both to the Jews, and also to the Greeks," but the same plan of salvation "repentance toward God, and faith toward our Lord Jesus Christ" (vs. 21).

But this is the farewell address. He is going to Jerusalem with some unrest of soul, some warning. They have not been mentioned as the warnings of the brethren in Tyre and Caesarea, as the next chapter will tell us, but the Holy Ghost had witnessed in every city that bonds and afflictions were ahead and that in connection with his trip toward Jerusalem!

But Paul was not afraid of bonds and afflictions. He was not afraid to die. He had come so close to it many times! He could say, "I die daily" (I Cor. 15:31). His great ambition was to "finish my course with joy, and the ministry, which I have received of the Lord Jesus, to testify the gospel of the grace of God." Hence the triumphant praise in II Timothy 4:6-8:

> "For I am now ready to be offered, and the time of my departure is at hand. I have fought a good fight, I have finished my course, I have

kept the faith: Henceforth there is laid up for me
a crown of righteousness, which the Lord, the
righteous judge, shall give me at that day: and
not to me only, but unto all them also that love
his appearing."

And we ought also to understand from his letters to the
Corinthians, and from Acts 24:17 that Paul hoped by bringing gifts to the poor in Jerusalem to win the favor of some
of the Jews and there have some of the proper respect which
had been his before he was converted.

Paul was the noblest of God's good men, but he was still
human. His motives were good, and he wanted to please
God, but he also wanted to win the favor of the Jews he
loved so much, and to get to preach to them. As Peter was
subject to error in compromising at Corinth, described in
Galatians 2:11-14, so Paul may have had a blind spot about
Jerusalem, so badly did he want to preach some to his people there.

But Paul has had some light from Heaven. He says, "I
know that ye all...shall see my face no more." He had
some inward pressure not to go by Ephesus. And now he
tells these elders of Ephesus he will never see even them
again!

Paul then gives a farewell charge to these preachers.
The Holy Ghost had made them overseers of the church.
They must remember that every Christian is purchased
with the blood of Christ. They must expect that after Paul
should leave "shall grievous wolves enter in among you, not
sparing the flock." And he warned them, "Also of your own
selves shall men arise, speaking perverse things, to draw
away disciples after them." Did he not know how Barnabas
had left him to please and use John Mark? Did he not know
how Alexander had left the faith or would do so (I Tim.
1:20), and do Paul much harm (II Tim. 4:14)? And in Rome
Paul would find "that all they which are in Asia be turned

away from me; of whom are Phygellus and Hermogenes" (II Tim. 1:15). That would include the people in Ephesus! And then in Rome he would say, "For Demas hath forsaken me, having loved this present world" (II Tim. 4:10).

Some think that a falling away in doctrine and life is a sign of the approaching end of the age. Not so! It is simply an evidence of the frailty of all our human hearts, of the inherent wickedness in the carnal nature which all of us have! As churches today fall into worldliness and sin and then into modernism and wicked unbelief, denying the faith, so then did some of the churches unto which Paul preached. Not a one of them is left today except that monstrosity at Rome which is the successor of that little group of devout Christians to whom Paul addressed his epistle to Rome! Every preacher who is faithful and strong will find, as Paul did, that some of those who love him will turn away from him and from the Gospel he preaches. So the churches in Galatia turned to legalism. So in Corinth many learned to prefer Apollos and Peter. The normal course of Christianity is not only for the Spirit-filled preacher to have riots and abuse and persecution and trouble, but for him to find with grief and disappointment that many who claim the Lord then do not remain true to Christ and loyal to those who win them.

I wonder how startled were those elders to whom Paul made this plain prediction. Some of these very men themselves would divide the churches, and selfishly "seek to draw away disciples after them."

Oh, Paul could speak with holy boldness. And the two great verses in this chapter which describe Paul's ministry are verses 20 and 31. Not only had he taught them everything needful, publicly and from house to house, but he reminded them that "by the space of three years I ceased not to warn every one night and day with tears." Notice this warning. Let's consider the ministry of Paul in Ephesus.

1. It was in public, preaching in the synagogue and the school of Tyrannus and elsewhere.

2. It was house to house, personal visitation, speaking to families, groups, individuals.

3. His ministry covered everything needful to Christian life and usefulness. "The whole council of God."

4. It was night and day. An unceasing time of warning, pleading.

5. It was a ministry with floods of tears, compassion, concern, indignation, pleading, burden! I do not wonder that he could say to them, "Wherefore I take you to record this day, that I am pure from the blood of all men." Oh, thou God of the Bible and our Saviour Jesus Christ, who sent Paul, create in us the same steadfastness, urgency, concern, sacrifice, labor and tears!

VERSES 32–38:

32 And now, brethren, I commend you to God, and to the word of his grace, which is able to build you up, and to give you an inheritance among all them which are sanctified.

33 I have coveted no man's silver, or gold, or apparel.

34 Yea, ye yourselves know, that these hands have ministered unto my necessities, and to them that were with me.

35 I have shewed you all things, how that so labouring ye ought to support the weak, and to re- member the words of the Lord Jesus, how he said, It is more blessed to give than to receive.

36 ¶ And when he had thus spoken, he kneeled down, and prayed with them all.

37 And they all wept sore, and fell on Paul's neck, and kissed him,

38 Sorrowing most of all for the words which he spake, that they should see his face no more. And they accompanied him unto the ship.

Paul's Good-By to Ephesian Elders

Now Paul had some closing words. He commends them to God. That is, Paul depends upon the Lord to help these preachers carry on the work that Paul had begun. And then he commends them "to the word of his grace." They have the Old Testament. They will have Paul's letters. These are "the word of his grace." And the Word of God is able to build them up and to give them an inheritance "among all them which are sanctified."

There is a Bible doctrine of sanctification. It does not mean necessarily sinlessness, but it means set apart. The term is used of Christians in such a way that we know that there are three stages of sanctification.

1. The death of Christ, paying for our sins, sets us, who trust in that blood, apart forever for Christ. "...we are sanctified through the offering of the body of Jesus Christ once for all" (Heb. 10:10). And again, "For by one offering he hath perfected for ever them that are sanctified" (Heb. 10:14). The one all-sufficient price for salvation has been paid. One who accepts Christ and depends upon Him is already set apart forever for God. His reaching Heaven and eternal blessedness will not depend now on anything he does or does not do. He is already born of God, set apart for God; he is made a partaker of the divine nature. Saved people, in this sense, are scripturally sanctified.

2. But there is a sense in which these Ephesian elders would be sanctified by the Word of God. So in the high priestly prayer Jesus prayed, "Sanctify them through thy truth: thy word is truth" (John 17:17). As one masters the Word of God and becomes mastered, colored, moved, hounded and driven by the Word, so one becomes set apart for God in a peculiar sense. He fits another world better than this world. So people are sanctified by the Word, Paul says.

3. Practical sanctification will be finished when at the rapture we are changed in a moment and raised incorruptible and immortal (I Cor. 15:52, 53).

But the lesson to these Ephesian elders is a lesson for all

of us. We are to be sanctified as we become mastered by the Word of God.

But Paul has a holy honor at stake. Even at Corinth some had risen against him and had slandered him and Paul had felt a need to defend himself there, as we see in II Corinthians 10 and 11. And some at Corinth had evidently talked about his preaching for money, for he had written rather indignantly saying, "Behold, the third time I am ready to come to you; and I will not be burdensome to you: for I seek not your's, but you: for the children ought not to lay up for the parents, but the parents for the children." And he asked them, "Did I make a gain of you by any of them whom I sent unto you?" (II Cor. 12:14, 17). And before that in I Corinthians he had written:

"Even so hath the Lord ordained that they which preach the gospel should live of the gospel. But I have used none of these things: neither have I written these things, that it should be so done unto me: for it were better for me to die, than that any man should make my glorying void.... What is my reward then? Verily that, when I preach the gospel, I may make the gospel of Christ without charge, that I abuse not my power in the gospel."--I Cor. 9:14, 15, 18.

So Paul felt he must make it so clear that when some of these started to go astray and lead disciples after themselves, they would remember, "I have coveted no man's silver, or gold, or apparel. Yea, ye yourselves know, that these hands have ministered unto my necessities, and to them that were with me." And then he calls to their remembrance a statement about Jesus Christ which is handed down to us here but is not quoted in the Gospels: "It is more blessed to give than to receive."

Ah, Paul, some would indeed accuse you of preaching for

money. So they have accused every honest preacher who preached with power down through the years! And like God's best preachers, you who are willing to do without the proper support so that you might make your boast that you were not chargeable to any man, could not be subject to any man's rules about your preaching!

Then they had a prayer meeting. And even as orientals do today, they hugged each other and kissed the cheek and sorrowed, because it was good-by forever. They would never see Paul again. And then these preachers accompanied Paul to the ship at Miletus, and down the coast he would go to Tyre and Caesarea, then up to Jerusalem.

ACTS 21

VERSES 1-3:

AND it came to pass, that after we were gotten from them, and had launched, we came with a straight course unto Coos, and the *day* following unto Rhodes, and from thence unto Patara:

2 And finding a ship sailing over unto Phenicia, we went aboard, and set forth.

3 Now when we had discovered Cyprus, we left it on the left hand, and sailed into Syria, and landed at Tyre: for there the ship was to unlade her burden.

From Miletus to Tyre

The trip toward Jerusalem continued by ship along the coast of the Mediterranean. First, they came "with a straight course unto Coos," then to the large island Rhodes. It would be well to follow this on your map. You will see that the Aegean Sea is full of islands. Coos, or Cos, is an island northwest of Cnidus. Rhodes is a larger island. And then they went to the city Patara, on the coast. There they changed ships and found a ship "sailing over unto Phenicia." That is the general area around Tyre and Sidon. Their port was Tyre. They sailed south of the island of Cyprus but within sight of land, leaving it on the left hand and came to the east end of the Mediterranean to the city of Tyre. This ship carried passengers, but principally it had a cargo to unload at Tyre. They would take another ship down the coast to Ptolemais, then to Caesarea and then they would go overland to Jerusalem.

One must be impressed with a vast commerce around and across the Mediterranean Sea. That sea put Rome in comparatively close touch with southern Europe, Asia Minor and Africa. Since there were no railroads, no automobiles or trucks, then sailing ships were the most important means of communication between countries. They had no mariner's compass but steered by the sun and by the stars.

So a ship usually stayed in harbor during winter and long periods of bad weather (Acts 27:13) and counted a good deal on landmarks, islands, shore lines, etc. So here the sailing is by short sections between known landmarks, and they "discovered Cyprus," though they did not land there but passed by it (vs. 3).

VERSES 4–6:

4 And finding disciples, we tarried there seven days: who said to Paul through the Spirit, that he should not go up to Jerusalem.

5 And when we had accomplished those days, we departed and went our way; and they all brought us on our way, with wives and children, till we were out of the city: and we kneeled down on the shore, and prayed.

6 And when we had taken our leave one of another, we took ship; and they returned home again.

The Holy Spirit Clearly Forbids Paul's Trip to Jerusalem

At Tyre Paul and others found disciples and stayed seven days. And these Christians "said to Paul through the Spirit, that he should not go up to Jerusalem." As the Scofield Reference Bible says, "Not, as in Acts 20:23, a warning of danger, but now an imperative command."

God's warnings about Paul's going to Jerusalem had extended for a long time.

1. When he first went back to Jerusalem after his conversion (Acts 22:17-21).

2. Repeatedly, as he told the Ephesian elders at Miletus, "...the Holy Ghost witnesseth in every city, saying that bonds and afflictions abide me."

3. Now the Holy Spirit through other Christians tells Paul plainly "that he should not go up to Jerusalem."

4. The next warning comes from Agabus in verses 10 and 11. Paul surely ought to have heeded these warnings.

He excused himself thus. He was taking gifts to the poor saints at Jerusalem. He was willing to be bound or to die for Jesus. He still wanted to witness to the Jews, although he had been sent primarily to the Gentiles. So he went headlong on to Jerusalem and God permitted and overruled it.

Those warnings of impending imprisonment and persecution were given only because Paul ought not to have gone. God had in a vision a man at Macedonia pleading with him to come over into Macedonia and help them. So Paul was led of God to go to Philippi, though there he was beaten and put in jail. God did not warn him against Lystra, though he was stoned at Lystra and left for dead. No, the warnings of God about Jerusalem meant that he should not go, meant the same as the plain command of verse 4, "that he should not go up to Jerusalem."

Paul and his party stayed some days at Tyre with these Christians. They must have felt, as did the Ephesian elders, that they would see Paul no more, so with wives and children, whole families came out to the seashore and there they had a prayer meeting and, we suppose, a tearful goodby. The words "when we had taken our leave one of another" indicate very fervent individual farewells. Then into the ship went Paul and his companions and proceeded.

VERSES 7-9:

7 And when we had finished *our* course from Tyre, we came to Ptolemais, and saluted the brethren, and abode with them one day.

8 And the next *day* we that were of Paul's company departed, and came unto Cesarea; and we entered into the house of Philip the evangelist, which was *one* of the seven; and abode with him.

9 And the same man had four daughters, virgins, which did prophesy.

A Noble Deacon's Spirit-Filled Daughters

Here Paul and his company were invited into the home of Philip the evangelist. He was "one of the seven" deacons selected in Acts 6:5 because he was "full of the Holy Ghost and wisdom" (Acts 6:3). A story of Philip's evangelism is told in Acts 8:5-40. He had a blessed, great revival at Samaria, winning thousands, we suppose. He won the Ethiopian eunuch. The Scripture does not tell of his other work, but he is called here "the evangelist." That man, filled with the Spirit, had four daughters, virgins, "which did prophesy." But to prophesy means one speaking for God in the power of the Holy Spirit (See Acts 2:17, 18). So Spirit-filled Philip had four Spirit-filled daughters! How blessed! He was a soul winner and so were these, for to be filled with the Spirit meant witnessing for Jesus with power (Acts 1:8). They were not preachers for that is forbidden women in I Corinthians 14:34, 35 and I Timothy 2:11, 12.

It is surprising and sad that the children of great men of God are often poor Christians. Most of the twelve sons of Jacob were not godly men. We hear of nothing of importance from the sons of Moses. We never hear of the sons of Joshua. Of Samuel, the mighty prophet, we are told, "And his sons walked not in his ways, but turned aside after lucre, and took bribes, and perverted judgment" (I Sam. 8:3), a strange thing since Samuel as a child had been given God's message of condemnation for Eli because "the sons of Eli were sons of Belial; they knew not the Lord," and he did not restrain them (I Sam. 2:12). Most of David's sons were wild and wicked. Solomon started well but at old age went into idolatry. Ammon was guilty of rape, Absalom of murder and rebellion, Adonijah of rebellion and we never hear of a son of Elijah or Elisha or Samson or Isaiah or Jeremiah. Here Philip's godly, witnessing daughters are mentioned, but there is never a word about any child of

Peter or James or John or other apostles doing any service for God! Ah, it is a rare gift of God and rare faithfulness of God's anointed preacher when his children walk in the ways of the Spirit-filled, soul-winning Christians.

The Lord made special revelations to Abraham, "For I know him, that he will command his children and his household after him, and they shall keep the way of the Lord..." (Gen. 18:19). The way Isaac followed Abraham is blessed. In Hanani, the seer, who boldly reproved the good King Asa because he relied on the king of Syria instead of relying on the Lord (II Chron. 16:7-10), was followed by Jehu, the son of Hanani, who rebuked Jehoshaphat, the son of Asa, for yoking up with King Ahab (II Chron. 19:1-3). Paul had no children and we suppose John the Baptist had none, but how blessed if Peter had sons who preached like Peter.

We suppose Philip had no sons. But what a rich heritage he had in seven godly daughters, Spirit-filled virgins, who prophesied in Jesus' name and witnessed for Him.

VERSES 10–13:

10 And as we tarried *there* many days, there came down from Judea a certain prophet, named Agabus.

11 And when he was come unto us, he took Paul's girdle, and bound his own hands and feet, and said, Thus saith the Holy Ghost, So shall the Jews at Jerusalem bind the man that owneth this girdle, and shall deliver *him* into the hands of the Gentiles.

12 And when we heard these things, both we, and they of that place, besought him not to go up to Jerusalem

13 Then Paul answered, What mean ye to weep and to break mine heart? for I am ready not to be bound only, but also to die at Jerusalem for the name of the Lord Jesus.

The Prophet Agabus Warns Paul

Agabus is a prophet who lived in Jerusalem. We met him in Acts 11:28 when he came to Antioch and "signified by the

Spirit that there should be great dearth throughout all the world: which came to pass in the days of Claudius Caesar." A prophet is simply one who speaks in the power of the Holy Spirit and sometimes the Holy Spirit reveals future events. At Pentecost the disciples were filled with the Holy Spirit and prophesied according to Acts 2:16-18. Judas and Silas, "being prophets also themselves, exhorted the brethren with many words, and confirmed them" (Acts 15:32). So witnessing for Jesus would sometimes include public speaking or preaching, but not always. To prophesy meant that they have supernatural wisdom. So the mob and soldiers struck the blindfolded Jesus and asked Him saying, "Prophesy, who is it that smote thee?" (Luke 22:64). There are many virtues and many spiritual gifts, but all should seek to prophesy, that is, to witness for Jesus in the power of the Holy Spirit. "Follow after charity, and desire spiritual gifts, but rather that ye may prophesy" (I Cor. 14:1). And so Christians are commanded, "Wherefore, brethren, covet to prophesy..." (I Cor. 14:39).

This Spirit-filled man, Agabus, then had had revealed to him there would come a great drought. Now he has it revealed to him that if Paul goes to Jerusalem, he will be bound and delivered to the Gentiles. And remember he said, "Thus saith the Holy Ghost." To prophesy is to speak that which is given by the Holy Spirit. In this case it was prophecy in the sense of foretelling the future.

Now there began a clamor that Paul should not go to Jerusalem. "...both we, and they of that place, besought him not to go up to Jerusalem." "We" here includes Luke and the group mentioned in Acts 20:4. And those who lived at Caesarea (vs. 8) with whom Paul's party were guests, besought Paul also. He should not go to Jerusalem.

Some were weeping, but Paul was inflexible, would not be persuaded. Thus he went on to imprisonment, two or three sad and relatively empty years before he got to Rome and before he could resume a large ministry.

VERSES 14–17:

14 And when he would not be persuaded, we ceased, saying, The will of the Lord be done.

15 And after those days we took up our carriages, and went up to Jerusalem.

16 There went with us also *cer-tain* of the disciples of Cesarea, and brought with them one Mnason of Cyprus, an old disciple, with whom we should lodge.

17 And when we were come to Jerusalem, the brethren received us gladly.

Paul Arrives at Jerusalem

Paul would not be persuaded. So the party went with him. They trusted his leadership.

"We took up our carriages," that is, their baggage. So from Caesarea on the seaport they went overland to Jerusalem, only sixty or seventy miles away. Some of the Christians at Caesarea went with them, and one old Christian, Mnason of Cyprus, had a home at Jerusalem where they would stay, and the brethren at Jerusalem received them gladly. Word of Paul's missionary journeys had spread everywhere, and Christians could not but be glad that the Gospel had been so well received and so many thousands had found Christ.

VERSES 18–26:

18 And the *day* following Paul went in with us unto James; and all the elders were present.

19 And when he had saluted them, he declared particularly what things God had wrought among the Gentiles by his ministry.

20 And when they heard *it,* they glorified the Lord, and said unto him, Thou seest, brother, how many thousands of Jews there are which believe; and they are all zealous of the law:

21 And they are informed of thee, that thou teachest all the Jews which are among the Gentiles to forsake Moses, saying that they ought not to circumcise *their* children, neither to walk after the customs.

22 What is it therefore? the multitude must needs come together: for they will hear that

thou art come.

23 Do therefore this that we say to thee: We have four men which have a vow on them;

24 Them take, and purify thyself with them, and be at charges with them, that they may shave *their* heads: and all may know that those things, whereof they were informed concerning thee, are nothing; but *that* thou thyself also walkest orderly, and keepest the law.

25 As touching the Gentiles which believe, we have written *and* concluded that they observe no such thing, save only that they keep themselves from *things* offered to idols, and from blood, and from strangled, and from fornication.

26 Then Paul took the men, and the next day purifying himself with them entered into the temple, to signify the accomplishment of the days of purification, until that an offering should be offered for every one of them.

Paul, to Pacify Jewish Christians and Other Jews, Takes a Jewish Vow

Now came the great temptation unto Paul, a temptation to which he gave way. Note some things we think are wrong about Paul's culminating his Jewish vow in the temple, offering sacrifices and appeasing these Judaizing Christians.

1. The motive was wrong. He was asked to do it to please and pacify thousands of Jews who were "all zealous of the law." These had heard rightly that Paul was teaching the Jews where he had been "that they ought not to circumcise their children, neither to walk after the customs." And thus he was to leave this impression among these Judaizers; "and all may know that those things, whereof they were informed concerning thee, are nothing; but that thou thyself also walkest orderly, and keepest the law." These Jewish Christians found it difficult, living in Jerusalem where the priests and the temple and the sacrifices were, to clearly turn loose of all these things. Now, to pacify unconverted Jews, they wanted Paul to give them some ammunition, and to thus undo some of the things he had done in telling people that the law was fulfilled. I say the motive

was wrong. He was trying to please people instead of God.

2. It was wrong also because the Jews wanted to leave the impression, and Paul allowed them to do so, that Jews were required to keep the law, even though Gentiles were not. In verse 25 they told Paul, "As touching the Gentiles which believe, we have written and concluded that they observe no such thing...." And yet they want Paul to keep these ceremonial laws! But Paul himself has written his own converts in Galatia (probably wrote them at Corinth before starting back on this journey to Jerusalem!), assuring these Galatian Christians, "There is neither Jew nor Greek, there is neither bond nor free, there is neither male nor female: for ye are all one in Christ Jesus. And if ye be Christ's, then are ye Abraham's seed, and heirs according to the promise" (Gal. 3:28, 29). The requirements for Jewish Christians and Gentile Christians were not different. The Jewish Christians were freed from the law the same as Gentile Christians. And the Gentile Christians were spiritually Abraham's seed, as were the Jewish Christians. For Paul now to leave the impression that the Jewish ceremonies were proper for Jews but not for Gentiles is contrary to the clear revelation God had given him and us. The ceremonial law had already served its purpose. "Wherefore the law was our schoolmaster to bring us unto Christ..." (Gal. 3:24). And again, "Wherefore then serveth the law? It was added because of transgressions, TILL THE SEED SHOULD COME to whom the promise was made..." (Gal. 3:19).

To go back to the law was to turn again "to the weak and beggarly elements" (Gal. 4:9). Later, Paul would write to the Christians at Colosse, "Let no man therefore judge you in meat, or in drink, or in respect of an holyday, or of the new moon, or of the sabbath days: Which are a shadow of things to come; but the body is of Christ" (Col. 2:16, 17). And in verse 14 above he had just said that Christ had forgiven all their trespasses, "blotting out the handwriting of ordinances that was against us, which was contrary to us, and took it out of the way, nailing it to his cross." So since the cross of Christ fulfilled all the prophecies and types and shadows, no one now is to be subject to the rules of the ceremonies of the law!

3. It was wrong for Paul to enter the temple, observe the rules of the Nazarite vow, offer lambs for sacrifice, etc., because thus he gave prestige and power to things that God had clearly forsaken. The temple was no longer the house of God. Jesus had already wept over Jerusalem and announced to it, "Behold, your house is left unto you desolate" (Luke 13:35; Matt. 23:38). Jesus had already announced that "the hour cometh, when ye shall neither in this mountain, nor yet at Jerusalem, worship the Father" but in Spirit and in truth (John 4:21). When Jesus died on the cross, "behold, the veil of the temple was rent in twain from the top to the bottom" (Matt. 27:51). The holy place in that temple was no longer set apart as the sanctuary of God on earth and we may be sure that the Shekinah glory dwelt there no more!

The temple of the Spirit of God is now the human body, and there is a temple in Heaven. God's worship is not to be identified particularly with a place. Paul was wrong to count that temple the same holy place the Jews counted it.

And the sacrifices are now done. The book of Hebrews goes into great detail proving that the old covenant is superseded, that the Levitical priesthood is superseded by the priesthood of Christ, that the sacrifices of the ceremonial law are now fulfilled in the crucifixion of Christ. And the contrast of the priest standing ministering an offering, ofttimes the same sacrifices which can never take away sins, is contrasted with the once-for-all sacrifice of Christ (Heb. 10:10-12). And we are told, "For by one offering he hath perfected for ever them that are sanctified" (Heb. 10:14). God has now a new covenant with people to put this law in their hearts and to remember their sins and iniquities no more. And "now where remission of these is, there is no more offering for sin" (Heb. 10:18). When Christ died, then no one ever has a right to offer any other sacrifice. We now do not need the shadow; we have Christ. We do not now need the schoolmaster; we have the lesson completed that the law has been teaching. To indicate that these priests at the temple were still the priests of God, that the temple was still the dwelling place of God on earth, that the lambs or other animals offered for sacrifice now had some meaning still as a legitimate form of worship--all that would suit and please Christ-rejecting Judaism. It is not New Testament Christianity. It taught what is contrary to the Gospel.

When we see how deep-seated in the consciousness of Paul and of Peter (Gal. 2:11-14) and these Christians at Jerusalem are the ceremonies and priesthood and sacrifices and mores of the ceremonial law, we can see why the extensive treatment given the subject in the book of Hebrews, and how God was trying to get them ready for the utter destruction of Jerusalem and the scattering of Jews to the ends of the world.

A Jewish rabbi told his daughter, and she told me with tears, that now the Jews had no genealogies for which they could know who was a proper priest; they had no temple; they could have no sacrifices. Why did God leave it so Jews can have no temple, no priesthood, no sacrifices? God is done with all of that! Christ is the sacrifice and Christ is the Priest. The temple is the human body, and God wants people to worship in spirit and in truth, not in Jerusalem nor in some particular sacred place.

And let us, then, see how sensitive is the heart to temptation on the lines of our own denominations, our religious practices, our holy places, our elaborate buildings and organs, our rituals. How God must hate the formal worship services, the candles, the altar cloths, the crucifixes, the robes and statues which delight the sensual heart of man!

Here are four men, evidently good men, Christians. They have taken a vow, verse 23 tells us, and I suppose it is the same vow of a Nazarite, a certain period of time set apart for sacrifice and special service for God such as Paul took, we think, at Cenchrea (Acts 18:18). Now they have fulfilled their time. According to Numbers 6:18 they are to shave their head at the door of the tabernacle or temple, take their hair and put it in the fire under the sacrifice or peace offerings.

But first each man must offer his offering, "one he lamb of the first year without blemish for a burnt-offering, and one ewe lamb of the first year without blemish for a sin-offering, and one ram without blemish for peace-offerings, And a basket of unleavened bread, cakes of fine flour mingled with oil, and wafers of unleavened bread anointed with oil, and their meat-offering, and their drink-offerings. And the priest shall bring them before the LORD, and shall offer his sin-offering, and his burnt-offering: And he shall offer the ram for a sacrifice of peace-offerings unto the Lord, with the basket of unleavened bread: the priest shall offer also his meat-offering, and his drink-offering" (Num. 6:14-17). And then each man will be ready to shave his head there at the door of the temple and burn the hair in the fire under the sacrifice. But then after certain ceremonies the priest would relieve these men of their Nazarite vow, now fulfilled!

It was expensive, it would require each of the men to have a number of animals. It would take some seven days. And it would thus acknowledge the authority of the temple and the unconverted priesthood and acknowledge the still binding authority of the Old Testament ceremonial law. And that was wrong.

O Paul, you should have remembered what Peter said on this matter before. "Now therefore why tempt ye God, to put a yoke upon the neck of the disciples, which neither our fathers nor we were able to bear?" (Acts 15:10). And Peter had said properly that God now put no difference between the Gentiles and Jews (Acts 15:9).

VERSES 27–32:

27 And when the seven days were almost ended, the Jews which were of Asia, when they saw him in the temple, stirred up all the people, and laid hands on him,

28 Crying out, Men of Israel, help: This is the man, that teacheth all *men* every where against the people, and the law, and this place: and further brought Greeks also into the temple, and hath polluted this holy place.

29 (For they had seen before with him in the city Trophimus an Ephesian, whom they supposed that Paul had brought into the temple.)

30 And all the city was moved, and the people ran together: and they took Paul, and drew him out of the temple: and forthwith the doors were shut.

31 And as they went about to kill him, tidings came unto the chief captain of the band, that all Jerusalem was in an uproar:

32 Who immediately took soldiers and centurions, and ran down unto them: and when they saw the chief captain and the soldiers, they left beating of Paul.

Paul Seized in the Temple
by Unconverted Jews

By this time we have seen that there was a great deal of commerce and travel throughout the countries around the Mediterranean. Jerusalem was the center for the Jews. On the day of Pentecost "there were dwelling at Jerusalem Jews, devout men, out of every nation under heaven" (Acts 2:5), that is, temporarily staying there during the feast of the passover and of the unleavened bread, etc. Jews regularly went up to Jerusalem for some of the annual feasts as Paul himself felt he must in Acts 18:21. The Ethiopian eunuch had come up to Jerusalem to worship (Acts 8:27). The high priest at Jerusalem had sent Saul in his unconverted days, some two hundred miles north to Damascus to persecute Christians there (Acts 9:1, 2). So it is not surprising that at this season many Jews from the province of Asia and throughout the region where Paul has been preaching have come to Jerusalem as well as Paul and his own

companions in travel. Unconverted Jews all thought of Jerusalem as the center of God's worship on earth and came
when possible for the annual feast.

Some of these saw Paul and stirred up the people. They
said about him, with some truth, "This is the man, that
teacheth all men every where against the people, and the
law, and this place" (vs. 28). It was not true as they
charged that he "brought Greeks also into the temple."
They were shocked before when he associated with Gentiles,
and shocked particularly when he brought Trophimus, a
Gentile from Ephesus, in the city with him. The deep burning fires of Jewish nationalism and some ceremonial observance that led the mob to insist on Christ's crucifixion,
and that stoned Stephen in Acts 7, now caused them to seek
Paul and "they went about to kill him."

But there was a Roman detachment of soldiers here at
Jerusalem as always. The chief captain heard about the
mob and the uproar and took some soldiers and centurions
and here they came, armed soldiers to drive out the mob
and seize Paul from the hands of those who were beating
him! O Paul, you did not listen to the warning of the Holy
Spirit! Your love for Israel has led you to compromise and
hence to trouble.

VERSES 33–40:

33 Then the chief captain came
near, and took him, and commanded *him* to be bound with
two chains; and demanded who
he was, and what he had done.

34 And some cried one thing,
some another, among the multitude: and when he could not
know the certainty for the tumult, he commanded him to be
carried into the castle.

35 And when he came upon the
stairs, so it was, that he was
borne of the soldiers for the
violence of the people.

36 For the multitude of the
people followed after, crying,
Away with him.

37 And as Paul was to be led
into the castle, he said unto the

chief captain, May I speak unto thee? Who said, Canst thou speak Greek?

38 Art not thou that Egyptian, which before these days madest an uproar, and leddest out into the wilderness four thousand men that were murderers?

39 But Paul said, I am a man *which am* a Jew of Tarsus, *a city* in Cilicia, a citizen of no mean city: and, I beseech thee, suffer me to speak unto the people.

40 And when he had given him license, Paul stood on the stairs, and beckoned with the hand unto the people. And when there was made a great silence, he spake unto *them* in the Hebrew tongue, saying,

Paul, Bound With Chains, Identifies Himself as a Roman Citizen and Speaks

They bound Paul with two chains, one I suppose on his feet, one binding his hands behind him. The Roman government was efficient. They were accustomed to these troublemaking Jews. A little later the rebellion of these same Jews and others would lead to the destruction of Jerusalem and that the Jews would be scattered over the whole world, in A. D. 70, some ten years later.

What was it all about? Mobs are illogical, inflamed by passion. No one could tell the chief captain what the charges were, for certain, against Paul, because people did not agree. But the mob was still so violent in the attack on Paul that he was lifted up and carried by the soldiers (vs. 35). And the mob followed and screamed for Paul's death.

They went into the castle (we suppose the castle of Antonio, where the Roman garrison stayed, where Pilate had had his judgment hall, and the stone floor of it still preserved in Jerusalem as I saw in February 1962). "May I speak unto thee?" Paul said courteously. The man was astonished that Paul could speak in the koine Greek, the common Greek language spoken by intelligent people all over the Roman Empire. Wasn't Paul a certain Egyptian who had led four thousand men, murderers, into the wilderness in rebellion, before now?

Out-and-out Christians, soul winners, should get accustomed to wild tales. They said of Jesus that He threatened to destroy the temple at Jerusalem and rebuild it in three days, though what He had said referred to His own body. The owners of the slave girl had said about Paul and Silas, "These men, being Jews, do exceedingly trouble our city, And teach customs, which are not lawful for us to receive, neither to observe, being Romans" (Acts 16:20, 21). So in England it was widely spread that John Wesley received money from France to enlist men to support the pretender to the English throne, when he should make an invasion in England! Men in Chicago wrote slanderous falsehoods to Scotland about D. L. Moody. In England when Charlie Alexander, song leader for Torrey, was to marry an English girl, enemies said he had a wife in America! In a West Coast city, wicked men spread it widely and asked others to spread it, that I charged a thousand dollars a day for my services, that I had run off with a pastor's wife in Montana, etc. Satan is a liar and the father of lies. Spirit-filled soul winners may expect to be slandered and misunderstood.

No, Paul said he was a Jew of Tarsus and a Roman citizen there, so a man of culture and of standing. The chief captain was impressed, and allowed Paul to speak. So he stood on the stairs of the castle of Antonio, held his hand high until deathly stillness settled over the hateful mob below him, then Paul began to speak to them in the Hebrew tongue.

"The Hebrew tongue." Dr. Robert Young in his Analytical Concordance says, "The language spoken by the Jews in Palestine in the time of Christ. It might more accurately have been called Syro-Chaldee, being a mixture of the Aramaean of Daniel and Ezra with the ancient Hebrew." We generally call it simply Aramaic. Now in Palestine Israel is restoring the ancient Hebrew language, requires it in the schools, but in New Testament times Hebrew people used the Aramaic, a kindred language to the old Hebrew they had left. And so Paul began his defence before that mob. No doubt he still hoped to gain the friendship and fellowship of these Jews he loved so much, despite all the warnings God had given him.

ACTS 22

VERSES 1–5:

MEN, brethren, and fathers, hear ye my defence *which I make* now unto you.

2 (And when they heard that he spake in the Hebrew tongue to them, they kept the more silence: and he saith,)

3 I am verily a man *which am* a Jew, born in Tarsus, *a city* in Cilicia, yet brought up in this city at the feet of Gamaliel, *and* taught according to the perfect manner of the law of the fathers, and was zealous toward God, as ye all are this day.

4 And I persecuted this way unto the death, binding and delivering into prisons both men and women.

5 As also the high priest doth bear me witness, and all the estate of the elders: from whom also I received letters unto the brethren, and went to Damascus, to bring them which were there bound unto Jerusalem, for to be punished.

Paul's Defence as a Good Jew

Probably Paul had, in his mind, rehearsed many times the content of this message which he had so long hoped and planned to give to Jews in Jerusalem. He tried hard to show them that he himself was a good Jew, although a Christian. Note how careful his defence.

1. "Men, brethren." He claims kinship, racially and religiously with them.

2. "...and fathers." A term of reverence and respect for the members of the Sanhedrin, the chief priests and elders of the Jews, some of whom were present. This may have been a very customary form of address, like "Mr. Chairman, ladies and gentlemen." Stephen used the same words in his message, "Men, brethren, and fathers" (Acts 7:2).

3. "I am...a Jew," Paul said (vs. 3). A converted Jew is still a Jew; a better Jew than an unbelieving Jew. No one is a good Jew for failing to trust in the Jewish Messiah or failing to believe the Jewish prophets.

4. Yet Paul was "brought up in this city," Jerusalem. He was their fellow townsman.

5. Better yet, he was brought up "at the feet of Gamaliel." This Gamaliel, we are told in Acts 5:34, was "a Pharisee, named Gamaliel, a doctor of the law, had in reputation among all the people...." He was a reasonable man who persuaded the Sanhedrin not to kill Peter and John. To be trained in the law and Old Testament, the Scriptures and Jewish traditions and interpretations by the famous Gamaliel would prove Paul orthodox in background and education.

6. And Paul was "taught according to the perfect manner of the law of the fathers." He was a good student; he had been thoroughly taught.

7. And more than all that, he was "zealous toward God." Zealous in the same sense this mob of Jews were. He had been, in the past, as furious at these Christians, as determined to destroy this new sect of Christian believers, as the angry Jews themselves were. And he could prove it by the high priest himself who was probably present and by all the other chief Jewish leaders. Because from them he had begged and received letters to Damascus, that the synagogues there should turn over to him any Christians and he would have brought them bound to Jerusalem, to be punished. Oh, Paul had been reared and trained after the most orthodox manner, and he had been as zealous as they!

He earnestly tried to break down the prejudice of these Jews, to get them to listen to his testimony.

Oh, Paul felt he himself was freed from the ceremonial law by the freedom in Christ, but his heart attachment to his people made him one of them. He had said in his letter to the Christians at Corinth, "And unto the Jews I became as a Jew, that I might gain the Jews; to them that are under the law, as under the law, that I might gain them that are under the law" (I Cor. 9:20). All the powers of love and reasonableness were brought to mind.

I wonder if it came to Paul's mind here that as he had persecuted, so he was now persecuted. When he said he himself in the past was "zealous toward God, as ye all are this day. And I persecuted this way unto the death..." (vss. 3, 4), did he realize that he was now reaping what he had sown? But he was now the victim of the same persecuting zeal which had slain Stephen with his consent and would have slain others at Damascus.

These Jews, as Paul had already written to the Christians at Rome, were "concerning the gospel...enemies for your sakes: but as touching the election, they are beloved for the fathers' sakes" (Rom. 11:28). And we may understand Paul's fervor here better when we read his statement in Romans 9:1-5:

> "I say the truth in Christ, I lie not, my conscience also bearing me witness in the Holy Ghost, That I have great heaviness and continual sorrow in my heart. For I could wish that myself were accursed from Christ for my brethren, my kinsmen according to the flesh: Who are Israelites; to whom pertaineth the adoption, and the glory, and the covenants, and the giving of the law, and the service of God, and the promises; Whose are the fathers, and of whom as concerning the flesh Christ came, who is over all, God blessed for ever. Amen."

He understood their fanaticism for he had been a fanatic, too, even a murderous fanatic, and so he could say, "My heart's desire and prayer to God for Israel is, that they might be saved. For I bear them record that they have a zeal of God, but not according to knowledge. For they being ignorant of God's righteousness, and going about to establish their own righteousness, have not submitted themselves unto the righteousness of God" (Rom. 10:1-3).

And we need not think that Paul was insincere in speaking so reverently to these Jews and identifying himself so carefully with them. In II Corinthians 11:22 he said about certain Judaizing teachers, "Are they Hebrews? so am I. Are they Israelites? so am I. Are they the seed of Abraham? so am I." To the Galatian Christians, he properly boasted, "For ye have heard of my conversation in time past in the Jews' religion, how that beyond measure I persecuted the church of God, and wasted it: And profited in the Jews' religion above many my equals in mine own nation, being more exceedingly zealous of the traditions of my fathers" (Gal. 1:13, 14).

To the Christians at Philippi, he wrote, "Though I might also have confidence in the flesh. If any other man thinketh that he hath whereof he might trust in the flesh, I more: Circumcised the eighth day, of the stock of Israel, of the tribe of Benjamin, an Hebrew of the Hebrews; as touching the law, a Pharisee; Concerning zeal, persecuting the church; touching the righteousness which is in the law, blameless" (Phil. 3:4-6).

Paul contended always that the law was good and he was proud that to what light he had, he had been blameless and a zealous Jew. And he reminded Timothy, "And I thank Christ Jesus our Lord, who hath enabled me, for that he counted me faithful, putting me into the ministry; Who was before a blasphemer, and a persecutor, and injurious: but I obtained mercy, because I did it ignorantly in unbelief" (I Tim. 1:12, 13). Paul's persecution of Christians was committed "ignorantly in unbelief." He was always sorry for the sin, but he could boldly proclaim that he had been trying to live right according to what light he had till God stopped him on the road to Damascus. And many, many in this mob who were trying to kill him were zealous of the law, as he had been. And God had already revealed to Paul, as he wrote plainly in II Corinthians 3:13-15:

"And not as Moses, which put a vail over his

face, that the children of Israel could not stedfastly look to the end of that which is abolished:
But their minds were blinded: for until this day
remaineth the same vail untaken away in the
reading of the old testament; which vail is done
away in Christ. But even unto this day, when
Moses is read, the vail is upon their heart."

Yet despite their blindness, Paul loved them. He tried so
hard to win them, knowing that they were deceived in their
blind zeal, as he had been.

VERSES 6-10:

6 And it came to pass, that, as I made my journey, and was come nigh unto Damascus about noon, suddenly there shone from heaven a great light round about me.

7 And I fell unto the ground, and heard a voice saying unto me, Saul, Saul, why persecutest thou me?

8 And I answered, Who art thou, Lord? And he said unto me, I am Jesus of Nazareth, whom thou persecutest.

9 And they that were with me saw indeed the light, and were afraid; but they heard not the voice of him that spake to me.

10 And I said, What shall I do, Lord? And the Lord said unto me, Arise, and go into Damascus; and there it shall be told thee of all things which are appointed for thee to do.

Paul Tells of His Conversion

Compare the three accounts of Paul's conversion. That which God gives by inspiration in Acts 9:1-8; the record here of Paul's testimony before the crowd at Jerusalem; and the record in Acts 26:12-18, where we have the inspired account of what Paul said before Agrippa. We should remember that in Acts 22 and in Acts 26, we have simply an inspired and infallible record of what Paul said. We think Paul's statement was reliable, but we can permit slight dif-
ferences in the way the matter is stated. We know the rec-

ord in each case is infallibly correct in reporting what Paul said happened at his conversion. But in Acts, chapter 9, we have God Himself speaking about Paul's conversion and not simply God telling us what Paul said happened.

For example, the Bible, by divine inspiration, tells us what Satan said in Job 2:4--"Skin for skin, yea, all that a man hath will he give for his life." But Satan was lying about Job. We have the infallible report of what Satan said, but God did not say it was true. In Acts 5:38 we have the inspired record that Gamaliel said, "for if this counsel or this work be of men, it will come to nought." It is infallibly true that Gamaliel said that, but his statement is not always true. Sometimes false doctrine and false cults do prosper, as do Romanism, Christian Science, Mohammedanism, etc. In Paul's case we have an accurate report of what happened, told by a noble, good man. And we also believe that God, by inspiring Luke to write it down in the book of Acts, put His approval on Paul's testimony in both cases.

Note slight differences.

1. Both in Acts 22:6 and in Acts 26:13 it was "about noon," and "at midday" when Christ appeared to Paul on the road to Damascus. In Acts 9 the hour of the day is not told.

2. In Acts 9:7 we are told, "And the men which journeyed with him stood speechless, hearing a voice, but seeing no man." Here in Acts 22:9, Paul says, "They that were with me saw indeed the light, and were afraid; but they heard not the voice of him that spake to me." Dr. Scofield properly explains, "A contradiction has been imagined. The three statements should be taken together. The men heard the 'voice' as a sound (Gr. phone), but did not hear the 'voice' as articulating the words, 'Saul, Saul,' etc."

Here is told that wonderful story that Paul loved to remember and loved to tell. Jesus had suddenly spoken to him! There was "a great light round about me." And he heard the words, "Saul, Saul, why persecutest thou me?" He had immediately inquired, "Who art thou, Lord?" And Jesus had answered, "I am Jesus of Nazareth, whom thou persecutest." No doubt this was the time when Paul saw the resurrected Christ, as he witnessed in I Corinthians 15:8, "And last of all he was seen of me also, as of one born out of due time." Just as the Lord Jesus will be revealed to a rebellious, fanatical and blinded race of Jews at His Second Coming to the earth, so Jesus appeared to Paul who himself was such a Jew. I think in his testimony about the resurrected Christ, Paul had in mind Zechariah 12:10 and Zechariah 13:1, 6. Since he was familiar with the law, all this might have come to Paul's mind when suddenly at his conversion he saw the Saviour! So Paul was "born out of due time." Born prematurely as a special representative of the Jews. And the sight and the glory of the light and perhaps of the face of the resurrected Saviour blinded Paul for some days (vs. 11).

Surely, surely spiritually minded Jews ought to have been impressed with this true story of how Christ had personally appeared to Paul and proven Himself the Saviour. But they were not.

As any honest, openhearted Jew, zealous for the Word of God, ought to have done, Paul had said, "What shall I do, Lord?" Or as it is quoted in Acts 9:6, "Lord, what wilt thou have me to do?" And he was told to go to Damascus and there one would tell him what he must do.

VERSES 11-16:

11 And when I could not see for the glory of that light, being led by the hand of them that were with me, I came into Damascus.

12 And one Ananias, a devout man according to the law, having a good report of all the Jews which dwelt *there,*

13 Came unto me, and stood, and said unto me, Brother Saul, receive thy sight. And the same hour I looked up upon him.

14 And he said, The God of

our fathers hath chosen thee, that thou shouldest know his will, and see that Just One, and shouldest hear the voice of his mouth.

15 For thou shalt be his witness unto all men of what thou hast seen and heard.

16 And now why tarriest thou? arise, and be baptized, and wash away thy sins, calling on the name of the Lord.

Paul and Ananias at Damascus

Paul was blinded by the glory of the light, could not see and was led by the hand into Damascus. Then Ananias came to him and said, "Brother Saul, the Lord, even Jesus, that appeared unto thee in the way as thou camest, hath sent me, that thou mightest receive thy sight, and be filled with the Holy Ghost" (Acts 9:17). And we are told, "And immediately there fell from his eyes as it had been scales: and he received sight forthwith, and arose, and was baptized."

But I wonder if some weakness of the eyes did not consciously remind Paul that he had a personal commission from Christ? He usually had a helper write his letters as he dictated. Romans 16:22 says, "I Tertius, who wrote this epistle, salute you in the Lord." First Corinthians starts out, "Paul, called to be an apostle of Jesus Christ through the will of God, and Sosthenes our brother." I think the inspiration came to Paul, but Sosthenes perhaps wrote the words down in Paul's dictation. And II Corinthians started, "Paul, an apostle of Jesus Christ by the will of God, and Timothy our brother...." In Galatians 6:11 the King James Version says, "Ye see how large a letter I have written unto you with mine own hand." But in the Greek it is, "With how large letters I have written unto you with mine own hand." Dr. Scofield suggests that "now, having no amanuensis at hand, but urged by the spiritual danger of his dear Galatians, he writes, we cannot know with what pain and difficulty, with his own hand, in the 'large letters' his darkened vision compelled him to use."

He had reminded those Galatians of his temptation or trial in the flesh (Gal. 4:14). And he said, "For I bear you record, that, if it had been possible, ye would have plucked out your own eyes, and have given them to me" (Gal. 4:15). So God may have reminded Paul again and again of that blinding vision he had met on the road to Damascus.

Remember, Paul is telling the story of his conversion and related events, as that story was useful with these Jews, and remember that Paul was repeating in his own words this time what had happened, as it had been recorded in Acts 9. Ananias had been a devout man according to the Old Testament law, with a good reputation among Jews. He had come and said, "Brother Saul, receive thy sight." Compare that with the statement in Acts 9:17, "Brother Saul, the Lord, even Jesus, that appeared unto thee in the way as thou camest, hath sent me, that thou mightest receive thy sight, and be filled with the Holy Ghost." There is no contradiction. Paul is simply reporting the matter in his own words.

And note verse 16. Some have tried to use this Scripture as teaching that baptism is essential to salvation. God taught nothing like that in Acts 9:18 and He teaches nothing like that here in the recorded testimony of Paul. Paul was speaking to a Jewish group who all their lives had forms and ceremonies, symbols and figures and types. All the spiritually minded among these devout Jews knew that circumcision in the body ought to mean also a certain separation in heart. They knew that the lamb of sacrifice pictured the Lamb of God that would come. They knew that Moses was a prophet and that another prophet like him would appear that they must hear (Deut. 18:15). And they had asked John the Baptist, "Art thou that prophet?" (John 1:21). So they would readily understand that baptism was a figure or symbol of a spiritual truth. Jesus had used that kind of language all the time. He had said, "I am the bread which came down from heaven" (John 6:41). He had said, "I am the door of the sheep" (John 10:7). Jesus had said regarding the bread broken at the first communion supper, "This is my body." Zealous Jews were accustomed to figures and object lessons and likenesses in religious ceremonies. In Acts 22:16, "Wash away thy sins," is certainly figurative language.

So about baptism in Romans 6:4 and 5: "Therefore we are buried with him by baptism into death: that like as Christ was raised up from the dead by the glory of the Father, even so we also should walk in newness of life. For if we have been planted together in the likeness of his death, we shall be also in the likeness of his resurrection." In baptism we are "planted...in the likeness of his death," and we are raised "in the likeness of his resurrection." And in I Peter 3:20 and 21 we are told, "Eight souls were saved by water. The like figure whereunto even baptism doth also now save us (not the putting away of the filth of the flesh, but the answer of a good conscience toward God,) by the resurrection of Jesus Christ." Baptism is a "like figure" of the way we are saved, "by the resurrection of Jesus Christ." Baptism is a picture of the resurrection and so a figure or a likeness of the way we are saved by the resurrection of Christ, in whom we have trusted.

The Bible makes it clear that "not by works of righteousness which we have done, but according to his mercy he saved us, by the washing of regeneration, and renewing of the Holy Ghost" (Tit. 3:5). And even there in Peter we are plainly told that it was not the putting away of the filth of the fleshly nature in baptism, but it was "the answer of a good conscience toward God," a conscience already forgiven and purged, before baptism. (See my book, Bible Baptism, an extended study of the Scriptures on this subject.)

VERSES 17-24:

17 And it came to pass, that, when I was come again to Jerusalem, even while I prayed in the temple, I was in a trance;

18 And saw him saying unto me, Make haste, and get thee quickly out of Jerusalem: for they will not receive thy testimony concerning me.

19 And I said, Lord, they know

that I imprisoned and beat in every synagogue them that believed on thee:

20 And when the blood of thy martyr Stephen was shed, I also was standing by, and consenting unto his death, and kept the raiment of them that slew him.

21 And he said unto me, Depart: for I will send thee far hence unto the Gentiles.

22 And they gave him audience unto this word, and *then* lifted up their voices, and said, Away with such a *fellow* from the earth: for it is not fit that he should live.

23 And as they cried out, and cast off *their* clothes, and threw dust into the air,

24 The chief captain commanded him to be brought into the castle, and bade that he should be examined by scourging; that he might know wherefore they cried so against him.

Paul's Argument With God About Jerusalem

Here Paul reminds us that when he first returned to Jerusalem after his conversion and baptism at Damascus, he had gone into the temple in fervent prayer and "was in a trance." And there God had plainly told him, "Make haste, and get thee quickly out of Jerusalem: for they will not receive thy testimony concerning me." We cannot doubt the fervor of the young convert. He had never gotten away from his love for Israel, his burden for their salvation, which was a "continual sorrow" in his heart (Rom. 9:2). And so the converted Saul had there in the temple argued with God. He reminded God how he had imprisoned and beaten the Christians, how he had consented to the death of Stephen and had held the garments of those that slew him.

Again, God had said unto him, "Depart: for I will send thee far hence unto the Gentiles."

So Paul had been clearly appointed "apostle to the Gentiles." The other apostles understood as he tells us in Galatians 2:7 and 8 that "the gospel of the uncircumcision was committed unto me, as the gospel of the circumcision was unto Peter; (For he that wrought effectually in Peter to the apostleship of the circumcision, the same was mighty in me toward the Gentiles)." And in Romans 11:13 he was inspired to write, "For I speak to you Gentiles, inasmuch as I am the apostle of the Gentiles, I magnify mine office."

And these plain instructions God had given him stayed with him in all his missionary journeys. So always, though he began with Jews and preached in the synagogues where he could, it ended up in his preaching to Gentiles and fulfilling the work God had given him to do.

But in Paul's testimony his emphasis that God would send him "far hence to the Gentiles" was an insult i ı their minds (vs. 21). It was hard enough to convince even the Christian Jews that Gentiles did not need to be circumcised and keep the law of Moses in order to be saved. These unregenerate Jews hated Gentiles, hated even the Samaritans who were half-breeds in religion and race. So now they began to scream out, "Away with such a fellow from the earth: for it is not fit that he should live." And so in rage they threw off their clothes, threw dust in the air. There was no chance that the truth would come out in such a raging mob, so the chief captain had Paul brought into the castle, "and bade that he should be examined by scourging."

That simply means that they intended to beat Paul until he confessed to whatever crime he was charged with or at least to find out any truth that he was hiding.

VERSES 25–30:

25 And as they bound him with thongs, Paul said unto the centurion that stood by, Is it lawful for you to scourge a man that is a Roman, and uncondemned?

26 When the centurion heard *that*, he went and told the chief captain, saying, Take heed what thou doest; for this man is a Roman.

27 Then the chief captain came, and said unto him, Tell me, art thou a Roman? He said, Yea.

28 And the chief captain answered, With a great sum obtained I this freedom. And Paul said, But I was *free* born.

29 Then straightway they departed from him which should have examined him: and the chief captain also was afraid,

after he knew that he was a Roman, and because he had bound him.

30 On the morrow, because he would have known the certainty wherefore he was accused of the Jews, he loosed him from *his* bands, and commanded the chief priests and all their council to appear, and brought Paul down, and set him before them.

Paul Saved by His Roman Citizenship

Here came the soldiers to bind Paul's arms, perhaps, around a marble pillar or perhaps to tie his hands and feet to iron rings in the stone floor. But Paul spoke up. He was a Roman citizen and he was uncondemned. It was against the Roman law for a Roman citizen to be scourged without a legal trial. The centurion (captain over one hundred men) in charge told the chief captain, "Take heed what thou doest: for this man is a Roman."

We must remember that only a few people were Roman citizens. Some had been given the freedom of the city of Rome because they had served in wars with some of the emperors; others because their fathers had. Some think that Paul being a native of Tarsus, a city favored by some of the Roman emperors and given the same privileges as the city of Rome, made him born free, a Roman citizen.

The captain himself was a Roman citizen, having purchased this freedom, this standing, with a great price. But Paul said, "I was free born," that is, his father or grandfather before him had earned this honor, this standing in the government and before the courts and before the Roman Senate.

The chief captain was greatly concerned. He had thought that Paul was, as Matthew Henry says, "a vagabond Egyptian" (Acts 21:37, 38). Instead he has found that Paul was not only a learned, cultured man, a citizen of a great city, but that he was a Roman citizen and he has had Paul bound, an indignity he ought not to have offered a Roman citizen.

We remember how concerned the magistrates were at Philippi when Paul insisted they come personally and escort them out of the prison (Acts 16:37, 38), and when the magistrates heard this, "they feared."

Paul seems to have been serene in these trying times. There is a dignity in his faith in God, a deep-seated self-respect and dependence on God for help.

The next day the chief captain took off Paul's bonds and brought Paul down and let him sit in the meeting of the Sanhedrin to hear their charges.

ACTS 23

VERSES 1–5:

AND Paul, earnestly beholding the council, said, Men
and brethren, I have lived in all
good conscience before God until
this day.

2 And the high priest Ananias
commanded them that stood by
him to smite him on the mouth.

3 Then said Paul unto him,
God shall smite thee thou whited
wall: for sittest thou to judge
me after the law, and commandest me to be smitten contrary to
the law?

4 And they that stood by said,
Revilest thou God's high priest?

5 Then said Paul, I wist not,
brethren, that he was the high
priest: for it is written, Thou
shalt not speak evil of the ruler
of thy people.

Paul and the Corrupt Sanhedrin

Paul, "earnestly beholding the council," felt reverent toward these men. He had worked with them before in persecuting Christians. They represented to him the highest
body of Jews. He was conscious that even by their own
standards, he, Paul, had been a good Pharisee.

Paul said, "I have lived in all good conscience before God
until this day." He had been, by Jewish standards, "touching the righteousness which is in the law, blameless" (Phil.
3:6). There had been a sincerity, a zeal for God in Paul or
Saul, the strict Pharisee, which was not evident in the other
Pharisees Jesus berated in Matthew 23. We think he did not
"for a pretence make long prayer" (Matt. 23:14). As a
Pharisee he had been unconverted, but there was a heart
honestly seeking righteousness, and that no doubt is why he
was quickly saved when God spoke to him on the road to
Damascus. Immediately, as soon as he had inquired, "Who
art thou, Lord?" and had learned, "I am Jesus whom thou
persecutest," then he, humbled and trembling, surrendered, said, "Lord, what wilt thou have me to do?" (Acts
9:5, 6). Paul's persecution of the Christians was very seri-

ous sin, and he himself later was inspired to say that he had been a blasphemer and a persecutor and injurious, "but I obtained mercy, because I did it ignorantly in unbelief" (I Tim. 1:13).

I think from all that Paul was inspired to give us about his unconverted state, we may believe that there was a hunger and thirst for God somewhat like that of the Ethiopian eunuch in Acts 8:28 and like that in the heart of Cornelius and his household (Acts 10:1, 2), which made them open to the Gospel.

"Smite him on the mouth," commanded the high priest! He was not willing to grant the sincerity of anybody who turned to Christ and so, he thought, dishonored the leadership of the Sanhedrin and the high priesthood, dishonored the Jewish traditions and the ceremonial law. This meeting of the Sanhedrin was not any honest effort to find whether or not Paul had a revelation from God. This was no impartial court.

Courageous Paul spoke up with holy indignation, "God shall smite thee, thou whited wall: for sittest thou to judge me after the law, and commandest me to be smitten contrary to the law?" Paul remembered that Jesus had called unconverted religionists like these "whited sepulchers" (Matt. 23:27). Paul knew God's divine law that men reap what they sow, that God punishes sin. And even here Paul could not cease to be God's preacher, God's prophet. These men had a pretended righteousness. They had sheep's clothing but were inwardly ravening wolves (Matt. 7:15).

But Paul had not recognized that the hateful and wicked man before him was a high priest and he remembered Exodus 22:28 which says, "Thou shalt not revile the gods, nor curse the ruler of thy people." So although the high priest was wicked, he was still the high priest. Since the Roman government left much of the control of the people in the hands of local governments, and in the case of the Jews this was through the Sanhedrin, the Jews' religious ruling body, Paul respected that authority. Jesus had said, "...The scribes and the Pharisees sit in Moses' seat: All therefore whatsoever they bid you observe, that observe and do; but do not ye after their works: for they say, and do not" (Matt. 23:2, 3). But Paul had little chance for a fair trial in this court.

VERSES 6-10:

6 But when Paul perceived that the one part were Sadducees, and the other Pharisees, he cried out in the council, Men *and* brethren, I am a Pharisee, the son of a Pharisee: of the hope and resurrection of the dead I am called in question.

7 And when he had so said, there arose a dissension between the Pharisees and the Sadducees: and the multitude was divided.

8 For the Sadducees say that there is no resurrection, neither angel, nor spirit: but the Phari-sees confess both.

9 And there arose a great cry: and the scribes *that were* of the Pharisees' part arose, and strove, saying, We find no evil in this man: but if a spirit or an angel hath spoken to him, let us not fight against God.

10 And when there arose a great dissension, the chief captain, fearing lest Paul should have been pulled in pieces of them, commanded the soldiers to go down, and to take him by force from among them, and to bring *him* into the castle.

Paul Appeals to the Pharisees About the Resurrection

Paul soon saw these Jewish leaders would not listen to the Gospel, would not hear his testimony about Jesus Christ. But he thought of a way to get part of these Jewish leaders on his side so that he would not be stoned to death as Stephen was stoned.

What is the great center of his Gospel? It is that Jesus Christ is risen from the dead and thus is proven to be the Christ, the Messiah prophesied in the Old Testament, God come in the flesh. The principal purpose of having twelve apostles, and so of electing one to witness instead of Judas, was "beginning from the baptism of John, unto that same day that he was taken up from us, must one be ordained to be a witness with us of his resurrection" (Acts 1:22). And so the resurrection of Christ was the principal theme at Pentecost (Acts 2:24-32), is the point Peter stressed in Acts 3:15 and in Acts 4:10. All along "with great power gave the apostles witness of the resurrection of the Lord Jesus" (Acts 4:33). The resurrection is the fact which the apostles witnessed before the high priest and the council in Acts 5:30 and 31. It was in Peter's message to Cornelius (Acts 10:40, 41). He preached it at Athens (Acts 17:31, 32). Paul had stressed the resurrection, too, at Antioch in Pisidia (Acts 13:30-37).

So here Paul would make an issue of the general principle of the resurrection. For a part of the Sanhedrin were Sadducees. "For the Sadducees say that there is no resurrection, neither angel, nor spirit: but the Pharisees confess both." So Paul said, "Men and brethren, I am a Pharisee, the son of a Pharisee: of the hope and resurrection of the dead I am called in question."

Well, the Pharisees were strictly partisan. If they could win a victory over the Sadducees by releasing Paul, they would; and so they strove and the chief captain was afraid "lest Paul should have been pulled in pieces of them." So he had the soldiers take him by force and bring him into the castle. And it must have been quite a tussle because Tertullus, the hired lawyer, later complained before Felix that "the chief captain Lysias came upon us, and with great violence took him away out of our hands" (Acts 24:7).

Paul said, "I am a Pharisee." Well, let us say that he had been a Pharisee, and he still believed in the resurrection.

VERSE 11:

11 And the night following the | hast testified of me in Jerusalem,
Lord stood by him, and said, Be | so must thou bear witness also
of good cheer, Paul: for as thou | at Rome.

The Lord Appears to Paul

How gracious that the Lord came to encourage Paul! He had needed it! So in Acts 18:9, 10, "Then spake the Lord to Paul in the night by a vision, Be not afraid, but speak, and hold not thy peace: For I am with thee, and no man shall set on thee to hurt thee: for I have much people in this city." So again, on shipboard in the storm, Paul will be able to stand and say, "For there stood by me this night the angel of God, whose I am, and whom I serve, Saying, Fear not, Paul; thou must be brought before Caesar: and, lo, God hath given thee all them that sail with thee" (Acts 27:23, 24). And there Paul could say, "I believe God," for that was the fourth time, including the vision on the road to Damascus, in which the Lord had appeared to him.

We are reminded of the way the Lord appeared to others in trouble and distress, to encourage them. So He appeared to Jacob, the erring, runaway young man, sleeping on the ground in Genesis 28:10-15. It was in a dream but very real. And so Christ, the Jehovah of the Old Testament, met Jacob in Genesis 32:24-30. He is called "a man" and we would think an angel, but Jacob said, "I have seen God face to face." We are told that "the angel of the Lord" appeared to Gideon to encourage him (Judg. 6). After the exaltation of a great victory on Mount Carmel had passed, Elijah "sat down under a juniper tree: and he requested for himself that he might die...." But an angel came, prepared him food and water, watched over him while he slept, fed him again, then God met him at Horeb to encourage and instruct him further (I Kings 19:4 ff). When the three Hebrew children in Babylon were cast into Nebuchadnezzar's firey furnace, they were not only kept without harm, but, astonished, Nebuchadnezzar said, "Lo, I see four men loose, walking in the midst of the fire, and they have no hurt; and the form of the fourth is like the Son of God" (Dan. 3:25).

When Daniel was cast into the lions' den, not only did God deliver him, but Daniel said, "My God hath sent his angel, and hath shut the lions' mouths..." (Dan. 6:22). So "the angel of the Lord by night opened the prison doors..." and brought out Peter and John and said, "Go, stand and speak in the temple to the people all the words of this life" (Acts 5:19, 20). So the angel came to deliver Peter from jail in Acts 12:7-11. Oh, those who were never in extremity for Jesus' sake do not know the sweet deliverance that He can give those who trust Him!

Now the Lord said to Paul, "For as thou hast testified of me in Jerusalem, so must thou bear witness also at Rome." Paul had been inspired to write to the Christians at Rome only a few weeks or months before: "For which cause also I have been much hindered from coming to you. But now having no more place in these parts, and having a great desire these many years to come unto you; Whensoever I take my journey into Spain, I will come to you: for I trust to see you in my journey, and to be brought on my way thitherward by you, if first I be somewhat filled with your company. But now I go unto Jerusalem to minister unto the saints" (Rom. 15:22-25). Again he said, "When therefore I have performed this, and have sealed to them this fruit, I will come by you into Spain. And I am sure that, when I come unto you, I shall come in the fulness of the blessing of the gospel of Christ" (Rom. 15:28, 29). He had had leading that he should go to Rome, but unwisely, we think, he had insisted on going to Jerusalem. Now he will go to Rome as a prisoner, but nevertheless, he will go to Rome as he had been inspired to promise the saints there, in his epistle to the Romans.

VERSES 12–22:

12 And when it was day, certain of the Jews banded together, and bound themselves under a curse, saying that they would neither eat nor drink till they had killed Paul.

13 And they were more than forty which had made this conspiracy.

14 And they came to the chief priests and elders, and said, We have bound ourselves under a great curse, that we will eat nothing until we have slain Paul.

15 Now therefore ye with the council signify to the chief captain that he bring him down unto you to morrow, as though ye would inquire something more perfectly concerning him: and we, or ever he come near, are ready to kill him.

16 And when Paul's sister's son heard of their lying in wait, he went and entered into the castle, and told Paul.

17 Then Paul called one of the centurions unto *him*, and said, Bring this young man unto the chief captain: for he hath a certain thing to tell him.

18 So he took him, and brought *him* to the chief captain, and said, Paul the prisoner called me unto *him*, and prayed me to bring this young man unto thee, who hath something to say unto thee.

19 Then the chief captain took him by the hand, and went *with him* aside privately, and asked *him*, What is that thou hast to tell me?

20 And he said, The Jews have agreed to desire thee that thou wouldest bring down Paul to morrow into the council, as though they would inquire somewhat of him more perfectly.

21 But do not thou yield unto them: for there lie in wait for him of them more than forty men, which have bound themselves with an oath, that they will neither eat nor drink till they have killed him: and now are they ready, looking for a promise from thee.

22 So the chief captain *then* let the young man depart, and charged *him*, *See thou* tell no man that thou hast shewed these things to me.

Radical Jews Vow to Kill Paul

Forty men vowed that at any cost they would kill Paul and would never eat nor drink until they had done so. Such a murderous conspiracy is shocking: but the more shocking is that these men regard themselves as serving God and the

Jewish religion and the Jewish people! Their vow, we judge, was counted a religious vow! And they took "the chief priests and elders" into their confidence and had their full co-operation! The whole Sanhedrin was to ask the chief captain to bring Paul down for further questioning on the morrow, and these Jews, even if it involved open battle with soldiers and perhaps that or imprisonment for some or all of them, would kill Paul!

I suppose there have never been any tortures inflicted on people like the persecution by religious zealots! The murderous hate of these Jews against Paul reminds us of the Spanish Inquisition, of St. Bartholomew's massacre, of the burning of Cranmer and Ridley at the stake, and the torture and murder of Protestants in Columbia, Peru, and in Mexico in recent years. There is no wickedness so terrible as that wickedness which claims to be blessed of God! This is the fulfillment of what Jesus had promised to His faithful disciples: "They shall put you out of the synagogues: yea, the time cometh, that whosoever killeth you will think that he doeth God service" (John 16:2).

How Easy It Is for God to Thwart Evil Plans and Defend His Own

It is said of God, who does not faint and is never weary, that "there is no searching of his understanding" (Isa. 40:28). God is never at His wit's end about how to protect His own. He could have a fish get a coin from the sand of the sea for Peter to use as tax money (Matt. 17:27)! He could have a gourd vine grow up to shade Jonah, or a worm to cut the vine (Jonah 4:6, 7). He could have a smooth stone from David's sling hit the giant Goliath in his carelessly uncovered forehead (I Sam. 17:49). He had a donkey to preach to Balaam (Num. 22:22-31), and a rooster to remind Peter of his sin (Luke 22:60-62). So here to protect Paul, God had a little boy in the right place to hear the conspiracy discussed. The little boy was Paul's sister's son. Since

Paul was a Roman citizen and so respected by the soldiers, the boy was allowed to see Paul and told the story. One of the captains or centurions then was called and the "young man" was brought to the chief captain and privately told him the story.

Note that the lad seemed to have been shy, because the chief captain "took him by the hand, and went with him aside privately" to hear his story. "Tell no man," the chief captain advised, and immediately he made his plans to thwart the conspiracy.

I wonder if all those forty men died of starvation, or whether they broke their vow to not eat nor drink till they had slain Paul.

We remember that the advice of Gamaliel was used to save the lives of Peter and John (Acts 5:34-39), although his advice would not necessarily always be good advice. God can take care of His own! And He had made a promise to Paul in verse 11 which He will certainly keep.

And let us remember, then, that the Christian, in the will of God, is always perfectly safe and all things work together for good to him. Nothing evil can happen to a Christian in the will of God. If it seemed evil, then wait until the full results are known and you will find that, though men meant it for evil, God meant it for good.

VERSES 23-35:

23 And he called unto *him* two centurions, saying, Make ready two hundred soldiers to go to Cesarea, and horsemen threescore and ten, and spearmen two hundred, at the third hour of the night;

24 And provide *them* beasts, that they may set Paul on, and bring *him* safe unto Felix the governor.

25 And he wrote a letter after this manner:

26 Claudius Lysias unto the most excellent governor Felix *sendeth* greeting.

27 This man was taken of the Jews, and should have been kill-

ed of them: then came I with an army, and rescued him, having understood that he was a Roman.

28 And when I would have known the cause wherefore they accused him, I brought him forth into their council:

29 Whom I perceived to be accused of questions of their law, but to have nothing laid to his charge worthy of death or of bonds.

30 And when it was told me how that the Jews laid wait for the man, I sent straightway to thee, and gave commandment to his accusers also to say before thee what *they had* against him. Farewell.

31 Then the soldiers, as it was commanded them, took Paul, and brought *him* by night to Antipatris.

32 On the morrow they left the horsemen to go with him, and returned to the castle:

33 Who, when they came to Cesarea, and delivered the epistle to the governor, presented Paul also before him.

34 And when the governor had read *the letter*, he asked of what province he was. And when he understood that *he was* of Cilicia;

35 I will hear thee, said he, when thine accusers are also come. And he commanded him to be kept in Herod's judgment hall.

The Chief Captain Sends Paul to Governor Felix at Caesarea

Tomorrow the forty conspirators hoped to kill Paul. So the chief captain, Claudius Lysias, wisely planned to send him away that night. He would be sent to Caesarea, which was now the capital of the province, since King Herod moved from Jerusalem there (Acts 12:19).

Caesarea had been founded by Herod the Great, on the Mediterranean Sea, perhaps seventy or seventy-five miles northwest of Jerusalem. There had been built a harbor, an amphitheater. It was a port and administrative center throughout the Roman period. Part of the ruins are now uncovered. So two hundred foot soldiers would travel with Paul all night, along with seventy horsemen and two hundred spearmen. They would leave at nine o'clock at night and Paul would ride. That night they reached Antipatris, slightly more than halfway to Caesarea. Then the next day the seventy cavalrymen took Paul on to Caesarea, and the soldiers returned to the castle at Jerusalem.

With two hundred soldiers (perhaps with the regular Roman short sword), and two hundred spearmen, and seventy cavalrymen, the chief captain was prepared for any mob that would try to take Paul. But the surprise move got him away without incident and so on the morrow night to Caesarea.

Note the letter of Claudius Lysias. He gives the facts about Paul except that he claims special credit for rescuing Paul: "having understood that he was a Roman." We know that that was not true because he had at first commanded Paul to be bound and "examined by scourging," and then was chagrined and embarrassed when he found that Paul was a Roman citizen (Acts 22:24-29). But he said that there was no evidence that Paul was charged with anything "worthy of death or bonds." So he had sent Paul directly to the governor and gotten the trouble out of Jerusalem where he would have been responsible, and sought some credit for having handled the matter well. He had sent Paul to the governor as an important man, a Roman citizen, whose death at the hands of a mob would be counted very serious, sent him away from the place of danger. Then the chief captain says he "gave commandment to his accusers also to say before thee what they had against him."

So the horsemen, with a centurion, brought Paul to Caesarea and presented him before the governor, Felix. Felix read the letter, found that Paul was from the province of Cilicia, and hence perhaps that there was no obligation to return him to Jerusalem for trial, and promised to hear Paul's case when the accusers should come, and Paul was to be kept imprisoned in Herod's judgment hall.

So Paul's life is spared, but there will be a dreary wait of years before he gets his expected journey to Rome.

ACTS 24

VERSES 1–9:

AND after five days Ananias the high priest descended with the elders, and *with* a certain orator *named* Tertullus, who informed the governor against Paul.

2 And when he was called forth, Tertullus began to accuse *him,* saying, Seeing that by thee we enjoy great quietness, and that very worthy deeds are done unto this nation by thy providence,

3 We accept *it* always, and in all places, most noble Felix, with all thankfulness.

4 Notwithstanding, that I be not further tedious unto thee, I pray thee that thou wouldest hear us of thy clemency a few words.

5 For we have found this man *a* pestilent *fellow,* and a mover of sedition among all the Jews throughout the world, and a ringleader of the sect of the Nazarenes:

6 Who also hath gone about to profane the temple: whom we took, and would have judged according to our law.

7 But the chief captain Lysias came *upon us,* and with great violence took *him* away out of our hands,

8 Commanding his accusers to come unto thee: by examining of whom thyself mayest take knowledge of all these things, whereof we accuse him.

9 And the Jews also assented, saying that these things were so.

High Priest and Sanhedrin Accuse Paul Before Felix

After five days Ananias and members of the Sanhedrin came from Jerusalem.

The high priest and the Sanhedrin must have felt it desperately important, a desperate urge to see Paul dead or all of them would not have made the long two days' journey to Caesarea. We can imagine the scheming, the plotting before they came. They employed "a certain orator named Tertullus" to present their case. Their great concern is a reminder that the Christian Gospel was turning many thousands of Jews away from the leadership of the temple priesthood, the Sanhedrin and high priest. Their political power, their prestige, their income was threatened.

Note the flattery with which Tertullus began. He credited Felix, thus: "We enjoy great quietness" and "very worthy deeds" and "thy providence." He said, "most noble Felix," and that these Jewish leaders of the nation accept Felix' benefactions "with all thankfulness."

Note the accusation. Paul is "a pestilent fellow, and a mover of sedition among all the Jews throughout the world, and a ringleader of the sect of the Nazarenes." They accuse him that he had "gone about to profane the temple." That was hearsay. In Acts 21:28 they had said that he "brought Greeks also into the temple, and hath polluted this holy place," supposing that had been true because they had seen him in the city in company with Trophimus, an Ephesian! He calls Paul "a mover of sedition," that is, of causing excitement and resistence to government authority. Actually, Paul had never caused any resistence to the government, but the Gospel he preached did lessen the authority of these Jewish leaders over Jews.

In Acts 16, the wicked men whose slave had her fortunetelling devil cast out by Paul and Silas accused them, "These men, being Jews, do exceedingly trouble our city, And teach customs, which are not lawful for us to receive, neither to observe, being Romans" (Acts 16:20, 21), but the charge was false then. At Ephesus the uproar caused by the silversmiths had been quieted by the town clerk who reminded them that no law had been broken. So Felix could obviously see that the words of Claudius Lysias were true. Paul had "nothing laid to his charge worthy of death or of bonds" (Acts 23:29).

But these Jews were pleading that in religious matters they had their own laws and the right to enforce them. They accused the chief captain of taking Paul out of the Sanhedrin meeting "with great violence." However, in Acts 23:10 we were told that "the chief captain, fearing lest Paul should

have been pulled in pieces of them, commanded the soldiers to go down, and to take him by force from among
them...." So Felix was now asked to examine these members of the Sanhedrin and the high priest, to question them
about Paul. "And the Jews also assented, saying that these
things were so."

VERSES 10–21:

10 Then Paul, after that the governor had beckoned unto him to speak, answered, Forasmuch as I know that thou hast been of many years a judge unto this nation, I do the more cheerfully answer for myself:

11 Because that thou mayest understand, that there are yet but twelve days since I went up to Jerusalem for to worship.

12 And they neither found me in the temple disputing with any man, neither raising up the people, neither in the synagogues, nor in the city:

13 Neither can they prove the things whereof they now accuse me.

14 But this I confess unto thee, that after the way which they call heresy, so worship I the God of my fathers, believing all things which are written in the law and in the prophets:

15 And have hope toward God, which they themselves also allow, that there shall be a resurrection of the dead, both of the just and unjust.

16 And herein do I exercise myself, to have always a conscience void of offence toward God, and *toward* men.

17 Now after many years I came to bring alms to my nation, and offerings.

18 Whereupon certain Jews from Asia found me purified in the temple, neither with multitude, nor with tumult.

19 Who ought to have been here before thee, and object, if they had aught against me.

20 Or else let these same *here* say, if they have found any evil doing in me, while I stood before the council,

21 Except it be for this one voice, that I cried standing among them, Touching the resurrection of the dead I am called in question by you this day.

Paul Makes His Defence Before the Governor

Notice how sensible and modest is Paul's language compared with the flattery of Tertullus. Felix was not a good governor, not a good man, and Paul did not pretend that he was. But one good thing: Felix had been for many years over these Jews and so he could tell whether Paul reported the facts correctly. Paul's answer was very simple. It had been only twelve days since he went up to Jerusalem (from the same city of Caesarea). He had not disputed in the temple, had not raised up followers or a mob, and the charges against him could not be proved.

But Paul did not miss the opportunity to testify to his faith.

1. Yes, they accused him as "ringleader of the sect of the Nazarenes." So he confesses "that after the way which they call heresy, so worship I the God of my fathers."

2. But it is a God of his fathers, the Jewish patriarchs.

3. He believes all things that are written in the law and the prophets. He follows the Jewish Old Testament.

4. He made an issue of the resurrection of the dead. This would appeal to the Pharisees.

5. He was careful to keep a good conscience morally and socially. He was a man of good character and reputation.

6. He had come to Jerusalem "to bring alms to my nation, and offerings."

7. His accusers had been "Jews from Asia" who carried on the same persecution they started in that province.

8. Paul confessed that the only thing they had a right to have against him was that he had the Pharisee position of a literal resurrection, which the Sadducees, including the high priest, did not believe.

It was a practical and sensible defense, so factual and clear that Felix must certainly have believed it.

VERSES 22-27:

22 And when Felix heard these things, having more perfect knowledge of *that* way, he deferred them, and said, When Lysias the chief captain shall come down, I will know the uttermost of your matter.

23 And he commanded a centurion to keep Paul, and to let *him* have liberty, and that he should forbid none of his acquaintance to minister or come unto him.

24 And after certain days, when Felix came with his wife Drusilla, which was a Jewess, he sent for Paul, and heard him concerning the faith in Christ.

25 And as he reasoned of righteousness, temperance, and judgment to come, Felix trembled, and answered, Go thy way for this time; when I have a convenient season, I will call for thee.

26 He hoped also that money should have been given him of Paul, that he might loose him: wherefore he sent for him the oftener, and communed with him.

27 But after two years Porcius Festus came into Felix' room: and Felix, willing to shew the Jews a pleasure, left Paul bound.

Felix Considers the Case of Paul

Felix "had more perfect knowledge of that way," that is, he had heard before now of the Christian faith, had heard certainly of the life of Christ, the stoning of Stephen, and the spread of the Gospel among the provinces through Paul and others.

He wanted more detail from "Lysias the chief captain" and would have him come down to Caesarea. One must be impressed with the sober uprightness of the Roman law. Even though Paul doubtless should have been released, Paul was kept in house arrest with a Roman officer to keep him. Any of his acquaintances could come to see him and could provide for his needs.

But Felix was interested not only in the legal aspects of Paul's imprisonment but in the Gospel he preached. So, with his wife, Drusilla, a Jewess, he sent for Paul and heard him "concerning the faith in Christ." How blessed it is to read that Paul "reasoned of righteousness, temperance, and judgment to come" before the Roman governor! So the gospel preacher always must, as Paul was inspired to command Timothy, "Preach the word; be instant in season, out of season; reprove, rebuke, exhort with all longsuffering and doctrine" (II Tim. 4:2). It would be no honest presentation of the Gospel that did not reprove and rebuke, that did not call men to repentance.

Felix was himself an evil man. Josephus says that although he suppressed the robbers and murderers who infested Judaea, "he himself was more hurtful than them all." He employed assassins to kill those whom he hated. He was cruel and rapacious. He hoped that Paul would bribe him to be released, so he kept him in jail and saw him often. He was willing to keep Paul in jail "to shew the Jews a pleasure" (vs. 27). And so Paul who had refused to flatter him when he was on trial now preached plainly about righteousness, temperance, and judgment! I do not wonder that Felix trembled!

I wonder what kept Felix from turning to God? Perhaps it was his wife Drusilla. How strange that Felix trembled, but his wife, a Jewess, as far as we know, did not!

He was covetous and thought to make money out of Paul.

He was a crooked politician seeking the support of the Jews even at the cost of an innocent man's freedom! And so bound by his sins, Felix did not repent. He trembled but never repented. Many a man has been convicted, has wept, has considered the claims of the Gospel but rejected Christ and went to Hell as, no doubt, Felix did. After two years Porcius Festus came to be governor of the province, in Felix' room, and Felix, to please the Jews, left Paul in jail.

Doubtless he had other ties among the Jews, having married a Jewess woman. He would seek support for his heavy tax program and other oppression, and so tried to please the Jews by his sinful treatment of Paul.

ACTS 25

VERSES 1-8:

NOW when Festus was come into the province, after three days he ascended from Cesarea to Jerusalem.

2 Then the high priest and the chief of the Jews informed him against Paul, and besought him,

3 And desired favour against him, that he would send for him to Jerusalem, laying wait in the way to kill him.

4 But Festus answered, that Paul should be kept at Cesarea, and that he himself would depart shortly *thither*.

5 Let them therefore, said he, which among you are able, go down with *me*, and accuse this man, if there be any wickedness in him.

6 And when he had tarried among them more than ten days, he went down unto Cesarea; and the next day sitting on the judgment seat commanded Paul to be brought.

7 And when he was come, the Jews which came down from Jerusalem stood round about, and laid many and grievous complaints against Paul, which they could not prove.

8 While he answered for himself, Neither against the law of the Jews, neither against the temple, nor yet against Cesar, have I offended any thing at all.

Chronology of Paul's Ministry

The key date about which we can be more nearly sure than others in the life of Paul from history is the accession of Festus who replaced Felix (Acts 24:27). Traditionally that date is taken as either 60 A. D. or 61 A. D. Ramsey says, "The great majority of scholars accept the date 60 for Festus...," but he thinks the date should be 59 for the recall of Felix. Smith's Bible Dictionary, David Thomas (The Acts of the Apostles) and Davis Bible Dictionary agree with many others that Festus probably assumed office late in 60.

The chronology then of the life of Paul given in Davis Bible Dictionary is as follows:

"G. T. P."

Paul Appears Before the New Governor, Festus

When Festus came into the province, he naturally felt that he must go to the religious center of the country, Jerusalem, and look over the situation there. Much of the administration of the province was left in the hands of the Jewish leaders, the Sanhedrin and the high priest.

Through two years, the hatred for Paul had not died down. With a burning hatred for the Christians, they determined still to kill Paul if they could. And they still planned to do it illegally, "laying wait in the way to kill him."

No, Paul would be kept at Caesarea. Festus would return there to his palace. As many as wished should come down and accuse Paul before him in Caesarea. So after ten days he left Jerusalem, returned to Caesarea and "sitting on the judgment seat" he commanded that Paul should be brought before him for further trial, in the presence of these leaders who, after two years, again faced Paul, demanding his death.

These Jewish leaders were hard put to it to accuse Paul. They "laid many and grievous complaints against Paul, which they could not prove." He answered simply that he had offended neither against the law of the Jews nor against the sanctity of the temple nor against Caesar and the Roman government. He had broken no laws.

VERSES 9–12:

9 But Festus, willing to do the Jews a pleasure, answered Paul, and said, Wilt thou go up to Jerusalem, and there be judged of these things before me?

10 Then said Paul, I stand at Cesar's judgment seat, where I ought to be judged: to the Jews have I done no wrong, as thou very well knowest.

11 For if I be an offender, or have committed any thing worthy of death, I refuse not to die: but if there be none of these things whereof these accuse me, no man may deliver me unto them. I appeal unto Cesar.

12 Then Festus, when he had conferred with the council, answered, Hast thou appealed unto Cesar? unto Cesar shalt thou go.

Paul Appeals to Caesar at Rome

Festus was a better man than Felix, but he had only recently come to Judaea. He naturally wished to please the people over whom he would rule. Since it was a religious offense charged against Paul, would Paul be willing to go to Jerusalem and there be judged before Festus but with whatever witnesses might be brought and facts determined there?

But Paul knew of the determination to assassinate him en route. He knew these Jews had not changed. He was a Roman citizen, had a right to appeal to the highest court, that is, to Caesar himself at Rome. Here Paul, before the Roman governor, stands at Caesar's judgment seat where he ought to be judged. There is no requirement that he should go to Jerusalem. No, as a Roman citizen, he claims his right. "No man may deliver me unto them," he said. "I appeal unto Caesar."

We can understand Paul's impatience at having been kept in prison for two years over unproven charges. He knew of the cupidity of Felix, his wicked attempts to please Jewish leaders by keeping Paul in jail. He also had an unceasing desire to go to Rome and a certainty in his heart that desire was of God. If he could not have justice here, he would claim it at the highest source at Rome. And as a Roman citizen, he had that right and must be sent to Rome. And so Festus, perhaps impatiently, said, "Hast thou appealed unto Caesar? unto Caesar shalt thou go." He may have thought that he would speedily release Paul. Certainly he was not aware of the murderous intent of the Jewish leaders. Now he would send Paul to Rome and get the matter out of his hands!

VERSES 13-27:

13 And after certain days king Agrippa and Bernice came unto Cesarea to salute Festus.

14 And when they had been there many days, Festus declared Paul's cause unto the king, saying, There is a certain man left in bonds by Felix:

15 About whom, when I was at Jerusalem, the chief priests and the elders of the Jews informed me, desiring to have judgment against him.

16 To whom I answered, It is not the manner of the Romans to deliver any man to die, before that he which is accused have the accusers face to face, and have license to answer for himself concerning the crime laid against him.

17 Therefore, when they were come hither, without any delay on the morrow I sat on the judgment seat, and commanded the man to be brought forth.

18 Against whom when the accusers stood up, they brought none accusation of such things as I supposed:

19 But had certain questions against him of their own super-

stition, and of one Jesus, which was dead, whom Paul affirmed to be alive.

20 And because I doubted of such manner of questions, I asked *him* whether he would go to Jerusalem, and there be judged of these matters.

21 But when Paul had appealed to be reserved unto the hearing of Augustus, I commanded him to be kept till I might send him to Cesar.

22 Then Agrippa said unto Festus, I would also hear the man myself. To morrow, said he, thou shalt hear him.

23 And on the morrow, when Agrippa was come, and Bernice, with great pomp, and was entered into the place of hearing, with the chief captains, and principal men of the city, at Festus' commandment Paul was brought forth.

24 And Festus said, King Agrippa, and all men which are here present with us, ye see this man, about whom all the multitude of the Jews have dealt with me, both at Jerusalem, and *also* here, crying that he ought not to live any longer.

25 But when I found that he had committed nothing worthy of death, and that he himself hath appealed to Augustus, I have determined to send him.

26 Of whom I have no certain thing to write unto my lord. Wherefore I have brought him forth before you, and specially before thee, O king Agrippa, that, after examination had, I might have somewhat to write.

27 For it seemeth to me unreasonable to send a prisoner, and not withal to signify the crimes *laid* against him.

Festus Discusses Paul's Case With Agrippa

King Agrippa, who ruled over the province of Galilee and part of Perea across Jordan, came to Caesarea to visit Festus, the governor of Judaea. With him was Bernice, his sister, with whom he lived in sin. This Agrippa was of the famous Herod family. He is Herod Agrippa II, the son of Herod Agrippa I of Acts 12:1, and the great grandson of Herod the Great who ruled in Judaea for the Roman Empire, when Jesus was born. The Herodian family had long been intimately associated with the Jews, and so Paul could say, "I know thee to be expert in all customs and questions which are among the Jews..." (Acts 26:3).

To his fellow governor, Festus told about Paul. Festus

had only recently come to take up the governorship of the province. The Jewish leaders had made serious charges against Paul. Paul had appealed to Caesar, but Festus did not know what he should write about the man. Would King Agrippa like to hear Paul also?

Note Festus' honest statement about Roman law in verse 16.

Festus had been disappointed about the charges against Paul. The Jews "had certain questions against him of their own superstition, and of one Jesus, which was dead, whom Paul affirmed to be alive." Festus did not feel that sufficient to write to Rome when he should send Paul there.

So on the morrow the visiting king was brought with great pomp to the judgment hall and Paul was brought forth. Festus announced that "all the multitude of the Jews" had cried that Paul "ought not to live any longer." But he found that Paul had "committed nothing worthy of death." The purpose of this examination was "that I might have somewhat to write." He would not displease the Jews by releasing Paul. He would do away with trouble in the province by shipping Paul to Rome. But there ought to be more serious detailed charges. So the hearing before Festus and King Agrippa and his sister Bernice.

ACTS 26

VERSES 1—5:

THEN Agrippa said unto Paul, Thou art permitted to speak for thyself. Then Paul stretched forth the hand, and answered for himself:

2 I think myself happy, king Agrippa, because I shall answer for myself this day before thee touching all the things whereof I am accused of the Jews:

3 Especially *because I know* thee to be expert in all customs and questions which are among the Jews: wherefore I beseech thee to hear me patiently.

4 My manner of life from my youth, which was at the first among mine own nation at Jerusalem, know all the Jews;

5 Which knew me from the beginning, if they would testify, that after the most straitest sect of our religion I lived a Pharisee.

Paul at Ease Before Agrippa

Porcius Festus was now the governor of Judaea, including Caesarea where Paul is imprisoned. Festus, "willing to do the Jews a pleasure," would have had Paul go back to Jerusalem where Jews waited to kill him, but Paul as a Roman citizen had appealed to Caesar and would be sent to Rome.

Meantime, King Agrippa, that is, Herod Agrippa II, ruler of provinces north of Judaea, had come to visit Festus and he asked to hear Paul.

This Herod Agrippa II was the grandson of Herod the Tetrarch called Antipas, the son of Herod the Great. That grandfather Herod had murdered John the Baptist. And we are told that "Herod feared John, knowing that he was a just man and an holy, and observed him; and when he heard him, he did many things, and heard him gladly" (Mark 6:20). He must have listened to the preaching and teaching of John and he reluctantly had John beheaded because of his oath to Herodias and Salome. But when he knew of Jesus his guilty conscience troubled him "and he said, that John the Baptist was risen from the dead, and therefore mighty works do shew forth themselves in him" (Mark 6:14). So the Herod family for five generations had known of the Scriptures and God's prophets and God's dealings with Israel.

So Paul stood forth before King Agrippa and his wife Bernice and before Governor Festus. "Then Agrippa said unto Paul, Thou art permitted to speak for thyself." Then Paul took over the proceedings with remarkable ease. It seems more like a sermon before an audience than the defense of a prisoner. He seemed more like a king's counselor than an accused criminal. So Paul stretched forth his hand dramatically and began to speak.

The ease of Paul before King Agrippa came, first, from long experience answering again and again those before whom he is tried since his arrest in Jerusalem.

1. He had defended himself before the multitude of Jews in Jerusalem standing on the stairs above the crowd, but under arrest by the Roman soldiers (Acts 22:1-21). And he had addressed the crowd, "Men, brethren, and fathers," that is, the fathers or spiritual leaders of Israel. There he had to remind the people of his training under Gamaliel, the most influential Jewish teacher; of his strict training in the law, of his persecuting of Christians and of his being sent as a representative of the Sanhedrin to Damascus where he told of his conversion, of the light from Heaven and the voice of God which would impress Jews. There he told them also of "one Ananias, a devout man according to the law, having a good report of all the Jews which dwelt there" (Acts 22:12) who had come and announced that he was called of God and admonished Paul to be baptized. The baptizing would greatly impress the Jews who long remembered everywhere the tremendous ministry of John the Baptist, baptizing multitudes. Also he used the figure of speech, "Be baptized, and wash away thy sins," to Jews accustomed to spiritual ceremonies with symbolic meaning.

2. On trial again before the Sanhedrin in Acts 23:1-6,

there with burning words he had reproved the high priest for commanding him to be smitten contrary to the law, there he had announced that he was a Pharisee, and that the question at issue was the resurrection. Pharisees believed in a resurrection; Sadducees did not. Hot arguments arose between the two parties. So the assembly broke up in disorder and Paul was taken by the centurion back to the castle.

3. Then Paul, when the centurion found a conspiracy against his life, was taken to Caesarea and there appeared before the governor Felix. There Paul talked briefly, denied the charges, reminded Felix that it had only been twelve days since he came to Jerusalem on the recent journey. And again, Paul had said the issue was the resurrection (Acts 24:15). And he also told of the disorder in the Sanhedrin when he had brought up the question of the resurrection.

4. Later Paul was brought again before Felix and his wife Drusilla, a Jewess, where Felix "heard him concerning the faith in Christ" (Acts 24:24, 25), and Paul "reasoned of righteousness, temperance, and judgment to come" so that Felix trembled, but took no stand.

5. But this was not all, for afterward Felix "hoped also that money should have been given him of Paul, that he might loose him: wherefore he sent for him the oftener, and communed with him" (Acts 24:26). So Paul had spoken familiarly with Felix a good many times. And Felix, "willing to shew the Jews a pleasure," left Paul bound whom he knew to be innocent.

6. When Porcius Festus became governor, the high priest and others in Jerusalem vigorously "informed him against Paul, and besought him, And desired favour against him, that he would send for him to Jerusalem, laying wait in the way to kill him" (Acts 25:2, 3). Then Paul was brought to the judgment seat before Felix. The formal charges were made again by leading Jews from Jerusalem,

we suppose members of the Sanhedrin, and perhaps the chief priests. Paul's answer was short and simply told. "While he answered for himself, Neither against the law of the Jews, neither against the temple, nor yet against Caesar, have I offended any thing at all" (Acts 25:8). And when Festus asked Paul to go to Jerusalem and there be tried, Paul appealed to Caesar and so must be sent to Rome.

And now again Paul comes to give an account of himself, a prisoner, before King Agrippa. But Paul is not awed by kingly robes or governmental authority, and with amazing poise he faces the king and queen and the governor and tells his story and preaches Christ.

Why Paul Was Specially Glad to Speak Before King Agrippa

In verses 2 and 3 Paul expresses his happiness that he is to answer before King Agrippa, "especially because I know thee to be expert in all customs and questions which are among the Jews." This is King Herod Agrippa II. He is the son of Herod Agrippa I, who had the Apostle James killed and planned to kill Peter in Acts 12, and after a great popular acclaim over his oration, we read of Herod Agrippa I in Acts 12:23--"And immediately the angel of the Lord smote him, because he gave not God the glory: and he was eaten of worms, and gave up the ghost." And that indicates that God held even that Herod to account more than He would an ignorant man who did not know the God of the Jews, of the Scriptures, of the Messiah.

This Herod Agrippa II before whom Paul now stands is the great grandson of Herod the Great who was ruling in Jerusalem when Christ was born. He had rebuilt the temple magnificently and although he was a wicked man and had innocent children killed trying to destroy the baby Jesus, there is evidence that he believed the Old Testament Scriptures. Matthew 2:3 tells us that "when Herod the king had heard these things," about the wise men who came looking for the Messiah, "he was troubled, and all Jerusalem with him." And again we find "and when he had gathered all the chief priests and scribes of the people together, he demanded of them where Christ should be born" (Matt. 2:4). He knew the Old Testament prophesied the coming of Christ, the King, and he inquired and found that the Messiah was to be born in Bethlehem of Judaea, according to Micah 5:2. So Herod the Great had known about supernatural predictions in the Bible and about the coming of the Saviour.

And Herod Agrippa I, who killed James and was otherwise wicked, yet was so disturbed about the supernatural events in Jerusalem that after he had the jailers killed, from whom the angel took Peter at night, "he went down from Judaea to Caesarea, and there abode" (Acts 12:19). And still God held him accountable and the angel of the Lord killed him "because he gave not God the glory" (Acts 12:23). So we can understand then that this Herod Agrippa is of a family that for four or five generations has known of the Jews, their worship, their Scriptures, their promised Messiah, the ceremonial law. And before such a man Paul felt free to speak.

The indication is that, of all the men before whom Paul had been brought, this Herod Agrippa was the most discerning of all, and though wicked, was spiritually instructed in a way that others had not been. And Paul could say, "King Agrippa, believest thou the prophets? I know that thou believest" (vs. 27). And we must bear this in mind as Paul speaks to King Agrippa.

Paul's personal defense has a small part in this witness before King Agrippa. He says in verse 4 that all the Jews knew about his life in Jerusalem, his strict training and stand as a Pharisee and his working as an agent of the Sanhedrin defending the rule of the high priest and the priesthood against the Christians (vss. 4, 5). And he says that really what he stands to be judged for is "the hope of the promise made of God unto our fathers" (vs. 6).

VERSES 6–8:

6 And now I stand and am judged for the hope of the promise made of God unto our fathers:

7 Unto which *promise* our twelve tribes, instantly serving *God* day and night, hope to come. For which hope's sake, king Agrippa, I am accused of the Jews.

8 Why should it be thought a thing incredible with you, that God should raise the dead?

Christ Is the Hope of Israel

Although Paul's life is at stake, the attack of Jewish leaders on him is an attack on Christ and is in truth an attack on God's blessings offered Israel and God's promises made to Israel. God had made great promises to Israel and in speaking only for the more spiritual Jews, Paul says, "Unto which promise our twelve tribes, instantly serving God day and night, hope to come." Remember Anna the prophetess and Simeon in the temple when Jesus was presented (Luke 2:25-38). Remember the revelation to Zacharias about the birth of a son John, who should be a forerunner, and of the glad joy of that righteous man in Luke 1. Remember the many who had asked John the Baptist, "Art thou the Christ?" (John 1:19-27; John 3:25-30). Remember that even the chief priests were familiar with the Scripture in Micah 5:2 where the Messiah should be born (Matt. 2:5, 6), and with many other Old Testament prophecies about Him. Nathanael, won by Jesus, although he had had the questions, had a seeking heart (John 1:45-49). Even the Samaritan woman, half-breed in religion and race, yet expected the Messiah and said, "I know that Messias cometh, which is called Christ: when he is come, he will tell us all things." And then she ran to the town saying, "Come, see a man, which told me all things that ever I did: is not this the Christ?" (John 4:25, 29). Those who were spiritually near to God and sought God, in all Israel, looked forward to the fulfillment of certain promises and had a certain hope, which could only be fulfilled in Christ and of these Paul spoke here in Acts 26:6 and 7.

That "hope of Israel" may be outlined briefly as follows:

1. It included the covenant with Abraham, the father of the race, that "I will make of thee a great nation...and in thee shall all families of the earth be blessed" (Gen. 12:2, 3). To Abraham, God had promised the land of Canaan when he was yet a stranger in it (Gen. 13:14-17). And that promise was to Abraham "and to thy seed forever." And that is explained by inspiration in Galatians 3:16, "Now to Abraham and his seed were the promises made. He saith not, And to seeds, as of many; but as of one, And to thy seed, which is Christ." And we are told, "And the scripture, foreseeing that God would justify the heathen through faith, preached before the gospel unto Abraham, saying, In thee shall all nations be blessed. So then they which be of faith are blessed with faithful Abraham" (Gal. 3:8, 9). This covenant was repeated to Abraham in Genesis 15:5 and 6 and in Genesis 17:6-8. But the Seed through whom the world would be blessed is Christ, and the true children of Abraham are those who have faith in Christ, as did Abraham.

2. God made a covenant with David in II Samuel 7:10-17 to establish the throne of David forever. "And thine house and thy kingdom shall be established for ever before thee: thy throne shall be established for ever." And that could not come to pass except through Christ in His Second Coming when He restores Israel to the land and sets the premillennial kingdom on earth.

That covenant is given also in I Chronicles 17:4-15. This promise of David's Seed to reign literally on the throne of David is repeated in Isaiah 11:1-12, in Isaiah 9:6 and 7.

The virgin birth of Christ as a sign to the "house of David" is promised in Isaiah 7:14. It is prophesied in Isaiah 32:1-5, in Isaiah 35. The reign of Christ on David's throne and regathering of Israel is very clearly prophesied in Jeremiah 23:3-8, in Jeremiah 33:12-26, in Ezekiel 34:11-31, in Ezekiel 36:22-28, and in Ezekiel 37:11-28.

Thus it is no wonder that the genealogy of Jesus given in Matthew 1:1 officially goes back to David and Abraham, "Jesus Christ, the son of David, the son of Abraham." And so when Jesus was to be born, the angel Gabriel had said to Mary:

> "And, behold, thou shalt conceive in thy womb, and bring forth a son, and shalt call his name JESUS. He shall be great, and shall be called the Son of the Highest: and the Lord God shall give unto him the throne of his father David: And he shall reign over the house of Jacob for ever; and of his kingdom there shall be no end." --Luke 1:31-33.

3. There had been a clear teaching that the nation Israel had been delivered from the conquerors and put back in their own land under their own king. Even in the time of Christ, Jews were scattered all over the then known world, and Judaea was a conquered province of the Roman Empire. The promised restoration and conversion of Israel is foretold in Deuteronomy 30:1-6. It will come, of course, at the second coming of Christ. That conversion and restoration of the nation Israel under the Saviour's kingship is foretold in Zechariah 12:10-14, Zechariah 13:1, 6 and particularly Zechariah 14, notably verses 4, 9, 20 and 21. Then the wonderful peace and plenty promised in Micah 4:1-8 will come to pass in Israel.

It is clear that not only the blessing of salvation through the Christ in whom Abraham trusted, but the restoration of David's throne and kingdom and the restoration of Israel to their own land under their own king, must await the second coming of Christ. And so when Paul spoke, these things for the nation Israel were still a future hope and promise, as Paul mentioned them in Acts 26, verses 6 and 7.

4. But the priesthood, the animal sacrifices, the ceremonies--all these could never be fulfilled but in Christ. Spiritual Jews knew that the blood of bulls and goats did not take away sin. These object lessons pictured some great Lamb of God who would come. The high priest pictured a High Priest who would come forever after the order of Melchisedec. The Shekinah glory resting in the tabernacle over the mercy seat pictured the Spirit of God who would dwell in temples not made with hands, that is, in bodies of Christians, who would have peace through the mercy of Christ accepted. Circumcision was only an outward form, meaningless unless it pointed to a supernatural mark, regeneration in the heart that would set God's people apart from the world. We may properly say that Judaism and all the Old Testament promises and prophecies, all the Old Testament ceremonies, all the hopes of Israel, could only be fulfilled in Christ Himself.

And that means, of course, that Christianity is but the proper projection and flowering of scriptural Judaism: not the flowering of the forms and ceremonies which Pharisees had added, but the flower of God's own revealed ceremonies, promises, pictures and prophecies. The only way one can be a true son of Abraham is to trust in Christ, as did Abraham. So we are told in Romans 4:1-8, so we are told in Galatians 3:6-9. And Jesus could face the wicked Pharisees and say, "...If ye were Abraham's children, ye would do the works of Abraham. But now ye seek to kill me, a man that hath told you the truth, which I have heard of God: this did not Abraham. Ye do the deeds of your father," that is, Satan (John 8:39-41). Oh, Jesus is the hope of Israel and the hope of every other child of Adam born in this sinful, lost race! But there are special promises to

Israel as a nation which are not given to other races as nations. Individually every person has the same offer of grace and mercy, every Christian has the same blessed promises. But as a nation God has certain plans for Israel which must be fulfilled. So Israel had a hope nationally, as well as the individual's hope of salvation through Christ.

All Depends on Christ's Resurrection

Paul's sermon was on the resurrection.

"Why should it be thought a thing incredible with you, that God should raise the dead?" (vs. 8).

1. The hope of Israel is possible only through the resurrection. What is the hope of Israel mentioned in verses 6 and 7? It is to be fulfilled in Jesus Christ, of course. BUT ONLY IF HE ROSE FROM THE DEAD! And so Paul launches into his theme with this startling, compelling question, "Why should it be thought a thing incredible with you, that God should raise the dead?"

The birth of Jesus saved no one. His marvelous ministry, His miracles, His teachings were wonderful, but His life, His teachings, His miracles do not save men. Only by dying for sin and then being raised from the dead could Christ save men. Jesus was "declared to be the Son of God with power, according to the spirit of holiness, by the resurrection from the dead" (Rom. 1:4). Jesus had declared that there would be no sign, no miraculous evidence of His deity, "but the sign of the prophet Jonas: For as Jonas was three days and three nights in the whale's belly; so shall the Son of man be three days and three nights in the heart of the earth," and then, of course, rising from the dead (Matt. 12:39, 40). There is no Christianity without the resurrection. The Gospel, as specially defined in I Corinthians 15:3 and 4, is, "...how that Christ died for our sins according to the scriptures; And that he was buried, and that he rose again the third day according to the scriptures."

Likewise, there could be no fulfillment of the hope of

Israel for a regathered and redeemed nation, no hope of the promise of Abraham's blessing to all the world, no hope of the reign of the Son on David's throne, and of an age of peace and righteousness and blessing on the earth, except as Christ is raised from the dead. That was the inspired argument of Peter at Pentecost, you remember, as recorded in Acts 2:30 and 31:

> "Therefore being a prophet, and knowing that God had sworn with an oath to him, that of the fruit of his loins, according to the flesh, he would raise up Christ to sit on his throne; He seeing this before spake of the resurrection of Christ, that his soul was not left in hell, neither his flesh did see corruption."

2. But why then should it be thought incredible that God should raise the dead? If there would be a God, He should act like a God, as Dr. Charles Blanchard has said (Getting Things From God). If there is a God who made men, He is greater than man, able to do what man cannot do. He would be a small God, a limited God who could not raise the dead. In view of the hope of Israel and all the promises and all the types, why should anyone not believe in the resurrection? You may be sure that here is the very core of wicked unbelief. The man who does not believe that Jesus rose bodily from the grave is not a Christian, does not hold any major part of the Christian content of faith. This is part of the "doctrine of Christ" in which, if one "transgresseth, and abideth not," he "hath not God" (II John 9). Any man who would leave out the miraculous, whether in the inspiration of the Bible, the miraculous virgin birth, the miracles of His life or His resurrection from the dead, is not a Christian. The very heart of this body of doctrine is the bodily resurrection of Christ from the dead, fulfilling prophecy and proving His deity. One who could believe that man, by inherent natural forces, rose from the amoeba or from the

ape by natural evolution; who believes that all the marvels of this orderly creation are the result of chance, instead of believing in the miracles of the Bible, is a credulous fool. He has gagged at a nat and swallowed a camel!

3. In all the story of his persecution of Christians and of his conversion, note that Paul is striving to prove the resurrection. He is showing that the most arrogant and confirmed unbeliever was convinced that Christ is really God come in the flesh. That person who spoke to him from Heaven on the road to Damascus is the risen Christ! That risen Christ has talked to Paul, has called him to preach, has delivered him again and again "from the people, and from the Gentiles" (vs. 17). And in verses 22 and 23 he says that his life is now summed up in witnessing to small and great, that all the prophets were true when they prophesied about Christ, that He should suffer and "that he should be the first that should rise from the dead."

In truth, the conversion of the Apostle Paul is a staggering argument for the resurrection. Paul, a fanatical, bloodthirsty Pharisee, holding the garments of those who stoned Stephen, arresting Christians and punishing them everywhere, compelling them to blaspheme, chasing them down even in strange cities to arrest them and bring them bound to trial, is now changed into a humble Christian, preaching the Gospel, losing all the things dear to men but the mightiest preacher of the Gospel, setting ablaze the rim of the Roman Empire in the first century! I am not surprised that the English skeptic Gilbert West was converted when he set out to answer the testimony of the Apostle Paul and his witness to Christ's Gospel and His resurrection.

4. We should remind you again that all through the book of Acts and in New Testament Christianity there is a predominate, overwhelming emphasis on the resurrection of Christ. (a) He showed Himself alive after His passion by many infallible proofs (Acts 1:3). (b) A witness was elected to take the place of Judas, a personal witness: "Beginning

from the baptism of John, unto that same day that he was taken up from us, must one be ordained to be a witness with us of his resurrection" (Acts 1:22). (c) At Pentecost the principal emphasis of Peter was on the resurrection (Acts 2:24-31). (d) In Acts 3 when Peter preached it was that "the God of our fathers, hath glorified his Son Jesus" and that these Jews had "killed the Prince of life, whom God hath raised from the dead; whereof we are witnesses" (Acts 3:13-15. See also Acts 4:2, 10, 32; Acts 5:30-32). (e) Stephen saw Jesus alive standing at the right hand of God and addressed Him publicly (Acts 7:55, 56). In Acts 9 Paul saw the resurrected Saviour. To Cornelius, Peter preached the resurrection (Acts 10:40). In Antioch of Pisidia Paul preached, "But God raised him from the dead" (Acts 13:30, 33, 34, 37). In Acts 17:31 Paul preached in Athens there was coming a judgment by Christ, "whereof he hath given assurance unto all men, in that he hath raised him from the dead." To a multitude when Paul was arrested, he told that the risen Christ had talked to him (Acts 22:7-10). Before the Sanhedrin he had said, "Of the hope and resurrection of the dead I am called in question" (Acts 23:6). Before Felix he had declared a hope "that there shall be a resurrection of the dead, both of the just and unjust" (Acts 24:15). And Felix had reported to King Agrippa that the Jews had concerning Paul, "certain questions against him of their own superstition, and of one Jesus, which was dead, whom Paul affirmed to be alive" (Acts 25:19).

The resurrection has a central place in the Gospel. And one of the first places Satan attacks the integrity of the Bible and the deity of Christ is on the book of Jonah. The unsuspecting one forgets that Satan's aim is to prove that Jonah was not brought forth after three days in the whale's belly, so Christ was not risen from the dead, and so the Bible is not literally true, and so Christ is not really God in the flesh.

VERSES 9–18:

9 I verily thought with myself, that I ought to do many things contrary to the name of Jesus of Nazareth.

10 Which thing I also did in Jerusalem: and many of the saints did I shut up in prison, having received authority from the chief priests; and when they were put to death, I gave my voice against *them.*

11 And I punished them oft in every synagogue, and compelled *them* to blaspheme; and being exceedingly mad against them, I persecuted *them* even unto strange cities.

12 Whereupon as I went to Damascus with authority and commission from the chief priests,

13 At midday, O king, I saw in the way a light from heaven, above the brightness of the sun, shining round about me and them which journeyed with me.

14 And when we were all fallen to the earth, I heard a voice speaking unto me, and saying in the Hebrew tongue, Saul, Saul, why persecutest thou me? *it is* hard for thee to kick against the pricks.

15 And I said, Who art thou, Lord? And he said, I am Jesus whom thou persecutest.

16 But rise, and stand upon thy feet: for I have appeared unto thee for this purpose, to make thee a minister and a witness both of these things which thou hast seen, and of those things in the which I will appear unto thee;

17 Delivering thee from the people, and *from* the Gentiles, unto whom now I send thee,

18 To open their eyes, *and* to turn *them* from darkness to light, and *from* the power of Satan unto God, that they may receive forgiveness of sins, and inheritance among them which are sanctified by faith that is in me.

Paul's Personal Testimony of His Conversion

Remember that there are at least two reasons for Paul's detailed account of his persecution of Christians. First, since his persecution was well known to all the Jews, his confession ought to be as widely spread as his sin. And, second, to admit what an arrogant and hardhearted and determined opponent he was of Christ and the Christians would give strength to his testimony that he had personally met Christ, had been convinced he was wrong, had been converted and changed by divine intervention and by meeting Jesus in person and trusting Him.

According to verses 4 and 5, all the Jews were familiar with Paul's life as a strict Pharisee persecuting the Jews. And even of King Agrippa Paul could say, "I am persuaded that none of these things are hidden from him; for this thing was not done in a corner" (Acts 26:26). Therefore, the detailed confession of verses 10 and 11. He had shut up the saints in prison. He had asked for and received authority to arrest Christians in synagogues far and near. When they were put to death, he gave his voice against them. Doubtless he had cried for the death of Stephen and held their garments who stoned him. He compelled Christians to blaspheme and went beyond Judaea. Wherever there were Jewish synagogues these synagogues were regarded as subject to the priesthood and the Sanhedrin in Jerusalem and Rome had very largely left the Jews to run their own matters, according to their own laws.

Consider elements in Paul's testimony to King Agrippa.

1. Note the miraculous element, the light from Heaven brighter than the sun, the voice from Heaven, the revelation that it was Jesus, the supernatural call. Oh, Paul had good reason to be convinced that Jesus was risen from the dead and is the Christ, the Saviour. And we may be sure that King Agrippa and Bernice were not unimpressed with this evidence.

2. Note some elements in the testimony here. They differ from other occasions when Paul told part of the same story. Here the Lord Jesus had added, saying to Saul, "It is hard for thee to kick against the pricks." Here Paul, no doubt, revealed for the first time the haunting of his conscience by the dying face of Stephen and of his testimony.

Here Paul does not mention his baptism. To the Jews, it would be very impressive to those who all knew about John's baptism and how that led into the ministry of Christ. It is not necessary to mention it here to Agrippa.

Ananias, that devout Jew, was greatly respected by Jews. It was not necessary to mention his part here in the story to King Agrippa.

Again, Paul was speaking to a distinguished man of the world who not only knew the Jewish race, their customs, their laws, their Scriptures and their hope, but also knew the Roman Empire. Then Paul tells more in detail of his call to preach to both Jews and Gentiles (see verses 16-18, and 23). This would explain Paul's missionary journeys which were doubtless known to Agrippa, as we see in verse 20.

And the end of all Paul's preaching was "to open their eyes, and to turn them from darkness to light, and from the power of Satan unto God, that they may receive forgiveness of sins, and inheritance among them which are sanctified by faith that is in me," that is, in Jesus who was thus speaking to Paul (vs. 18).

VERSES 19–29:

19 Whereupon, O king Agrippa, I was not disobedient unto the heavenly vision:

20 But shewed first unto them of Damascus, and at Jerusalem, and throughout all the coasts of Judea, and *then* to the Gentiles, that they should repent and turn to God, and do works meet for repentance.

21 For these causes the Jews caught me in the temple, and went about to kill *me*.

22 Having therefore obtained help of God, I continue unto this day, witnessing both to small and great, saying none other things than those which the prophets and Moses did say should come:

23 That Christ should suffer, *and* that he should be the first that should rise from the dead, and should shew light unto the people, and to the Gentiles.

24 And as he thus spake for himself, Festus said with a loud voice, Paul, thou art beside thyself; much learning doth make thee mad.

25 But he said, I am not mad, most noble Festus; but speak forth the words of truth and soberness.

26 For the king knoweth of these things, before whom also I speak freely: for I am persuaded that none of these things are hidden from him; for this thing was not done in a corner.

27 King Agrippa, believest thou the prophets? I know that thou believest.

28 Then Agrippa said unto Paul, Almost thou persuadest me to be a Christian.

29 And Paul said, I would to God, that not only thou, but also all that hear me this day, were both almost, and altogether such as I am, except these bonds.

Paul Presses the Matter of Salvation Upon King Agrippa

What causes the burning eyes, the fervent heart, the tearful and yet bold and impassionate plea of Paul? He was not disobedient to the heavenly vision! He tells King Agrippa that all his missionary journeys were to teach both Jews and Gentiles to repent. And this is the background of his arrest in Jerusalem.

Verse 22 tells us that all of his preaching was based upon the Old Testament, those things "which the prophets and Moses did say should come: That Christ should suffer, and that he should be the first that should rise from the dead, and should shew light unto the people, and to the Gentiles."

But the matter was getting personal. Even King Agrippa evidently showed some signs of concern and conviction. Festus the governor felt he need intervene, so he interrupted loudly, "Paul, thou art beside thyself; much learning doth make thee mad."

But Paul would not be diverted. King Agrippa, it seems, more than any of the Sanhedrin, more than Festus or Felix, understands the great principles about which Paul was speaking and was more stirred and convicted in his heart. So Paul continued boldly, "I am not mad, most noble Festus; but speak forth the words of truth and soberness. For the king knoweth of these things, before whom also I speak freely." None of these things Paul speaks of are hidden from King Agrippa. And then boldly facing the busy

king, Paul said, "King Agrippa, believest thou the prophets? I know that thou believest." In other words, are you
ready to admit that Christ fulfilled the promises that He is
the Messiah? Are you, Agrippa, ready to face the same
Gospel Paul has preached in all his missionary journeys,
that Christ is the only way to forgiveness and salvation,
both to Jews and Gentiles?

In our King James Version we have in verse 28, "Then
Agrippa said unto Paul, Almost thou persuadest me to be a
Christian." The American Standard Version has it, "With
but little persuasion thou wouldest fain make me a Christian." I do not believe that particularly changes the meaning. King Agrippa was convicted. Paul was pleading for a
clear-cut decision now. The Scofield Reference notes say,
"The answer might be paraphrased: 'It will require more
than this,' etc. or, 'A little more and you will make me a
Christian.'" In any case, Agrippa was convicted. He must
answer to God for clear light on this matter. If he was not
saved, his condemnation will be all the more because of the
great enlightenment he had. Millions of others have really
turned away after being greatly convicted, saying, "Almost
thou persuadest me to be a Christian." But "almost saved"
is still altogether lost.

I do not wonder that Paul said, "I would to God, that not
only thou, but also all that hear me this day [Festus, Queen
Bernice, and others he means], were both almost, and altogether such as I am, except these bonds."

And a familiar song comes to mind.

> "Almost persuaded," now to believe;
> "Almost persuaded," Christ to receive;
> Seems now some soul to say,
> "Go, Spirit, go Thy way,
> Some more convenient day
> On Thee I'll call."

"Almost persuaded," come, come today;
"Almost persuaded," turn not away;
Jesus invites you here,
Angels are ling'ring near,
Prayers rise from hearts so dear,
O wand'rer, come.

"Almost persuaded," harvest is past!
"Almost persuaded," doom comes at last!
"Almost" cannot avail;
"Almost" is but to fail!
Sad, sad, that bitter wail,
"Almost," but lost!

And not so well known but infinitely sweet and moving are the words of the song by P. P. Bilhorn:

Almost I trusted in Jesus,
Almost I turned from my sin;
Almost I yielded completely
To the sweet striving within.

Almost I said, "Jesus, save me,"
Almost submitted my will:
Almost persuaded to serve Him,
But I rejected Him still.

Almost, but still I resisted,
Almost, but never believed;
Almost, but waited and waited,
Till the sweet Spirit was grieved.

Almost at one time I yielded,
Almost at one time was saved:
Almost, but drifted and drifted:
Satan thus held me enslaved.

Almost,—why longer refuse Him?
Almost, O lost one, believe;
Almost,—swing open thy heart's door,
Jesus the Saviour receive.

Chorus:
Now is the time to receive Him,
Now is the time to be saved;
Now, while the Spirit is pleading,
Now, Jesus waiteth to save.

VERSES 30–32:

30 And when he had thus spoken, the king rose up, and the governor, and Bernice, and they that sat with them:

31 And when they were gone aside, they talked between themselves, saying, This man doeth nothing worthy of death or of bonds.

32 Then said Agrippa unto Festus, This man might have been set at liberty, if he had not appealed unto Cesar.

Paul Might Have Been Released: Now Will Go to Rome

The interview was over. The king and the governor and Bernice "and they that sat with them," (we suppose a considerable crowd of retainers had heard the Gospel) went aside.

Herod and Festus said, "This man doeth nothing worthy of death or of bonds." And Herod Agrippa said to Festus, "This man might have been set at liberty...." Indeed! So the Pharisees among the Sanhedrin had known (Acts 23:9). And Felix knew it, too, for he had kept Paul in hope of a bribe to release him (Acts 24:26). And Festus had kept him "willing to shew the Jews a pleasure" (Acts 25:9). Paul has appealed unto Caesar. So the case must be carried to the highest court and that is to Rome.

ACTS 27

VERSE 1:

A ND when it was determined that we should sail into Italy, they delivered Paul and certain other prisoners unto *one* named Julius, a centurion of Augustus' band.

Paul to Be Sent to Rome

Paul was now to be sent to Rome. As a Roman citizen, an honor that few men had, he had special rights under Roman law. He had appealed to Caesar, to Caesar he must go.

So "Paul and certain other prisoners" were delivered unto a certain centurion or captain of the Roman soldiers, named Julius, an officer of a regiment or group named after Caesar Augustus and perhaps a man whose headquarters was in Rome. They would go by ship and the government would buy space in shipping eastward in the Mediterranean Sea until they would come to Rome.

1. What a comfort to Paul that the long wait is over! He has been a prisoner now more than two years (Acts 24:27). In that time he has preached only to the soldiers or to those who came to him on the occasions of his trial, etc. Two of the long years must have seemed very empty during the reign of Felix. We have no record of what Paul did during that time in jail. He had been again and again in danger of his life. Fickle governors would have taken him back to Jerusalem. Jews had a conspiracy to lie in wait and kill him en route. Governors and officers who knew him to be unworthy of the charges against him, yet for political reasons kept him prisoner. And now at last these long weary and seemingly fruitless years are over and Paul will go to Rome!

2. How much and how long Paul had planned to go to Rome! And I think those plans were of God for they are re-

corded in the divinely inspired Epistle to the Romans. How penitently Paul had written to these! They were in his prayers without ceasing (Rom. 1:9). He was continually "making request, if by any means now at length I might have a prosperous journey by the will of God to come unto you" to Rome (Rom. 1:10). Paul did not know what that "by any means" would mean going as a prisoner! He longed to impart some spiritual gift to them and be comforted by them, he says. And he had "oftentimes purposed" to come to them, but hitherto had been hindered (vss. 11-13). So he was ready to preach the Gospel at Rome also (Rom. 1:15). With this in mind, note how Paul had stressed in his letter to the Romans that he was "apostle of the Gentiles" (Rom. 9:13). Note how that he had somewhat outlined the history and the nature of his ministry in Romans 15:15-21.

But all along in his mind he had hoped to come to Rome, and these great missionary journeys are the reason for the delay. "For which cause also I have been much hindered from coming to you. But now having no more place in these parts, and having a great desire these many years to come unto you; Whensoever I take my journey into Spain, I will come to you: for I trust to see you in my journey, and to be brought on my way thitherward by you, if first I be somewhat filled with your company" (Rom. 15:22-24).

Then he tells how he is going to Jerusalem with offerings for the Jewish Christians and says, "When therefore I have performed this, and have sealed to them this fruit, I will come by you into Spain. And I am sure that, when I come unto you, I shall come in the fulness of the blessing of the gospel of Christ" (Rom. 15:28, 29). Then he pleaded with them to pray for him that he might be delivered "from them that do not believe in Judaea....That I may come unto you with joy by the will of God, and may with you be refreshed" (Rom. 15:31, 32).

Those passages in Romans are inspired. So God had revealed to Paul that he would go to Rome. Incidentally, since this is inspired, we know that there must have been two imprisonments of Paul. He must have been released for a season because he had plainly been inspired to write, "I will come by you into Spain." And he did not go to Spain before the book of Acts closes. To the Philippians he wrote, while in Rome, "And having this confidence, I know that I shall abide and continue with you all for your furtherance and joy of faith; That your rejoicing may be more abundant in Jesus Christ for me by my coming to you again" (Phil. 1:25, 26). And that "coming again" would require a release from imprisonment. And to Philemon, Paul wrote from Rome, "But withal prepare me also a lodging: for I trust that through your prayers I shall be given unto you" (Philem. 22).

So now Paul is to go to Rome. It was not God's first and best plan that he should go this way, we think. He had been warned again and again against going up to Jerusalem (Acts 21:4; Acts 21:10, 11) and as Paul himself had had direct instruction from God in Acts 22:17-21. But still Paul was God's man; God had determined for him to go to Rome and had revealed it to Paul. And now at last Paul was ready to go to Rome a prisoner.

One should consider in this connection all the friends whom Paul knew by name at Rome. Read Romans 16. He names twenty-seven people who are to be greeted, and a number by households and others who are not called by name! That illustrates the fact that Rome was the center of the world and as an old proverb says, "All roads lead to Rome." So among those Paul had met far and near and among those he had won to Christ, many were now at Rome. He longed to see them. And he was inspired to send greetings to all of these, because he intended to come to Rome.

3. What other prisoners went with Paul to Rome? "Paul and certain other prisoners" were delivered unto Julius the centurion to take them to Rome. Not all of them are named. Aristarchus is one of them. He had been Paul's companion in travel, was in the riot in Ephesus (Acts 19:29), possibly

had been arrested also because of complaints of Jewish leaders. Other prisoners are not named here. But the inspired writer again and again says "we" (vss. 4, 5, 7, 18, 19, 37). So Luke, the inspired writer, was evidently present with Paul, with Aristarchus and those others. "Aristarchus...being with us," Luke is inspired to write (vs. 2).

VERSES 2-13:

2 And entering into a ship of Adramyttium, we launched, meaning to sail by the coasts of Asia; *one* Aristarchus, a Macedonian of Thessalonica, being with us.

3 And the next *day* we touched at Sidon. And Julius courteously entreated Paul, and gave *him* liberty to go unto his friends to refresh himself.

4 And when we had launched from thence, we sailed under Cyprus, because the winds were contrary.

5 And when we had sailed over the sea of Cilicia and Pamphylia, we came to Myra, *a city* of Lycia.

6 And there the centurion found a ship of Alexandria sailing into Italy; and he put us therein.

7 And when we had sailed slowly many days, and scarce were come over against Cnidus, the wind not suffering us, we sailed under Crete, over against Salmone;

8 And, hardly passing it, came unto a place which is called the Fair Havens; nigh whereunto was the city *of* Lasea.

9 Now when much time was spent, and when sailing was now dangerous, because the fast was now already past, Paul admonished *them*,

10 And said unto them, Sirs, I perceive that this voyage will be with hurt and much damage, not only of the lading and ship, but also of our lives.

11 Nevertheless the centurion believed the master and the owner of the ship, more than those things which were spoken by Paul.

12 And because the haven was not commodious to winter in, the more part advised to depart thence also, if by any means they might attain to Phenice, *and there* to winter; *which is* a haven of Crete, and lieth toward the southwest and northwest.

13 And when the south wind blew softly, supposing that they had obtained *their* purpose, loosing *thence*, they sailed close by Crete.

The Journey by Sailing Vessel

Here we get some light on the dangers and inconveniences of traveling by sail ship. All the ships were of wood. The only power was that of the wind on the sails. Some war-ships had one, two, or three banks of oars manned by slaves, sometimes chained, but that was too expensive in man power. And sailing ships were faster and better than any other means of communication by land or sea. So, before the days of railroads, nearly all the principal cities of the world were on the seacoast or on large rivers so goods and people could move by boats or ships. The centurion found a ship in the harbor at Caesarea with the home port of Adramyttium up the coast north near Troas in Asia Minor. So they planned to sail "by the coasts of Asia," the province for that name covered part of the peninsula. It now belongs to what we call Asia Minor. The next port north was Sidon and there they stopped. Paul had friends and was allowed to go to their home to refresh himself; possibly a soldier went with him. But he was given great liberty. Then they sailed on north. It was intended to go northwest, but "the winds were contrary," so they went near the shore and east and north of Cyprus, and thus near the land "over the sea of Cilicia and Pamphylia" to Myra, a city of Lycia.

It will be good for you to see a map of Paul's missionary journeys and familiarize yourself with all of this eastern end of the Mediterranean Sea. Thus you can find where Paul preached, find the relationship of Macedonia, Thessalonica, Athens and Antioch in Greece to the area of Asia Minor where Paul had his first ministry. They stopped at the port of Myra. The ship they have used is bound still further north, we suppose to Adramyttium, but they wanted to sail due west to Rome. So they found another ship and rented space.

Again, the wind was contrary, they sailed slowly, trying, we suppose, to tack against the wind from the west. They came opposite Cnidus on the seashore and then not being able to sail directly westward and by the tip of Greece, they turned south and sailed "under Crete," that is, east of the end of Crete and along the south shore. They passed Salmone on the eastern tip of the island and then along the south shore until they came to the harbor called The fair havens. The winds had been against them. They had not made the time they hoped to make.

But now it was going into the fall. "The fast was now already past." It was getting into the time of wintry winds on the Mediterranean. That fast was on the tenth day of the seventh month, according to Leviticus 23:27-29. It is dangerous to sail on. But the harbor was not "commodious to winter in." The captain of the ship was anxious to discharge his cargo, collect his money. Besides, on the northwest end of the island of Crete there was another harbor, larger, called Phenice.

Note the warning of Paul in verses 9 and 10: "Sirs, I perceive that this voyage will be with hurt and much damage, not only of the lading and ship, but also of our lives." Evidently he had warning from the Spirit of God that the trip through the winter season would be dangerous. We are not to suppose that Paul knew more about sailing ships than did the captain of the ship. But God tells his servants what He will do, if they obey Him and live near Him. So the south wind blew softly. They could adjust their sails and make their way westward; and so they started sailing along the southern coast of Crete.

VERSES 14–20:

14 But not long after there arose against it a tempestuous wind, called Euroclydon.

15 And when the ship was caught, and could not bear up into the wind, we let *her* drive.

16 And running under a certain island which is called Clauda, we had much work to come by the boat:

17 Which when they had taken up, they used helps, undergird-

ing the ship; and, fearing lest they should fall into the quicksands, strake sail, and so were driven.

18 And we being exceedingly tossed with a tempest, the next *day* they lightened the ship;

19 And the third *day* we cast out with our own hands the tackling of the ship.

20 And when neither sun nor stars in many days appeared, and no small tempest lay on *us,* all hope that we should be saved was then taken away.

In Peril of the Sea

Paul had been often on ships sailing along the coast of the Mediterranean Sea in his missionary journeys. Before his last trip to Jerusalem and his arrest, Paul had written about his sufferings for Christ. Already he could say, "Thrice was I beaten with rods, once was I stoned, thrice I suffered shipwreck, a night and a day I have been in the deep; In journeyings often, in perils of robbers, in perils by mine countrymen, in perils by the heathen, in perils in the city, in perils in the wilderness, in perils in the sea, in perils among false brethren" (II Cor. 11:25, 26). Already three times he had suffered shipwreck. He had spent a night and a day, evidently clinging to a mast or in a lifeboat in the sea. He could write of perils of waters, "perils in the sea." So the peril of this journey is not the first such testing Paul has had.

Before long a storm arose. It was rather expected each winter, we suppose, and had a name "Euroclydon."

Concerning the Euroclydon, a note in the Encyclopedia Britannica is interesting. In the item about the island of Malta in the Mediterranean the article says:

"Pleasant northeast winds blow for an average of 150 days a year, cool northerly winds for 31 days, east winds 70 days, west for 34 days. The northwest 'Gregale' (Euroclydon of Acts 27:14) blows about the equinox and occasionally, in the winter months, sometimes with almost hurri-

cane force for three days together; it is recorded to have caused the drowning of six hundred persons in the harbor in 1555. This wind
was a constant menace to shipping at Anchor;
the breakwater on the Monarch Shoal was de-
signed to resist its ravages."

In the American Standard Version the term used for
Euroclydon is Euraquilo, the word for "northeaster." And
another article in the Encyclopedia Britannica says Euroclydon comes from the northeast instead of from the northwest. It probably varies, but comes fairly regularly about
the last of September.

There is a small island south of Crete called Clauda.
And they "ran under" it, that is, they were out of the way to
the south of it instead of directly west. They "had much
work to come by the boat." We suppose that a smaller boat
used for loading and unloading, etc., was trailed on a rope
behind the sail ship. They brought it aboard. They used
cables or ropes undergirding the wooden ship, so heavy
loaded, unless the pounding of the waves should open some
of the seams.

One of the great dangers in sail ships was to be blown
upon shore and have the ship broken. So they took down the
sails and were driven before the wind. Nothing they could
do would control the ship's course.

The next day they were so burdened that "they lightened
the ship," that is, they cast out much of the merchandise
which filled the cargo space and much of the deck, we suppose.

"And the third day we cast out with our own hands the
tackling of the ship." We suppose that this means Paul and
Luke helped. The ship's officers were in such distress of
mind and in so dangerous a situation that even the extra
cordage and sails were tossed overboard. It was a dis-
consolate group of 276 people (vs. 37). On a ship driven

blindly before the wind, they could not see sun nor stars, thus could not judge where they were. Possibly they had a compass, as some sailing ships did in those days. This ship may not have had.

VERSES 21–38:

21 But after long abstinence, Paul stood forth in the midst of them, and said, Sirs, ye should have hearkened unto me, and not have loosed from Crete, and to have gained this harm and loss.

22 And now I exhort you to be of good cheer: for there shall be no loss of *any man's* life among you but of the ship.

23 For there stood by me this night the angel of God, whose I am, and whom I serve,

24 Saying, Fear not, Paul; thou must be brought before Cesar: and, lo, God hath given thee all them that sail with thee.

25 Wherefore, sirs, be of good cheer: for I believe God, that it shall be even as it was told me.

26 Howbeit we must be cast upon a certain island.

27 But when the fourteenth night was come, as we were driven up and down in Adria, about midnight the shipmen deemed that they drew near to some country;

28 And sounded, and found *it* twenty fathoms: and when they had gone a little further, they sounded again, and found *it* fifteen fathoms.

29 Then fearing lest we should have fallen upon rocks, they cast four anchors out of the stern, and wished for the day.

30 And as the shipmen were about to flee out of the ship, when they had let down the boat into the sea, under colour as though they would have cast anchors out of the foreship,

31 Paul said to the centurion and to the soldiers, Except these abide in the ship, ye cannot be saved.

32 Then the soldiers cut off the ropes of the boat, and let her fall off.

33 And while the day was coming on, Paul besought *them* all to take meat, saying, This day is the fourteenth day that ye have tarried and continued fasting, having taken nothing.

34 Wherefore I pray you to take *some* meat; for this is for your health: for there shall not a hair fall from the head of any of you.

35 And when he had thus spoken, he took bread, and gave

thanks to God in presence of them all; and when he had broken *it*, he began to eat.

36 Then were they all of good cheer, and they also took *some* meat.

37 And we were in all in the ship two hundred threescore and sixteen souls.

38 And when they had eaten enough, they lightened the ship, and cast out the wheat into the sea.

Paul, Comforted by God's Angel, Comforts the People

It is a fact often referred to in the Scripture that God has a way of revealing His plans to those who are very near Him and thoroughly committed to please Him and serve Him. Paul had known ahead of time that he was going to Rome, and a number of times had mentioned it in his letter to the Romans. God revealed to him, though he would not hear, that he should not go to Jerusalem lest he should be bound and imprisoned. Later the Lord revealed to Paul that his death approached and Paul said, "I am now ready to be offered, and the time of my departure is at hand" (II Tim. 4:6). So the Lord has revealed to Paul ahead of time that this voyage leaving The fair havens and winter coming, would be with loss and danger (vs. 10).

God had revealed to Abraham His plans to destroy Sodom and Gomorrah saying, "For I know him, that he will command his children and his household after him, and they shall keep the way of the Lord, to do justice and judgment ..." (Gen. 18:19). God revealed to Rebekah that she would bear twins, "and the elder [Esau] shall serve the younger [Jacob]"(Gen. 25:23). God revealed to Jacob so he could tell his sons "that which shall befall you in the last days." And he told them, "And when Jacob had made an end of commanding his sons, he gathered up his feet into the bed, and yielded up the ghost" (Gen. 49). The Apostle Peter was inspired to write, "Knowing that shortly I must put off this my tabernacle, even as our Lord Jesus Christ hath shewed me" (II Pet. 1:14).

Two years before he died, my own father had a stroke and was given up to die. When I rushed home from a revival campaign to see him, he was sitting up and while he was in pain and could not breathe lying down because of his heart condition, yet he told me frankly, "Son, my time is not yet. God will tell me before my time comes." Two years later, when he seemed in greatly improved health, he told at least two people that his time was now at hand, made a last visit to me in a revival campaign, won four men, heads of families, to Christ in two days, then came to my quarters sick and in an hour was gone!

I am suggesting that if Christians walk close to God, we could not only have comfort in every storm at sea, but reassurance and help whenever we need them. So the angel of God stood by Paul in the night and said, "Fear not, Paul; thou must be brought before Caesar: and, lo, God hath given thee all them that sail with thee."

Paul must have remembered joyfully that time in Corinth when "then spake the Lord to Paul in the night by a vision, Be not afraid, but speak, and hold not thy peace: For I am with thee, and no man shall set on thee to hurt thee: for I have much people in this city" (Acts 18:9, 10). Oh, the man or the woman who is near the Lord and in the will of God and who has learned to trust, can have peace and assurance which "passeth all understanding" in time of stress and trouble. So Paul told the people, "Wherefore, sirs, be of good cheer: for I believe God, that it should be even as it was told me. Howbeit we must be cast upon a certain island."

The storm had continued for two full weeks. In some way the shipmen now felt they were approaching land, the ship with bare masts, blown without sails. They sounded and found the water twenty fathoms deep (120 feet). Then it was fifteen fathoms or ninety feet deep. They cast four anchors out of the stern to hold them off the land and waited anxiously for daytime. The sailors were about to let down the boat on a pretext to flee away and go to land and save themselves. Paul called attention of the centurion to their device. The ropes were cut, the boat fell off, and all were left together on the ship.

They were a frightened and frail group. For fourteen days they had eaten nothing, as we understand from verse 33. Again, Paul reassured the 276 people, "For there shall not an hair fall from the head of any of you." And he took bread and ate before them. Then they also took food and ate and cast even the extra wheat out into the sea.

VERSES 39-44:

39 And when it was day, they knew not the land: but they discovered a certain creek with a shore, into the which they were minded, if it were possible, to thrust in the ship.

40 And when they had taken up the anchors, they committed *themselves* unto the sea, and loosed the rudder bands, and hoised up the mainsail to the wind, and made toward shore.

41 And falling into a place where two seas met, they ran the ship aground; and the forepart stuck fast, and remained unmoveable, but the hinder part was broken with the violence of the waves.

42 And the soldiers' counsel was to kill the prisoners, lest any of them should swim out, and escape.

43 But the centurion, willing to save Paul, kept them from *their* purpose; and commanded that they which could swim should cast *themselves* first *into the sea*, and get to land:

44 And the rest, some on boards, and some on *broken pieces* of the ship. And so it came to pass, that they escaped all safe to land.

God Delivers Them All Safely to Land

The daytime came after the long weary night. What a bedraggled group they were, weak and with two weeks of fasting, doubtless with bedding and clothing wet from spray of the storm, 276 people crowded into a small ship (small by present-day standards). What would they do? There was a creek--they could see the mouth of it on land. They hoped to drive the ship into that little estuary. They released the anchors and committed themselves to the sea. They loosed the rudder bands, hoisted the mainsail, and made toward the shore.

The wind was such that on one side of the island the waves came from one direction and we suppose on the other side they came from a slightly different direction, and here they met. They ran the ship aground. The fore part stuck in the sand and the back of the wooden ship was broken to pieces by the waves.

Would the prisoners escape? The soldiers thought the sensible thing was to kill the prisoners, including Paul. "But the centurion, willing to save Paul, kept them from their purpose." Those who could swim jumped into the sea. Others on boards and broken pieces of the ship floated till they could wade ashore. All escaped safe, with not one loss!

May we suggest some lessons from the shipwreck. First, "in the world ye shall have tribulation" (John 16:33). Paul spoke to the new converts of his missionary journey in Lystra, Iconium, and Antioch, "confirming the souls of the disciples, and exhorting them to continue in the faith, and that we must through much tribulation enter into the kingdom of God" (Acts 14:22). We should remember:

> **"Faith of our fathers! living still**
> **In spite of dungeon, fire, and sword."**

It costs something to be a good Christian and it ought to. The servant is not better than his Lord.

But thank God for a second lesson. A Christian need never be in danger alone. He need never be in poverty without a God who can supply his needs. A Christian need never be in sorrow without comfort. A Christian may be in a storm at sea and have perfect peace and the angel of God reassure him!

Yes, Paul must go to Rome! And God will care for it and see that he gets there! A Christian, in the will of God, is perfectly safe. No one can harm him without the consent of God. He cannot die except by the will of God.

ACTS 28

VERSES 1, 2:

AND when they were escaped, then they knew that the island was called Melita.

2 And the barbarous people shewed us no little kindness: for they kindled a fire, and received us every one, because of the present rain, and because of the cold.

The Shipwrecked Company Lands on the Island of Melita

The modern name of Melita is Malta, an island in the Mediterranean Sea about 17 1/2 miles long and 9 miles broad. There are four other small islands, two of them inhabited, in the Maltese group. Malta is about 60 miles from the nearest point of Sicily, 140 miles from Italy, 180 miles from Africa.

There is a bay on the northeast island now called St. Paul's Bay. St. Paul's Bay is where it is thought the shipwrecked group landed.

The island was originally peopled from Phenicia and they are called here in verse 2 "the barbarous people" because they had not been included in the Grecian or Roman civilizations and language. So William Ramsey has dealt extensively with the topography of the era in his book, St. Paul the Traveler.

VERSES 3–6:

3 And when Paul had gathered a bundle of sticks, and laid *them* on the fire, there came a viper out of the heat, and fastened on his hand.

4 And when the barbarians saw the *venomous* beast hang on his hand, they said among themselves, No doubt this man is a murderer, whom, though he hath escaped the sea, yet vengeance suffereth not to live.

5 And he shook off the beast into the fire, and felt no harm.

6 Howbeit they looked when he should have swollen, or fallen down dead suddenly: but after they had looked a great while, and saw no harm come to him, they changed their minds, and said that he was a god.

Paul Miraculously Healed of Snake Bite

The people on the island were kind. It was raining and relatively cold, although in that Mediterranean area it rarely gets colder than forty-five degrees. And the rainfall on the island of Malta averages about twenty-one inches a year. But this was in the rainy, stormy season and the shipwrecked people shivered in the cold. So the kindly people kindled a fire and the 276 people of the shipwreck crowded about to warm.

It was like Paul that although he was the most distinguished man present, he, too, gathered sticks and laid them on the fire. God uses men for soul winning who are busy, thrifty men, men who try to carry their part of the load.

But as Paul laid sticks on the fire, there came a viper, a poison snake, out of the heat and bit his hand.

Immediately the native people, who may have known Paul was a prisoner, thought that here was judgment of the gods, or whatever god they worshiped, on a murderer who had escaped. It is interesting to note that even the heathen have a moral sense. As Romans 2:14 and 15 says: "For when the Gentiles, which have not the law, do by nature the things contained in the law, these, having not the law, are a law unto themselves: Which shew the work of the law written in their hearts, their conscience also bearing witness, and their thoughts the mean while accusing or else excusing one another." Men, by nature, know that they are accountable for sin. Men who do not know the true God, yet feel that there must be a God who brings sin to judgment. For God who created man created a conscience to remind men of God.

But Paul shook off the poison creature in the fire and felt no harm. Then the people thought that he was a god! Paul would remember that when he had been used of God to heal a lifelong cripple at Lystra they had thought he was a god. "And when the people saw what Paul had done, they lifted up their voices, saying in the speech of Lycaonia, The gods are come down to us in the likeness of men. And they called Barnabas, Jupiter; and Paul, Mercurius, because he was the chief speaker" (Acts 14:11, 12). And they would have offered oxen before him as sacrifices, but Paul restrained them.

This healing of the poisonous snake bite is the only case we have recorded in the New Testament where Mark 16:18 was fulfilled. There we are told that among the signs to follow those who have faith for them was, "They shall take up serpents; and if they drink any deadly thing, it shall not hurt them; they shall lay hands on the sick, and they shall recover." There were many miraculous healings of sick people in the New Testament, but this is the only case of poison snake bite healed that is definitely recorded.

Certainly this was a miracle. And equally certain, I think, a Christian today, if he had need, would be right to pray for supernatural intervention. There is nothing in the Bible to indicate that God wants us to tempt Him by deliberately seeking snake bite. Ignorant and publicity-seeking people bring reproach on the cause of Christ by their snake-handling in certain mountain areas. Yet it is true that if one were snake-bitten he would be right to pray, and if God should give the faith for healing, God would give the healing as He did in the case of Paul.

Incidentally, we believe that the closing part of Mark's Gospel is authentic and that there is nothing promised there but what fits in with other promises throughout the Bible for those who put their trust in the Lord in time of need and depend on Him for help.

I think we may see here also in the miraculous healing of

Paul, as in other cases in the New Testament, that God's healing in answer to prayer opened the doors for testimony. I know that it is not always God's will to heal. I know that sometimes God wants people to die and sometimes He wants them to be sick until some spiritual end is obtained. But many times surely it is the will of God to heal and sometimes to heal instantly and miraculously, as in the case of Paul. And no doubt it is true in this matter as in many, many other matters that "ye have not, becaus﹖ ye ask not" (Jas. 4:2). It seems clear from James 5:13-15, that it is intended that God's preachers shall sometimes be called to fervently pray for the sick, and that God often intends to heal such sick people in answer to prayer.

VERSES 7–10:

7 In the same quarters were possessions of the chief man of the island, whose name was Publius; who received us, and lodged us three days courteously.

8 And it came to pass, that the father of Publius lay sick of a fever and of a bloody flux: to whom Paul entered in, and prayed, and laid his hands on him, and healed him.

9 So when this was done, others also, which had diseases in the island, came, and were healed:

10 Who also honoured us with many honours; and when we departed, they laded us with such things as were necessary.

The Healing of Publius' Father

The chief man of the island was Publius. Tradition says that he became the first bishop of the island or built the first Christian church building. However, the tradition is Roman Catholic and the word bishop to them does not mean, as it does in the Bible, simply a New Testament pastor of a local congregation. The chief man of the island "received us, and lodged us three days courteously," verse 7 says. Did that include simply Paul and Luke and Aristarchus and perhaps other Christians? Would it not include also soldiers or guards? Or does he mean the whole 276 people

from the ship? We do not know. Since the group stayed
there three months (vs. 11), all those people would need to
scatter out to seek accommodations.

But "the father of Publius lay sick of a fever and of a
bloody flux: to whom Paul entered in, and prayed, and laid
his hands on him, and healed him" (vs. 8). And that led
many others who had diseases on the island to come and
they too were healed. It is not surprising that they honored
Paul and his Christian friends with many honors and supplied their needs. Tradition says--and we believe it--that
Paul left many Christians on the island after the three
months.

VERSES 11–16:

11 And after three months we departed in a ship of Alexandria, which had wintered in the isle, whose sign was Castor and Pollux.

12 And landing at Syracuse, we tarried *there* three days.

13 And from thence we fetched a compass, and came to Rhegium: and after one day the south wind blew, and we came the next day to Puteoli:

14 Where we found brethren, and were desired to tarry with them seven days: and so we went toward Rome.

15 And from thence, when the brethren heard of us, they came to meet us as far as Appii Forum, and the Three Taverns; whom when Paul saw, he thanked God, and took courage.

16 And when we came to Rome, the centurion delivered the prisoners to the captain of the guard: but Paul was suffered to dwell by himself with a soldier that kept him.

On to Rome

Through the stormy winter a ship of Alexandria had wintered in the island of Malta Harbor. Paul's company (and
perhaps many or all of the others) secured passage on this
ship and embarked for Italy. The first port of call was
Syracuse on the eastern coast of the island of Sicily, south

of Italy. The three days there no doubt were to take on cargo and supplies.

From Syracuse their ship went north to Rhegium, now called Reggio di Calabria, a city on the very toe of Italy. They "fetched a compass," probably having to sail tacking against the wind instead of sailing nearly straight north. There they waited only one day till a south wind blew, and they came to Puteoli. Puteoli, with the modern name Pozzuoli, is on the northern part of the bay of Naples. It was originally the chief seaport of Rome, and so was a natural landing place for these travelers toward the capital city of the Empire.

There the Christians found Christian brethren and were allowed to tarry seven days. Paul was a distinguished visitor and was given every courtesy. But word went on ahead to the city of Rome, and some Christians came down the road to meet them. Some of the brethren from Rome met them at Appii forum, the market of Appius, some forty miles from Rome. Others met them at The three taverns. Paul was greatly encouraged to meet Christians, and now, with anticipation, he goes forward into Rome where he had long hoped to be. Rome is the center of the ancient world, the capital city of the Empire.

Paul had had seven days with Christians at Puteoli. But other Christians had met him at Appii forum and The three taverns.

They walked perhaps or may have ridden beasts of burden. They went, no doubt, the Old Appian Way which was begun over three hundred years before Christ, paved with large stones. It is still the base for some of the highway which we traveled from Rome to Naples in February 1962, with only a black top covering the old stones. Some of the ancient bridges are still in use. Some places the road leaves the ancient highway, but it can still be followed.

Now Paul was come to Rome. The centurion delivered them to the captain of the guard of the emperial palace in charge of important prisoners and those awaiting trial under the emperor. Hence Paul could later write to Philippi, "All the saints salute you, chiefly they that are of Caesar's household" (Phil. 4:22). Evidently Paul won some of these soldiers who guarded him. But since he was a distinguished prisoner, a Roman citizen, "Paul was suffered to dwell by himself with a soldier that kept him."

VERSES 17–24:

17 And it came to pass, that after three days Paul called the chief of the Jews together: and when they were come together, he said unto them, Men *and* brethren, though I have committed nothing against the people, or customs of our fathers, yet was I delivered prisoner from Jerusalem into the hands of the Romans:

18 Who, when they had examined me, would have let *me* go, because there was no cause of death in me.

19 But when the Jews spake against *it*, I was constrained to appeal unto Cesar; not that I had aught to accuse my nation of.

20 For this cause therefore have I called for you, to see *you*, and to speak with *you*: because that for the hope of Israel I am bound with this chain.

21 And they said unto him, We neither received letters out of Judea concerning thee, neither any of the brethren that came shewed or spake any harm of thee.

22 But we desire to hear of thee what thou thinkest: for as concerning this sect, we know that every where it is spoken against.

23 And when they had appointed him a day, there came many to him into *his* lodging; to whom he expounded and testified the kingdom of God, persuading them concerning Jesus, both out of the law of Moses, and *out of* the prophets, from morning till evening.

24 And some believed the things which were spoken, and some believed not.

Paul Meets Jews in Rome

In all of Paul's missionary journeys he had the custom of seeking out first the Jews and speaking whenever possible in

Jewish synagogues. With Jews he would meet people of the
same language and some who already knew something of the
Old Testament Scriptures and the ones with whom revival
and gospel preaching ought to begin. Here in Rome he could
not go to the synagogue since he was a prisoner, so he
called the chief Jews of Rome together. We remember that
Jews were scattered all over the Roman Empire, including
Rome.

To these Jewish leaders Paul told the story of why he was
a prisoner, of his appeal to Caesar, and thus is now in
Rome. And again to these Jewish friends he said, "Because
that for the hope of Israel I am bound with this chain." He
identified himself with the cause of God, the cause of the
Old Testament and the cause of Christ. Scriptural Judaism
is Christianity as far as it goes. Abraham was a Christian
in that he had trusted in Christ. All the Old Testament
pointed to the coming of the Saviour, and Christ is really
the fulfillment of it. He is now and will be in the future, all
the fulfillment of the hope of Israel.

These Jewish leaders had not heard about Paul. It is
many a mile from Rome to Jerusalem. There are no tele-
graph wires, no railroads, no postal system, so they had
not heard of Paul's arrest. They had heard of Christ and
the rise of Christianity and "for as concerning this sect,"
they said, "we know that every where it is spoken against."
There were Christians in Rome to whom Paul had addressed
his epistle to the Romans. And those Christians bore the
reproach of Christ, as good Christians everywhere must
do.

So they requested Paul to set a day when they could gather
a crowd and they would come to his lodging house and there
he would expound and testify the kingdom of God, "persuading them concerning Jesus, both out of the law of Moses,
and out of the prophets, from morning till evening." They
came and Paul spent the whole day with them.

Were they saved? "And some believed the things which

were spoken, and some believed not." Some of them may have been converted. Others were mentally more or less convinced and others were not.

In any case, there was not a great breaking-out revival and soul winning among the Jews.

VERSES 25-31:

25 And when they agreed not among themselves, they departed, after that Paul had spoken one word, Well spake the Holy Ghost by Esaias the prophet unto our fathers,

26 Saying, Go unto this people, and say, Hearing ye shall hear, and shall not understand; and seeing ye shall see, and not perceive:

27 For the heart of this people is waxed gross, and their ears are dull of hearing, and their eyes have they closed; lest they should see with *their* eyes, and hear with *their* ears, and understand with *their* heart, and should be converted, and I should heal them.

28 Be it known therefore unto you, that the salvation of God is sent unto the Gentiles, and *that* they will hear it.

29 And when he had said these words, the Jews departed, and had great reasoning among themselves.

30 And Paul dwelt two whole years in his own hired house, and received all that came in unto him,

31 Preaching the kingdom of God, and teaching those things which concern the Lord Jesus Christ, with all confidence, no man forbidding him.

Paul Turns to the Gentiles

Was Paul surprised that the Jews did not turn as readily to hear him as Gentiles had in his other missionary journeys? I do not think he was surprised. He had already written to the Christians here in Rome about three years before, "For I would not, brethren, that ye should be ignorant of this mystery, lest ye should be wise in your own conceits; that blindness in part is happened to Israel, until the fulness of the Gentiles be come in" (Rom. 11:25).

He had already told them in verse 28 of the same chapter, "As concerning the gospel, they are enemies for your sakes: but as touching the election, they are beloved for the fathers' sakes." Besides, Paul knew and had emphasized even in his letter to the Christians here at Rome that he, Paul, was the apostle to the Gentiles and that his principal ministry would be among Gentiles (Rom. 11:13; Rom. 1:13).

But Paul quoted to them a passage from Isaiah 6:9 and 10. When God had called Isaiah to preach to Israel, He had warned that their heart would be fat, their ears heavy and their eyes shut to the Gospel he would preach. And Jesus preached and quoted the same passage to the Jews of His day in Matthew 13:14 and 15. And Jesus made reference to this great truth from Isaiah again in John 12:38-40.

So here Paul the apostle says the same thing to the Jewish people.

Therefore, Paul now turned his attention to preaching to the Gentiles in Rome.

Some hyper-dispensationalists have thought that Acts 28:28 was a turning point. Some have taught that all of the New Testament up to this point was a transitional period and some think that baptism after this Scripture is not commanded. They think that since it was begun with the Jews, baptism was ceremonial and Jewish. However, they miss the point entirely.

When Paul turned from these unbelieving Jews in Rome to preach to Gentiles, he did exactly what he had been doing everywhere he went before!

For instance, the missionary journeys of Paul and Barnabas began in Acts, chapter 13. And there we see when Paul and Barnabas preached in Antioch of Pisidia and the Jews, when the Gentiles heard the Gospel, "were filled with envy, and spake against those things which were spoken by Paul, contradicting and blaspheming. Then Paul and Barnabas waxed bold, and said, It was necessary that the word of God should first have been spoken to you: but seeing ye put it from you, and judge yourselves unworthy of everlasting life, lo, we turn to the Gentiles" (Acts 13:45, 46). That was not a turning point in dispensations and neither is this similar case in Rome.

When Paul and Silas came to Thessalonica, "Paul, as his manner was, went in unto them, and three sabbath days reasoned with them out of the scriptures" (Acts 17:2). But soon these Jews turned against Paul. At Athens Paul first "disputed...in the synagogue with the Jews," and then preached to the Gentiles in the market place and on Mars' Hill (Acts 17:17-22).

In Acts 18:4-6 we find that Paul at Corinth "reasoned in the synagogue every sabbath, and persuaded the Jews and the Greeks. And when Silas and Timotheus were come from Macedonia, Paul was pressed in the spirit, and testified to the Jews that Jesus was Christ. And when they opposed themselves, and blasphemed, he shook his raiment, and said unto them, Your blood be upon your own heads; I am clean: from henceforth I will go unto the Gentiles."

Again Paul said, "Henceforth I will go unto the Gentiles." So when at Rome, in Acts 28:28, Paul announced he would go to the Gentiles, he was only following the custom he had followed in every city where he had preached the Gospel--to go to the Jews first, then to the Gentiles.

In fact, when Paul was converted, the Lord said to Ananias, "Go thy way: for he is a chosen vessel unto me, to bear my name before the Gentiles, and kings, and the children of Israel" (Acts 9:15). But God had told Paul far more than that, as he reported it in Acts 22:17 and 18: "And it came to pass, that, when I was come again to Jerusalem, even while I prayed in the temple, I was in a trance; And saw him saying unto me, Make haste, and get thee quickly out of Jerusalem: for they will not receive thy testimony concerning me." And again verse 21 says, "And he said unto me, Depart: for I will send thee far hence unto the Gentiles." And as Paul reported his conversion and call to King Agrippa, it was thus: "But rise, and stand upon thy feet: for I have appeared unto thee for this purpose, to make thee a minister and a witness both of these things which thou hast seen, and of those things in the which I will appear unto thee: Delivering thee from the people, and from the Gentiles, unto whom now I send thee, To open their eyes, and to turn them from darkness to light, and from the power of Satan unto God, that they may receive forgiveness of sins, and inheritance among them which are sanctified by faith that is in me" (Acts 26:16-18).

In Galatians 2:7 and 8 Paul had written, "But contrariwise, when they saw that the gospel of the uncircumcision was committed unto me, as the gospel of the circumcision was unto Peter; (For he that wrought effectually in Peter to the apostleship of the circumcision, the same was mighty in me toward the Gentiles.)."

When Paul turned from the reluctant Jews to preach to the Gentiles in Rome, he followed a regular custom which he had followed in every city where he preached, and he followed the plain instructions of God, to major on preaching to Gentiles.

Not the Close of Paul's Ministry

The inspired account here says in verse 30, "And Paul dwelt two whole years in his own hired house, and received all that came in unto him." But if Paul had been executed at the end of that two years, surely Luke in this inspired account would have told us. No, he only claims to tell this far in Paul's ministry. The death of Paul is not mentioned and there are a good many reasons why we think it could not have happened at this time. Note the evidence that Paul was released for a season and had a second imprisonment.

1. In his letter from Rome to the Philippians, Paul, after telling of great blessing on his preaching of the Gospel in Rome, said, "For I am in a strait betwixt two, having a desire to depart, and to be with Christ; which is far better: nevertheless to abide in the flesh is more needful for you.

And having this confidence, I know that I shall abide and continue with you all for your furtherance and joy of faith; That your rejoicing may be more abundant in Jesus Christ for me by my coming to you again" (Phil. 1:23-26). Paul says here, "...I know that I shall abide and continue with you all...that your rejoicing may be more abundant in Jesus Christ for me by my coming to you again." Remember that the words of the Scriptures are God-breathed. Whatever Paul thought in this case may have coincided with what God said. But God Himself guarantees the truth of the Scripture.

Here in divinely inspired writing, Paul told the Philippians that he knew he would come to them again from his imprisonment from Rome.

2. Writing to Philemon in Colosse from Rome, Paul was inspired to say, "But withal prepare me also a lodging: for I trust that through your prayers I shall be given unto you" (Philem. 22). We ought to take that as an inspired statement. Paul was to be released and to visit Philemon at Colosse.

3. In Romans 15:24 Paul wrote the Christians at Rome, "Whensoever I take my journey into Spain, I will come to you: for I trust to see you in my journey, and to be brought on my way thitherward by you, if first I be somewhat filled with your company."

And again in Romans 15:28 he says, "When therefore I have performed this, and have sealed to them this fruit, I will come by you into Spain."

Now it is clear that God had revealed to Paul he would go to Rome. I think it is equally clear He had revealed to Paul he would go to Spain. But he did not go to Spain before going to Rome; therefore, he must have been released and made his trip to Spain and to Colosse and to Philippi before his last imprisonment.

4. The second epistle to Timothy is written from Rome and evidently soon before Paul's death, for he said in II Timothy 4:6--"For I am now ready to be offered, and the

time of my departure is at hand." But a number of Christian workers are mentioned here in II Timothy that were not mentioned in Paul's first journey to Rome. Demas, Crescens, Titus and Tychicus are all mentioned as having been with Paul in Rome. They are not mentioned in the account of his arrival, of his journey to Rome, nor of his two years' stay there. In his missionary journey heretofore, we were particularly told in the book of Acts when Barnabas or Silas or Titus or Timothy or Aristarchus was with him. See Acts 20:4--"And there accompanied him into Asia Sopater of Berea; and of the Thessalonians, Aristarchus and Secundus; and Gaius of Derbe, and Timotheus; and of Asia, Tychicus and Trophimus." So it seems unlikely that all these workers named in II Timothy had been with Paul at Rome, and they are not mentioned at all in connection with his coming or during his two years' stay there.

5. In II Timothy 1:15 Paul wrote Timothy from Rome, "This thou knowest, that all they which are in Asia be turned away from me; of whom are Phygellus and Hermogenes." Had Paul then been back to the province of Asia and met them and been rejected by leaders there? We could understand that if after his first imprisonment he went back to Philippi and then to Colosse and been through the little province of Asia. But how would Paul be an issue among them, he in far-off Rome, with almost no communication? We think Paul must have been back in that area after his first imprisonment.

6. In II Timothy 4:13 Paul wrote to Timothy, "The cloke that I left at Troas with Carpus, when thou comest, bring with thee, and the books, but especially the parchments." Does he refer to a cloak left four or five years before at Troas, books and parchments? I think not. I think that he speaks of a recent visit at Troas.

7. In II Timothy 4:20 Paul says, "...But Trophimus have I left at Miletum sick." Miletum is another name for Miletus. Now Trophimus was with Paul when he left Macedonia

and went into the province of Asia and on to Troas, as we see from Acts 20:1-5. He is particularly mentioned in verse 4. And on that journey to Jerusalem, Trophimus was with Paul and Paul stopped at Miletus to speak to the elders of Ephesus. However, he did not leave Trophimus there at Miletus, for we find that he accompanied Paul on to Rome, and in Acts 21:29 we find that when Paul was arrested they had this excuse: "They had seen before with him in the city Trophimus an Ephesian, whom they supposed that Paul had brought into the temple." So Paul did not leave Trophimus at Miletus on the trip toward Jerusalem.

But Paul from that time was in prison at Caesarea, and then was taken to Rome. Was Trophimus with him on that journey? Trophimus is not named on the journey, as you see from Acts 27:2 and then in that entire journey the ship did not stop at Miletus and Paul could not have left Trophimus there.

When, then, did Paul leave Trophimus sick at Miletus? After Trophimus had been with him at Jerusalem? Evidently on some other journey between two imprisonments Paul had been released and had visited at Philippi, Colosse, at Troas and Miletus.

So it seems clear there was another imprisonment, and when the book of Acts closes it is not the close of Paul's ministry.

Besides the Bible evidence, tradition is strong that Paul was released, then later suffered another imprisonment and death at Rome. Davis Bible Dictionary says:

"Although the book of The Acts leaves Paul a prisoner at Rome, there is abundant reason to believe that he was released after two years' confinement and resumed his missionary journeys. The evidence for this may be summarized as follows: (1) The closing verse of The Acts

accords better with this view than with the sup-
position that the imprisonment which has been
described ended in the apostle's condemnation
and death. Luke emphasizes the fact that no one
hindered his work, thus certainly giving the impression that the end of his activity was not
near. Moreover (2) Paul fully expected to be
released (Phil. i:25; ii:17, 24; Philem. 22), and
this expectation was fully justified by the treatment which he had always received at the hands
of Roman officials.

"It should be remembered that Nero's persecution of the Christians had not yet begun; that it
was a sudden outbreak, preceded by no official
ill-treatment of them; and that in the view of Roman law, the Christians were as yet only a sect
of the Jews, whose liberty to maintain their religion was fully recognized. It is, therefore, altogether probable that, when Paul's case came
before the imperial tribunal, he was acquitted of
any crime of which Roman law could take cogni-
zance. No doubt also the report of Festus was a
favorable one (see Acts xxvi. 31), nor do the
Jews appear to have sent any accusers to Rome
to appear against him (xxviii. 21). (3) The tradition that he was released and resumed his
journeys, and was again arrested dates from an
early period. Clement of Rome, A. D. 96,
seems clearly to imply that Paul went to Spain,
for he says that in his journeys 'he reached the
limit of the west.' His journey to Spain is also
mentioned in the so-called Muratori Fragment,
A. D. 170. With this agrees the history of
Eusebius, A. D. 324, which reports, as the
common tradition, that 'after he [Paul] had made
his defense, the apostle was sent again on the

ministry of preaching, and a second time having come to the same city [Rome] , he suffered martyrdom.' It must be admitted that this traditional evidence is not sufficiently strong to be absolutely demonstrative; but it is early and strong enough to confirm the rest of the evidence, and no sufficient counter-evidence can be adduced. (4) The epistles to Timothy and Titus may be proved to be Pauline by abundant external and internal evidence. No place for them, however, can be found in the history of Paul related in The Acts. They must, therefore, have been written later, and that fact compels us to accept the tradition given by Eusebius.

"We must, therefore, believe that Paul's appeal from Festus to Caesar resulted in his release. His subsequent movements can only be inferred from the allusions contained in the epistles to Timothy and Titus and from tradition.

        *   *   *   *   *

"The release of Paul from his first Roman imprisonment probably occurred in A. D. 63, and his subsequent activity lasted about four years. According to Eusebius, his death took place in A. D. 67; according to Jerome, in A. D. 68. How he came to be rearrested we do not know. There are a few slight hints furnished, however, by the Second Epistle to Timothy, which was written from Rome shortly before his death. We should remember, moreover, that in A. D. 64 Nero's persecution of the Christians in Rome broke out; and it was doubtless followed by sporadic outbreaks against them in the provinces (1 Pet. iv. 13-19). It may be, as some have supposed, that Paul was informed against as a leader of the now proscribed sect by the

Alexander mentioned in 2 Tim. iv. 14. At any rate, and wherever he was arrested, he was sent to Rome for trial, either because, as before, he appealed to Caesar, or because he was charged with a crime committed in Italy, perhaps with complicity in the burning of Rome, or because the provincials wished to gratify Nero by sending so notable a prisoner to the capital. Only Luke, of his former friends, was with him when 2 Tim. was written (2 Tim. iv. 11). Some had even deserted him (i. 15; iv. 10, 16), while others had gone away on various errands (10, 12). Yet when arraigned before the tribunal he was at first not condemned (17), though he continued to be held on some other charge. Possibly he was able to disprove a charge of criminal conduct, but was retained in custody because he was a Christian. He speaks of himself as a prisoner (i. 8) in bonds (16), as if an evildoer (ii. 9), and regards his fate as sealed (iv. 6-8). No doubt he was finally condemned to death simply because he was a Christian, in accordance with the policy begun by Nero in A. D. 64. Tradition relates that the apostle was beheaded, as became a Roman citizen, on the Ostian Way."

So the last days of Paul are not revealed in the book of Acts but in II Timothy particularly.

For a complete list of books available from the Sword of the Lord, write to Sword of the Lord Publishers, P. O. Box 1099, Murfreesboro, Tennessee 37133.